YOU'RE WONDERING NOW

First published in Great Britain in 2009 by Cherry Red Books (a division of Cherry Red Records Ltd.), 3a Long Island House, Warple Way, London W3 ORG.

Copyright © Paul Williams 2009

ISBN: 978-1-901447-51-4

Front cover: Photographed by Mike Laye/image-access.net.
Special thanks to Nick Davies for the caricature on pages 244/5.
Specials lyrics reproduced by kind permission of Plangent Visions Music Ltd.

Design: Dave Johnson

YOU'RE WONDERING NOW

THE SPECIALS

from Conception to Reunion

– 30th Anniversary Edition –

Paul Williams

DEDICATION

For Ruth Lilico -
My beautiful personal Editor-in-Chief and a wonderful lady,
Who lights up my life. She made it all possible.
Her enthusiasm and support knows no bounds.
I am so indebted to her. This is for you babe.

WITH THANKS

I would like to thank the following:
Roddy Byers, Terry Hall, Lynval Golding, Horace Panter, Neville Staple, John Bradbury, Jerry Dammers, Phill Jupitus, Steve Blackwell and Michelle Golding. Mike Cornwell and Stu Rennie the dynamic duo who have helped me above and beyond the call of duty. Aaron, Zoey and Terry for being my fantastic kids. Miggy Sinclair, Nick Welsh, Rhoda Dakar, Chris Foreman, June Golding, Pete Chambers, Nick Davies, Jason Weir, Michael Sanderson, Hazza and The Rough Kutz, Miles Woodroffe, Sean Flynn, Sam 'Skabilly' Smith, Seamus Flynn, Nikolaj Torp, Dave Wakeling, Chalkie Davies & Carole Starr, *Coventry Evening Telegraph,* Special Brew, Marc Wasserman, Linda Lee and the Ska-cumentary team New York, George Marshall, Andy Clayden and Bob Heatlie. Also, little Alice for her patience while letting me dominate the computer for so long. So many more people I could mention, all greatly appreciated. I would like to express my gratitude to the many publications (such as *Sounds, Record Mirror, NME, Melody Maker, Smash Hits,* plus various tabloids and broadsheets) for their unintentional help via my vast collection of cuttings. Thank you and goodnight.
In memory of Nana, Mike Williams and Callum 'Benny' Caird – sorely missed. With respect to Dave Jordan.

CONTENTS

FOREWORD

*I*t's difficult to tell the story of my love of music without devoting a large portion of it to the Specials. Let me give you some context. At the time of writing (winter 2008) I am a 46 year old survivor of Glam, Prog, Punk, New Wave, Power Pop, Acid House, Baggy, Big Beat, Britpop and any number of those less enduring musical genres and movements. Each of them usually came into my life in the same fashion. I'd hear the music on the radio, usually on the John Peel show, and then I'd read about them in inkies such as *Sounds*, *Melody Maker* or the *New Musical Express*. And then, depending on their success or hipness, I'd get to see them in action for the very first time on either *Top Of the Pops* or the *Old Grey Whistle Test*. Living in the hinterlands of Essex on a limited income, my own gig going didn't really take off until I got my first job in the wines and spirits department of Tesco's in Basildon at Christmas in 1980. Early shows I took in were by Blondie, Siouxsie and the Banshees, the Members and the Clash. The last two bands were my own favourites because of their integration of the downbeat grooves of reggae in amongst the power of their electric guitars. I vividly recall moonstomping my way through the Members' 'Offshore Banking Business' or the Clash roaring through a spirited version of Junior Murvin's 'Police And Thieves'. The co-ordination required to make the downshift from the chaos of pogo-ing to the loopy grace of the skank remains of my favourite memories of the whole gig going experience.

Towards the end of the Seventies, I was blagging my way through Sixth Form College. I remained academically incompetent while having the time of my life socially. Unruly teenage mobs of us armed with our meagre Saturday job earnings would get the train into Fenchurch Street and then on to venues such as Hammersmith Palais, the Music Machine, the Rainbow, Hammersmith Odeon, the Marquee, the Lyceum and many others to spend a scant couple of hours feeling like young lions with the world at our feet. The Ship in Wardour Street, the Marquis of Granby in Covent Garden, the George Robey in Finsbury Park, we would always go and get pissed before the show in nearby pubs, our adrenalin battling with the alcohol for dominance of our robust teenage constitutions. No matter how much we tried to time our arrival at the venue to a tardy, cool perfection, we always somehow arrived just as the support band was finishing up their set. Those of us who had saved up enough would invest in some badges or a tee shirt, those who were thirsty enough would pay the exorbitant venue price for watery lager. Then we'd slowly but surely edge our way towards the front of the stage. Each venue had its own pitfalls. At the Palais, you had to edge in from the sides, at the Music Machine you'd just barge your way forward through the frantic mob and at the Marquee, it was every man for himself in the sweaty melee. For my contemporaries, the ritual of the whole gig going experience was rooted in the familiar, the journey, the pub, the banter, the queue. The gig itself started to become just the excuse for a boozy night out, and often we were so drunk that we could barely remember the shows we had seen. Then one night at the Palais for me that all changed.

YOU'RE WONDERING NOW

The Specials were already firm favourites on my turntable at home. The debut album was a lesson in dance floor economy, brilliant track after brilliant track would burst out of my speakers with all the bounce and energy of a live gig. They cemented their reputation with the Number 1 'Too Much Too Young' EP, seven essential inches of vinyl that perfectly captured a great live band at their frenetic best. By this point in time most of my cash was being spent on a then girlfriend who was at a university some miles away. The result of this was that I didn't get to see the Specials until they toured their second album.

The London shows for the *More Specials* tour took place at Hammersmith Palais, and our tickets were picked up from a branch of Keith Prowse in the City. The month spent waiting for the date to come dragged by incredibly slowly. But once I was inside the sprung floor splendour of the legendary venue, my heart began to race. Earlier that year I'd seen the Clash, who were quite extraordinary. I was not expecting that experience to be bettered but it was.

Many critics and fans had not taken to Jerry Dammers' lounge psychedelia dub vision of the Specials. The second album had taken a sharp left turn from the upbeat precision of their debut. Swirling organs, mariachi trumpets and electronic rhythm boxes underpinned the bleakness of the lyrics. Tales of sexual infection, despondency, misery and drunkenness never sounded so good. The chaotic rhumba of 'Stereotype' giving way to the savage mosh of 'Gangsters' is to this day the finest transition between two songs I've ever seen at a gig. Our journey homewards on the X1 bus on the A13 was a muted affair. Usually we'd be bubbling with tales of how close we got to the front, chatting up girls by the bar or how we nearly got dragged into somebody else's ruck. But that night we were quiet and reflective, through a mixture of exhaustion and wonder. The meaning of Dammers' lyrics started to seep into our consciousness, the maturity of the arrangements sent me hunting for ever more eclectic sounds in my own record collection, the sheer energy of their live show made us all feel we'd made erroneous career decisions. It was in short a life-changing gig.

For me they remain a life-changing band. A few months ago, I stood in the pouring rain, six miles from the place of my birth on the Isle Of Wight and watched open mouthed as six of those life-changing individuals took to a stage once more. I recalled that the last time I saw them I was in exactly the same position in the front row, pressed up against the barrier at the Rainbow. It was as if I'd shut my eyes in 1981 and opened them again in 2008 and everything was as it had been.

When I talk to other fans about the Specials, they get quite enthusiastic; it seems I'm not the only one who was affected so deeply by their work. So was Paul, who wrote this book, and I bet you were too...

Phill Jupitus
December 2008

From JA to UK
THE ORIGINS OF SKA

*t*O UNDERSTAND the 'Dawning of a New Era' in the late Seventies, when ska became a household word in Britain through the explosion of 2Tone, you may want to know a little history…

'Ska' is a strange but exciting looking word, fittingly suited for the music it depicts. But ska isn't something that just exploded one day into an unwitting world. The origins of this hypnotic, up-tempo music we call ska essentially began life way back in African culture and tradition. The source of all Caribbean music can ultimately be traced back to the slave trade. In the late 17th and early 18th centuries, white European slave masters enslaved thousands of Africans and sent them to work in various parts of the British Empire, a large influx finding themselves on the islands of the West Indies. These slaves were sold off to land owners and in the process tribes and familes were split up. The result of this abhorrent practice was that, because of the mix of numbers of Africans from so many different and places and cultures, a fusion of traditional African musical styles developed. When the differing styles merged into one the music still heavily relied on rhythm. Later these fusions would draw in some European influences from the slave owners.

Moving forward to the late 19th century and early 20th century the sound of the Caribbean was calypso, which originated on the island of Trinidad. Calypso-style songs of the time were often risqué (a trend exploited by the Jamaican ska scene some decades later), topical to the islanders and sung in an African/French patois. The main topical verse was sung in an African language, whilst the chorus was made up of a local patois. Calypso, coming from the African word 'Ka'iso' was used by slaves to ridicule their owners without fear of reprimand, reprisals or worse. This form of musical insult was in the tradition of the African 'Griot' or 'Jali.' The Griot was a poet or wandering musician who collected and memorised a repository of oral traditions. These were important to the African tribes and therefore to the slaves who had no form of written history. The Griot chronicled their collective of histories, ancestry and genealogy. He would know many traditional songs off by heart, but also used his vocal talents to improvise and ad-lib on current events, incidents and the scenes he beheld. Griots had devastating wit and entertained through history, gossip, satire, and political comment. This is reflected in black music today through 'Toasting', as demonstrated by Neville Staple of the Specials, and is present in rap and hip-hop.

While calypso became Trinidad's main genre of music, in Jamaica, originally an island home to the Arawak Indians, a style of music was emerging from 'Kumina'. Kumina was introduced through the slave trade and it is believed its roots lie in the Congo. It is an amalgam of religion, music and dance and is the most African of Jamaican cults. During a Kumina ceremony, the exponents call on their ancestral spirits to guide them through events such as births, deaths and thanksgivings. The ceremonies consist of a dance ritual, similar to the polka, set to Kumina music. Kumina music has a heavy bass-line, which was originally played through the branch of the 'trumpet tree.' The music includes two types of drums, which provide a rich and highly charged musical background for the dancers, and helps to invoke the spirits of the ancestors. The larger and lower-pitched drum plays a steady 4/4 rhythm with accent on the first and third beats. This is significant to ska music as it could be seen to be the forerunner of the offbeat rhythm, which is unique to the Jamaican sound. Other instruments used are 'scrapers', (usually made of a simple kitchen grater which produces a scratching sound when another metal object is pulled across its surface), 'shakas' (gourd or tin-can rattles), and 'katta sticks' (two pieces of sticks used to play a steady rhythm on the back of the drum). Sometimes an empty rum bottle tapped with a spoon was used as an impromptu instrument. This style of music was most prevalent in the parish of St Thomas and is still played today.

After World War 2, the island's music began to transform. By the end of the Forties calypso was still prevalent in Jamaica but the country was quietly developing its own musical identity and mento was becoming the more popular sound. Mento is a laid-back, acoustic style of music with a distinctive rural or folk flavour. It was originally described as 'country music' by those who played it on the island. Mento draws on the musical traditions brought over by the slaves. The tradition of the Griot is reflected in the lyrics, which deal with aspects of everyday life in a light-hearted, humorous way and comment on political topics such as poverty, poor housing and other social issues. The lyrics also include thinly veiled sexual references and innuendos (often said to be the precursor of 'slackness' in dancehall music). Also reflected are aspects of the Kumina with its makeshift instruments cunningly crafted from what was available. Mento uses a huge range of more traditional and hand-crafted instruments including the saxophone, flute, banjo, bamboo fifes, PVC pipes, acoustic guitar, katta (or rhythm) sticks, shakas and the rhumba box. The rhumba box is a large 'thumb piano' made from wood. A number of tuned metal tines are stretched over a circular hole in the box; they are plucked to produce bass notes. The music of this period in mento, distinguished by its many instruments, was a prototype of what is known today as the reggae chop.

The influence of European music on mento is also strong. In the days of slavery, slaves who could play musical instruments were often required to play music for their masters. The Masters were enthusiastic about the ballroom, or set, dances of the courts of Europe such as the quadrille, and the lancer. After slavery ended the harmonies and melodies of these dances and accompanying music continued to contribute to the mento sound. Mento is also sometimes known as 'Jamaican Rumba' after the Australian born pianist Arthur Benjamin. Benjamin reproduced the mento form in his 'Jamaican Rumba' composition, which was published as sheet music in 1938. The music, akin to what was later known in the UK as 'Skiffle', brought him popular acclaim in the UK and made him a household name. The Jamaican government gave him a free barrel of rum every year for his contribution to making the country known.

In the Fifties mento had many popular stars but its best known exponents were the Jolly Boys, Lord Flea, Lord Fly, Lord Power, Lord Kitchener, Harold Richardson and the Ticklers and Count Sticky. The mento genre was given exposure by early Bob Marley and the Wailers recordings before he moved on to ska and ultimately Reggae, the area in which Marley went on to achieve global acclaim. Joseph Gordon, better known as Lord Tanamo, despite being known as one of Jamaica's top ska performers, was in fact an established mento star before he later turned his hand to R&B and then on to his court on the ska and reggae scene. When Jamaica became a huge favourite of tourists in this decade, mento bands performed at the docks, and by the pools, beaches and hotels up and down the island. Laurel Aitken, renowned worldwide as the 'Godfather of Ska', began his career performing his blend of mento and calypso for the Jamaican Tourist Board to entertain visitors alighting at Kingston Harbour.

It had been during World War 2 that the stationing of American Military forces on the islands first allowed Jamaican youths to listen to military broadcasts of American music, predominantly Big Band music and Jazz. During the Fifties the prominent radio stations on the island were 'Radio Jamaica Rediffusion' and the 'Jamaica Broadcasting Corporation', who were mainly responsible for churning out the contemporary pop sounds of North America. The youth of Jamaica, however, were simply outgrowing this mainstream fare and were ready to expand their musical tastes. They turned their attention to radio transmissions from the Southern United States which, weather permitting, the islanders could receive. The majority of these broadcasts came from stations in New Orleans and Miami, and for the first time they heard full-blooded R&B played by the likes of Count Basie, Fats Domino, Louis Jordan and Professor Longhair. These sounds lit up the Island's youth and it wasn't long before musicians incorporated the style into their own forms; by the mid Fifties the musical tide was turning in Jamaica. There is a theory that the delay effects (an important ingredient in the ska/reggae sound) may have originally been inspired by the oscillations in the radio signals from these faraway stations! With renewed energy and vigour, Jamaican bands and musicians began covering the US R&B hits they heard and interpreting them in their own style, which by now included jazz as an essential component.

Also at that time, smaller musical groups were superseding the Big Bands in America with a more Bop/R&B sound. This influence was brought back to Jamaica by Islanders who had travelled to the States. In the mid Fifties that sound combined with jazz and mento created yet another new form called shuffle. In the earliest days of shuffle, songs were all instrumental but the style was extremely derivative of North American artists. It was around this time that artists began to record their music for the first time. The shuffle sound gained ground as a favourite through the works of artists like Neville Esson, Owen Grey and the Matador Allstars. Many of the acts used studio musicians and so the mantle 'Allstars' was added to credit the back-up bands on records. By now, recording studios and like-minded companies began surfacing to hone new-found talent. The Jamaica Broadcasting Corporation, once cast as a somewhat generic station, brought their shows up-to-date with the developing popular sounds of the Island. This, in turn, stimulated young musicians into delving deeply into their respective genres.

Perhaps motivated by a desire to have recordings of local music to sell in his namesake department store, Stanley Motta was the very first producer to recognise the mento style and issue a few 78rpm records on his fledgling MRS (Motta's Recording Studio) label. In 1951, Motta built a small studio at 93 Hanover Street in Kingston, just around the corner from his department store. The studio itself was hardly a studio at all. Situated in the back room of a woodwork factory, it consisted of a 12 to 14 foot square space with insulated ceiling boards. The bands, musicians and their equipment were all crammed into the same small space. Recordings were captured through one microphone and the cutting machine only had one volume knob. Motta also utilised the one recording desk at the Rediffusion Radio Station. Stanley Motta is known as one of the first Jamaicans to produce records and would later set up a licensing deal with Emil Shallit's 'Melodisc' label for mento tracks to be released in the UK. Musical matters shifted again when the Sound Systems came into vogue and R&B dominated. This new form had a pulsating, raw, and heavy beat, a sound welcomed across the generations, both young and old succumbing to its infectious rhythms.

Sound System owners travelled to the States to buy the latest records, or employed agents to ship over the sought-after discs. Competition between the systems was fierce and the battle was to get the newest, freshest sounds for your system. Popular songs were repeated throughout the night as the systems brought in the crowds. Two sound systems well and truly above the others were located in Kingston, with Duke Reid formulating his legendary Trojan Sound System, and the celebrated Clement Dodd developing his famous Sir Coxsone Downbeat. These two icons of Jamaican music competed for over ten years and their eagerness to outdo each other meant they became major channels for the growth of the Jamaican music industry. Originally, the systems had no choice but to play American records, until Stanley Motta changed things when he built his recording studio. In the ghettos of Kingston, the DJs would set their system up by packing a truck with a generator, turntables, and huge speakers and then set up street parties that would rage for hours. Eventually, in order to move on from playing nothing but records from the States, the two sound system legends turned their keen eyes to record production. Initially, they produced only singles for their own sound systems, which came to be known as 'Exclusives'. The Jamaican producers introduced to their work some of the original elements of the indigenous Jamaican sound, rhythm guitars strumming the offbeat and a snare-drum emphasis on the third beat.

This new musical form became more popular and both Dodd and Reid moved more seriously into music production. Coxsone's production studio became the world famous Studio One', later dubbed the Motown of Jamaica. It soon became home to artists such as Theophilius Beckford, The Skatalites, Don Drummond, Bob Marley and Lee Perry, to name but a few. Meantime, Duke Reid would go on to found another JA giant, 'Treasure Isle', named after the family store he ran after being a police officer for ten years. He recorded the likes of Justin Hinds, U-Roy and Dennis Al Capone and would later specialise in Rastafarian roots music. All this recording activity meant that ska was burgeoning on the horizon.

There are various schools of thought about the development and naming of this new exciting genre. Guitarist Ernest Ranglin laid claim to the naming the sound with the term he coined as the 'skat! skat! skat!' scratching guitar strum. Double-bassist Cluett Johnson claimed that he had instructed Ranglin to 'play like ska, ska, ska' during a recording session, although Ranglin denied this, stating that Johnson could never tell him how to play! Another theory is that it derived from Johnson's word 'Skavoovie', the phrase he was known to greet his friends with. Founding Skatalites member Jackie Mittoo insisted that the musicians themselves called the rhythm 'Staya Staya' and that it was Byron Lee who eventually shortened this term to 'ska'. The last theory about the origin of ska is that the genre's biggest export and worldwide star, Prince Buster (born Cecil Bustamente Campbell) had created it during the inaugural recording sessions for his own new record label, Wild Bells. The session was financed by Duke Reid, who was supposed to get half of the songs to release. However, he only ever received one, which was a track by trombonist Rico Rodriguez, another talented musician who would go on to be an integral part of the Specials in 1979. It was during these sessions that Prince Buster told guitarist Jah Jerry to 'change gear, man, change gear.' The guitar began to emphasize the second and fourth beats in the bar, creating a completely new sound, which he complimented with a traditional Jamaican marching beat drum. In essence, to generate the ska beat, Prince Buster had essentially flipped the R&B shuffle beat to emphasize the offbeat with the assistance of the rhythm guitar. There will always be debate over who was the founder of ska, but we are all happy about its ultimate creation!

Early ska had few vocals and relied heavily on instrumentals. There was also an emphasis on horns and saxophones, which came as no surprise as the majority of ska artists were primarily experienced jazz musicians. The first ever ska records were created on Coxsone's Studio One and WIRL (West Indies Recording Limited) Records in Kingston, Jamaica with the chief producers being Coxsone, Reid, Prince Buster, and Edward Seaga, the owner of WIRL who dramatically went on to become the Prime Minister of Jamaica in 1980. The early records were about the Jamaican 'Rude Boy', or local gangster, who became staple subject matter for ska artists. The ska sound coincided with the celebratory feelings surrounding Jamaica's independence from the UK in 1962, and the event was commemorated by songs such as Derrick Morgan's 'Forward March', The Skatalites' 'Freedom Sound' and Lord Kitchener's 'Jamaica Woman'. Byron Lee and the Dragonaires performed ska with Prince Buster, Eric 'Monty' Morris, and Jimmy Cliff at the 1964 New York World Fair as the Jamaican sound was taken to America.

As music changed in the United States, so did ska. In 1965 and 1966, when American soul became slower and smoother, ska changed its sound accordingly and evolved into rocksteady before reinventing itself into what is known as reggae. The mass immigration to the UK from Jamaica via the ship *Empire Windrush* in 1948 meant that Jamaican influences and styles would inevitably follow, but it wasn't until the mid to late Sixties that the styles and sounds would be appreciated by the British. Artists such as Prince Buster, Laurel Aitken, The Pioneers, The Maytals, Harry Johnson, The Ethiopians, Desmond Dekker, Pat Kelly and Max Romeo made a huge impact on the UK music scene and it was their sounds that brought together young white, working-class youths and young Jamaicans in dance halls. This mix brought about the Skinhead youth cult, as the styles of the Jamaican Rude Boy were blended with those of the British mod as a celebration of the melding of the two cultures.

In Coventry, during the late Sixties and early Seventies, the throbbing beat of ska captivated a young man called Jerry Dammers and he began to formulate a plan. If 'You're Wondering Now' then read on…

PART ONE

THE DAWNING OF A NEW ERA

"We don't play Jamaican music...We play English music."
Jerry Dammers 1980

*I*F YOU ask anyone to name a city known for its contribution to music the answer will no doubt be London, Liverpool or Manchester. Few would think of the City of Coventry, but the town which nestles in the Midlands of England, better known for the antics of Lady Godiva, World War Two bombings and that enigmatic phrase 'being sent to Coventry', was also, in the Seventies, the birthplace of Britain's last great youth movement, 2Tone. 2Tone grabbed the British music charts by the throat, and for a short and volatile time turned the country into a sea of black and white chequers. The seven young men at the heart of this musical revolution were the Specials, a band whose music and ideals would leave such a legacy that, even today, their momentum is still felt on the on the face of the fickle British music industry. The Specials led the way for other bands that joined the 2Tone movement, such as the Selecter, Madness, the Beat, the Bodysnatchers and the Swinging Cats. Their music gave a voice and cause to disillusioned youth up and down the country, showed them how to stomp on the dancehall floors and shake the dust from the rafters. If you were young at that time and embraced the sounds and styles, you got a real sense of belonging. If you were part of it then you know how it felt. A simple Specials' button badge immediately linked you with total strangers who treated you like part of the club, and that's what 2Tone was – one big club. To be part of it all you needed was a love of the music.

The musical, political and social vision behind 2Tone was the brainchild of just one man: Jeremy David Hounsell Dammers. Jeremy, later to be known as Jerry, made his way into the world on May 22nd 1954 in Ootacamundi in Southern India, son of the Right Reverend Alfred Hounsell Dammers and his wife Brenda. Jerry's father lead an amazing life dedicated to serving others through the church. Born in 1921 in Great Yarmouth, he became known as 'Horace', a name given to him by his teacher after the Roman poet. He was a staunch Labour Party supporter all his life and a Cambridge scholar who, during the war years, became involved in the church and slowly rose through its ranks. He travelled extensively before arriving in Coventry in 1965. Eventually he became the Dean of Bristol where he set up a chapel used for peace and anti-apartheid vigils and supported the city's homeless and other minorities. In 1972, he founded the 'Life-Style Movement' that encouraged people to give up their luxury items, he also wrote several books on the subject of faith. Jerry's father had a profound influence on his son's ideals and beliefs, especially on the anti-racist front.

As a child Dammers had been made to sing in church choirs, something he detested, and as he grew he started to rebel. It became apparent that his strict, respectable upbringing was going to lead to a clash of personalities and that trouble would follow. Jerry was certainly the most unconventional member of his family. His brother went on to become a doctor and his two sisters took up social work. He had been into music at an early age when, much to the amusement of his brothers and

Very early Specials flyer

sisters, Dammers recorded a tape and sent it to John Lennon! Aged 13, Jerry was forced to take up piano lessons but he soon gave them a wide berth, although in hindsight they were to prove invaluable in his later life. At 15, he became what he later described as a mini-mod, before adopting the hippy look, hair and all. Together with a friend, he escaped the humdrum of reality and fled to a small island off the Irish coast that John Lennon had previously bought for use as a commune for peace-loving dropouts.

"God, it was awful." Jerry later recalled, "They put us to work ploughing the fields and every night we'd be given a bowl of flour and water. The fields were laid out in the letters of the word L-O-V-E. That was when I stopped being a hippy and became a Skinhead."

Aged 15, Dammers gained his trademark missing two front teeth when he went over the handlebars of his bike; he was left with a huge brace and stitches in his face.

One night at a youth club in Baginton, a village just outside Coventry, a progressive rock band were playing, albeit terribly, and after they had left the stage, the disco erupted to 'Liquidator' by Harry J's Allstars, an original reggae track. As Dammers watched the few Skinheads in attendance diving around to the tune, something switched in his head: "Once you're hooked on Reggae," he explained, "it becomes a bit of a cause. 'Live Injection' by The Upsetters is probably the most ecstatic dance record ever made. Of course, I thought it had something to do with Skinheads then, I didn't know it was Lee Perry working his African magic across continents – but we were all misled and still are. I might have been stupid but I can remember thinking then, if only the skins weren't, according to the stereotype, kicking the shit out of hippies or immigrants, or each other at football, if only all that energy and anger was directed into something positive and against the system, which brutalised them in the first place. I was very idealistic, some might say bonkers."

Jerry left school at 16 with one art 'O' level to his credit, which scuppered his mother's plans to send him on to university. Instead, he became a student at Nottingham Art School for a year or so before transferring to Lanchester Polytechnic in Coventry. He spent most of his time there making films and cartoons, drinking and getting into youthful trouble. His career of vandalism came to an abrupt end one day when he started to jump up and down on the roof of an occupied car and fell straight through! Luckily, nobody was injured but Dammers collected a £250 fine and the gravity of a court appearance put him back on the straight and narrow. While at college, he made three intricate animated films. One concerned the Fifties boxing match between Rocky Marciano and British champ Don Cockell, another was entitled *Disco*, which included a reggae soundtrack composed by Jerry and a fellow student from the year above whom he had befriended and whose name was Horace Panter.

"*Disco* was about two minutes long," said Jerry, "there was a lot of work in all of them and I did all the animation myself. The soundtrack was pretty good and I was really pissed off when I discovered it had been nicked from college."

Jerry's third film was an epic: "It was a mixture of live film and animation set in Seventies Coventry. It started with someone walking down the street and you'd see all these people doing things. Then suddenly it would change to animation. There was a bloke running along, a sort of football hooligan, who throws a brick through a window and in animation, you saw the glass smashing. Then there was this old tramp, a mate of mine really, who falls over and spews over the pavement. The camera zoomed into on the spew and it was all bones and things bubbling away. There was an old woman crossing the street who gets run over. Some of it was full animation, but a lot of it was done with cut-outs, a very tedious business. It was about that time the IRA were going round and at the end a bloke puts a bag under a car and the whole street gets blown to pieces, guts flying everywhere."

Tom and Jerry it certainly wasn't! Dammers eventually got his degree, but dismissed it out of hand: "The actual degree was irrelevant, really; that was just a by-product of what I was really doing which was just using the college facilities to do what I wanted, which was to make cartoons. I hate the idea of degrees and all their connotations of privilege and success. I hate privilege, that's why I never collected my degree from them."

Apart from film, making music was another of Jerry's burgeoning passions. He based his decision to become a musician on two things; one was hearing Graham Parker's number 'Not If It Pleases Me' that made Jerry think that he could do things on his own. The other was when he saw the the Who perform 'My Generation' on TV, although he was taken solely by the music, rather than the band's approach. His own musical preferences included reggae from his Skinhead days and a whole range of bands from the Small Faces to Slade. His first taste of ska came courtesy of his brother: "I borrowed my brother's records all the time. One day I was sitting on the floor sifting through them when I found Prince Busters 'FAB-ulous Hits'. I listened to it and it had a great effect on me. I really took to the record."

After college, Jerry played in a number of bands that weren't really to his satisfaction. Some of them had curious titles including Cissy Stone Soul Band, Peggy Penguin and the Southside Greeks, Ricky Nugent and the Loiterers, and the Lane Travis Country Trio but undoubtedly the best was Gristle. He also had a stint with Ray King. Ray King was a local Coventry legend and it is fair to say that without him the 2Tone phenomenon may have never got off the ground since the majority of 2Tone musicians cut their musical teeth with him. His real name was Vibert Cornwall, and his band, well respected in the local area, was originally called Suzi and The Kingsize Kings. He acquired the stage name Ray King and the band mantle changed to the Ray King Soul Band. Their reputation quickly grew, and they were soon asked to play at the Playboy Club in London. They later recorded an album at that venue and signed to major labels such as Pye and CBS before splitting in the Seventies.

Ray had acquaintances in the town of Gloucester called Lynval Golding, Silverton Hutchinson, Desmond Brown and Charley Bembridge, all of whom later became big players in the 2Tone movement. Ray moved the Gloucester boys over to Coventry and formed another band, with himself on vocals, called Pharaoh's Kingdom. Hutchinson had a friend called Neol Davies who turned up to rehearsals and he brought with him Jerry Dammers. A couple of guys called the Smith brothers also joined up and a new group, Night Train, was formed. Ray King had wanted to play out-and-out ska but Dammers himself was not overly keen to play in this style at that time and left, and not long after Davies followed. Ray King himself carried on in music for a while, then ended up in management and devoting time to helping the local West Indian community.

With the advent of punk Jerry became heavily involved in song writing and took on the persona of Gerald 'The General' Dankey, most of his early compositions at this time being embryonic forms of future Specials tracks. He became well known in the close-knit Coventry music scene and by early 1977 was trying to put together his own band. Dammers joined forces with old friend Neol Davies to record some demos on an old Revox tape recorder in Jerry's living room. They needed to involve other people and so recruited bass player and college acquaintance Horace Panter. Horace was born Stephen Graham Panter on August 30th 1953 in Croydon, and was later adopted and moved to Kettering where his nickname of 'Horace' was given to him by a schoolteacher. He was working as a van driver and playing bass with the soul band Breaker when Jerry went to see them play in Coventry and afterwards asked him to play on a track he had written.

"After the gig I remember Jerry coming up to me," said Panter, "and as he talked he spat saliva over me. He wanted me to help him with some demos so I said okay. After he had gone I wondered what I was letting myself in for!"

In Horace's book *Ska'd for Life* he said: "I did recall him from college, one of the new boys who were loud and aggressive and didn't seem to give a toss, with his tartan trousers, sideburns and grown-out mod haircut."

Jerry reflected on those times, and added: "We used to wreck the hippie parties, play Prince Buster records. I had this band playing dodgy versions of Desmond Dekker's '007'. We used to gob at each other on stage. I was like a forerunner of punk but I suppose realistically punk was a bit of a musical dead end for me. I went to punk gigs but enjoyed the reggae they played between sets more. I thought the Sex Pistols played boring power rock, though I related to punk's lyrics and anarchic attitude. People felt able to write their own songs and about their own lives. I got thrown out of a local band for wanting to play our own material so it was then that I decided to form my own band."

Horace went along to rehearsals and was introduced to a true form of reggae, which he wasn't used to playing. He eventually mastered the sound and became a fully-fledged member of the group, now going by the name of the Hybrids. The inclusion of Horace as bassist had a bitter taste for one young graduate called Andrew Calcutt. He thought it should have been him taking his place in history but it was not to be: "Straight after my finals I moved to Cambridge to join Jerry and a couple of local graduates, one of them a Coventry kid like us, in forming a band of wannabe rude boys," said Calcutt. "I borrowed the phrase from Jamaican slang via the NME and introduced it at a rehearsal the previous summer, to general hilarity! Except that JD didn't show up as I thought we had agreed. A year or so later I received a phone call asking me to go hear him play at an American airbase, ('Soul Showband' or 'Rock'n'Roll Revival', it could have been either) somewhere in East Anglia. When I couldn't go, I got a message to the effect that if I wanted to join up where we had left off, I'd better get back to Coventry quick because of another good bass player in the offing. The other good bass player was Sir Horace Gentleman, and the off-ing happened to me, not him. Horace and I have a history, though we have only ever exchanged the briefest of pleasantries. He plays bass; so did I. He played bass in a band with Jerry Dammers; so did I (though when we started playing together, Jerry was still 'Jeremy'). I gave Jerry my organ, the cast-off my dad got cheap from the church where he was priest-in-charge."

Calcutt remained a musician and recorded with the band Ersatz, later going on to obtain an MA in Journalism and Society at the University of East London.

Dammers also grabbed the services of Tim Strickland, a gawky youth, on vocals. Strickland couldn't really sing a decent note, a fact which Strickland does not deny. He told writer Andy Clayden's ska and reggae website: "Hey! This was the time of punk mate, anything went! I was with the band for about nine months. Jerry had seen me perform, very badly, but enough to convince him that I was the one, at least for a short time, with a college band called Dave and the Ravers. I was the token punk although I thought I had more of a James Dean fixation! We rehearsed and gigged mainly in a pub called the Heath Hotel and regularly filled the place, which still amazes me! We were good, although I still never saw myself as musical or a pop star. I used to read the lyrics (all Jerry's) off sheets of paper, which I thought was appropriately punk and used to sit on the edge of the stage through the instrumental bits. We did record three or four songs as demos live in the Heath Hotel but I don't know what happened to them. Jerry invited me to rehearse with the band following a meeting on a train. I later worked at the Virgin record shop and as manager employed Brad (John Bradbury), later the drummer with the Specials, as assistant manager."

Strickland moved into band management, later being involved with Terry Hall's mid-Eighties combo the Colour Field and then becoming creative director of the doomed Museum For Popular Music in Sheffield that opened its doors in 1999 and closed in 2000. Also in the fledgling line-up was drummer Silverton Hutchinson who came from Barbados, and who was well known in close circles for his mood swings. He was an expert reggae drummer who had played with Dammers in Pharaoh's Kingdom.

The man who would later give the Specials their essential offbeat ska rhythm,

Lynval Fitzgerald Golding, came next. Lynval was born on July 24th 1951, in the Mendez District of St Catherine in Jamaica (a place that until the early Eighties didn't even have electricity). Life changed forever for Lynval when he was 10 years old. His mother sent him and his sisters to Gloucester, England with his aunt who would eventually bring them up. Lynval recalled: "I thought my mother was coming with us. I had no idea my mother was staying behind. When I was going on the ship, I was half way up, looked back, and saw my mother on the dockside crying. I wanted to run back but my aunt was shouting at me, everyone was walking up. For years, I didn't understand why she sent us away from her. Now I can see what an amazing, selfless act it was. It must have been the hardest decision she ever had to make. Sending her children to England because she believed it would benefit us. And she was right. I wouldn't be sitting here talking to you if it wasn't for that woman. I wouldn't have done the Specials or anything else in music. I wouldn't have had any of those opportunities. Can you imagine sending your children thousands of miles away because you knew they'd have a better life away from you? I'm forever grateful to her for the sacrifices she made to give me the life I've had. Before she passed, we had some very special moments that I'll treasure forever. I learnt a lot from her."

Lynval fondly told *Rockers Revolt* in 2008 about his early years in Jamaica: "It sounds like a cliché but we didn't have anything in Jamaica. We made our own toys, jigs and trucks and played marbles. They were cheap to buy. I used to love when it rained. The downpours were torrential, but pass just as quick is they started. We loved playing out in them. Everyday, first thing, we'd go and fetch the water from the well; there was no running water there. Then we'd move the goats to feed, then back home to wash, then walk the two miles to school. It was a very simple life, but a very happy one, surrounded by love and music everyday."

The transition to life in England was a hard one for young Lynval to make and he was miserable. He hated it here and thought it was very cold, missing the Jamaican climate, but the first summer he had in England was long and hot so that seemed to help him settle down. The family first lived in Southampton, then spent time in Birmingham and Gloucester, where Lynval went to school, before settling in Coventry. Once he had moved to Gloucester he enjoyed school, but after a while the larger kids at school subjected him to racial taunts: "School was the thing that got me. School in England was the first time I experienced racism. I didn't know what it was! I had no idea! I couldn't understand why these kids were calling me 'gollywog' and all these different names they had for black kids. I hadn't experienced racism in Jamaica. We had three white kids in our school in Jamaica and we just thought our job was to look after them. School in England were the worst years of my life. I hated it. The older kids spat at me and called me names. I just wasn't used to that kind of thing because in Jamaica prejudice didn't exist. There was no 'Oh, you're white so I'm not gonna talk to you.' In my school days in England there were only ten or so black kids, but nowadays it's a lot more mixed with Asians and West Indians, so at least its better for them."

Lynval's only real interest was music. His first guitar, a Fender, was purchased from his own pocket at the age of ten and funded by money he had made doing odd jobs. When he was 16, he left school and desperately wanted to be in a band but he began to tinker around with car engines, which got him a job as an apprentice motor mechanic. However, music had a magnetic attraction for young Golding and he was soon in his first band, the Merrytones, a soul-influenced combo that existed on covers of Otis Redding and Sam & Dave. By the time he was 20 he was married with a daughter and was an accomplished guitarist: "I don't think my father thought I could really make a creative career for myself in the music scene," said Lynval "so I intended to prove him wrong."

Later, as already documented, he teamed up in Coventry with Charlie 'H' Bembridge, Desmond Brown and Ray King in Pharaoh's Kingdom and it was during this time he met and befriended Jerry Dammers. Lynval already lived a mere fours doors away from him, they met frequently in the local pub The Pilot, and the friendship blossomed, with Dammers eventually asking him to join his band, the Hybrids. They played their first gig in 1977 at the Heath Hotel and went down quite well, well enough anyway to gain them a fortnightly residency along with some punk bands.

It was just after this that Jerry spied a singer in a local riotous punk band called Squad. He had seen the band wrecking some show in Coventry and phoned Horace Panter stating 'We need this guy in the band!' Jerry dragged Horace off to catch the group and its sullen, enigmatic young singer a couple of times before it was decided that Tim Strickland would have to go. His replacement would come in the shape of the soon-to-be former singer of Squad, Terence Edward Hall, a volatile 18-year-old who was known to perform gigs with his back to the audience. He possessed a perfect punk sneer and stage presence, based around one of his punk heroes, Johnny Rotten.

According to Terry there had been a bit of hero worship: "He was amazing. It was just the way he stood on stage and gazed for half an hour. I'd never seen anything like it. His stance was like an extension of standing still, it was like a meaningful glare. But I don't stand still."

Born on March 19th 1959, Terry had a happy upbringing in the city of Coventry. His father, Terry senior, worked as a technical author at the Rolls-Royce Parkside car plant in the city while his mother Joan worked as a trimmer at the Talbot car plant. Hall spent his early childhood tucked away in corners avidly reading copies of *The Dandy* and *Beano* and recalled his only major upset as a child was at Christmas one year when he was given what he thought was a cheap Johnny Seven GI figure when he had set his heart on an authentic Action Man! However, as is often the case, his rebellious streak soon started to develop.

He thoroughly hated school. Whilst attending the Frederick Bird Primary School in Swan Lane he actually jumped off a wall in an attempt to break his arm so he wouldn't have to attend. It didn't work, although he recalled he had a sling made up to make him look the part! As he approached his early teenage years, he began to break away from his parents, particularly when the original Skinhead movement arrived in the late Sixties to early Seventies: "I remember I wanted a pair of real Oxford Brogues," explained Terry "and my mum said she would get me a pair. She came back with these boots and they were (and I mean no disrespect to spastics) like spastic boots. I was supposed to be a Skinhead and I was going out done up like a spastic!"

Hall moved on to the Sidney Stringer Comprehensive School in Cox Street, now a community technical college, where he was duly picked on and constantly bullied. Terry said: "People thought that I was a poof because I didn't go around pretending I'd slept with every girl in the class."

His days of being tormented by the school thugs soon ended when one day three boys who regularly bullied him were waiting for him in a subway: "One of them hit me," Terry recalled, "so I punched him hard in the mouth and kicked hell out of him. I felt much better for it."

At the age of 13 he was a promising footballer and was signed up by Coventry City's youth team as a centre forward but his destiny as a professional striker was cut short when he discovered the charms of the opposite sex. "I used to make a right twat out of myself when it came to girls," he said, "I used to find them all difficult really. I never knew what to say to them. My first girlfriend was called Valerie and she was fat and quite horrible. We were both 14 and I used to blow kisses outside her bedroom window. It was acutely embarrassing. I wasn't even aware I was going out with her until someone told me! As I got older, though, they became less and less of an irritation and more and more a pain in the arse."

Terry realised there was more to life than going to school when he joined a local gang called Blackfoot. It was here he was involved in gang fights and where he first ran into a young Lynval Golding. He left school at 15 and never regretted it. He went straight into employment working with the disabled. He would often sort through the jumble sent in to raise funds and help himself to anything worthwhile, as did the other employees, especially searching out decent working radios. He later tried his hand as an apprentice bricklayer, as a clerk, and even considered hairdressing: "I remember working on a building site," he said, "and I was bored and I thought I wanted to go off and cut hair for a change, but that's as far as it got!"

His last main job was as a numismatist working for David Fletcher Ltd in Coventry's Station Square where his elegant job description meant that he dealt in coins and medals. Fletcher recalled his young apprentice: "Yes, I remember Terry Hall; he was employed by me at our stamp and coin shop by Coventry railway station sometime in the Seventies. His main duties were packing orders and dealing with the mailing. He seemed a decent young man. I think working for me was one of his first jobs after leaving school. I was quite surprised to see him all over the Coventry newspapers and TV with his group."

It was whilst sitting bored in this job that he realised his true vocation in life; music: "It may sound like a sob story," Hall explained "but having left school with no qualifications I was just bumming around in and out of about 20 different jobs. The only thing that remotely appealed to me was singing and music. I loved the early days of being in the Specials. I was also a bit over-awed – I used to sit there like a good lad and listen and try to work out what it was all about. I was 17; I had a lot of belief in Jerry. He was about five years older than me; they all felt a lot older than me at that time. They felt like grown-ups."

This led to Terry's riotous romp with Squad and after seeing him in action Dammers wanted him in his band, now known as the Automatics. So, in a shot, they voted in the sullen, broody Hall and Tim Strickland was out: "The move to replace me," said Strickland "was a little more organised. The band rehearsed Terry Hall, from Cov punk band Squad, and called round to take me for a pint and broke the news none too gently. I was already suspicious, as Jerry had never bought me a pint before! I was mildly pissed off but not really surprised and would never have had the dedication to go through what the Specials did after that. To my great embarrassment I did throw half a pint of beer over Terry one night when they had a support slot at Tiffany's!"

Strickland worked with Hall many moons later and there were no grudges borne over the beer-throwing incident!

The line up of what was to be the Specials took another major step forward with the conscription of lead guitarist Roddy Byers, known locally as 'Roddy Radiation'. Roderick James Byers was born on May 5th 1955 in the mining town of Keresley near Coventry, where he would stay for the first 18 years of his life. His father, Stan, played trumpet for a number of bands in the sixties and was very well known around the Midlands. When

YOU'RE WONDERING NOW

Roddy was 11, Stan introduced him to the trombone and his brother Chris to the trumpet, but a couple of years later young Byers found what he was looking for in the shape of rock 'n' roll. Out went the trombone and in came the electric guitar. Roddy joined a few school bands and gained a few youth club gigs and it was in these early days when he first encountered Jerry Dammers. The 15-old Dammers was in a band called Gristle when Roddy tried out for the group but it was only years later that they both realised they had been in the same band!

"Jerry was playing drums but he was a terrible drummer," said Roddy, "but the guitarist was even worse. I really didn't like him but he was someone to play with. The trouble was that no one else liked him either so I was always getting beaten up for playing with him!"

As school finished Roddy joined a band that played tunes during the interval at the bingo in the local Top Rank and he joined the local authority as a painter and decorator, which enabled him to buy a new guitar and a much-needed amp. Roddy soon upped the ante in his musical direction by joining a club show band called Heaven Sent, who played at working men's clubs, the hardest of all musical training grounds. Roddy's musical preferences and fashions changed in the Seventies and he adopted a Ziggy Stardust-style persona and the guise of Roddy Radiation, a moniker given to him by his brother Chris in reference to the fact that Roddy's face glowed when he had had one too many drinks! Roddy decided to keep the name when punk crept into the scene. Around this time, he wrote the track 'Meanest Creature' in Bowie-esque style and then expanded his musical boundaries, getting heavily into Iggy Pop, Lou Reed and the New York Dolls, which propelled him to form his first real group. With spiky hair, drainpipe trousers and safety-pins the order of the day, the Wild Boys became known as one of the better bands on the Coventry scene and played mainly covers interspersed with five or six songs that Roddy had written including 'Eighties Teddy Boy' and a song called 'Concrete Jungle' which would later become part of Specials folklore. The original line up of the Wild Boys included the UK Subs' Pete Davies. They played mainly local gigs apart from a highlight in Manchester where they played support to Buzzcocks. Jerry Dammers took Horace Panter to see them in action: "We went to see them at the Golden Cross. They were deafeningly loud and I didn't stay very long."

Also around this time, Roddy met Terry Hall. He was still screaming with Squad, who supported the Wild Boys at one show. The association did not last long because by the time the Wild Boys had come on stage Squad had broken all the microphones and spat over the crowd: "Me and Roddy were in the first group of punks that ever appeared in Coventry," said Terry Hall. "People just took the piss all the time. That only made us more hardened to the ridicule and afterwards things didn't worry us again."

Coventry muso Kevin Harrison recalls his good friend Roddy: "Everybody I know celebrated the arrival of punk. The Sex Pistols and the Clash played Coventry Lanchester Polytechnic. I met Joe Strummer, friendly, positive, and Johnny Rotten, snotty, negative. Perfect! The gig was a great inspiration, that is until some cretin pogo-ed on my Lynda's foot! We met 20 or so other punk revellers requiring medical attention in Casualty at Cov and Warwick Hospital including my good mate from Keresley, Roddy Radiation, who later would pop round to our gaff and record a few demos."

Neville Staple remembered Roddy from around Coventry. Apparently, he had been hard to miss! "I used to see Rod around Cov, with his safety pins, spiky hair and eye make up. I thought to myself 'what the bloody hell's goin' on there?'"

The Wild Boys split in 1977 just before Punk truly burst out nationwide. Roddy left but his brother Mark, known then as 'Mark Extra', carried on and they remained a draw to Coventry punters. They eventually recorded, and the track 'We're Only Monsters', written by Roddy, appeared on the album *Sent From Coventry* released by Cherry Red Records. It was to be through alcohol that Byers would soon be recruited by Dammers to join his burgeoning band the Automatics: "Me and Jerry Dammers were party animals in those days," recalled Roddy, "and trying to find a late drink was pretty difficult in Coventry in 1979. A curry or a dodgy club was the only way to get a late beer.

"One such club was called 'The Domino', which had been a gay hangout, but in 1978-79 had been taken over by punks and various degenerates and criminals. It was there that Jerry asked me to play guitar on a demo they (the Automatics) were doing in London. After many pints I staggered off home and next morning I was awoken by someone banging and kicking my front door."

At the front door was Jerry and a local DJ, Pete Waterman. Waterman, of course, would go on to be a pop-music supremo in the Eighties, but when he was involved with the Automatics he was DJ at a local night club called Mr George's in Coventry's Precinct. He would later go on to say he was the man that discovered the Specials. The Automatics had a Monday night residency at Mr George's and were slowly building up a good-sized following. Waterman had taken a shine to the band, their unique weird mix of punky reggae capturing his attention. He offered to take them into the studio, saying he "knew a few people" and stumped up £600 to pay for the session, which was to be recorded at Berwick Street in London's Soho district, and now he was banging on Roddy's front door.

"I explained the situation to my missus, slung on my clothes, then Jerry and Pete helped me load my Vox AC30 and Gibson Les Paul into a taxi and we caught the train to the Big Smoke."

The demos were recorded and Waterman tried to get various record companies to share his interest in the band but nothing came to fruition. Back to square one. Pete Waterman later recalled: "It's very easy to doubt your own abilities when people all around you are questioning your judgements. I remember being very disillusioned with the whole music industry when I managed the Specials. I had a great act on my hands, a really talented bunch of lads, and yet no one wanted to sign them. I began to think that maybe my gut instincts were wrong and reluctantly I had to let them go. Then the whole 2Tone thing exploded and I wondered why I had ever let them beat me down. Over the years, I have had quite a few times like that, and now I refer to my difficult periods as 'Specials Situations'. Whenever I start to self-doubt, I just think of them and that soon puts me back to my normal self! But I was their biggest fan and biggest champion. I knew how socially right their songs were. People know I was the first with the Specials, people knew I was the one that took these songs to them like 'Too Much Too Young' and 'Jaywalking'."

Lynval Golding told of how impressed Waterman was with singer Terry: "We were down in Berwick Street doing the demos when Terry comes in to do the vocal and he nails it all in one take! One take! He had only been with us a couple of months really. Pete comes in after and says 'Fuckin hell! Where the fuck you get him from? He is fuckin' brilliant!'"

"Terry taught me something," said Waterman, "which I thought was one of the greatest things you learn as a record producer. Really, Terry couldn't sing but what Terry had was a unique voice. The public does like people with unusual voices, something distinctive, and let's face it when you hear Terry you know exactly who it is. Then you had

Lynval and Neville who were really toasters, great characters, but to be honest how Neville got in the band I will never know. I think 'cos he was one of their mates and he was a bit of a Jack the Lad? I remember him saying he was singing in the group. I still can't believe it to this day! But there was one lad with a vision and he was Jerry Dammers. He was the creative dynamo."

As well as Waterman touting the demos around various record companies, Dammers himself was doing a similar job and sent one tape to Radio 1 DJ John Peel, the champion of all things new and alternative, but unfortunately for the band nothing came of that transaction.

"Pete Waterman was the first guy to demo us," said Jerry. "He tried to teach Terry Hall to dance some hip-swinging cross between the Watusi and the Shag. So, that was him sacked! Nothing against him though. I realised trying to teach Terry to dance was wrong; Pete was from a different variety really. I mean he was trying to teach Terry to swivel his hips and if anyone has seen Pete Waterman swivelling his hips it's enough to put you off for life!"

The demos recorded with Waterman's cash were lost for 15 years before they were found and released by Receiver Records in 1993 under the title *Dawning Of A New Era – The Coventry Automatics AKA The Specials*. The recordings gave a fascinating insight into a group who didn't sound any better than your average pub band but were only 18 months or so away from some major-league success.

As mentioned in the above album title, the group name was the Coventry Automatics, and the reason for the change in the title was that another band called the Automatics had signed to a major label, thereby scuppering the Midlands boys' plans to use it. The word 'Coventry' was added to make them distinguishable from the signed group.

London loomed again on the band's horizon and they ventured south once more to record more tracks, but again nothing happened as a result of these recordings. About this time Jerry was introduced to Chris Gilbey, the manager of UK-based Australian punk band the Saints. At their meeting, the Coventry Automatics were offered a support slot to the punks at the legendary Marquee Club in Wardour Street. The gig was successful, but as Horace Panter, who had now acquired the stage title of Sir Horace Gentleman (given to him by Lynval in parody of his middle class accent and mannerisms), said: "For one of the world's greatest rock stages the place was a shit hole. It stank."

The group were so short on cash that they had to borrow the petrol money to get back to Coventry but as Lynval Golding enthused: "It was rough, it was tough, but man, they were the real good old days. Just going from gig to gig, just scraping by, sitting on our equipment in the back of a little van, listening to tapes."

Back home, after the latest capital city jaunt, the band were quietly perfecting their punky reggae sound, gaining plenty of local gigs and venturing further a field to places like Manchester. They had a growing crowd of followers, but the next step on their road to national recognition came courtesy of one of the more well-known bands of the day, the Clash. A man the band knew called Dave Cork was acting as tour manager for the Clash and he owed Jerry and the boys a big favour after an earlier gig in Birmingham, where they had also been booked to support the Clash. The gig had gone awry when Joe Strummer et al had failed to turn up, leaving the Automatics to play on their own to a crowd expecting to see the Clash. As recompense, Cork managed to squeeze the band on to the bill as support on the 'On Parole Tour' while the real support act, US band Suicide, made their way over to the UK to join up with the tour.

Fate connects the two bands in another unconfirmed story. Well known for thinking on a grand scale, Dammers had originally wanted Johnny Rotten to join the band following the demise of the Sex Pistols, and while on a trip to search him out, Jerry left some tapes with one of Rotten's supposedly big contacts. But the cassettes never reached him. Instead they were heard by a man who was going to have a big effect on the career of the Automatics, Clash manager Bernie Rhodes who, along with Malcolm McLaren, was one of the most powerful managers around at that time. Rhodes was something of a mystery character, well known for his forthright approach to management, and was someone who rarely gave interviews. As a result, not a lot is known about the man and the eccentric reputation he holds as a tough, hard-nosed negotiator who loved to philosophise and who only worked on his own terms.

Rhodes was not a great self-promoter, but was very meticulous in his projects and possessed a rapier-sharp mind. As a result of not pushing himself forward in the media, his influence is often overlooked, but he was responsible for some major achievements. Aside from the Clash, he was the man who brought Johnny Rotten into the Sex Pistols and would have a hand in nurturing the careers of bands like the Specials, Dexys Midnight Runners and Subway Sect. Paul Simonon, the Clash bass player, told Pat Gilbert in *Passion Is A Fashion*: "You can't over-estimate Bernie's importance. He set up the whole punk scene basically. He saw how non-musicians like myself and John Lydon could contribute."

Rhodes was born in the East End of London, England, just after his Jewish mother had fled persecution in Russia in the wake of the Second World War. He grew up with an entrepreneurial attitude, always trying to cut himself a good deal. Come 1974 he was already designing and printing T-shirts for Malcolm McLaren and was a part-time mechanic, but his association with McLaren took him into musical circles, an area where he would thrive. He set up what was going to be the Clash after meeting Joe Strummer at a Sex Pistols gig, putting him together with Mick Jones and Paul Simonon. The rest, as they say, is musical history.

When the Automatics got some dates as support on the Clash tour, Dammers was determined to gain more shows and so harassed Strummer, singing the band's merits. Strummer warmed to the Automatic's strange punk-reggae style and was convinced that they were a safe bet. In due course Strummer told Bernie Rhodes he wanted them for the whole tour. After seeing them, Rhodes was less convinced, but gave in. On the opening night of the 'On Parole' tour the band announced themselves as 'The Special AKA The Automatics' but, as often happens with these things, someone shortened it to the Specials.

"Ah, well," Dammers would later say in 2005, "the group name the Specials was supposed to be like saying the word 'Sex Pistols' when you were pissed and slurring your words. That's true – not a lot of people know that, but they do now!"

Chris Long, former member of 2Tone band the Swinging Cats, and otherwise known as 'The Rhythm Doctor', recalled: "We were walking home from the pub one night, when Jerry asked me 'What do you think of the name the Specials?' to which I replied 'That's crap, it reminds me of the Special Constabulary.' But Jerry stuck to his guns and history speaks for itself. I also have a quirky memory of Jerry playing his organ in the crowd, facing the band onstage, and waving his hands like a conductor."

Journalist, musician and TV presenter Garry Bushell saw the first gig where the band that supported the Clash were billed as the Specials: "I was at the Aylesbury Friars club when they did that first gig billed as the Specials." said Garry, "I was working for the *Sounds* music paper and the first on that bill that night were the Specials. I was really intrigued by that mix they had, that punky reggae party thing going on. More than anything I always remember Neville; he was a ball of energy."

Predictably, the Clash went down a storm but support band Suicide suffered some abuse from the manic crowds. For the Specials it was an immense eye-opener, and they also received a hostile reception. In Aberdeen the band were pelted with flashcubes and spat at, and other gigs were little different. The hordes of drunken punks who were only interested in the Clash and their sound-a-likes, did not appreciate their mixed sound. For a measly £25 a night it wasn't anyone's idea of fun and even when the Clash forced Bernie Rhodes to double the Specials' meagre earnings, the Coventry boys must have wondered whether it was worth all the hassle. In Bracknell, the gig had been disrupted by Nazi skinheads, who were fervently aligned to the mighty and notorious Sham 69. The National Front had developed a plan of seek, approach and convert and they had infiltrated football hooligan and skinhead gangs. Their idea was to promote aggro at gigs and soccer matches as a way of courting the media's interest. Earlier that year, skinheads, rioting and sieg heiling as they went, had caused £7,500 worth of damage at a Sham 69 concert at the London School of Economics.

"In Bracknell," Jerry Dammers recalls, "the Sham Army turned up, got onstage and attacked the lead singer of Suicide, the other support band. That was the night the Specials concept was born. I idealistically thought 'We have to get through to these people.' It was obvious that a mod and skinhead revival was coming and I was trying to find a way to make sure it didn't go the way of the National Front and the British Movement. I saw punk as a piss-take of rock music, as rock music committing suicide, and it was great and it was really funny, but I couldn't believe people took it as a serious musical genre which they then had to copy. It seemed to be a bit more healthy to have an integrated kind of British music, rather than white people playing rock and black people playing their music. Ska was an integration of the two."

Despite the disruptions, the tour did have one bright spot, the arrival of the group's final member, Neville Staple. Neville recalls his experiences on the Clash tour: "It was great backstage, the Clash loved us and we loved the Clash, we got on with all of the members of the Clash and even now we still all talk."

Neville was a Coventry legend before he joined the band. Known as a loveable rogue, he began turning up to Automatics gigs and was an acquaintance of the group drummer Silverton Hutchinson. Horace Panter knew of his reputation around the town. In his book Ska'd For Life, he said: "Neville was street-wise in a way I wasn't and I kept him at a respectable distance until I got to know him better."

Neville Staple was born in Christiana, Jamaica on April 11th 1955, to a family with two sisters and a brother. Nev's father left for England in the late Fifties. When Nev was five his father sent to have him brought over to the UK. The original Rude Boy, he was often in trouble, especially with his father, who was extremely strict. When school finished for the day at quarter to four, Neville and his brother had to be home by four o'clock and were in bed normally by six, but they both began to sneak out of the bedroom window and get involved in wayward behaviour. Neville ran away from home three times when he was nine years old and slept rough in graveyards. He attended Rugby Secondary Modern School in the Midlands and spent more time in the headmaster's office than in lessons. He bunked off classes to go meet girls and by the time he was 13 he would walk off school premises to go to the local cinema and creep in the back door to watch what were then X-rated movies. During this period, he took up part time work as a grocery boy, but this didn't last long because he left when things got a little hot under the collar due to the fact he was skimming money from the till to fund his desire to own a motor scooter.

He left school at 15 and got a job as an apprentice TV engineer, which he stuck at for two years or so before working in a slaughterhouse, then moving on to a road gang. In his spare time, he was heavily into music, with his influences coming from the likes of John Holt, Gregory Isaacs and Linton Kwesi Johnson. Neville would often relieve his boredom by jumping in his car at night and speeding all the way down the M1 motorway to London with his music blaring out of the windows. As soon as he reached the first roundabout outside of London, he would turn around and drive straight back to Coventry, sometimes twice a night! He teamed up with best friend Trevor Evans (later to be a Specials road manager) to run a local reggae sound system, and it was through the sound system that both he and Evans ended up, in true Rude Boy stylee, serving time at Her Majesty's Pleasure: "We used to go around the clubs," said Neville. "We used to spend all our money on records and go around nicking wood to make the speaker boxes. We had to get cash to get a bigger sound but we got into a lot of trouble when the coppers caught us burgling some houses in Rugby."

These incidents, along with charges of affray and driving getaway cars, landed Neville and Trevor prison sentences. Neville spent time in detention at Winson Green before spending six months in Wormwood Scrubs: "Very depressing," explains Neville. "I was banged up most of the time while I was there, sometimes on my own, sometimes with a bunch of four or five others. I'd like not to go back there, ever. Yeah, it's fair to say I'm the original rude boy, I used to be really, really rude. I say rude, I used to get into loads of mischief, if it weren't for the Specials I'd probably be doing long time right now. I was literally from the street, I grew up on the street, I used to get up to all sorts of stuff. Detention centres, prison. I was bad before."

After release from prison, Neville and Trevor headed straight for the clubs and it was on one of their rounds of local venues they heard about the Automatics. Neville remembers their first sight of the group: "We had heard about this gap-toothed bloke doing the rounds with this band that had a couple of black guys in. We wanted to see what it was like, so me and Trevor went along to see what kind of sound they had and it wasn't bad."

Neville then started his own disco dancing troupe called Neville and the Boys, who made an appearance at Coventry's Locarno at one of the DJ nights, run by none other than Pete Waterman. Along with Evans, Neville now started to follow the Automatics around the city. After a while, the two resourceful men gained employment as roadies for the band and Neville's eventual inclusion into the outfit came on the Clash tour. In Leeds, whilst the band were tinkering on a soundcheck and going through their version of the ska classic 'Monkey Man', Neville plugged in a microphone at the sound desk and began toasting over the top of the track. The group were perplexed as to where the sound was coming from and tracked it back to Neville. They invited him to do the same onstage that night. After the show at the Music Machine in London, Neville was voted in as co-vocalist to Terry Hall and would later also take up some percussion duties.

"Often," said Jerry Dammers, "we'd hear a bit of singing coming from nowhere. At first, we didn't know what was happening and then I found out that Neville had plugged in a mike at the mixing desk and was toasting over the top of our numbers. It was a good decision to make him full time."

Neville recalled: "The atmosphere then was bloody electric, and I remember hearing the lads running through 'Guns Of Navarone' so I just plugged in the mike and off I went."

After the Clash tour, Dammers dropped a bombshell; if the group were to make a solid effort at pursuing a musical career, then he wanted total commitment, and so he told the employed members of the band, Terry, Roddy and Horace, that they should quit their jobs. It was a massive decision for them, especially the latter two, but it seemed to be the only realistic way forward if the band's ambitions were going to be met, so they agreed.

The next step in the master plan was to warily contact Bernie Rhodes to see if he could help them any further. Although Rhodes was never officially their manager, he worked with the band closely for some time and had them live in London for a six-month period, which almost brought about their demise. The boys' accommodation in the big smoke was an old, grim warehouse in Camden where they would occasionally practice their set. The group stayed in London for four or five days at a time before going back to Coventry to claim their dole, then turning about-face and racing back to London for more misery. The forbidding monstrosity that became a temporary home for the band was originally an old gin distillery, and at one stage housed a huge turntable for re-routing trains.

In June 1976, whilst it was still derelict, in true Bernie Rhodes bare-faced blagging style, he somehow convinced the local authority that under-privileged and disadvantaged local youths needed some space to rehearse their various bands, and the powers-that-be granted him the lease on the property. Rhodes had originally brought the Clash there to experience its harsh dreariness and oppressive atmosphere, believing something along the lines of 'maketh the man- maketh the band'. The building became known as 'Rehearsal Rehearsals' and represented a truly miserable time for the Special AKA. They had to sleep in one room that was infested with vermin, and after a period of thumb-twiddling and sharing half pints of beer, the group approached Rhodes about his seeming lack of effort to progress the band's career. Rhodes still expressed an interest in the seven weary Coventry boys, despite the fact that he thought they were 'still not quite right', and started to discuss contractual terms. To try to instil some enthusiasm back into the group, he organised a trip to Paris.

Mickey Foote, Rhodes' second in command and the man instructed to take care of the Clash when Rhodes was not around, was to accompany the band on the fateful Paris sojourn. Rhodes organised a hire van, loaded the band's equipment into it, and off it went down to Dover for the ferry crossing. Remarkably, Rhodes then instructed the band to unload the van, push the equipment up on to the ferry via the available trolleys, and said a driver and van would meet them in Calais. Hilarity ensued when Dammers' suitcase burst open on the ramp sending his underwear and clothing blowing around in the wind.

"Jerry was always clumsy," said Roddy "and untogether in ordinary ways, if not in music or his drive to succeed."

The alarm bells started ringing when Rhodes then gave Foote some money and bid his goodbyes. "We thought he was coming with us!" exclaimed Lynval Golding.

The crossing, as if a precursor of things to come, was rough, but a few beers all round managed to calm the unsuspecting Specials. Disembarking in France, Dammers, forever the eccentric, jokingly claimed France for England by dropping to his knees and putting a handful of foreign soil into his mouth. The jovial mood soon changed, however, when it was time to check through passport control. The band members had their passports but drummer Silverton Hutchinson, coming from Barbados, posed the problem. For him to play he needed a work permit, which he obviously didn't have and the French authorities demanded his return to London. Hutchinson had to oblige, despite Dammers' offer of a back-hander to the gathered gendarme and port officers. They agreed that Hutchinson get the work permit required and rejoin the group in Paris.

The fun continued when, after sorting six out of seven members through passport control, they emerged and were greeted by their French transport to Paris: "This bloke," said Lynval Golding, "had come in this tiny 'Interflora' van. There was no way we were gonna fit all the gear and the band into this one small van, so we came up with this plan that some of the guys should hitchhike from Calais to Paris. I looked around and thought me first time in France; the majority of the people were white. I knew one thing and that was I wasn't gonna hitchhike being black. Me and Neville looked at each other and we knew there was no way anyone would give us a lift, we just assumed that they had the same racial problems in France as we did in England, so we made sure that me and Neville squeezed into the van with some equipment on top of us and went straight to Paris."

With Lynval and Neville's fears about being left on the roadside in a foreign land miles away from home understood by the remainder of the line up, it was decided by Terry, Roddy, Jerry and Horace that it would be they who would chance their arm at hitch hiking to Paris. Lady Luck smiled on them briefly and they managed to flag down a Rolls-Royce! It took one more car to finally transport the weary Specials to the French capital: "We all went to the club where we were supposed to be playing the first night," said Roddy Byers, "and the caretaker set his dog on us!"

Jerry remembered the farce when they arrived: "Once we got dropped off in Paris it was the middle of the night. The trains weren't running and we didn't have enough money for a cab, but Bernie had given us a map so we spent the rest of the night dragging our amps, guitars and luggage across Paris. At dawn, we arrived at the club where we were due to play that night but it was closed of course. After waiting around for about eight hours someone arrived to open the club and we asked if we were at the right place. He didn't seem to like the look of us and told us we were at the wrong club and gave us the name of another venue, where he said we were definitely playing – this was apparently his idea of a joke. So we set off, dragging the gear, to the other venue, which he said was just around the corner, but turned out to be a circus about two or three kilometres away. After getting directions from lots of different people, we finally reached this circus and asked if we were playing there that night. The gypsy guy in the booth leapt over the counter and tried to attack us! So we had to lug the amps, guitar and luggage all the way back to where we started out from, at which point the rest of the band had arrived."

What was to follow would influence the writing of the band's first single 'Gangsters'. The band settled in at their hotel and after a couple of days, Silverton Hutchinson, now legal, arrived. It seemed things were beginning to look up, but that proved to be a short-lived state of affairs. As the band prepared for their first night as part of a residency at a Paris club, a woman approached them. She was the hotel owner and she wanted to know if they were from England. The wary band affirmed that they were, and from that moment the situation descended into farce. The woman, satisfied that her suspicions that they were English had been confirmed, vehemently explained to them an English group which had stayed in her hotel (later revealed to have been the Damned, managed by Rick Rogers, of whom more later) had smashed it up badly. The Specials, thinking it an odd statement, deemed it a warning from the woman to behave and stay out of trouble on her territory. They continued to laze around the hotel, strumming and tuning guitars, when two men came up and immediately grabbed the guitars belonging to Lynval and Roddy. The woman reappeared and directly told the perplexed boys that they should pay for the damage from the Damned's visit, and if no payment was forthcoming then she would not return the guitars. The band, thinking at first it was a joke, tried to laugh off her protestations, but it soon became obvious that she was in no laughing mood. At that point, all hell broke loose, with Roddy and Lynval demanding the return of their instruments.

"I went mad!" says Lynval. "It was my cream Telecaster guitar, it meant everything to me! I'd had to struggle to get it, I'd had to pay for it and I wasn't working, so for me it was tough."

The argument grew and the band ended up being pushed downstairs. Dammers had been dragged out of his shower, naked, and threatened with a beating. The argument, now at fever pitch, spilled into the lobby area. The hotel owner wanted the band thrown out and in the ensuing melee, pushing, and shoving the glass entrance door to the hotel was smashed. The Police arrived and seemed quite uninterested in what was going on, which allowed matters to escalate. The trouble only ceased slightly when the man who ran the club they were playing at also showed up and spoke directly to the angry, raging woman. The man from the club suggested the band go straight to the venue, which they gladly did. To their surprise and relief, by the time they arrived there all their equipment, including the confiscated guitars, was ready and waiting for them.

Roddy was extremely happy with the return of the equipment.

"We thought, how did they do that?" he said. "Then the manager of the club arrived, he offered me and Terry a mint. As he opened his jacket we saw a gun!"

"I thought wow! These guys were wicked," enthused Lynval. "How did they do it? Well, they pulled back their guns and demanded the guitars! There you have it. THAT is 'Gangsters'!"

The dates they played went well, but all in all the group were relieved to find themselves back in Blighty. However, they had no money to get back to the Midlands. Horace Panter worked some magic and eventually they managed to get all the instruments and the group back to Coventry. In the cold light of day, they were no further forward in their careers under the guidance of Bernie Rhodes. It was unanimously decided that they would have no more to do with the man, but things were starting to get desperate. Nobody had any money; under the circumstances, it was inevitable that arguments within the band would reach new levels. They had become disillusioned, and everything was on the verge of collapse, but after all his planning and hard work Jerry Dammers was hardly going to throw in the towel, and his guiding hand ensured they saw the new year in with the group amazingly still intact.

They had now started to rehearse in the back room of the Binley Oak pub in Coventry, but with Silverton Hutchinson regularly absent from practice more tension brewed, and Bernie Rhodes words about 'changing direction and getting their jumble of punk and reggae sorted out once and for all' haunted them. Jerry and Horace wanted to experiment with a music called ska, another export from Jamaica, and the father of reggae. Lynval, also a ska fan, shared their enthusiasm, Silverton was far from happy with the idea, but since he was absent from rehearsals the group tried out the ska sound. As if it were a gift from the gods, the band's true direction and musical identity was revealed, with their fast punky breaks now running hand in hand with the dancier, offbeat sound. At this point, Silverton quit – he had a family to think about and couldn't see the band going anywhere.

The SPECIALS – from conception to reunion   *29*

He was a volatile character, but his absence from the rehearsal room had mainly been due to the fact that he was looking for full-time employment because he had a mortgage to pay. He felt as if the band would never be able to pay him a living wage. The introduction of ska also made Roddy Byers think about quitting: "I'd been with the group for over a year," says Roddy, "and I'd worked out all these guitar things that I really liked. When Jerry brought in the ska, I was at bit of a loss. A lot of the guitar stuff I'd done didn't fit with ska, so I had to completely rethink my guitar playing over again for every song. Having to do it just like that was a bit of a shock for me, discovering ska really, plus I hadn't heard a lot of the original ska stuff. I didn't know how songs like 'Monkey Man' went, so I just played the first thing that came into my mind, sort of Chuck Berry, Duane Eddy, Johnny Thunders licks, trying to fit white rock guitar into a reggae feel."

Roddy would soon develop his own unique ska style, and he began to compose songs that would later get him recognition as an accomplished songsmith, second only to Dammers in the band.

Soon enough Bernie Rhodes raised his head again and offered one of the most valuable pieces of advice he'd ever given the band. He was a firm believer in selling an artist/group as a package, focussing on their artistic merits. His time with the Clash was a good example; in his eyes, a band with a good image had more of a chance of making it to the big time than a band without one. With the Specials now playing ska and reggae, Rhodes pointed them towards the attire of the West Indian rude boy and the British skinhead to solve their image problems. Roddy was a big fan of the change because he had long admired the Clash's Paul Simonon from afar. Simonon had adopted that mix of rudie/skinhead during his Clash days, something that Dammers himself had also taken note of. Terry Hall had been a skinhead, so he knew what was needed clothes-wise and helped to create their new style, which would become the definitive ska look of tonic suit, loafers and pork pie hat.

"Bernie Rhodes was right," says Terry. "Clothes are important. As far as I'm concerned, the clothing is almost as important as the music. They really are important to the whole thing."

Lynval Golding remembers the time he had a run in with Jerry Dammers over the clothing issue: "We were playing one night, can't remember where. I'm sat in my white T-shirt before the gig. Jerry comes in and says to me 'Er...Lyn, you gotta shirt?' so I tells him 'Yes, Jerry, I have a shirt.' He says to me 'Er...you wanna wear that shirt tonight then Lyn?' So I said 'No Jerry I'm wearing my white T-shirt tonight! I'm not asking your permission mate. I'm wearing my white T-shirt!' Anyway, we had an argument about that, but he did have this image visually in his mind, especially about what the band should look like, you know?"

With the image question resolving itself, Dammers worked on the next part of his master plan. He had a vision of what could be if the band proved successful. He had been captivated by the way Berry Gordy and Motown had evolved, and that is what he wanted to reproduce, a movement along the lines of Motown which also incorporated elements of the punk phenomenon. He quickly realised that a design or logo, which would be instantly recognisable and connected to the band would help with promotion. He and Horace Panter came up with some pop art-inspired designs that would eventually prove as a central to 2Tone as the music itself, and much later would be the symbol for ska bands recognisable worldwide. They considered names such as 'Satik' and 'Underworld' before the description '2Tone' thrust its way into their consciousness.

It turned out that Dammers thought of the idea for the black and white chequers whilst brushing around the gaps in his teeth with his black and white checked toothbrush which was, in later years, displayed in the Herbert Museum in Coventry.

"I came up with the '2' over the top of the 'Tone'" Horace recalled in his book, "but it was Jerry that used the idea of black and white checks and the 2Tone man. This was a caricature of Peter Tosh taken from an early Wailers album. It was a brilliant image. Simple, which said everything about us."

"That look is defiant, Jamaican and hard," said Dammers of Tosh's stance on the album cover.

The 2Tone character became the legendary "Walt Jabsco"; his name came from the label on the inside of a bowling shirt that Dammers owned. However, it wasn't just a band logo or label design, it was a statement of intent, and the black and white chequers symbolised the black of ska and white of punk in the mix of the music and the multiracial make up of the band. With the logo, name and design concepts in place, Walt Jabsco was ready to lead the charge of the 2Tone cavalry to bring British ska to an unsuspecting public.

Jerry had already made plans to launch his own record label, which would come to be known as 2Tone. He wanted 'Gangsters' to be the first release, but there were two major stumbling blocks. First, the Specials lacked any financial backing, and second there was a distinct lack of a drummer since the departure of Silverton Hutchinson. Neville had helped with percussion duties, but they really needed the services of a sticksman before they could go into the studio. Problem one was overcome when the band made the acquaintance of a Coventry 'businessman' of Irish descent called Jimbo O'Boyle. For a percentage, Jimbo agreed to lend them the £700 they needed to afford a studio session to record 'Gangsters'. The song title pretty much summed up the group's new benefactor; there were stories of guns in car glove boxes and physical manhandling! Roddy Byers later said: "I was once trying to point out to a relative of his that Jimbo never actually managed the band. He almost beat me up!"

The band were not put off and went ahead with the recording, and it turned out to be a sound investment.

The second hurdle was conquered with the arrival of John Edward Bradbury. Born on February 16th 1955 in Coventry to Irish parents, Brad (later known as Prince Rimshot) left Binley Park Secondary School, where he showed a flair for poetry, to attend Hull Polytechnic, where he achieved a degree in art (although this was fine art and not the same as Dammers' degree). It was whilst at Hull that Brad joined a local soul band as a drummer and toured the working men's club circuit. He returned to Birmingham as an art teacher, but also had various jobs such as a market stall assistant and concrete screener before landing work as a teacher of English as a second language to immigrant children in a community education centre in Coventry.

Brad's big musical influence was soul, and Stax in particular, but his first real taste of ska and reggae came while he was working as a sales assistant in the same Virgin Records shop as former Automatics singer Tim Strickland. Brad eventually amassed a huge record collection which instilled in him a love for Jamaican music rivalling his affection for soul. He had been involved in the music scene around Coventry on and off for years, including bands such as Nightease and Nack-Ed-En, whose members also included lead guitarist Loz Netto (later of Sniff and The Tears) and bassist Neil Richardson. Richardson remembers: "In 1970 the then drummer of Nack-Ed-En, Steve Harrison, introduced me to this band, asking me to bring some of my lyrics to a rehearsal at a pub in Primrose Hill Street one Sunday afternoon. It was the first time I'd met the band [apart from Steve], but I got to see a lot of them later on, especially Loz. They were a tight three-piece with high-octane musicianship. The second week I went along with my lyrics, Steve had been replaced by John Bradbury.

"Brad was a stand-out drummer even back then, ten years before the Specials. No long, messy drum solos, his breaks were terse and highly skilful [as in 'Gangsters'] and he seemed to have a great sense of song structure and band leadership. Because Steve left, my songs didn't get used, but we went to the Dive Bar after the Primrose Hill rehearsal and sat with a local guitarist Chris Jones, and they read through the lyrics. I remember Brad reading them and saying 'Who is he?' I wasn't sure if that was good or bad, but again, as soon as the band formed they seemed to split, so I never really got anywhere. As far as I remember the music was mainly R & B, but had an impressive progressive element, with John Bradbury's jazz rock skills and Loz's interest in bands like King Crimson."

Later, Brad would play in a number of outfits like the Bowl Alley Men and later the influential Transposed Men (the name coming from a Sixties sci-fi book cover), a group that also included Neol Davies, Desmond Brown (both later of the Selecter), well known Coventry musician Kevin Harrison and Steve Wynne (AKA Vaughan Tive). This line-up would rehearse embryonic versions of 'On My Radio', 'Street Feeling' and material that would later be performed by the Selecter and appear on the *Too Much Pressure* album on 2Tone Records. The Transposed Men had recorded demos in Brad's cellar in Warwick, but nothing else really happened for the band despite interest from Virgin Records. When Brad was poached by the Specials, the Transposed Men fell apart, with Neol and Desmond combining forces with local reggae band Hardtop 22 and recruiting female vocalist Pauline Black to form the Selecter. Kevin Harrison later joined the Urge and would tour as support to the Specials.

At the time of the Transposed Men and Silverton Hutchinson's sharp exit, Brad and Dammers were sharing a house. So Dammers' search for a new drummer took him as far afield as his kitchen! Jerry asked him initially to take the sticks just for 'Gangsters', and indeed, according to Horace, there had been doubt in Jerry's mind about whether Brad was exactly what he was looking for. The other band members then over-ruled any ideas Jerry may have had. The line-up was now complete. It has often been said, particularly by Lynval, that Brad's superb drumming was what gave the Specials their beefy sound but Brad, in turn, credits it to Lynval's classic offbeat chop!

By early 1979, the group had a number of fully written, composed and ready to record songs. 'Gangsters' was a clever and complete reworking of Prince Buster's bluebeat hit 'Al Capone'. In fact, the screeching brakes intro to the Special AKA (they were to revert to one of their original monikers for the first release just to complicate matters) are direct samples from The Prince's record. The opening line of "Bernie Rhodes knows...Don't argue!" is a sharp stab at the man himself, but it immortalised him on vinyl. The icy, poignant lyrics capture the band's ill feeling towards record companies and the music business as a whole, in particular those involved for the money rather than a love of music, as well as being a document of their eyebrow-raising trip to France.

"I wrote that song," explained Jerry Dammers, "straight after we came back from that disastrous trip to Paris. We were practising at Rhodes' rehearsal place in Chalk Farm. We were well and truly pissed off about that time. There were seven of us sleeping in that one room. I just stayed up all night and wrote it. That song was written on Joe Strummer's guitar. Basically, we were pissed off with the whole show like the club owners and the managers. What we set out to prove with 'Gangsters' was that you can do it yourselves really. You don't need those types of people and, besides, the song wasn't just about him. We were taking the piss out of him. I didn't hate him for anything, but he had been very tight."

Roddy was also a bit wary of Mr Rhodes: "He wanted to split us up. He wanted Terry to join the Black Arabs. He likes to put musicians together like that, but you can't do that with people."

On the subject of 'Gangsters', Lynval Golding echoed Dammers' feelings: "It's proof that groups can do things for themselves. We've been through so many guys who claimed they could manage us. They claimed they can do this and do that, and in the end, they do fuck all. That's when we said we'd do our own single and fuck them all! We tried to do everything the normal way to get the record out, but were told by some record labels 'Ah, they're a bunch of fuckin' wankers, fuckin' waste of time, get out of it. Send em back to Coventry' sort of thing y'know. Nobody wanted to know us."

Terry Hall said about the record: "We wrote 'Gangsters' about our manager, but also about the club promoters in and around Coventry. We weren't paranoid; we were just used to being threatened."

The money the band had borrowed would only stretch to the recording of 'Gangsters' and the recording of a B-side was sidelined. The band ensconced themselves in Coventry's Horizon 8-track studio on Warwick Road, which had been a railway building. It had been converted in 1977 by Barry Thomas, a former Coventry landlord who put a lot of his money into the new top-floor studio. The studio was upgraded to a 16-track in 1979 and was also purported to be haunted by the ghosts of an young art student, who had painted some of the décor at Horizon before succumbing to a drug-related death, and that of a former rail worker. Musicians recording there had reported being brushed past and something breathing heavily down their necks, as well as lights turning themselves on and off! It was intended that 'Nite Klub' would be recorded as the first single, but it was felt that the band could not get the right vibe on the day and as Terry Hall put it: "To be honest it was a no go with 'Nite Klub'. That is a late-night drinking song, best recorded at night."

With 'Gangsters' safely in the can, the only problem now was the lack of a B-side. This was when Jerry Dammers called upon long-time friend Neol Davies. Davies had composed an instrumental track called 'Kingston Affair' featuring himself on all instruments apart from drums (performed by none other than John Bradbury) and trombone played by Barry Jones, a local newsagent and sweet shop owner. Davies credited the song to the Selecters (the name they loosely wrote and recorded under and the forerunner of the Selecter) and wanted to record it. Enter Coventry legend and record producer Roger Lomas.

"By 1977," said Lomas, "I had taken time out of playing and I was more into the recording side of the business. I built a 4-track studio in the garden of my house in Broad Street, Foleshill. Then one day Neol Davies knocked on the door, he said 'I've got this great song I've written and I want to make a demo'. Neol at that time was known as a rock musician around town, so I was surprised to find that it sounded like old ska. But I have a commercial ear, which is necessary if you want to be a successful producer. I recognized that he'd written something good, even though it was not my kind of thing. We made a proper track and spent a week on it, which was unheard of in those days. It was just an instrumental track featuring a trombone solo, which I put through a flanger and used long delay echoes on it. Everybody was pleased with the results. I did the rounds with it, because I had a lot of contacts in the music business, but nobody was interested it. I think it was too soon for that sound. It was 18 months before the Specials recorded 'Gangsters'. I didn't know the Specials then, because I wasn't into the punk thing. I knew this song was good though."

The track was hastily renamed 'The Selecter by the group The Selecter' (which up until that point did not even exist) and was used to fill the gap on the Specials' disc. 'Gangsters' was given the catalogue number TT1 and 'The Selecter' became TT2, and a double A-side assault on the nation was almost underway.

"I remember hearing John Peel playing my track for the first time," said Selecter's Neol Davies "and he called it 'The Selecter by The Specials'. So I rang him up to put him straight."

1,500 copies were printed, and a set of rubber stamps were made up depicting the words 'The Special AKA – Gangsters' and 'VS The Selecter' and it was left to Horace Panter and Terry Hall to painstakingly ensure that all the 1,500 sleeves were stamped individually. Luckily, no cases of Repetitive Strain Injury were reported! The next problem was distribution, but this didn't prove too much of an obstacle when Dammers approached Britain's largest indie distributor of that time, Rough Trade. They heard the single, knew the band and quickly agreed to handle it. The first batch sold out, and Rough Trade took over and pressed further copies. Jerry originally wanted another 2,500 but Rough Trade decided to press 5,000!

With Panter and Hall happily rubber-stamping singles, Jerry realised that to distribute all those copies he was going to need help. This came in the form of Alan Harrison, who was a lecturer at the Lanchester Polytechnic; Harrison had shared a house in Crouch End with a publicist called Rick Rogers, who at the time was working in PR for Stiff and Chiswick Records. Eventually Rogers went his own way and formed the management group Trigger, which was based in London. His first inkling of the Specials came when Harrison had tried to get Rogers interested in them when they were called the Coventry Automatics. Harrison told Jerry of Rogers' existence and shortly afterwards Dammers made an appointment to see him. Rogers was, at that time, managing riotous punk band the Damned (sudden flashback to the hotel fracas in Paris).

At this meeting, Rogers sat and listened to this 'strange' young man, who at first didn't seem to have much going for him, and agreed to listen to the tapes that Dammers had brought with him. On hearing them, Rogers knew immediately he had to see the Special AKA in the flesh, and so that same week he travelled up to Coventry to catch them on the group's so-called '34th Tour of the Town.' He saw the band at the almost home ground of Warwick University, where a good local crowd helped make it a great gig, and Rogers was impressed: "I was totally knocked out," said Rick. "They were brilliant. The band had so much energy and enthusiasm. They mixed politics with having a good time; I knew they were destined for bigger things."

After the gig, Rogers felt he had to speak with the group, and a short while later he was confronted with a wary-looking bunch of exhausted Specials. He chatted to them and quickly offered to manage them. The boys cautiously agreed: "Only when I got really talking to the band did I realise what a huge part Jerry was playing in the game. He desperately wanted to get this 2Tone thing in operation. He had everything worked out, even the artwork. He wanted it to become a movement. Yeah, that's what he wanted to do, create a movement and a sound to go with it, a sort of British equivalent of Tamla."

On returning to London, Rick Rogers swung the Trigger Management press and

YOU'RE WONDERING NOW

promo machine into action and was determined to get the group some gigs in the nation's capital. He contacted friends and business associates and word of the group soon spread. With the rising success of 'Gangsters' in the independent charts, and excellent reviews from various fanzines and music magazines, there was a snowballing of popularity and recognition. Radio 1 legend John Peel heard 'Gangsters' and played it every night on his show for two weeks, he pencilled them in for one of his 'In Session' live studio performances. To promote 'Gangsters' the band played any gigs they could get, anywhere in the country and Rogers ensured they came thick and fast. He lined up a series of what would be very important London shows, some at smaller clubs and others as support band in larger venues. Their first gig was at the famous Hope & Anchor, but a mere 30 or so people attended. Their electric exuberance made up for the lack of audience, and as the gig-list increased, attendance began to rise swiftly. Word of mouth definitely worked in favour of the band.

On April 8th 1979 the group were placed on the bottom of a triple bill at the Lyceum Theatre, a building that had stood as a theatre since 1794 and was about to be assaulted by the punks of the 20th Century! Rick Rogers had his band the Damned playing as headliners, along with the upcoming UK Subs, and he pushed the Specials on in place of the billed Spizz Oil. Their now refined concoction of British punk and Jamaican ska won over the gathered skinheads who had come to see the Subs. Those same skinheads began to show up at other Specials gigs in the capital.

On May 3rd, a mere couple of weeks since the hideously low turnout at the Hope & Anchor, the Specials played the Moonlight Club in West Hampstead, a night that would go down in Specials' history. It was the eve of the General Election and the coming of Margaret Thatcher, and the boys delivered an intense and powerful set, introduced by Terry Hall: "As I've got nothing to say, it's the eve of the election and 'Its Up To You!'"

The venue was packed with a crowd of 300 kids, including skins, punks and the newly spawned rudies. The Specials were becoming the hottest property in the music business. Musicians of the time, such as Chrissie Hynde and Elvis Costello turned up to see the shows, as did A&R men from record companies such as Warner Brothers, Island, A&M and Virgin. Rolling Stones Records were also there and Mick Jagger turned up to experience the live power of the Specials. Rick Rogers recalls meeting up with Jagger and his entourage: "We obviously knew who he was when we saw him, but he didn't interest us in the slightest. We wanted to sign to a company that had an identity and quite frankly, Rolling Stones Records was never going to be a viable avenue for us. We just looked at him as this old man. He didn't fit in with us at all."

On the other hand, Jagger gave his reasons for chasing the Specials at that time: "I think the Specials are great. They're into a music with deep roots and that's something I like. I really get off on the Specials."

The first pressing of 'Gangsters' had by now sold out completely, and in the next few weeks the speed of developments was staggering. During the search for a record label, it became obvious that some companies saw the 2Tone ideals as a drawback. The group and Rogers emphatically declared their demands which, in a nutshell, were 'you take us, you take 2Tone.' They wanted a distribution deal for all 2Tone releases plus total control of which bands were signed to the label and the records to be released. Some bizarre offers were made. Jerry Dammers and Rick Rogers went to see Muff Winwood at CBS Records where they were offered an EP deal and were told that CBS would see how things develop from there. Their offer was branded as crap by Dammers who laughed with hysterical derision on the way out of the building.

However, present on that auspicious evening at the Moonlight Club was an A&R man from Chrysalis Records called Roy Eldridge. It was his wisdom and foresight that would eventually be responsible for signing the band to Chrysalis, despite them actually receiving better cash offers from other labels. The fact that Chrysalis would accommodate the idea of the separate 2Tone identity persuaded the group to sign on the dotted line. There were concerns from staff at Chrysalis who frowned on the deal, but the majority knew that the Specials were just too good to let go.

"The major labels couldn't entertain the thought of not retaining their corporate identity except Chrysalis." said Rick Rogers "It was an extremely unusual deal as the idea of little labels within big labels didn't exist then."

The victorious Roy Eldridge, stunned by the group at the Moonlight Club, takes up the story of his conquest: "I went to the Moonlight Club in Hampstead expecting nothing special," said Roy. "I'd been singularly unimpressed with a bunch of mod revival groups doing the club rounds at that time and had been told, very wrongly, that the Specials were part of that little movement. So, I turned up on my own expecting to be out of the club within 15 minutes or so and on to the next, but what a night! They were, and still are, the best unsigned live group I've ever seen. Energy, passion, politics, they made you dance, they made you think. Sensational! As soon as they came offstage, I talked my way backstage. Thankfully, I knew the manager Rick Rogers as I'd talked to him once about working for Chrysalis. I remember the group were shattered, they were always drained after a show and they were kind of suspicious, but we arranged to get together for a meeting. They outlined what they wanted, I agreed, and the rest as they say is history."

Rick Rogers found Eldridge to be the most sincere of all the chasing A & R hounds: "Roy was bursting with enthusiasm and raved about what he had seen. He didn't start throwing money like the rest of them, he was simply engrossed in the band and the music, and above all else that counted more than anything."

Eldridge's enthusiasm was certainly his driving force in securing the band to Chrysalis. He later recalled: "I was seriously going to give them a few minutes to impress me but was mesmerised by their musical up-beatness but lyrical darkness in such songs as 'Concrete Jungle' and 'Too Much Too Young'. They were full of contradictions; Terry was Mr Deadpan while Lynval and Neville were going crazy. Jerry wanted their own label and to release singles by groups he hadn't even found yet with no obligations. I didn't care what it took, as long as I got them."

In accordance with the Chrysalis signing, 2Tone Records were leased to record ten singles a year and had a £1,000 budget to record each single. The Specials signed a five-album deal with options for more, when, or if necessary. The group also secured a £20,000 advance, with half to be delivered on completion of the first album. They also signed to a music publishing deal with Plangent Visions Ltd. Although it seemed that 2Tone was a label in its own right, it was still Chrysalis who pulled the initial strings, and bands were signed to Chrysalis and not directly to 2Tone.

The other interesting thing that happened on that night in the Moonlight Club was that the gig was recorded. Next door to the club were the UK studios of Decca Records. The label was planning to record a charity album of acts that had appeared at the Moonlight Club, and on that night had set up a live audio feed from the club into the studio. The charity album never materialised, but ten of the tracks recorded live on that fateful night were released as a vinyl album, the most famous of the Specials bootlegs to emerge.

YOU'RE WONDERING NOW

Later that same month the group were to appear at a gig for the Rock Against Racism campaign. Rock Against Racism (RAR) was a project set up in 1976 in the wake of comments made by two of the top recording artists of that time, Eric Clapton and David Bowie. On stage in Birmingham, Clapton had made a drunken declaration of support for controversial Conservative MP, Enoch Powell. Clapton said that the country had 'become overcrowded' and asked the assembled crowd to vote for Powell to stop the UK from becoming 'a black colony'. Two men, rock music photographer Red Saunders and his friend Roger Huddle, from the CAST Theatre group, responded by writing a letter to the *NME* music paper expressing their opposition to Clapton's comments, which they said were "all the more disgusting because he had his first hit with a cover of reggae star Bob Marley's 'I Shot The Sheriff'." Further support for RAR came after David Bowie said in an interview that Britain was ready for a fascist leader; he also allegedly did a Nazi salute while riding in a car. Bowie later retracted his comment and claimed that he said it as a result of being under the influence of a 'substance'.

Around this time the Anti-Nazi League were in force to counteract the growing wave of racist attacks in the UK, and to thwart the growing menace of the National Front. So, in 1978, 100,000 people marched six miles from Trafalgar Square to the East End, for what was to become a renowned open-air concert staged by the Rock Against Racism group. The concert featured the Clash (as seen in the film *Rude Boy*), Buzzcocks, Steel Pulse, X-Ray Spex, the Ruts, Sham 69, Generation X and the Tom Robinson Band. More recently, the ideals of RAR were reborn under the guise of Love Music Hate Racism. However, it has been said that 2Tone, in its short life, did more to help racial matters than RAR: "We started out at the same time as RAR," said Jerry Dammers, "so it was all part of the same thing. For me, it was no good being anti-racist if you didn't involve black people, so what the Specials tried to do was create something that was more integrated."

The Specials got involved in RAR through a gig staged at the Hope & Anchor pub. Although the event was for a worthwhile cause, another step was made in the rise of the 2Tone phenomenon. In the crowd, that night was a young skinhead and his friends who were in a band that played a similar style of music to the Specials. He was very impressed with the set delivered by the Coventry boys, got chatting to Jerry Dammers afterwards and, before they parted, they had swapped addresses and phone numbers. The young man was Graham 'Suggs' McPherson, and his band were a little-known North London outfit called Madness.

"They played in the Hope & Anchor in North London that we all drank in," said Suggs at the time. "We hadn't heard of them really, but they were similar to us. Funnily enough the first thing I had heard about them was a half-page article on the Specials in the *Melody Maker* paper, you know the sort of thing, championing a band before they had really achieved anything, you know? I could see they dressed the same as us in a way. We were using the Hope & Anchor as a focal point at that time, all meeting up there regularly, monopolising the jukebox, playing obscure ska and bluebeat tracks. That night though the Specials were fantastic. Jerry Dammers stayed at my flat that night and we talked long into the night about pop music and he talked about his vision and future that was to be 2Tone."

May 27th saw the Specials back at the Lyceum Theatre, this time as bottom of the bill with the Mekons above them and the Gang Of Four headlining. The Specials didn't just steal the show; they took it right out of the hall, chucked it in their van and had

Coventry Automatics (before Specials) 1978 – Canley College. Photo by R.Byers

Coventry Automatics – Canley College 1978. Photo by R.Byers

driven away before the Gang Of Four had even come on stage. Pete Thomas, a member of Elvis Costello's backing band the Attractions, was asked by gathered journalists if there was any chance of him persuading Costello, a self-confessed Specials convert, to take the group on tour with them, to which Thomas replied: "You're kidding. They'd blow us off every night!"

The Specials then played a packed Fulham Greyhound. Despite agreeing to sign to Chrysalis, A&R men still climbed in through windows to get a glimpse of the band of the moment. The group and Rick Rogers were continually harassed by other labels desperate to get them to sign up. One such label was Virgin Records, who, at every available opportunity, offered to double any Chrysalis offer and individual cash incentives were waved about as sweeteners. This did not impress the Specials, who saw the underhand dealings as one side of the music business they would prefer to avoid, and had even lambasted in 'Gangsters'.

May 23rd found the group in the BBC studios at Maida Vale to record a session for iconic DJ John Peel, to be broadcast to the nation on the 29th. The songs they chose to perform were 'Gangsters', 'Too Much Too Young', 'Concrete Jungle' and a bouncy cover of the Maytals' 'Monkey Man'. The recording of this session became available to the public in 1987 when it was released on vinyl through Strange Fruit Records. The band would record two more sessions for Peel; the first was recorded on 15th October 1979, and featured fantastic live studio renditions of their set, such as 'Rude Boys Outa Jail', 'Rat Race' and 'The Skinhead Symphony in Three Movements' (a compilation of 'Long Shot Kick De Bucket',' Liquidator' and 'Skinhead Moonstomp'). The set was aired on Radio 1 a year later on 22nd October 1980. The second session was recorded exactly a week after the first broadcast, and consisted 'Sea Cruise', 'Stereotype' and 'Raquel', it was aired on December 1st 1980. These recordings eventually got the digital treatment and were issued in 1998 on compact disc via EMI, who at the time of writing, own all the Specials and 2Tone recordings.

Back in 1979, with the Chrysalis deal signed and sealed, more copies of 'Gangsters' were pressed and instead of using a plain sleeve, the black and white checks and the unmistakable countenance of Walt Jabsco adorned the covers. Now, with major label backing and on national release, sales of the single began to rocket and an eight-week tour of Britain's clubs was arranged. Before it started, Jerry and Horace travelled to London to see the band Madness play: "I had originally seen their name carved on a toilet door," said Horace Panter. "That was my first introduction to Madness."

Jerry Dammers had a similar experience: "I remember seeing 'Chalky n Suggs ov Chelsea' scraped into toilet doors and on walls."

Madness put on a great performance, and Dammers was convinced that the group were a safe bet. He was handed a demo by the band: "We handed Jerry a demo of 'The Prince'," said Madness guitarist Chris Foreman AKA Chrissy Boy. "We thought it was awful, but I guessed he must have liked it because it became our first single and the second 2Tone release."

Dammers had not particularly enjoyed the recording: "The demo they gave me of 'The Prince' was really, really bad. There was no record company going to sign them at that time in their career except 2Tone. I did see the potential though and signed them up."

As well as the offer of a single on 2Tone, that night Madness were also offered support slots on some Specials gigs, the first one being the forthcoming show at the Nashville Rooms in Kensington on June 8th. The Nutty Boys immediately agreed. At

Coventry Automatics 1978 – Canley College. Photo by R.Byers

the Nashville gig, the Specials played under the banner of 'The Rude Boys Return', and were a huge success.

"That was an amazing night. Great time had by all," said Horace Panter. "From then on I think we knew things were going to really take off, but by how much we never imagined."

Madness' drummer Dan 'Woody' Woodgate said of the momentous evening: "It was amazing! We walked in and everyone was in all the suits and the whole gear. It was like 'What is this? This is amazing!' A massive great room full of Mikes and Suggs and Lees and what have you."

The event was covered briefly in the Madness biographical film *Take It Or Leave It*. Not all of the Specials' ever-increasing army of supporters could fit into the room, and hundreds were turned away at the door. Those outside were none too pleased at the prospect of not getting to see their newfound favourite band, and the disappointment turned into sporadic outbursts of trouble. The police rushed to the aid of the panicking management and halted what could have been a very nasty episode. The lesson was learned, and 20 days later, when the Specials returned to the Nashville with Madness, it was made an all-ticket event.

Reviews of the Specials' gigs in the music press were more than favourable and gushed with praise, sparking even more interest in the group of Coventry upstarts who were taking London by storm. The band had quickly picked up a huge following, and people were being turned away from almost every venue because there was never room to accommodate the group's burgeoning army. The group would let a few of the audience backstage after every show to have a drink and hang out, a good-natured gesture by the exhausted group to show their willingness to include the paying public and fans. Initially the bands hardcore fan base consisted of mainly skinheads (a hangover from the UK Subs crowd). Within weeks, a new breed of youth was on the scene, the rudeboy or rudie. Rude boys were originally small time gangsters and street thugs in Sixties Jamaica; they dressed in sharp suits and pork pie hats and had no immediate connection to ska music. The ska connection in the UK came when emigration brought rude boys to England, where they played their indigenous ska, rocksteady and reggae in discos, and mixed with the early skinheads who had just broken away from the mod subculture and were looking for a totally separate identity.

Ska and the Jamaican influence, as well as the gang mentality, took root in the British skinhead psyche, but it wasn't until the advent of 2Tone that rude boys became associated with ska. Rude boys were immortalised in ska music by legends such as Prince Buster and Laurel Aitken. Neville Staple's Specials alter ego, the right honourable Judge Roughneck, was based around a character in the Prince Buster track 'Judge Dread' which, in turn, was based on a real life Jamaican magistrate who was extremely harsh when sentencing the original rudies in Jamaica. Through the Specials and 2Tone, rude boys became as British as bangers and mash. 2Tone brought original roots music to life through its covers, and inspired a generation to explore the roots of ska and ultimately music in general, something to which this author can testify.

Back on tour, one of the biggest nights was scheduled for July 21st at the Electric Ballroom on Camden High Street. Topping the bill were the Specials, and support came again from Madness, who were now a bona fide 2Tone band after Dammers had secured their signatures for a one off single record release. First on the bill were the newly created the Selecter, another 2Tone recruit, who hailed from Coventry and were fronted by the Specials' old sparring partner Neol Davies: "Madness were definitely the fun element." said Neol, "Us? I always said we were like a raging bull running amok in a field. A very dangerous band. The tension and danger in our line-up made our show what it was."

The Electric Ballroom was a magical night and again crowds queued right down the street to get in. The Selecter performed their set, and even though they had been together for little over a month, they were well received. Their dark, deeply skanky sound, which set them apart from their label mates, went down well. Madness, with their growing posse of London based 'nutty' fans, turned up the temperature for the home crowd, but it was the Specials who took the show by the scruff of its neck and belted out the searing numbers that sent the 2Tone army into a stomping, skanking frenzy. At the end of the unforgettable evening all three bands brought the house down when they joined forces on stage, along with some of the audience, for a rousing rendition of the Pioneers' 'Long Shot Kick De Bucket'. The evening was an out-and-out triumph and proudly heralded the true coming of 2Tone.

The rise of the 2Tone label saw 'Gangsters' established in the charts in a time when the charts still meant something to those genuinely interested in music. The UK listings at that time were a mish-mash of different musical styles, with the likes of grand rockers Queen, ELO and Cliff Richard keeping up appearances for the old school, and the Brotherhood of Man touting the obligatory Eurovision Song Contest entry. However,

'Save Your Kisses For Me' sounded tame and dated when it came up against the new punk sound of Sham 69's 'Hersham Boys', The Sex Pistols' 'Great Rock'n'Roll Swindle' and the Damned's 'Smash It Up'. 'Gangsters' climbed to the dizzy height of Number 6 in the charts, which meant an appearance for the Coventry boys on *Top Of The Pops*, and as history tells us, feisty young musicians and the straight-as-a-die BBC do not easily mix. Roddy Radiation takes up the story of the Specials at the BBC studios: "Well, I remember it was like being back at school; being told what to do, stay in your room, stand there etc. Also, the studio didn't look very large and the audience were about 30 kids moved about in front of the cameras. We took the piss mostly, stamping about trying to wreck the stage, but they have a bar at the top of the building, which you are allowed to visit just before they film you for real, and you have to be there for about 11.30am in the morning for the several rehearsals. Usually after driving to London from wherever we had been playing, we would have had maybe three hours sleep before getting to the Beeb. I was escorted from the bar after an argument with a BBC boss who pushed in front of me and got served first, so I complained. He said 'I suppose you're with *Top Of The Pops*' as he looked down his nose at me. Then a uniformed doorman

Causing trouble at Top Of The Pops 1979. Photo by R.Byers

The SPECIALS – from conception to reunion **43**

grabbed my arm and led me outside! I remember being so drunk on the first time we did the *Pops*, that I thought I'd played a gig and spent a long time looking for the backstage entrance so I could find the group's van! It was a stupid programme, but it would have been a dream come true had I still been a young teenager not a 20-year-old punk rocker! I also remember seeing Doug Trendle [Buster Bloodvessel of Bad Manners] in a dress outside the dressing rooms! We all thought he'd lost it, not knowing he'd recorded a version of the 'Can Can!'"

Meanwhile, Madness had retreated into the famed Pathway Studios to put down material for their 2Tone debut. During the session, they recorded three tracks for consideration for the single, due for release on August 10th. This was to be their only 2Tone release, in accordance with the contract between themselves and Dammers. The chosen single would be Madness' sax player Lee Thompson's tribute to Prince Buster, 'The Prince', with the B-side track 'Madness', another Buster original and the group's signature tune. It was their first ever record, the second ever release on the 2Tone label, and became an instant hit, propelling the band towards the title of one of Britain's most successful bands ever.

For Suggs McPherson they were exciting times: "When we got the first copies of 'The Prince', the first record we had ever made, and also the second record on 2Tone, it was the label itself that was my biggest memory I have of those early days. I just remember thinking of how it summed up everything in one visually striking way. It was a fabulous feeling not having to compromise on anything."

The graphic identity and design of 2Tone record covers and promotional work came from Chrysalis Records' design team of Dave Storey and John 'Teflon' Sims. Senior designer Sims (nicknamed 'Teflon' by his Chrysalis compatriots for the way he handled a table tennis bat in the record company's games room) was born in Farnborough and grew up with a love for drawing and football. He left school to work in a commercial art studio, but within six months became a trainee artist working on film and TV advertising including *Dr Zhivago*, the *Carry On* films, *The Man From Uncle* and *The Avengers*. He then spent a year in an advertising studio sweatshop that led to a job as general artist for the Russell James studio working on national and provincial theatre accounts including shows like *Godspell*, *The Rocky Horror Show* and *Jesus Christ Superstar*. After becoming freelance, Chrysalis Records became one of his clients, and he did artwork for the likes of Leo Sayer and Jethro Tull. He was then offered a permanent job at the company, which lead him to Dave Storey and the 2Tone project. Dave was born in Cumbria, and came fresh from Middlesex University of Art and Design.

Refinement was not an artistic problem in the 2Tone design work – it was quite the reverse, the difficulty lying in achieving amateur-looking effects. Jerry Dammers, technically the art director, spent much of his time telling Storey and Sims to roughen up their work with repeated photocopying or by hacking bits off with a scalpel. Despite its rough and ready outward appearance, the team's output was anything but, with influences coming primarily from the formal Swiss typography of the early Sixties. The team's 'anti design' ideas later influenced designers such as Jean Paul Gaultier. Storey and Sim's work for 2Tone led to other music industry commissions, many of which they fulfilled together. Storey's client list would include the Fun Boy Three, the Colourfield, the Housemartins, the Lightning Seeds, Iggy Pop, the La's and Norman Cook.

Teflon was heavily into ska and the sounds of 2Tone after being a bit of a mod in his youth. With the emergence of 2Tone in the vibrant post-punk ska era his work

YOU'RE WONDERING NOW

flourished. He would later go on to work with the Fun Boy Three, A Flock Of Seagulls, Comsat Angels, Salt'n'Pepa, and DJ Jazzy Jeff & Fresh Prince.

"Any talk of an art movement or 'ism would have raised a laugh with Jerry," said Storey. "Stiff had popularised the 'Fuck Art, Lets Dance' slogan and that was very much the bottom line. There was a purity and honesty to what Jerry did, like punk in a way but not as snarling, something softer."

Storey and Sims remembered seeing the Specials for the first time: "They were an impressive bunch, quite frightening to look at; Jerry without any front teeth, and all their skinhead haircuts. But talking to them, they were thoughtful, even charming characters, though Jerry didn't suffer fools gladly. In that respect, we got on well with him, especially us just having left college. They were such a breath of fresh air. We were more used to pop stars coming in on clouds of aftershave. Jerry would just shuffle in anonymously with a carrier bag full of bits and pieces. What made 2Tone different to everything else was that Jerry directed all the visuals. He'd say 'run the checkerboard right across, move this figure two millimetres to the left.' We'd sometimes create these immaculate images, as we did for all Chrysalis artwork but he'd insist we rough things up."

By this time, it was August, and the Specials were busy laying down foundations and material for their forthcoming debut album, as well as fulfilling a hectic tour schedule up and down the country. However, they managed to find time to jet to the continent for a date at the long-standing Bilzen Jazz Festival in Belgium. The event was an annual three-day festival, along the lines of the Reading Festival, where British record companies tried to crack the lucrative European market. Appearing that weekend were the Police, the Pretenders, the Cure and hairy Australian rock gods AC/DC. It had rained consistently for days before the event, and over the three days of the festival, it had been torrential, except for a miraculous 45-minute spell where Coventry's finest turned up and stole the show with a rip-roaring set. It seemed that 'Our Father Who Art in Heaven' was a fan of the new red-hot sound of live British ska!

The gig got underway with 'Dawning Of A New Era', the punky opener to all the early Specials sets, which struck a chord with the normally placid Belgians. Terry Hall's dry wit and classic one-liners were fast becoming legendary, and he introduced 'Do The Dog' to the mud-soaked and now bouncing Belgian crowd with: "This one's for anyone who's got dog shit on their wellies!"

There was a number of the crowd who were intent on winding up the security men who were standing cross-armed and menacing in front of the high steel fence unreasonably erected to separate the crowd from the foot of the stage. The pushing and shoving created a definite air of tension as the crowd surged forward to dismantle the offending fence and the security men got very heavy-handed. The Specials' performance of 'Too Hot' was brought to a halt by Terry Hall, not one to tolerate security staff at the best of times, who calmed the melee by voicing his disdain: "Just leave it. It's not worth it. You know they [the security] have the mentality of a house brick."

"The first time we went to Europe we played this festival to a field of Belgians who'd never seen us before," said Horace, "but fences still got torn down. I remember thinking 'this is it; this is what it's all about!' We were speechless."

Back home, 2Tone mania was gripping the nation. Madness' 'The Prince' had peaked at Number 16, and new signings the Selecter were ready to launch themselves with the release of their debut single 'On My Radio'. On returning to Britain, however, the Specials headed straight for the studio, this time to record the long awaited album. Waiting for them in the producers chair was renowned new-wave recording artist and newly converted Specials fan Elvis Costello.

The man chosen by the group to collaborate with them was born Declan Patrick MacManus in London, England in 1954. He was the son of British bandleader Ross MacManus, who had played with the famous Joe Loss orchestra and found 'fame' as the singer of the 'R White's Secret Lemonade Drinker' song for the Seventies advert. Costello eventually took his stage pseudonym from Elvis Presley, and his mother's maiden name, Costello. His career began professionally in about 1969 when he played in a number of bands in London, before forming part of successful pub-rock band Flip City in the mid-Seventies. He got his first record deal with Stiff Records in 1977, while still holding down a fulltime job as an early computer operator. His first album *My Aim Is True* was a hit in the UK and landed Costello a worldwide deal with Columbia records. Over the next decade, Costello recorded a number of popular and influential albums with memorable hits such as 'I Don't Want To Go (To Chelsea)', 'Watching The Detectives', 'Oliver's Army' and 'I Can't Stand Up For Falling Down'. He is still regarded as an extremely influential singer/songwriter and performs all over the world. Back in 1979, he had a good reputation and, as a lover of reggae music, had turned up to a few Specials gigs and liked them immensely.

"I don't think we had really met a famous person before we met Elvis," said Jerry Dammers. "I remember being in the pub with him and there would be all these crowds around staring at him. Very off-putting."

Some of the tracks were recorded, and it was decided to release one of them as a single, so the Specials resumed their 7" career with a rendition of the Dandy Livingstone ska classic 'A Message To You Rudy' (CHS TT5). It was an excellent cover and included two new faces who would go on to become honorary Specials. The first was Jamaican trombonist Emmanuel 'Rico' Rodriguez.

Born in 1934, he attended Kingston's famous Alpha Boy School, an institution for wayward boys and for children from the wrong side of the tracks. He was taught to play the trombone by the strict Catholic nuns that ran the school, and by the age of ten, had become a good player. Later he honed his skills under the tutelage of legendary ska pioneer Don Drummond of the Skatalites. At the age of 20, Rico tried his hand as an apprentice mechanic, and he also became a Rastafarian, a religion that would be close to his heart all his life. He often worked under the direction of the renowned ska and reggae producer Duke Reid, and became one of Jamaica's most highly regarded session musicians. In 1961, Rico moved to England where he worked in car factories and played in various reggae bands including the Undivided, who were mainly employed as a backing band for Jamaican artists that were touring the UK. In 1967, Rico played trombone on Dandy Livingstone's original 'Rudy, A Message To You'. When Island Records resurfaced as a major player in the reggae genre, Rico was on their list of session musicians. His first session took place in 1975, for Toots and the Maytals' *Reggae Got Soul*. In 1977, he finally saw his album *Man From Wareika* released to rave reviews. With that critically acclaimed solo album under his belt, Rico was quickly signed up as a support act for Bob Marley and the Wailers on their 1978 European tour.

The second conscript was Dick Cuthell, possessor of the best moustache in music. Dick began his musical career in Liverpool, in the next generation of bands that came in the wake of the Beatles and Gerry and the Pacemakers. His band, originally called the Washington Soul Band, eventually moved to London where they changed their name to Selofane, and their style moved from jazz/soul to pop. Dick left shortly after and in the years that followed he played with a number of bands, including Rich, Grimes, Babylon

46

and Trifle. When he was signed up to Island Records as a part-time engineer his path in music changed and he worked with the label's ska and reggae musicians. He became involved by chance when Chris Blackwell heard some demo tapes he had put together: "I had recorded a lot of reggae down at Hammersmith," said Dick, "and guys would come down and say 'We want a Roots sound', and I'd think, 'Well, what you talking about? Here we are with a brand new studio, with all the technology you need and it's all clean up the sound and make it beautiful.' Anyway, we did some demos, three tunes just to see what they thought. We were using various people, Eddie Thornton, Byron on drums, Philip Chen on bass, Bunny McKenzie, Tony Washington, Ferdinand Dixon, and Ijahman doing some vocals. It took a long time for Chris to hear them but he did and then I was sent off to Jamaica."

This brought him to the attention of Rico Rodriguez and a long-lasting and revered partnership was forged. Cuthell was recording for six weeks, although he was supposed to be there for only three originally, in the famous Jamaican drummer and bandleader Count Ossie's camp in the Wareika Hills, where Rico had become a Rastafarian. Recording was held up briefly after Ossie was killed in a car accident. The sessions were a real eye opener for Dick: "It was really strange up at the centre of Count Ossie in Wareika Hills," he said, "I didn't feel as if I was on Earth at all, and it wasn't because I was high on smoking or anything, it was, I don't know, all the drums going and all the percussion. Rico was just blowing, and he said to me 'blow!', so I got my horn, I was all breathless from running with it 'cause it's so hot there, and I wasn't used to not having any structure to play with, you just have the drums with you, and Rico was just blowing and blowing and blowing and I found myself trying to find the bass to hold me down or a guitar to give me a chord to change key or something. But it wasn't that at all, it was just the drums, and as Rico says, 'It's a matter of breathing'. You can play exactly what you want, and it sounds great. We just ran the cassettes that I had with me and blew all night."

Cuthell, a man of many musical talents, (he could also play bass, keyboards and percussion as well as compose and arrange) was primarily known as a cornet and horn player. His skills were employed on Rico's Island album *Man From Wareika* which Cuthell also produced. At about that time Rodriguez and Cuthell teamed up with Godfrey Maduro on sax and became the formidable horn section christened the Hammersmith Horns. They played with the likes of Burning Spear, Steel Pulse and Aswad and performed on the London club circuits, but Rico and Dick were about to be offered an unusual career move. In an interview with *Reggae Vibes*, Rico recalled the day Dammers came calling: "Oh yes, I used to go over to the south-east of London everyday to see a friend live there. And one day me daughter, one of me daughters, say 'Some people look fe you, man, and them call every day and them would really like to get in touch with you.' And so me say yes, and one day when me there them call me an' say them look for me, for them would a like me to join up with their band. So me tell them 'Say me no really join band, for when the band breaks up it's like you come in the wilderness, y'know.' So me practice me instrument an' go about the show business an' get to know people myself. But they convinced me it would be good to join them, OK? I decide fe join them an' start the recording. I realised they like what I was playing, so they asked me to join them. So I join them an' play."

So Rico and Cuthell made their appearance on the Specials' 'A Message To You Rudy', which had a message to all the young skins, rude boys and youths who found themselves involved in trouble. The message simply said that getting involved in confrontations and acts of violence would lead to nothing but time spent at Her Majesty's pleasure.

"When we did that song," said Lynval Golding, "it was like a message to any of the heavy skins who came along to our gigs just for the trouble. It was a message to the rude boys saying that if you come out looking for aggro then the only place you're gonna end up is jail 'cos that's where all the bad rude boys end up. Its not on to go to a gig for fighting, you go there to enjoy yourself. When we used to get into fights in Coventry, it would sometimes get very heavy, though it's cooled down a lot since those days. Sometimes it would get really bad and people would end up in hospital and that would really shake me up."

Neville Staple was well versed in what happened to unruly rude boys; he had experienced prison life and had this to say about the record's message: "If you go around in gangs you're going to force yourself into a lot of trouble. You get sent to prison and that's not the place to be. If you can't look after yourself in there, you just get kicked around. Most guys going around fighting think it's fun but when you get put inside you realise that's it's not worth it but by then it's too late. From the time I left home I used to think it was the in thing to go fighting but now I know different."

Terry Hall also had a bit of a reputation for getting involved in trouble in his younger days. He had been a frequent visitor to Coventry City's Highfield Road football ground, where he and the other Coventry skins and punks would go out of their way to clash with rival supporters: "My days as a football hooligan," said Terry, "came to an end one Saturday afternoon after being kicked in the balls against Stoke City. Stoke was always one of the worst grounds I went to. I got hit four times and I got chased with a pickaxe. We travelled a lot to Manchester United games, five or six of us used to go from Coventry and Rugby. There were a lot of games where we used to get into trouble but everybody did then. What would happen is, we would all sleep at our house on the Friday night and somebody would have a car because the trains were often too expensive so we'd leave as soon as we woke up and drive at about 6am, and we would get to a town about eight in the morning and wander round the town all day. Trouble found you really."

After choosing 'A Message To You Rudy' for the A-side, the Specials chose 'Nite Klub' for the B-side. One of the outstanding features of the track is the booming, loping bass-line provided with ample venom by Horace Panter. For a large number of Specials fans 'Nite Klub' is the pick of the two tracks on the single.

The band easily scored a second Top 10 hit with 'Rudy', but the big test was to come with the release of the band's debut album. Two weeks before it was to be issued to the eagerly awaiting public, they suffered a setback when bootleggers almost scuppered their plans. The group's performance at the Moonlight Club, as recorded by Decca Records, had drifted out on to the market in a vinyl LP format. The music scene clamoured to get hold of the album and gave it red-hot reviews. However, this left the Specials and their cohorts in a state of apprehension as to how the official studio album would be received and compared to the live bootleg. There was only ever going to be one way to find out, and that was to get the finished product out. Everyone held their breath, and a fortnight later, the debut album was released. They needn't have worried.

Simply entitled *Specials* (CDL TT5001), one of the classic albums of all time was born. The front cover featured a black and white shot of the band looking mean and moody (taken by rock music photographic team Chalkie Davies and Carole Starr, now successful designers based in New York), standing in the empty Coventry Canal Basin, a run down and dilapidated area that summed up the angst imparted in the album. The basin is now refilled and after much regeneration is surrounded by flats, craft shops and cycle lanes. The cover was to become an iconic design. The word 'Specials' had a small chunk of the letter C missing at the bottom to portray an 'iron-on' transfer. A thoroughly thought through piece of artwork, a symbolic and striking image which grabbed you before you even got past the cover and into the music. The album is also exceptional because it manages to capture on vinyl what the live experience was all about.

"When we started recording the album," Terry Hall remembered, "it was a typical sort of late night drinking album. I remember that punctuality wasn't our greatest asset really but I was always very keen to get in there. Plus, there were songs on the album that I liked playing live like 'Nite Klub', which was great live. That track captured what we were all about, it was raucous and yes, everybody was drunk and it captured what Coventry was about. To be honest its only in the last two or three years that I've realised what sort of impact that the first Specials album made and that was by meeting up with musicians who were referring to our album on their work as an influence such as bands like the Libertines and Blur and it's rewarding 'cos it means people listened and took something from it."

Suggs of Madness was also a big fan of the album: "They really encapsulated the sound of what it was like to see the Specials live. A great job and quite unusual."

Even though that album got some scintillating reviews, some critics dared to say that the album lacked any real rhythm and producer Elvis Costello came in for his fair share of criticism too, but the polished result was good enough for Jerry Dammers: "I thought Elvis caught our feelings just right. He did a good job. We chose him because he had often said that he'd like a go at producing us. He had shown a lot of faith in us by coming to all our gigs. He got interested in us and we clicked together. He was the only man for the job."

At the time, Roddy Radiation was a bit more conservative: "I don't think Elvis quite understood what we were aiming for," argued Roddy. "I think he still thought that it was like one section of reggae, then the next section's a heavy section, then another section comes along. But I'm not knocking him at all. He got a great drum sound, and he was a lot better than having some hot-shot producer who wouldn't even let us in to the mixing sessions. It would be nice if we could do it ourselves next time, though. Then you've got no-one to blame."

Costello himself also gave high praise to the band he had just produced: "I saw the Specials' early shows," he said, "in the days when they'd have bonfires on the beach after gigs with their travelling gang of mates. I wanted to produce them the way they sounded best before someone professionally fucked them up. We used a basic 24-track studio to get the right sound but you could only stay in for a limited time because it shared an air-vent with a laundromat and the smell kept on coming in. All the crew and the band's mates were in and out of the studio, so we shoved them all into the cubicle one day, turned out the lights and recorded 'Nite Klub'. One day Neville let off this replica gun in the control room, as a gag, which no one realised would deafen you! We had to go home after that. They were a proper band, know what I mean? the Specials sang about things that were obvious but which were direct."

Also in the recording booth was engineer Dave Jordan, who became an integral part of the Specials' studio set-up.

"Dave Jordan, the engineer, did a lot of work in the studio," explained Roddy. "Dave did the legwork while Elvis would be getting Terry to record a vocal in a toilet or somewhere, or breaking bottles for the background noise in 'Concrete Jungle'."

Elvis may have been a fan, but around the time of the album recording sessions, he approached Jerry Dammers with the remarkable advice that the band part company with guitarist Roddy Radiation.

"He told the band to get rid of me!" exclaimed Roddy. "I think after he had done his 'Watching The Detectives' he started digging into the past and got into the early Jamaican ska stuff. He couldn't really hear my rock'n'roll punk guitar fitting in with that. I'm not sure he understood what we were aiming at. Maybe he thought we were going to 'revive' the music and do it exactly the same but Terry's vocals were hardly Prince Buster or Desmond Dekker."

Terry Hall saw truth in Roddy's argument: "It's not that we are just trying to revive ska. It's using those old elements to try and form something new. In a way, it's still a part of punk. We're just trying to show another direction, you've got to go back to go forward."

The general consensus was that the album was a breath of fresh air and a screaming success. Punk was dead and Britain had begun to stagnate, until the stinging lyrics and biting social observations of the Specials washed away the decay with a fresh and strident new sound. It was stark and powerful and it was hard to shake the tunes out of your head.

Side 1 kicked off with the group's latest 7" offering 'A Message To You Rudy' the aforementioned warning on behaviour:

> *"Stop your foolin' around,*
> *Time you straightened right out,*
> *Better think of your future,*
> *Or else you'll wind up in jail."*

This was followed by one of the albums many highs, 'Do The Dog', which had originally been recorded by Georgie Fame in the Sixties but had been completely rewritten by Dammers to contain his bitter cynicism:

> *"All you punks and all you teds, National Front and natty dreads,*
> *Mods, rockers, hippies and skinheads,*
> *Keep on fighting 'til you're dead,*
> *Who am I to say? Who am I to say?*
> *Am I just a hypocrite? Another piece of your bullshit?*
> *Am I the dog that bit the hand of the man that feeds it?"*

The third track, 'It's Up To You', was a refined example of their ska/punk hybrid sound, and courtesy of Neville includes some fine toasting, snapping out the vitriolic prose:

> *"In London town you can hear the youth them say,*
> *Take warnin',*
> *It's up to you what you really want to do,*
> *For you were standin' on the corner givin' trouble,*
> *When the police man come he says you have to move on the double,*
> *So steppin' up the street with my little rude girl,*
> *With her sta-press to her ankles,*
> *It's up to her what she really want to do,*
> *It's up to you, you, and strictly you and you."*

50

It was followed up by the sleazy 'Nite Klub', a rollicking poke at the trendy inner city club scene. The lyrics still ring true today and are best loved for their icy wit and the celebrated line:

> *"I won't dance in a club like this, 'cos all the girls are slags and the beer tastes just like piss."*

"I never liked that line." recalled Jerry Dammers, "It didn't sit right with me."

Lynval Golding, on the other hand, enthused about the lyrical sound bite: "That's such a great line! It fits perfectly. It fits because that's how we talk as guys. We say those kinds of things."

> *"Nite Klub, is this the in place to be?*
> *Nite Klub, what am I doing here?*
> *Nite Klub, watching the girls go by,*
> *Spending money on...*
> *Hey, hey, I don't work,*
> *'Cause I don't have to,*
> *I don't have to work,*
> *There's no, no work to do."*

Next on the roll of soon-to-be classics was the track 'It Doesn't Make It Alright', a gentle, rolling number advocating racial tolerance, an area that would be further tackled by the band over the coming months. The song sums up their ideal with the lines:

> *"Just because you're a black boy,*
> *Just because you're a white,*
> *It doesn't mean you've got to hate him,*
> *Doesn't mean you've got to fight,*
> *It doesn't make it alright."*

A blistering example of the Specials' punk edge came with 'Concrete Jungle'. Composed by Roddy Radiation in his days with 'The Wild Boys', it would become a Specials anthem. Roddy took over the lead vocals in place of Terry Hall. Roddy remembers: "On 'Concrete Jungle' I played with the whole band but I got to sing the track as well. Dammers told Costello that I had sung it when we were the Coventry Automatics so he let me do it, or maybe Terry wasn't around at the time, I dunno."

> *"I won't fight for a cause,*
> *I don't want to change the laws,*
> *Leave me alone just leave me alone,*
> *I want to get out on my own,*
> *I'm walking home tonight,*
> *I only walk where there's lots of light,*
> *In the alleys in the doorways,*
> *They smash a bottle straight in your face."*

This high speed hurtle through inner city life then rolls into a lilting mellow cover of

Prince Buster's rude boy ode 'Too Hot' to close side one.

> *"The soldiers came back to you without them,*
> *The police force are afraid they can't even touch them,*
> *They said you think you're bad,*
> *Why don't you come out yourself,*
> *These boys are spoiling for a fight,*
> *Fighting tonight they don't lie,*
> *It's too hot."*

Side 2 commenced with another cover, one of their favourite songs from the live set, Toots and the Maytals' party piece 'Monkey Man'. The tune opened with Neville declaring 'This ones for the bouncers!' a sampling taken from the Moonlight Club bootleg that introduced the same song. It has become a popular piece with many ska bands, the bouncy skanking tune sees Neville's toasting at its best:

> *"I was on my way to Banbury Cross,*
> *Then I see a monkey upon a white horse,*
> *With rings on he fingers, bells on him toes,*
> *Sing a little song, wherever he be,*
> *'Cos he's a monkey, 'cos he's a monkey,*
> *'Cos he's a weedy weedy weedy little monkey man."*

The aptly-titled 'Dawning Of A New Era' came next, another heavily punk-influenced track with a great sniping vocal from Terry Hall (although it was said somewhere that he sounded a bit like Norman Wisdom!) and the whole track dominated by the licks and twangs of Roddy Radiation's guitar.

"That song is really made up of lyrics about different things that had happened to me," said Jerry Dammers. "'Area 3' was about Chelmsley Wood in Birmingham and there's a bit in it about a doormat, well I'd slept on that in Hillfields in Coventry. A bit of everything in that one."

> *"We climbed the stairs to the 14th floor,*
> *The key wouldn't fit the door,*
> *This is the dawning of a new era,*
> *She said she had a beautiful flat,*
> *We had to sleep on a mat,*
> *This is the dawning of a new era."*

Following on from that riotous song comes the bluesy 'Blank Expression' which features some explosive drumming from John Bradbury complemented by marvellous work from the rest of the rhythm section. This track shows the true raw power of the Specials, its tale of a miserable winter's night in uptown Coventry (hear the jingle bells ring!), out for a beer and some unsociable drinking and meeting an uninterested girl:

> *"I walk in a bar and immediately I sense danger,*
> *You look at me girl as if I was some kind of a total stranger,*
> *Where did you get that (blank) blank expression on your face?"*

The traps of relationship disharmony and youthful matrimony are given plenty of derisory comment in the hilariously constructed song 'Stupid Marriage' that sums up teenage weddings (still apt these days but perhaps the marriage aspect wouldn't ring so true). The tune sees the appearance of the enigmatic character Judge Roughneck, portrayed with gusto by Neville Staple, shouting out his judgements across the court room to Terry Hall's rude boy in the dock who is facing a charge of criminal damage and stalking (another 'modern' phenomenon). Hall, in full witty retort, gives his explanation of the sorry event, but unfortunately for Terry, Neville AKA Roughneck shows no sympathy and sends him off to jail before the manic choral ending : "Silence in the court! Order! Rude boy, you have led me to believe that you was going out with a girl and she left you and married someone else. So you got drunk and smashed up your ex-girlfriend's property. I have come to one conclusion, that is to sentence you to five months in prison. Before they take you down to the cell, what have you got to say for yourself?...

> "He wanted to be something but he knows he never will,
> She's got him where she wanted and forgot to take her pill,
> And she thinks that she'll be happy when she's hanging out the nappies,
> If that's a happy marriage I prefer to be unhappy."

The subject of blowing away your youth continued in the next track 'Too Much Too Young', with its warning tale of social security dependency and the story of being an unmarried teenage mother. The tune, based loosely around the original ska classic 'Birth Control' by Lloyd Terrell, was about a girl who Dammers had known, who had fallen into teenage pregnancy (another tale that sits as relevantly with today's society as it ever did). Full of derisive lyrics and told with punk venom, over the next few months this track brought the Specials global attention:

> "You've done too much, much too young,
> Now you're chained to the cooker,
> Making currant buns for tea.
> Oh no, no gimme no more pickney,
> Ain't you heard of the starving millions?
> Ain't you heard of contraception?
> Do you really want a programme of sterilization?
> Take control of the population boom,
> It's in your living room,
> Keep a generation gap,
> Try wearing a cap."

The album continued towards its climax with yet more disdain from Terry Hall, in an early Dammers song 'Little Bitch', a real frenetic crowd pleaser.

> "And you think it's about time that you died,
> And I agree, so you decide on suicide,
> You tried but you never quite carried it off,
> You only wanted to die in order to show off,
> And if you think you're gonna bleed all over me,

You're even wronger than you'd normally be,
And the only things you want to see are kitsch,
The only thing you want to be is rich,
Your little pink up-pointed nose begins to twitch,
I know, you know, you're just a little bitch."

Then the album closer, a cover of Doreen Schaeffer's 'You're Wondering Now', which was the perfect set finisher and delivered in the familiar contemptuous fashion. The track would become another Specials anthem as the group made the track their own in their unique British ska style.

"Curtain has fallen, now you're on your own,
I won't return, forever you will wait,
You're wondering now what to do,
Now you know this is the end,
You're wondering now who will pay,
For the way you did behave,
You're wondering now what to do,
Now you know this is the end."

What an exhilarating compilation of songs! Any doubts about the success of the album were quickly dispelled when it went straight into the album charts at Number 7. While most of the songs were Dammers creations, apart from the covers and Roddy's 'Concrete Jungle', it was felt that everybody contributed.

"I might throw in a couple of odd lines here and there," Terry Hall commented at the time, "but Jerry wrote most of the songs that we're doing at the moment. I'd feel uncomfortable about singing those words if I didn't agree with them. What he's basically saying is what I agree with, and what the rest of the band agree with, otherwise we wouldn't be in the same band. I've got the same feelings about girls as I have for boys. A boy could be a slag as far as I'm concerned. And a song like 'Too Much Too Young', about the girl not dealing with contraception, it's just as much on the boy's head as it is on the girl's. You've got to have two people to use contraception, and two people not to."

The group were staying at a hotel in Redcar, Cleveland at the time of the album's appearance, and two telegrams arrived for them. The first was from Elvis Costello heralding their success, the second offered congratulations on the album from a certain Paul McCartney of the Beatles. That same night the McCartney telegram was stolen.

"We weren't too bothered about that really," said Rick Rogers, "though it was nice of him, but the one from Elvis meant more to us anyway."

The Specials and 2Tone had by now captivated a generation's imagination. At the time, increasing unemployment and poverty lead to disillusionment among the young, who needed some hope to cling to, and although it was never likely to change circumstances or fortunes, 2Tone came along at a time when its sentiments rang true. At this time, Madness, now signed to Stiff Records after their one 7" contract was fulfilled with 2Tone, were riding high in the charts with their debut album *One Step Beyond*, which incidentally also bore a monochrome cover. The Selecter were wooing people up and down the country at their gigs, and the speed of this collective success was certainly breathtaking.

Roddy Radiation was enjoying the ride, but was determined that they should all keep their feet firmly on the ground and not get swept away with their success: "This game can be a bit dangerous in that you get too much praise. That's a problem with groups, you get to the stage where you start believing all the stuff in the papers and you feel you have to live up to it. Then once you get into what we're doing now you start going to certain clubs, where all the other bands go, and that's where you get the rock elite thing. I don't like it. I've been to a couple of these show-business parties and they're really boring."

Another drawback, the boys found, was that as their popularity increased they were starting to be recognised in the street and it was posing the odd dilemma. In Coventry, things weren't overly problematic because they had all been quite well known around the city before hitting the big time, but in other places they were stopped to sign autographs, causing crowds of people to clamour around them in the process. For some it was an enjoyable experience but for Terry Hall it was becoming a bit strained: "I don't mind if people approach me at a gig" said Terry, "but in the street or wherever, I just go to pieces. It's an embarrassment thing really, I don't see myself as a star, I'm just an ordinary bloke. I don't want to be on a big stage with bright lights with kids gawping up at me. My worst moment so far was when I was buying some groceries when the assistant on the till suddenly recognised me and asked for my autograph. There was a huge queue behind me and they weren't too pleased at the delay. I don't think I've ever signed my name so quickly in my life. It may sound silly but it's the way I am."

Jerry Dammers had noticed that attitudes towards them were changing now they were popular. It was well-documented that celebrity did not sit well with him: "Everywhere you would go, everyone acts abnormal. People were like 'He's in the Specials, act abnormal!' It's like entering the Twilight Zone or something. It can be a bit weird, to put it mildly, especially as it happened really quickly."

What happened next is still remembered by many people as the ultimate experience, a massive 40-date nationwide '2Tone Tour'. The tour mostly sold out, with the ticket price capped at only £3, a carefully-considered arrangement which was designed to further spread the gospel according to Walt Jabsco. The mouth-watering line-up saw the Specials, the Selecter and Madness on the same bill, ready to decimate the country's dance halls.

Madness were only contracted to do half the tour as they were pencilled in for a small tour of the US by Stiff Records. They were asked to come on board despite the fact that, technically, they were no longer on the label, because they were still big favourites of the 2Tone army. The Specials were due to spend three days in rehearsal before the tour commenced (not that they really needed it after months of solid gigging) but according to Horace Panter in *Ska'd For Life*: "That turned into half a day's filming for the 'Rudy' video and two days' worth of shopping."

The promotional video to accompany 'A Message To You Rudy' also magnified the 2Tone theme a step further when it showed the band decked out in black and white clothes, performing in a totally white studio, all strictly pop art. The video was interspersed with actual documentary footage of real life skins and rudies on the streets. 2Tone trademark Walt Jabsco got in on the act, dancing to the fading track to close the promo.

On October 19th, the bands all travelled together, squeezed into a 48-seater coach, to the tour's opening night at the Brighton Top Rank. The revue went down a storm and was celebrated afterwards with much inebriation and partying well into the night. The following day a crop of heavy-headed, dark-spectacled 2Toners were reluctantly ushered on to the famous Brighton Beach, with its connotations of mods v rockers, for a photo-shoot for *The Face* magazine. The bands all sat together on the pebbles in what was to be another archetypal 2Tone image.

"One of my best early memories," said Suggs of Madness, "was sitting on Brighton Beach with Jerry Dammers from the Specials; he was throwing a cassette player in the air and shouting 'Sputnik!'"

During both the Specials' and Madness' sets at Brighton, over-zealous fans had invaded the stage, and this swiftly became the norm at 2Tone gigs. These invasions continued despite the actions of security and the obligatory unlicensed 'bouncers' who were often a little too hasty to wade in with fists and boots to clear the stage, even if the bands had invited the audience to come up and join the party in the first place.

"Who am I to say the kids can't invade the stage?" Terry Hall said at the time. "We're not bothered, it bothers other people. They have wrecked equipment sometimes but its only equipment isn't it? That can be replaced. What gets me is the attitude of some people that the venues employ as bouncers. They're supposed to stop the trouble not start it. It really pisses me off when they've got nothing to do so they decide to kick the shit out of a group of kids on the front row and then blame them for causing the trouble. It not only spoils it for the kids but it spoils it for us."

Some of the stages on the tour could not accommodate a full stage invasion and safety became an issue. When the crowds were at a crescendo it was left to frontman Terry to clear the stage, which he did in his familiar droll fashion: "This stage is our prison. We don't want you to have to become prisoners of the record industry, so please clear the stage."

Terry said: "It was so chaotic, on and offstage. You felt like it was a seven-piece gang, which then turned into a lot more people, which felt like a part of you. We had kids travelling all over with us, it just grew and grew. Then there was Madness and the Selecter as well, there were so many people! Everybody got on."

Word of mouth was also spreading about the band that would let you dance on stage with them, as Neville Staple explained: "One night, early on, at a gig somewhere, somebody got onstage and we didn't kick them off. It just grew from that, word got around. Some clubs used to get annoyed with it, we used to tell 'em to leave these kids alone y'know? They were alright! That's why the kids liked us; we used to stick up for them if the bouncers tried to kick them off. It was brilliant! A lot of people thought it was frightening but it wasn't at all. You had the odd one or two dickheads who'd try to nick our stuff that was why we had the roadies keepin' an eye out. It only affected the music by making us more into it, making us more involved with the audience and closer to them. That way we knew they were getting off on it. Which was getting us off on it. Soon, it was like they were fucking ALL onstage, so you couldn't see the other members of the band!"

On the tour, the coaches (other vehicles would ferry the crew around the country) would pull into town and word would spread like wildfire that the 2Tone label had arrived. Unemployed fans, and there were many of those around in 1979, would flock to the venues during the day, as would kids that had played truant from school to catch a glimpse of their new-found heroes. The Specials were very decent to those who had come to the concert halls before the gigs and would often invite a few ecstatic fans in to watch the soundcheck or go for a drink with them in nearby watering holes. Fans were carried on the coach as well, doing their own tour and sleeping on any spare floor in the band's hotel. A true sense of camaraderie and community made everyone feel included, this was the 2Tone way. During the tour, as the label rose in the national consciousness, so the demand for more shows grew. Rick Rogers had to stop in many phone boxes as they travelled the country trying to book additional and bigger venues to accommodate the surge in interest.

Drinking was a feature of life in the Specials (as well as the occasional dabble in less legal substances) and the group and entourage would often partake of a beverage through sheer boredom whilst hanging around in venues and hotels. The pressures of living up to the rock'n'roll lifestyle and living up to the dream often made temptation too much to bear for the young lads.

"There was too much drinking going on in the band," recalled Rogers. "Way too much. The group once had a wardrobe case made up for putting their stage suits and stuff in. A great big thing it was but that didn't last long because in time it was filled to the brim with beer and spirits; it became a travelling bar."

The tour was barely a week old when a violent incident threatened to bring it to a juddering halt. On 27th October, the tour rolled into Hatfield where the bands were due to play at the local polytechnic, now the University of Hertfordshire. Early on in the gig a large group of men were refused entry (the management always reserves the right, remember) and quietly departed without any sign of trouble. However, during the Selecter's set, the same men, apparently declaring themselves the Hatfield Anti-Fascist League, burst back into the venue via a fire door and into a bar area that was separate from the actual dance hall. They started to lash out with cutthroat razors, knives and broken bottles, windows were smashed. As a result of the incident ten people were hospitalised, eleven were arrested and over £1,000 worth of damage was caused. When the Specials arrived at the venue from their hotel the fracas had ended and their dressing room was being used to treat the injured and walking wounded. If the marauders had got into the dance hall, the injuries and damage could have been potentially disastrous. In the crowd that day was TV and radio personality Gary Crowley who had gone along with a girl called Siobhan Fahey, later of Bananarama: "I remember going to the 2Tone tour at the Hatfield Polytechnic with Siobhan, whose sister I was going out with at the time" said Crowley, "It was a riot. It took place in the reception area and we had to take cover behind the merchandise stall; it went off completely."

Terry Hall recalled his memories of that incident: "Hatfield was horrible, really bad. I remember turning up to that gig and going into the dressing room to be greeted by loads of kids with cuts all over their faces. It was really nasty. That was the gig for me where I started questioning what was going on a bit. Its all very well trying to stop incidents as they happen but I think you have to take responsibility for it, I also had a bit of grievance with Madness about it, 'cos I didn't think they were taking responsibility for this, I think they should have made a stand really at that point. They were on the same tour as us and it was up to them to denounce it. It was a nasty period..."

The crowd, however, remained undaunted and all three sets by the bands went ahead unhindered.

Violence at gigs is not a common occurrence these days but it was an all too familiar feature back in the late Seventies and early Eighties, whether it was racially-motivated or football-related.

"We deplore violence at any of our gigs," said Jerry Dammers. "We don't need it, the audience don't need it and I've said this before but if anyone is thinking of coming with the sole intention of causing trouble then none of us want them there. Our gigs are about having a good time and that message is imperative."

The other problem which began to raise its ugly head at concerts was racism. The 2Tone bands, despite their obvious multi-racial stand, attracted many skinheads into their audience. These naïve young men were prime targets for the National Front and British Movement, who at that time were slowly building support across the country. The National Front had attracted attention to itself during the Seventies through the violence associated with its demonstrations in areas with large black and Asian populations. In response, the Anti-Nazi League was formed by members of the Socialist Workers' Party to counteract the National Front marches and to contain the British Movement. In 1979 the NF fielded their largest ever group of parliamentary candidates in the hope of cashing in on the scaremongering surrounding multi-racialism.

They tried to preach to the country that multi-culturalism would not work and implied that the black community were taking jobs. In the climate of unemployment and dissatisfaction, the parties recruited more members and the British Movement saw a large influx of so-called 'white power' skinheads. The media seized upon the image of a racist skinhead, especially since early skinheads had been seen to be involved in 'Paki-bashing'. It must be stressed that, while there were some skinheads conscripted to the Neo-Nazi cause (these tended to be called boneheads to differentiate them from average skinheads) not all skinheads were racist. Racists, under a false sense of kinship, suddenly took on the skinhead image and attempted to pollute the minds of the naïve.

The extreme right began to use these skinheads as foot soldiers for their own political means. The recruiters sought out these disillusioned young men and persuaded them that they would be serving some great cause. Getting a group of these disaffected people to wreck 2Tone events was yet another way of getting the National Front and British Movement's racist message across. As a result skinheads became persecuted by the media (who still use the same stereotypical image when commenting on skinheads today) whether they supported the extreme right or not. It was assumed that a skinhead was a racist and a thug. The irony of a racist skinhead listening to a black genre of music and paying money to see the multi-racial bands of 2Tone, who preached racial unity, simply served to show that the majority of those roped into far-right activities had no clue what they were doing, or what the NF and BM really stood for.

The problem was that 2Tone and its overtly anti-racist stance was attracting the far right who were instigating the disruption at gigs. With the Specials and the Selecter's strong anti-racist policy evidently put into practice in the flesh, the main focus of the right-wing fans became Madness, the only 'all white' band. Not only were Madness, along with other 2Tone bands, popular with the skinhead crowd but it was said that the band members themselves were associated with the subculture. The group's relationship with their skinhead following was quite uneasy. Mike Barson, the keyboard player with the band, was discontented with the skinhead following, and was concerned that so many were present at performances.

"Personally that sort of thing makes me a bit sick," he said. "Sometimes I look at them all and think 'Who the fuck are these prats?' you know? It really makes me angry and I'll say to Chas, 'These are your mates, what the fuck are you bringing them here for?' You can say that, and then again, if you're chatting to them they're all right. They're mates, y'know? I mean they're not particularly mates of mine; they're more mates of Chas. Well, they're all sort of mates of ours."

Before he became a band member, it was documented that Chas Smash had been involved in fights with skinheads at performances, but the one major event that woke Madness up to what was going on occurred on November 18th, 1979. Madness were supported by Red Beans and Rice, who were going through their set. The group had a black lead singer and the band were heckled and harassed throughout their performance by some racist 'skinheads'. It became so unbearable that the band could not continue. Chas, real name Carl Smyth, takes up the story: "Me and Suggs liked Red Beans and Rice, they did R&B covers but they were getting lots of grief from a particular obnoxious minority, you know, really making their presence felt. So me and Suggs went out onstage, shitting it a bit, and asked them to respect and give them time and they did. We couldn't believe they listened to us!"

Suggs had roused himself to realise that he was actually in an influential position.

"Yeah I am [in an influential position]. You see it's just kids like that vote NF and stuff because they do we're supposed to tell them to fuck off. Whereas I'd rather have it like this, to sit and talk about it, the way everyone else I know does. I think the worst thing about racism is that it's a really touchy subject. Nobody will talk about it without being on one side or the other, really going mad or over the top about it. It's like a dirty word."

That said, however, it did not stop a large group of right-wingers from Nazi saluting at the end of the show. Matters took a further downturn in a 1979 *NME* interview when Madness' Chas was quoted as saying: "We don't care if people are in the NF as long as they're having a good time."

This added to the growing media worries that Madness were a racist band with allegiances to the National Front, which truthfully and wholeheartedly the band members denied. It was just that the group, with their carefree 'nutty' attitude, weren't bothered with politics. They were out to have a good time and their inexperience in expressing themselves effectively on the matter added to the debate. They responded quickly with Smash saying he was totally misquoted and misrepresented. The matter encouraged him to write the track 'Don't Quote Me On That' about the affair. The subject was revisited in the late Eighties when it was discovered that in the Seventies Suggs had been a friend of Ian Stuart, the right-wing skinhead who fronted the band Skrewdriver. Stuart had been drinking with Suggs and friends in London and offered Suggs the job as roadie for Skrewdriver so that Suggs wouldn't have to pay entry to their gigs. It has to be stressed that this was in the days before Skrewdriver were any part of the National Front set up, they were merely a punk band signed to Chiswick Records who were picking up good reviews and even did a John Peel session. The racist element of the band did not appear until 1982 when they re-formed after a split in the late Seventies, by which time Madness were in full swing. Ironically, Stuart's friendship with Suggs saw him land a very small part as a member of a skinhead gang in the Madness bio movie *Take It Or Leave It*.

Carl Smyth observed: "When you are writing about rude boys, which encourages a rude boy, skinhead and mod following, it makes for a volatile mix. Madness got into trouble for being the only white band, guilt by association and all that, but we wouldn't be doing a tribute to Prince Buster in 'The Prince' if we were racists. I still reckon that the right wing thought they had a potential base of new members and the kids got conned into it. You'd always see an older guy causing trouble and then suddenly vanish. It's ok to talk about the fascist troubles but you have to remember, it will be remembered as a joyous time too. It lent an edge and the stage invasions were incredible. Jerry Dammers loved them too, Terry Hall didn't."

The fracas about the Madness *NME* interview seemed to have been a storm in a teacup, and the band realised they had to make some sort of stand. This they did, as I can testify, when they played Leeds in the early Eighties. A group of far-right sympathisers began sieg heiling, Madness stopped the show, and had them removed, Suggs offered apologies all round.

"Most skinheads aren't a real problem at all," said Jerry Dammers "they're very discriminated against really. They look a bit intimidating that's all, its not a political statement the way they dress and its just not true at all that if you're a skinhead you've gotta be in the National Front. They've crippled the skinhead cult but we can tell everybody that if they're into the NF or British Movement and they want to come to our gigs, we just don't want them there. They're just not welcome, if they've bought tickets, well, that's just tough, we won't give them their money back. We just don't want them there."

Neville Staple, a prime target for the right wing element, had his own way of dealing with the racists.

"Sometimes," he said, "we'd run off stage to eject some horrible Nazi skinhead and throw him out of the building. They'd chuck money at me and Lynval, spit at us and taunt us. It got to me but never put me off. The message was there in the music."

The sporadic violence did not hamper every Specials gig and the group took no prisoners in quelling trouble, especially if it was race-related.

"I remember one gig," said Roddy Radiation "when a contingent of National Front skinheads turned up and started on Neville and Lynval. Neville, being a bit of a fucking hard case, jumps in to have a go. Lynval does too and he's no fighting man, so I jumped in to help. I didn't realise that the stage was ten foot high and I misjudged it completely and fell flat on my face. I eventually got back up and started swinging my guitar around my head, then someone said 'Ere, the fights over there' pointing 200 yards down the hall. You couldn't tell the good skinheads from the bad ones, then Nev comes back up and says 'Give me your guitar.' I gave it to him and he ran off and broke someone's arm with it. When I got it back, the neck was all split, falling apart. Then when Madness played in Coventry and I saw some lads kick the hell out of this one guy, one looked up at me and said 'This is your concrete jungle Roddy'. It was mindless violence."

Another problem for the bands were the bootleggers and counterfeiters that had caught on to the 2Tone boom and were cashing in on all things 2Tone on the black market. Everything was copied, posters, badges, patches, scarves, T-shirts, and even headbands and sweatbands. It was a common sight to see the spivs parading up and down the queues of kids outside venues offering their very cheap, poor-quality wares. In those times of destitution, and with official merchandise sometimes out of the price range of the fans, the fakers made a nice bundle of cash. Some of this merchandise was terrible; one wash of the clothing and it fell apart. The reproduction of the Sixties-style clothing that 2Tone helped to bring back into vogue also got the same treatment.

Suggs of Madness recalled the clothing boom once 2Tone had taken off: "It was obvious that the fashions we were all into were very Fifties/Sixties-orientated, partly because you could still get good Fifties/Sixties suits in the second hand shops. I don't think there will ever again be a trend started from an Oxfam shop. The mass-produced stuff really was depressing, I remember horrible see-through Harrington jackets. Harringtons were great jackets but they stopped making real ones in 1972. The mass-produced stuff became a travesty of the original thing. Also, the new gear was always made from nylon and what was it with those cardboard pork-pie hats? It got really depressing for me seeing hordes and hordes of kids dressed identically but it was just unfortunate 'cos really we were sort of preaching individuality which is not what it became. It was supposed to be larger than life but was smaller than life. Inevitable, really."

With the 2Tone tour taking the country by storm, the label's meteoric rise was celebrated in traditional British style on November 7th with the Specials, Madness and the Selecter all set to make an appearance on that evenings *Top Of The Pops* show. However, on the night of the broadcast the three bands were due to play the Top Rank in Cardiff. After lots of hair-tearing and frantic negotiations it was decided that the Selecter would remain in Cardiff to start the proceedings, so *TOTP* had to use a tape of their performance of their debut 'On My Radio' from the previous week's show. The Specials performed 'A Message To You Rudy' and Madness did 'One Step Beyond'. Acts on *Top of the Pops* in those days were billed as playing live but often mimed along to their tracks. The 2Tone bands poured disdain on the charade by making it blatantly obvious through their onstage antics.

The Specials and Madness turned up at the TV studios at the BBC (no doubt the Director General was nervous that day) and played for the programme. As soon as the technical clearance was given, they had to make a crazy non-stop dash to get back to Cardiff in time for the concert. Madness took the quickest route possible and flew back by private helicopter. Meanwhile, Coventry's finest had more time to spare and so caught the train from Paddington station. The Specials made it to Cardiff in good time but there were no signs of Madness. The Nutty Boys had been forced off course by inclement weather and eventually made it to the gig with just five minutes to spare!

"Madness still gave a great show," said Specials manager Rick Rogers. "Only the Specials could top a Madness performance and Cardiff was no exception. The adrenaline of the day gave the citizens of Cardiff one of the best shows I've witnessed."

Once the tour hit the middle of November, Madness said their goodbyes and headed off to fulfil their booked US tour in an attempt to try to crack the lucrative American market. The Madness departure was done in true Nutty Boy style when the band walked across the stage during the Specials' set carrying their suitcases!

"Such great memories of that tour..." said Suggs. "I can remember giving Rico the bumps for his 60th birthday and me and Jerry trying to drive a speedboat over a water ski jump à la James Bond style and getting stuck halfway up the ramp! Fantastic times! We wanted to keep really friendly with the Specials. It was so easy to fall into needless bickering and it just wasn't fuckin' worth it. We were both after the same things, we had got the same problems and thought probably the same lifespan. We were all really young, so when it was all over we'd be able to do things together. Their contract ended with Chrysalis after four years and so did ours with Stiff. Hopefully, we thought, we would have enough bread by then to get a really good, proper label together. That's what I'd really like to have done."

The Selecter's wild dreadlocked bass player Charley Anderson recalled the impact of the 2Tone Tour: "That tour could never be repeated! Whoever witnessed it will never forget. And we had it for 41 dates! We shook some dust off the venues up and down the country. It was very hectic. Like the night when we didn't know if Madness or the Specials were going to make the gig venue, but the Selecter were there holding the fort. Madness was to come by helicopter and the Specials by train, both from the BBC's *Top Of The Pops* studios. We just kept playing 'til the first one arrived. So that was what the real spirit of 2Tone was like. The 2Tone Tour was fantastic. The audiences got their money's worth, they got to sweat three, maybe four times over, with so much energy. Sometimes we could actually feel the whole building shaking!"

Madness were replaced by the Birmingham soul band Dexys Midnight Runners, who were more or less well appreciated by the hordes of the 2Tone army, as their brassy Sixties soul sound was not entirely removed from that of 2Tone. According to sources, Dammers offered Dexys a deal to release a record on the label, which was immediately dismissed by Kevin Rowland when he spat condescension on any plans by telling people he 'didn't want any part of any movement.'

Dexys guitarist Al Archer said: "We'd rather be our own movement. If we had seriously wanted to jump on the bandwagon, we could have been Secret Affair ages ago. But we were very conscious of the fact that we might become too closely associated with that very strong 2Tone image, when in fact we're into a whole different approach. A lot of people have already come to expect a certain type of music, a particular beat and a most definite image from every new band signed to the label and automatically it's all down to whether or not you're as good as the Specials."

As far as the 2Tone tour went, the band proved somewhat aloof with their 2Tone associates and kept themselves to themselves. As the tour progressed to Belfast and Dublin, Dr Feelgood supported the Specials and both the Selecter and Dexys Midnight Runners stayed on the British mainland.

November 25th saw the Specials' set at the Lyceum Theatre, London recorded for posterity and the same happened when they played an emotional homecoming gig at Tiffany's in Coventry on November 29th. The club's capacity of 2,000 was met and the fans gave the band a tumultuous reception. Fans queued for up to four hours prior to the gig to see their heroes and there were problems with ticket forgeries and touting. Large quantities of forged tickets were seized before the gig but only two people were caught trying to gain entry with them. It's widely known that the Coventry show was one of the best the band ever played:

"It was a fantastic night," said Roddy. "Definitely one of the best I'd had. I think we were all a bit overwhelmed."

With the gig played on home turf it was an opportunity for the band's parents to see their offspring in action and Terry Hall's parents were glowing with pride: "It was out of this world," said Terry Hall Senior. "I never believed it could be so good. I've seen him on television but it was never as exciting as this!"

Hall's mother Joan was equally impressed: "It's just amazing that my son has come from working in an office to this. I think the whole thing is fantastic!"

Such was the clamour to see the Specials that new shows were being organised and three more dates in London and a matinee performance for the band's younger followers in Coventry were arranged. They also played another two nights back at Tiffany's and again the scene was frantic and spectacular. Horace Panter recalled: "This is probably going to sound pretentious but those two shows just before Christmas 1979 turned into a celebration for a city that desperately needed something to celebrate. The atmosphere was unbelievable. Playing up there onstage, trying not to get in the way of Roddy's guitar lead, narrowly missing a shirtless Neville Staple, trying to get to the front of the stage. I felt as proud of the people in that club as they felt proud of us. I might have cried!"

In a year that would have left the more faint-hearted musician for dead, the Specials rounded off an exhilarating 1979 at the Hammersmith Odeon in a charity concert for UNICEF. The event spread lasted from December 26th to the 29th and it proved to be one of the largest gatherings of British music talent ever assembled for a single event. The show, which grew out of meetings between the then UN secretary Kurt Waldheim and Paul

McCartney (who was plying his trade with Wings) saw all the artists and road crew donate their services to the cause for free. The first night was a full show by big-haired rockers Queen, the night after was Ian Dury and the Blockheads, the Clash and Matumbi. Night number three, December 28th, saw the Pretenders and the Specials onstage as support to the Who. The Specials pulled out all the stops to steal the show with a passionate set. A collection of songs from the event was released on a double album vinyl format by Atlantic Records entitled *The People's Concert for Kampuchea* (Atlantic ATL 60153). The double album featured highlights from the sets delivered that night but disappointingly, the Specials only feature on one track, 'Monkey Man'. The event was also recorded on film and was originally aired on ITV – its highlight must be Neville Staple toasting whilst climbing a rope which nearly reached the lighting rig!

It was the last gig of a frenetic year for the band. From playing small clubs and pubs only nine months earlier, they had graduated to running their own record label and had 'made it' in terms of national recognition and music chart success. There had been no time for the boys to assimilate their dramatic rise and for some of the band it had not registered. Drummer Brad summed up the bewildering pace of their year by saying: "If I sit and think about everything we have done this year, I'll go mad."

The *NME* published its readers poll for 1979 which saw the Specials eighth in the list for Best Group (won by the Jam), Jerry Dammers voted sixth Best Keyboardist but the Specials romped home to top both the Best New Act category, and Best Record of 1979 with 'Gangsters'.

Even though the Specials had shut up shop for the end of the year, the 2Tone label hadn't. The label had been swamped by demo tapes from would-be ska bands from all over the country and while some were abominable, the odd cassette shone. One of these was from a Birmingham band called the Beat. The band, originally formed by vocalist/guitarist Dave Wakeling and friend Andy Cox, was a six-piece outfit boasting a 50-year-old sax-player and they had already been touting a unique brand of punky reggae around Brum for a few months.

"Ska had yet to reach Birmingham," said Dave Wakeling, "but there was punk and

In the dressing room prior to filming Gangsters promo video 1979. Photo by R.Byers

reggae wherever you went. We had lots of house parties and we noticed that people burned out really quickly if you just played punk but if you mixed it up and played a reggae tune, then a couple of punk tracks, people would stay on the dancefloor longer. One night Andy said, 'Wouldn't it be great if we could do this as a band?' That was our moment of realisation."

Thinking that the group were on to something new they were shot down in flames when Cox brought a copy of the *Melody Maker* music paper to rehearsal and announced that a band had beaten them to it!

"Well, a week after that," explained Wakeling, "we were playing in town and the Specials and the Selecter came to see our show. I can remember Jerry Dammers dancing at the front like a lunatic."

Dammers was impressed with what he witnessed and offered the band some gigs supporting the Selecter in London: "The Beat's first London gig was supporting the Selecter," said Beat co-vocalist Ranking Roger. "About 90 per cent of the audience were skinheads. I'd spoken to those guys before in Birmingham but to see them going 'sieg heil' for the first time freaked me out! But as 2Tone got the hits, the audiences changed. You genuinely had black, white and Asian kids dancing under the same roof. It was great."

After a show at the Electric Ballroom, London, Dammers asked the band if they would like to release a single on 2Tone.

"Of course, we jumped at the chance," said Dave Wakeling. "This was in the August and by September we were in the studio. There was this strange thing whereby whatever song we released Chrysalis would have owned it for five years, so we decided to do 'Tears Of A Clown' and keep most of our songs for ourselves."

With 'Tears Of A Clown' recorded and their original composition of 'Ranking Full Stop' as its B-side, the Beat wanted to get the single out in time for Christmas but Dammers wanted to release it in the new year. This caused a lot of friction, particularly since it was becoming increasingly difficult to get hold of Dammers due to his commitments with the Specials. When the Beat did manage to get hold of him they complained that all they got were three girls giggling in the background and an incomprehensible Dammers grumbling excuses into the telephone. After a lot of pressurising the Beat got their way and notched up their first success and another accolade for 2Tone when 'Tears Of A Clown' hit Number 6. Like Madness before them the Beat were only signed to 2Tone for one single. In a deal that was similar to that of 2Tone and Chrysalis, they eventually signed up to Arista Records who agreed to let them set up their own label, Go-Feet.

Another band which attracted the attention of Dammers was London-based outfit Bad Manners. This zany nine-piece, formed in 1976 and originally called Sissy Solo and the Sheet Starchers, was fronted by the larger than life Douglas Trendle under his stage name Buster Bloodvessel (a mantle taken from the bus conductor in the Beatles movie *Magical Mystery Tour*). They had started out playing pub-rock style numbers before progressing to R&B and reggae. By some quirky twist of fate, at a similar time, they were playing similar sounds to that of their London cohorts Madness and Coventry's Specials. They hadn't realised there was to be a revolution in British music and they would be part of it, albeit away from the 2Tone label.

"Jerry Dammers was the leading light in ska at the time," recalled Buster. "I remember him coming to see us for the first time and he said 'You gotta do more ska in your set.' So we had this toothless man coming down to us from Coventry telling us what to do. We thought 'Who's he talking to?' We did include ska but that was just one of the aspects of our sound. We started out doing things like 'Liquidator'. We was R&B ska. The only songs we could write ourselves were reggae ones and whenever we started dropping 'em out of the set to do something different people would say they wanted to hear them back again, so we took it from there."

Dammers could see the potential in this big band with its awesome brass section and he offered Bad Manners a deal to record and release on 2Tone: "But we didn't have a demo tape or anything," said Buster about the offer, "so we got one together and by the time 2Tone came back to us there was other companies after us. And because we thought 2Tone was more of a stepping-stone for groups who couldn't get a good contract and we already had Magnet and others offering us a lot of money we let it pass. And 2Tone had only offered us a one-off single anyway. We would've been famous if we had've gone on 2Tone but there again we were making it on our own merits, not on the label's merits."

The Specials and the Selecter were the label's hard hitters and now Madness had some company in the padded-cell department with the arrival of Bad Manners.

"They were a fun band, somewhat more than ourselves at times," said Suggs "they were polar opposites to the Specials. They were the Pontin's chalet to the Specials' villa in Tuscany."

Bad Manners signed up to Magnet Records for a six-figure sum and the review from their debut album *Ska'n'B* from the *NME*'s Mark Ellen (who later went on to present the *Old Grey Whistle Test*) summed up the band and expressed the idea that turning down 2Tone may have been a wise step: "Let's make it crystal clear before we board this bus: Bad Manners are about having fun, dressing up snappy, dancing, getting pissed, making an unholy din and very little else besides. It can't be denied that for the newer ska-based bands ploughing through the exhaust fumes of the ever-accelerating 2Tone tank, sympathy is starting to wear thin. Bad Manners, to their credit, don't attempt to wave the chequered flag but offload any political sentiment and simply assume the basic position, a ska backbeat, to make this logical diversion: Ska'n'B. Sure, there's a lot of porkpie hats and shades in evidence but otherwise 2Tone references are indirect and unobtrusive. Bad Manners set their sights down low and win outright. At a time when life expectancy is nearing rock bottom (especially for predominantly 'live' bands and in ska circles) a debut this good is no mean achievement. Get it tomorrow: dance it to death."

The image the band portrayed hid the fact they were accomplished musicians and readily accepted by the 2Tone army of supporters. Despite the warning of a short life expectancy in Ellen's review, Bad Manners found longevity beyond all the 2Tone bands and they would later appear on 2Tone by default. Another band with a very brief alliance with 2Tone were a seven-piece outfit from the Midlands (but not Coventry). Strictly reggae outfit UB40 were desperate to inform the public that they were not a ska band or connected with 2Tone: "They're all our mates," said Robin Campbell, lead guitarist and co-vocalist about the 2Tone contingent, "but the press seem to have got hold of the idea that because we've done a few dates with the Selecter and the Beat we're a ska band. We've even been billed as that."

The group had been around for six months when 2Tone shot to prominence and they started getting gigs and playing further afield.

"Ska has opened the door for reggae, y'know, made it more acceptable," said lead vocalist Ali Campbell. "Reggae is, after all, a natural progression from ska like, the original ska of the Sixties developed into reggae, and I think modern ska is heading the same way. Ska today will become reggae tomorrow, and people'll be listening to us then, instead of the 2Tone bands."

A prophetic statement, and that was it for UB40 and 2Tone. Although Lynval Golding did spend time trying to convince Jerry Dammers that they may be right for 2Tone, there was never any deal offered to the boys from Brum despite rumours to the contrary. UB40 went on to have major hits worldwide and sustained a long fruitful career as one of the premier reggae bands in the world.

With barely enough time to recharge their batteries over the festive season, 1980 came all too soon for the Specials. The blistering pace resumed in January when BBC2 called for the channel's series *Rock Goes To College* who wanted to put the band on at the Colchester Institute in Essex. They played to a crowd mainly made up of students but some locals from Coventry had made the journey down to offer their moral support. The compère of the show was former Radio Luxembourg DJ Pete Drummond who engaged the crowd with a two-minute potted-history of the 2Tone story. The performance, broadcast on 21st January, was a masterclass for the nation and became something of the Terry Hall show as he was on top sardonic form, as demonstrated by his introduction to the track 'Rat Race': "This one's for those of you who are going to walk out of here missing your mothers and fathers and you'll have your little degree tucked under your arm."

Terry, often the chief placator when it came to crowd trouble, showed his contempt for security even whilst broadcast into the nation's living room when he became involved in a quarrel during 'Long Shot Kick De Bucket'. Two Coventry skins attempted to clamber on to the stage for a dance and were ruthlessly restrained in front of millions of viewers. Once Hall had clocked what was happening he swiped at one of the security with his tambourine, expressing his thoughts at the manhandling of the audience. As soon as the song blended into 'Liquidator' more youths leaped on to the stage to join the party and the scene became surreal as Hall exploded halfway through the tune and from one end of the stage hurled his tambourine with vicious force at the security! He continued to berate them and they soon relented and allowed the stage to fill with eager kids who wanted to get up and dance with their heroes.

BBC2 remained on the scene and followed the band with the intention of producing a documentary based around the Specials and 2Tone. It was presented by a young journalist called Adrian Thrills who was a massive fan of the group and even adopted the new rude-boy fashion.

"The band were playing a gig at the Moonlight Club in West Hampstead just a stone's throw from my flat, and with the entrance fee being a mere 75p it was a gamble worth taking for the chance to see an up-and-coming band. They delivered a set of almost frightening musical intensity. 1979 had been a good year for me. I had been doing reviews for the *NME* and chasing interviews, and after seeing that night at the Moonlight I was keen to be the first writer to champion the Specials."

Thrills did just that, following the band and getting all the important interviews as well as capturing the 2Tone explosion on film for the Beeb. He would go on to have a successful journalistic career, and at the time of writing is working for the *Daily Mail* newspaper. The documentary, titled *The Rudies' Return*, was for the BBC2 flagship arts programme *Arena*, and was due to be broadcast towards the end of January. It proved to be a fascinating insight into the world of the Specials, and featured a vast amount of previously unseen concert footage and rare behind-the-scenes shots of life at 2Tone HQ.

The group were the reluctant main stars of the programme but it also featured the Selecter and extolled the virtues of 2Tone. Jerry Dammers was seen showing Thrills around the shabby-looking office that was actually Jerry's flat in Albany Road. With, to some extent, unintended sarcasm and a comedic trait, Dammers seemed to be either carried away with the exposure or was embarrassed to be the subject in front of the camera. He flashed various cheque books, clearly showing contempt for their financial use, tore up a number of so-called contracts and then disrespectfully threw various demo tapes around the office saying: "As you can see, we've been inundated with tapes..."

The TV critics didn't like it and some said it looked like 2Tone had grown too big for its Doc Martens, with apparent success going to its creator's head. The 2Tone boom had led to other bands adopting the ska sound and image with hopes of being signed to the label and, good or bad, it was harsh to witness their dreams being strewn around an office. However, overall, the documentary caught the feeling of what 2Tone was about.

Meanwhile, 2Tone was beginning to be dragged into a legal battle with an old sparring partner Elvis Costello, who had been releasing records on his own Radar label, distributed by WEA Records. Radar had ceased to be, and WEA proceeded to claim the right to all of Costello's recordings. Elvis' manager Jake Riviera, a co-founder of Stiff Records, came up with the idea of finding a label to release a one-off single to bridge the gap until a new company could be found to issue Costello's *Get Happy!!* album, and that label was to be 2Tone. Costello had recorded a cover of Sam & Dave's 'I Can't Stand Up For Falling Down' and it was this which was earmarked for 2Tone release. Copies were pressed and given the catalogue number TT7 and it was all systems go to get the single out. While the planning for this was taking place, Riviera was on the verge of forming a new label for Costello to work from. Originally entitled 'FuckBeat', which no doubt would have incurred the wrath of any watching media censor, it was eventually changed to 'F-Beat.' Unfortunately for Costello, WEA gained information on the 2Tone single and, feeling disgruntled about the way they had been treated after distributing Costello's previous hits and obviously thinking they had some investment in him, went to court to get an injunction to stop 2Tone.

The law found in favour of WEA, and 2Tone found itself lumbered with a few thousand copies of a record it could not release. These were handed out as freebies at gigs in London, and Riviera had more pressed up to give away at shows in the US. Ironically, later, once the legalities were sorted, WEA took up distribution of F-Beat releases and the single saw light of day via that outlet. The 2Tone single would become one of the label's most sought after collector's items, still commanding good money for a 7" in present day terms at between £15-£40, although in New York, where copies were given away, the record is known to go for around $5.

After the Costello farce, the agenda transferred to a few dates arranged in Europe, and to the new Specials single. It was time to pack the suitcases, hire a coach, get a stiff upper lip and face the challenges of the continent. Gigs were booked in France, Belgium, Holland and Germany. On 17th January, the band appeared on the German version of *Top Of The Pops*, called *Musikladen*, to perform 'A Message To You Rudy'. The group put on a real piss-take of a performance with hilarious antics. They obviously enjoyed themselves and after they watched Madness performing 'One Step Beyond' from the audience, both bands really got stuck into some serious dancing to 'Rockabilly Rebel' by Matchbox. The frolics were captured for posterity and are viewable on video hosting site YouTube where Dammers, adorned in trademark flat cap, dances like a man possessed and even grimaces at the screen, alongside a pork-pie-hatted Chas Smash, an avid Suggs and a skanking Neville Staple.

The Specials played the Market Hall in Hamburg and gave a great account of themselves in what would later emerge as a top Specials bootleg vinyl LP called *Nite Klubbing Monkey Men*.

The new 7" was to be released on 26th January and was to be an exceptional release as it was to be an EP (extended play- a recording consisting of 3-5 tracks) and was recorded live in concert. For some reason the EP was released under their original handle of the Special AKA and the headlining track was 'Too Much Too Young' (CHS TT7), followed by 'Guns Of Navarone' recorded at the Lyceum in London. The other track was the sublime 'Skinhead Symphony' consisting of covers of the Pioneers' 'Longshot Kick De Bucket', Harry J's 'Liquidator' and Symarip's 'Skinhead Moonstomp' recorded live at Tiffany's in Coventry at the band's homecoming gig. Notably the EP was given the old Costello catalogue number of TT7. The release superbly captured the true sound of 2Tone and seemed to sum up all that the band were about in one recording. It bristled with raw energy and oozed excitement and is often regarded as their best 7" recording.

Given that, by normal standards, live singles traditionally fared poorly on the UK music chart listings (although Chuck Berry's live record 'My Ding-a-Ling' went to Number 1 and was, by some weird twist of fate, also recorded at the Lanchester Polytechnic in Coventry, a favourite Specials venue on their home turf), 'Too Much Too Young' ripped into the Top 40 on the day of its release. The *NME* review said: "More like the souvenir of the tour than a brand spanking new Specials effort. In the old Sixties (creak, groan) spirit of combining business with pleasure, Coventry's finest have opted for a selection of live material that is better showcased on an EP than an album. Breezy vibrations get compromised slightly by the muddy mix, but I can't see the fans baulking at such technical niceties."

The fans certainly didn't baulk at the technicalities and the single shot up the charts.

After a host of successful gigs in France and Germany, the Specials' bus rolled into Amsterdam, Holland. The gig, at the Paradiso, was another fine Specials exhibition but almost didn't happen when a bizarre event occurred in the afternoon on the day of the gig. The band and friends had gone down to the local fleapit to see a screening of *Monty Python's Life Of Brian*, the hot film of the time. When the credits rolled at the end of the film, the house lights remained down and when the filmgoers tried to leave the auditorium they found that all the doors were locked. A long period passed before the doors were eventually opened but the newly-freed cinemagoers were offered no explanation. Horace Panter reckoned it was God's way of reproaching them for laughing at the blasphemous storyline on screen!

Rico Rodriguez, meanwhile, was dropped by his label Island Records. It was a peculiar move by the company, especially as he was now getting more publicity than he ever had. He had had a couple of non-starters after the release of *Man From Wareika*, so it looks as if that must have been the main reason for his release, but it could have been the perfect time for Island to capitalise on his new-found celebrity. There was a strange proposal by Island to release a live version of 'Guns Of Navarone' with the Specials as Rico's backing band but that was shot down rapidly by 2Tone HQ. Without an official statement, Rico was dropped from the Island roster.

"We thought it'd be good for him," was the Island stance.

Jerry instantaneously solved the problem for Rico: "We could be paying him a

68

session fee," said Jerry, "but he gets the same as all of us and we're gonna bring his next album out on 2Tone."

Europe, it seemed, was really a warm-up for the forthcoming tour of America, which loomed large on the horizon. The American tour is covered in fine detail by Horace Panter in his account of the events in his book *Ska'd For Life*. The many short tours of the UK and Europe could not have prepared the band for the onslaught of shows in the US but even so, the group and entourage were hopeful and good spirited. The band had a day off from their European jaunt before they jetted across the Atlantic, ready to give Uncle Sam a good time and introduce them to raw British ska. On arriving in the 'land of the free', a press conference was organised to introduce the innovative septet whose first album had started to make a dent in the charts.

"Considering they weren't used to things like press conferences they did a pretty good job at handling the Americans." said Specials manager Rick Rogers.

When pressed on the subject of how he was finding life in the States, Terry Hall was unassuming: "It's alright. It's funny," he said, "I can't really take it all in as yet. In another few weeks I might be able to understand some of it but at the moment it's just like some giant fun-fair."

Jerry, on a natural high during his early time in the US, attempted to be a little more aloof: "Being in America is more like a holiday for us. Something to spend the money from 'Message To You Rudy' on." Guitarist Roddy had some concerns of his own, and in a spooky premonition said: "Will the Specials break America or will America break us?"

After the media grilling, they headed to the hotel. The tour was to bring many band tensions to the fore and for Rick Rogers hotels were just one of the headaches he had to oversee.

"I had to go ahead before the Specials came over to seek out places to stay. I had to check that the hotels were not too flashy for Jerry. It sounds odd but if Jerry had walked into a hotel foyer and seen a chandelier, he'd have walked right back out again and gone into a YMCA or something. It was nothing 'arty' concerning his attitude to things, it was nothing like anti-star, it was simply the way he was. Jerry firmly believed no-one was special including himself. Another factor, believe it or not, was Rico. He had a penchant for wanting a chicken sandwich at 4am and if he couldn't get food at all hours he would want to burn the building down. When I checked out places to stay I had to make sure they were down to earth with no status symbols and had 24-hour room service!"

"A lot has been said about my attitude to driving in flash cars and staying in exotic hotels," said Jerry. "Maybe a vicar's pay was actually low enough to teach me some respect for money. We didn't travel in the van with the gear, we travelled in a normal tour bus and the hotels were fine, with a few exceptions."

The US tour exploded into life on January 25th at Hurrah's in New York, although the group did arrive two hours late. A well-respected club, Hurrah's was a popular place to play for many a group in the Eighties and this night saw it packed wall to wall. The group delivered an inch-perfect set and expended so much energy that if it had been harnessed they could have lit up New York for a week. The Americans were astounded by the show on the small stage, the frenzied mania that emanated from the Specials. The crowd couldn't get over the enthusiasm and onstage antics and responded likewise by creating a great atmosphere. Terry Hall would either stand still or glower and prowl the stage like a wolf, eyeing the audience as his prey, snarling lyrics and cynicism as he went. To the gathered journalists and media: "If you're here to analyse us, don't bother, just join these and dance."

Before launching into 'Too Much Too Young', he declared: "This is your last chance to dance before the third world war. Who's touching on a subject?"

Then as 'Gangsters' kicked in to its instrumental booming trombone solo piece towards the end of the song he told the crowd: "You got lots of fuckin' trouble! What about the poor bastards you're fighting over? This is where you fight Iran, this is where you fight the Russians!"

All part of the incomparable Hall repertoire.

Neville and Lynval never stopped moving and ran riot all over the stage, initiating mock battles. Mad-professor-esque Dammers bounced and wrecked his keyboards. Horace bopped to the side of Roddy, who stood mean and moody, hammering out his riffs with intent to rock, while Brad kept the whole show together with his precise rhythms. Total captivation and a raging triumph, a great beginning to the tour. The group were more than ready to show the US what 2Tone was all about. The Americans were bowled over. Early reviews after the show compared Terry to the Sex Pistols' Johnny Rotten. The feeling of the moment is perfectly captured by contemporary journalist Richard Grab's review from the 16th February 1980 edition of the NME: "This 2Tone thing is constantly referred to in terms of its ska connection. In the Specials' case that's of course an influence, but this is no ska 'revival.' No, we've got something here so clever that it eludes any really appropriate categorisation. Three cheers! Over this side of the pond, reggae and ska have hitherto been of slight influence on the local sounds. But what the 2Tone crew have provided is the most exciting live music seen for some time.

"Madness broke the ground; the Specials were media stars before they arrived. Their debut was a full-scale scene-making event, the 'Be There Or Be Square' hype laid on thick and swallowed whole; the all-time record for stuffing bodies into Hurrah's. The Specials lived up to whatever anybody may have thought they had to live up to, and gloriously. The opening chords of 'Dawning Of A New Era' hit like a landing party guns blazing, which I suppose it was really. American audiences supposedly being a hard nut to crack, the Specials figured they had a challenge here. It didn't matter that this being Hiptown, you know, this audience was already committed. It was the right thing, it made them play hard. They sounded like they were giving it all they had, through a series of hot fast album cuts.

"Singer Terry Hall was all nerves and agitation. Jerry Dammers was a sight to behold, leaping around behind his organ like a demented puppet. But the standout was singer Neville Staple. Bits of the sharp dash of Wilson Pickett, the soul voice of Sam Moore, the wit of Prince Buster and the audacity of Trinity or the Lone Ranger, all wrapped up into one non-stop spectacle. He was pure locomotion, all over the stage, on top of the speaker stacks, into the crowd, over the top. And while Hall is not as dynamic, Staples doesn't upstage him. Like a shell game, the Specials keep everything moving, moving so fast you don't know where to look; a trick that seems to push back the walls and makes room for everybody.

"The sheer luxury of having so much going on at once is a visual feast. But the band's idea on how to project their act in America resulted in a curious on-stage attitude, articulated by Hall between songs. A song called 'Rat Race' was prefaced by laboured invective against students; other times he pointed to the back of the club and lectured those who were standing, not dancing. If this had been the general case, Hall would've been justified, but most of the club was one mass of heaving pandemonium. However, if someone would rather stand and watch, calling them 'shitheads' seems a bit out of order. But that's a minor bone to pick, when one is delivered such a set. Horn men Rico and Dick Cuthell were in place and perfect. Staple's Judge Roughneck routine got its laughs. The audience's excitement was a force like waves, falling just slightly for unfamiliar numbers like 'Guns Of Navarone' or 'Rude Boys Out Of Jail', and then rising with a palpable rush when something like 'Concrete Jungle' followed. We're talking here about body reaction, and soaking up a great show.

"The Specials are up to more than that, both in their lyrics and in the social implications of their presentation. Hall can deliver a song like 'Doesn't Make It Alright' with just the right mixture of sincerity and matter-of-factness. Nothing screams 'message' but there's a lot to listen to and learn. The last encore. Rico's 'Man From Wareika', was a reggae-wise instrumental that the Specials' rhythm section handled like they were born doing it. A perfect way to ease down and cushion the fall.

"The uncanny thing about the Specials' package is the way they've connected themselves to all those outside references, while putting together an identity that's self-contained, purely their own. And here, where those references are themselves still exotic, the effect is double-whammy impressive. Never saw nuthin' like it in this little town."

In 2007, American veteran cameraman Bob Zabawski brought the Hurrah's gig back into the limelight when some grainy old Super-8 film footage was added to an inadequately constructed DVD called The Specials – Too Much Too Young. The DVD was released in the US only and showed the band at their best on the Hurrah's stage.

The tour moved on to a gig in the jazz city of New Orleans, Louisiana, known as 'The Big Easy' a reference to the easy-going, laid back attitude to life that jazz musicians and local residents indulged in. It seemed entirely fitting that the group were bringing their refreshing brand of ska to New Orleans because, without a doubt, had it not been for the city's radio stations in the Fifties broadcasting the R&B music that had been picked up on the airwaves in Jamaica and re-interpreted by Jamaican youngsters, ska might not have evolved. The Specials were bringing events full circle.

The band were to play in a big warehouse that was situated by the city's sprawling railroad stockyards as support to British supergroup the Police, and a huge crowd was expected. The gig went ahead to a gathering of 3,000 old-school hippies, who had really come to see the Police, but the Specials pulled out all the stops and had at least a quarter of them pogo-ing and skanking before they had finished their set. They were followed by thunderous, uplifting shouts for an encore and they happily obliged, much to the dismay of Sting and Co. who had worryingly witnessed the conversion of the crowd. After headlining the gig, the Police left the stage to spiritless, half-hearted appreciation!

The group then made for Oklahoma City, in Middle America. They were booked to play in an edge-of-town suburb called Norman, in the prissy, quintessentially American Boomer Theatre, owned by the giant RKO film company and a favourite haunt of the local students. Around 700 people turned up and were initially reserved, with no idea what to expect. The band wowed the ultimately rabid crowd with their unique Midlands rhythms. Jerry Dammers was left feeling over-awed: "I really envy them," he said in reaction to the joyous chaos that had erupted in the Boomer Theatre "Can you imagine it? Fancy being able to hear all that great music for the first time. The whole bit: ska, mod, great! How can you not be knocked out?"

That night the group retired to their beds happy. During the night, the phone rang in Rick Rogers' room. It was good news all the way from England: "I was woken up at 1am with a phone call from Britain." said Rick "'Too Much Too Young' had gone to Number 1. I leapt out of bed, rushed into Jerry's room and woke him with the news. It's the only time I've seen an artist genuinely not care about their success. He went straight back to sleep! The rest of the band weren't much better."

The tour would continue for another three weeks, with some more shows as support to the Police, one at the PNE Gardens auditorium (now a school for circus arts!) in Vancouver, Canada. That gig saw the Specials really blast Sting and friends off the stage when they were applauded back for two encores! The headline in the local newspaper summed it all up with big bold type reading 'POLICE GOOD, SPECIALS INCREDIBLE!' Sting went to see the Specials, to try to get them to tone down their performances, but not too surprisingly was sent packing

After the PNE gig, the band were grateful to have a couple of days off to see a bit more of Vancouver and taste some of the nightlife. Such was the appeal of the group following the PNE that they were offered a stint at the Commodore Hotel in the town. Word the spread like wildfire and within 24 hours the gig was sold out, but it was in Vancouver that the first cracks in the Specials touring machine appeared. As exhaustion took hold, there was a downturn in behaviour and wayward comments made to the media. Rick Rogers did his utmost to keep the tour flowing from city to city, venue to venue, as well as managing everyday matters, but erratic personnel pushed the whole setup towards a crisis they did not want to face. Horace Panter said: "After the Commodore gig I was doing an interview when Rod, Jerry and Terry came in and fucked it up. They hadn't acted like it in England. I thought we were all about talking to people, not taking the piss out of them."

Backstage in San Francisco, Roddy had tried to chat up a good-looking female journalist, when he caught sight of Terry pulling faces behind his back, so Roddy punched him. Terry later replied by throwing a drink in Roddy's face. This fuelled a fantastic performance, with Roddy declaring Terry was "better than Jimmy Pursey" on the night.

One of the largest undertakings of the tour was the four-day stretch at the legendary Whisky A Go Go club on Sunset Strip in Los Angeles. By now, although the band were shattered and smiles were pretty much painted on, the success of the Specials album in the US charts was causing great excitement at Chrysalis USA. The album had reached Number 84, selling over 100,000 copies solely on reviews and the promotion of the group. With this feat in mind, some employees of the Chrysalis post-room approached their superiors with an idea to decorate the exterior of the club with black and white checks to make the four-day run a real 2Tone occasion. The post-room boys did the job themselves but on arrival at the club, Jerry Dammers was outraged and accused the record company of hype. He was not impressed and didn't back down despite Rick Rogers pointing out that it had nothing whatsoever to do with hype: "Poor Jerry," said Rick. "He just couldn't see the wood for the trees. He couldn't distinguish between record company hype and what was a sincere gesture from some lads in the Chrysalis post-room. He didn't like America at all."

The first of the four nights was for the record company executives and gathered media. The weariness manifest within the Specials unit was there for all to see, and the performance was not great, with onstage arguments and malfunctioning monitors. Afterwards, no-one was in the right frame of mind to be interviewed, but it had to be done. Just as the protest over the decoration of the club had died down, Dammers increased the tension by telling one reporter he had had more fun on a school trip to Russia than he was having in America.

"It was one of the stupidest things to ever happen to the Specials," Dammers later remembered. "Onstage we're putting everything in to it. Playing two shows a night was like putting someone in for two boxing matches a night, it made no sense at all. I hate to say it, but that really broke the spirit of the band. We were completely exhausted. After that, everybody stopped getting on."

"We were shattered," said Roddy, "partly due to non-stop partying, but mainly exhaustion. The Chrysalis USA guys came in wearing suits and ties, smoking cigars and wanted us to have a photo taken with them. This was in-between sets, towards the end of our residency. On this particular night, we came off stage after the last gig and the business suits from the record company were there. We were all hot and sweaty and one of them said to me, 'Oh I love that song of yours 'On My Radio' [a Selecter song] and could you teach me how to pogo?' That shows how much they knew about us as a band. Jerry just told them to fuck off and most of the band joined in. They stopped pushing the record, but I must say it felt good! Maybe today, if we had been good little English boys, we might have a little more money in the bank! But we considered ourselves revolutionaries with Jerry as our leader. But it felt great at the time telling them to fuck off!"

Terry Hall summarised the American experience when he told reporters: "It's been like gig-sleep-get up-travel-gig-sleep non-stop, and most of the time playing two gigs a night. It's hard to make much sense of it. Personally, I don't think 2Tone will be as popular over here as it is in England. Fashions don't tend to catch on in a big way over here, the country's too big."

Lynval Golding was by then tired, a little disheartened, and had even suffered racial discrimination whilst on the US sojourn. It was something he hadn't foreseen and which shattered a few illusions of the American dream: "I walked into this shop in Chicago to buy a watch for my sister, me and Rex our roadie," said Lynval, "and the guy says 'Hey, you can't come in here' and I said 'What's the matter with you?' and as soon as he heard our accents it was 'Can I help you, sir?' I told him to stick his shop up his arse. Can you imagine how they treat American blacks in that state? Another time I was in this bar in Boston wearing a green hat, and this guy turned round with his mate and said 'I like that hat…only trouble is I don't like it on you.' It's the same the whole world over."

The American experience wasn't altogether unpleasant; there had been a few belly laughs. Jerry had been asked to do an interview with the media after a wild night out in New Orleans. He proceeded to get up out of bed, much the worse for wear, and without warning walked directly past the awaiting journalists into the hotel swimming pool, where he vanished, fully clothed, underwater. Another time, Rico stayed up throughout the night trying to hide his dope in his bible before going through Canadian customs, only to be busted for smuggling oranges, of all things, as Canadian law prohibited the importation of fresh fruit! Sometimes the band acted like lunatics at petrol stations, all staring eyes and strange muttering delirium, as modelled on the *One Flew Over The Cuckoo's Nest* video they had been watching on their tour bus. The *LA Times* newspaper provided unintentional amusement when it described Terry Hall as an 'energetic Jamaican'.

However, with the media alienated and Chrysalis fuming over the 'Russia' comment, promotion on the debut album stopped immediately and it plummeted out of the charts as quickly as it had gone in. The tour rolled unenthusiastically through the final furlongs of a number of small towns towards the finishing post in New York (and an overall loss of $50,000).

The penultimate gig at was at the Diplomat Hotel in the Big Apple. There was much ado over sky-high ticket prices and the money grabbing antics of promoter Ron Delsener (the group would dedicate 'Gangsters' to the unwitting Delsener that night) but nevertheless the concert was sold out. That gig was attended by music dignitaries such as David Bowie, Specials fan Mick Jagger, Debbie Harry, the Jam's Bruce Foxton plus entourage, Robert Smith of the Cure and the Go-Gos, an all female pop-rock outfit who had played as support to the Specials at the Whisky A Go Go. The Go-Gos were touted, even by Jerry Dammers, as a very possible future 2Tone signing. Again, the show was somewhat jaded but that didn't stop the crowd from bouncing off the walls and demanding encore after encore. It was the old football adage of 'If you can win when you are playing badly, then you are doing something right,' and they were.

The final gig arrived (to a huge exhalation of breath all round) at the Speaks Club in Long Island and it proved to be a classic Specials gig. After being introduced onstage by Debbie Harry, a ding-dong end of tour finale ensued. The band were inspiring, with seven magnificent individual performances leading to many encores. The climax saw the band members leap into the audience, a more or less naked Neville sat on top of a collapsed Dammers, Lynval throwing Horace Panter into the crowd, Terry Hall wishing everyone bon voyage and Brad, caught up in the passion of the event, wrecking his drum kit! It was a beguiling display. America was done, but was it conquered? That would remain to be seen.

From the time of the Specials conception, the thrill of simply being in a band had been an enjoyable experience for those involved, but, as is often the case, hard times are good times and the boys had felt the satisfaction of struggling to succeed. However, as their popularity grew, the US tour, the hangers on, the yes-men, the exploitation and the disorganised hectic schedule of dates all conspired to take the shine off what should have been pleasurable. It was real work experience and a massive learning curve, not just about the 'machine' but about each other. With the satisfaction of completing the tour and having made a good job of it, the boys had a small amount of time off before they would have to return to the UK to get their British career back on track. Eventually, back in Blighty, it was time for reflection. Jerry confessed that the US tour, despite its palpable highlights and victorious conversion of the audiences, was not, in his mind, as successful as he would have personally wished: "By the time the last few dates came round," he said, "we were actually getting to the stage where we weren't enjoying playing. I've never felt that before. That's what it does to you and if you're not enjoying it then there's not much point in going on. In future we might just do the odd gig there instead of big tours."

Terry Hall was equally philosophical about the big American adventure: "It was a whirlwind. All of a sudden, it turns into a machine and you get an itinerary at the start of the tour; this is where you are going to be in ten days' time, this is when you get an hour off. It felt job-like. The gigs at the Whisky, four days, two shows a night. It was literally; get off the plane, go to soundcheck. You're in LA and you know? Where am I? What am I doing here? When you're 18 you stay up all night drinking. You get tired, really, really tired."

Whilst in the States, plans had been made about what was going to happen next on the recording front. There had been talk of an album for Rico Rodriguez and, more surprisingly, the original ska and rock-steady legend Desmond Dekker had even submitted a tape for consideration. The band had new songs, Lynval Golding wanted to do his own album and drummer John Bradbury had a version of Rex Garvin's 'Sock It To 'Em JB' which he wanted to release. There was also another signing in the offing, a

Coventry based group called the Swinging Cats (or 'Three Brothers and an Auntie' as Terry Hall liked to call them). There was also an idea for Neville Staple and Madness's Chas Smash to do a one-off single, with Neville to appear again as Judge Roughneck trying Chas in court for dancing too mechanically. Thinking even further ahead, there were dreams of the Specials owning their own recording studio and even possibly opening a club in Coventry. Terry Hall, however, wanted to keep the roots of the label firmly in the ground and on course to achieve its goals: "We just want to make sure it stays a natural process," said Terry, "not get pushed in directions we don't want to go. It may seem to have happened fast to you but, really, it's the culmination of years of having nothing. We're not exactly rich now; the royalties won't really come through 'til later next year. But we wanna keep ploughing money back, which doesn't mean we're gonna go round saying we're gonna help Tom, Dick and Harry but we will be an alternative for people who deserve the help and who want to use us."

Roddy, still with on eye on the bigger picture, was still holding out hope that the hustle of the last year would not affect their future approach.

"People keep asking us what it's like now, but it's very hard to see the overall picture of what's going on. It's all a bit of a rush, which is a bit worrying, and another thing I've thought about recently is that when we start writing some more songs, instead of writing about things we wrote about in the past we're going to start writing about things we're doing now. Which is a bit like a sell-out to the kids, but I write about what I'm going through at the time. Imagine if I wrote a song about falling over in a Holiday Inn! Bloody hell! Holiday Inn? There's so much emphasis on what you say now, so you have to try and say it right. It takes a bit of thinking about to put it over to the best of your abilities."

Their last single 'Too Much Too Young' had topped the charts for two weeks in January, only to be displaced by country star Kenny Rogers' 'Coward Of The County' (yes it was a time when the charts and record companies catered for all tastes and ages!). Still 2Tone's grip on the UK listings continued into 1980, with two releases from the Selecter and another from new signing the Bodysnatchers.

The Bodysnatchers were a seven-piece all-female outfit led by bassist Nicky Summers. She was another person who had caught the Specials at their awe-inspiring Moonlight Club gig and, from that night, she had wanted to form her own ska band. The group were hastily assembled after Summers put an advert in the music weeklies declaring 'Calling All Rude Girls'. Shane McGowan (later of the Pogues) introduced Nicky to Rhoda Dakar, a well-known face on the London gig circuit. Nicky asked if Rhoda could sing and Dakar agreed to have a have a blast at vocals, placing the final piece in the original girl band's jigsaw. Nicky Summers said at the time: "Rhoda was the last to join. I just saw her image and everything and thought 'God! I've never seen anything like it.' I just went up to her and asked her if she could sing. She said yeah and came down to the next rehearsal and that was that."

Despite the unconventional way the band had been thrown together they soon got a few dates around London. It was as support to McGowan's band of the time, the Nips, that they were seen by Jerry Dammers who was at the gig with Pauline Black of the Selecter. The gap-toothed maestro offered the band a spot on the current '2Tone Tour Part 2' in which the Selecter and the Beat played around the country together as a package. As part of the offer, the Bodysnatchers would sign to 2Tone and release a record.

"We played our first gig and then a week or two later we played our second gig and there was Jerry Dammers and Pauline Black," said Rhoda. "We never even got a chance to get going and we were offered things! It was just through being girls and being in the right place at the right time. We only had one original song and the rest were covers. It was all a bit 'Oh yeah, that's alright. They can do it'. I don't know how we got it! It was mad really!"

There were people within the 2Tone stable that had reservations about the girls' inexperience. They would have their fair share of critics, some scathing, but although unproven as performing artists some of the band were competent musicians, they were pretty tight live and had a very distinctive sound of their own. Within weeks, they were in the studio, with Roger Lomas as producer, recording a cover of Dandy Livingstone's 'Lets Do Rock Steady', which gained them a Number 22 hit and a TV appearance on *Top Of The Pops*. Thanks to 2Tone, the group were catapulted from obscurity to success in a matter of months, but only time would tell if their success was premature. They became the first band to feel some of the inevitable backlash that 2Tone had started to receive under the old media philosophy of 'build em up, knock them down'. The Bodysnatchers were exposed to the talons of the music press and in one of the music weeklies, who were beginning to show a lack of interest in the ska boom, they received a sarcastic review: "*The much-touted Bodysnatchers offer no real surprises, dragging out the inevitable shiny vinyl organ, farting sax and wandering single-string guitar for an ever-so-polite Rocksteady-A-Go-Go rhythm. Not so much a song with any real substance but one of those repetitive mid-set riffs used to introduce the band, the overall impression is of a soundtrack for a 'Do The Climb' type dance routine. By virtue of association, its self-conscious charm will ensure a respectable chart placing whilst fending off those cynics just sharpening their quills for the time when a 2Toner doesn't automatically chart with all the thrust of an Apollo rocket.*"

The press were interested in discovering the next big thing, but 2Tone wasn't ready to exit stage left. Such was 2Tone's success that it had inadvertently resurrected the careers of original ska stars like Laurel Aitken, the Pioneers, Toots and the Maytals, Desmond Dekker and Prince Buster. The original stars had all started gigging again and were enticing a new generation of fans with their pure ska beats. Labels, especially the famous Trojan, also joined in the party by re-issuing a huge back catalogue of original recordings. Indeed, repackaged for the new record buying market, Prince Buster's 'Al Capone', the Pioneers' 'Long Shot Kick De Bucket', Harry J Allstars' 'Liquidator' and Symarip's 'Skinhead Moonstomp' all found their way into the lower reaches of the charts largely thanks to the Specials' patronage. Neol Davies recalled the glut of records released around the time: "There was so much available! We snapped them all up. Stuff by the Upsetters, Owen Gray and the Pioneers. It was weird to realise it was ourselves that had caused the boom in this material but it opened us up to some great forgotten tracks."

With the Bodysnatchers signed and operating for the 2Tone cause, the Specials returned to their old hunting ground of Europe for a date. They ventured to the Pavilion Boultard in Paris where, a week before the Specials arrived, British new-wave mod outfit the Jam and their fans were attacked inside and outside the Pavilion by knife-wielding French skinheads. Still drained and weary from the US tour, Coventry's finest were prepared for trouble. The sound that night was terrible for a Specials gig, and out-of-tune equipment and atrocious acoustics inside the hall only made matters worse. Three minutes into the gig and the group had just finished the opening number 'Dawning Of A New Era' when things began to go wrong. Terry and Neville stood precariously at the edge of the stage and their tempers were being severely tested by a group of Parisian skinheads attacking a small bunch of London and Coventry skins who, in turn, were trying to defend themselves.

David Connor, a student at the time and now a successful graphic designer, was there that fateful evening: "Myself and two friends were travelling around the world back then, we were making our way back from the Far East. We were holed-up in France for two weeks and when we found out that the Specials were down to play we were well up for it. In the end, it was a shambles. The band were good but the crowd were real shits. There was fighting breaking out all over the place. It was pointless, we didn't understand what had set it off but a French lad next to us at the back of the hall said skinheads were involved. The scuffling came our way and I saw one lad take a few blows but it was French attacking French from what I could make out. The band were stopping and starting their set and we got pissed off with the whole thing and left halfway through and went to a jazz club up the road. Not a nice place to be."

As if having to endure their travelling support being assaulted was not enough, a huge shower of saliva was being aimed up at the Specials as the troublesome crowd began gobbing at the band. To try and distract from the fighting the group restarted by running through 'Do The Dog' but once the song ended a hail of spit descended on to the two Specials frontmen. Terry Hall was fuming: "Right! Just one thing!" he shouted, pointing an accusing finger at the disruptive area of the audience, "If anyone fucking spits, we fuck off. You start spitting we fuck off, so let's get that clear alright?"

The group burst into 'It's Up to You' but again at the end of the number another cascade of dribble splattered over Neville. He then marched up to the edge of the stage and pointed in the direction of one of the Paris skinheads: "Next time? Right! You fucking animal!" Neville was not amused.

The tension continued throughout the strained performance and after the completion of 'Blank Expression' Neville had had enough and leapt into the crowd to sort out the degenerate. After that, the spitting and verbal abuse ceased, only to be substituted by full and empty beer cans being thrown. Terry took a direct hit on the forehead from one of the empty cans and it was clear that he had lost hope. He picked up the object and showed it to the crowd: "It says 'Kronenbourg,'" he sighed. "It also says you drink it and when you've finished drinking it you put it on the floor, you don't throw it at us."

The concert was shambolic, but after the 'Skinhead Symphony' the band showed true character and resolve by returning for a 'Madness' and 'You're Wondering Now' encore. Terry Hall had the last word as usual: "You've been very naughty tonight. You've fought with us, spat at us and generally shit on us but WE'VE had a good time. Thank you and goodnight."

With that, he picked up a crunched can, balanced it on his head, flicked it off and volleyed it into the auditorium before slipping away with the rest of the band. Backstage, remnants of what had taken place could be seen as some battered Coventry skins were being tended to. A skinhead from Willesden was being calmed down after the merchandise stall he was operating on behalf of the band had been turned over by the French skinheads, who had then stolen or maliciously destroyed a large amount of the gear. As for the Specials, it was unanimously agreed that the quicker they returned home the better.

Following the grind of the US tour and the unpleasantness in Paris, and already under mounting pressure from the popularity of the 2Tone label, Jerry Dammers suffered a major personal setback when his girlfriend, Valerie, left him citing a change in him over the last few months. Lynval Golding saw how hard it hit him: "Jerry's girl was great. After she had gone, it affected him badly, especially as he'd been with her for a few years. One of the things he hated was any kind of violence and things like the National Front and he gave up everything to fight for that cause. I'm not saying they split up because of that but she couldn't stand the strain and pressure of living with him I suppose."

There had definitely been a shift in the band's fortunes. Perhaps it was, unfortunately, predictable, as Roddy noted: "Our private lives had radically changed, whether we liked it or not. I had crowds of youngsters hanging around outside my house and Terry could hardly go out. Jerry's girlfriend split 'cos of the pressure, to name but a few of the problems our fame had brought us."

Allowing no time to dwell on personal matters, the release of the Specials' new single was scheduled for May 1980. It was to be the superbly acerbic 'Rat Race' (CHS TT11), written by Roddy Radiation. The song had been part of the set list for about six months and work to tweak it had been done whilst the band were in the US. The song was a solid, direct poke at students, which Roddy had written as he sat in the Lanchester Polytechnic Students Union bar watching the world go by and listening to the bollocks spouted by those in attendance. A promotional video was to be recorded and was finally filmed at the Lanchester Poly, using real students as part of the cast. In the video, the group dress up in various teacher-like guises with Jerry in tweed jacket, Doc Martens, skirt and wig to steal the show. In fact, when the video was shown on *Top Of The Pops*, angry parents were enraged at the sight of a skirt-clad Dammers playing a Head Teacher and kids around the country were scared by him!

"The song slags off some students and we were given real students to play the parts in the video," said Roddy. "They didn't understand the lyrics, otherwise they would have walked off. 'Rat Race' was a track we had recorded on the BBC *John Peel* show and had been in our live set for several months. A song that has been much misunderstood. I wrote 'Rat Race' after a night in the local college bar, while sitting and supping, I chanced to hear several well-to-do students in conversation. They were discussing the jobs their parent had lined up for them when they finished college. It struck me that their places in college would be better used by students of a less wealthy background, but not everybody understood the sentiment; in fact, I was told I was anti-education! We did the video in the hall below the college bar where I had overheard the conversation. I've often wondered whether those rich kids were there. The video was filmed on FA Cup Final day. It was the only time it could be fitted in; anyway, it got to Number 5, not bad for my first effort! I'm still happy to play that tune because the people I wrote it about know who they are and it still gets up their noses."

'Rat Race' heralded a shift in responsibility for song writing from Dammers to other band members. As well as Roddy's composition being the main track, the B-side was the stylishly titled 'Rude Boys Out Of Jail', a jaunty, rhythmic melody in the ska tradition of paying homage to the rude boy. The track was in fact a tune that Nev and Lynval put together while jamming, then Horace took ten minutes to jot down some lyrics. With both 'Rat Race' and 'Rude Boys Out Of Jail' pressed on the same vinyl it became the first Specials record not to contain any Dammers lyrical input. The single put the band back into the top 5 of the UK charts but the punishing schedule continued as they all ventured into Horizon studios, this time to face the more serious business of trying to get their collective heads together to plan what is widely known in music circles as the 'difficult second album'.

The Specials' success seemed unaffected by an undercurrent of malaise towards 2Tone and ska, but the effect felt by the Bodysnatchers and was now a problem for the

Selecter. The Selecter's latest offering 'Missing Words' had been rocked by some dubious reviews. The NME said: "Another 2Tone record, not unlike all the other 2Tone records. As such, you'll already know whether you're going to buy it, no matter what I say. 'Missing Words' lacks the easy grace that characterises the best of the genre, and generally sounds just a little too pompous for its own good. To be brutally frank, it bores the balls off me."

Some critics were talking about 2Tone losing its appeal, trying to stir up some response from the record buying public. For every review celebrating the 2Tone explosion there was another waiting for signs of collapse. Madness had now started to drift in style and wanted to distance themselves from the movement as they attempted to broaden their charm, intending not to be written off when British ska was no longer flavour of the month. Slowly but surely the tide was beginning to turn but the fans put speculation behind them and continued the party that had started a year ago. With Margaret Thatcher's misguided political and economic philosophy slowly destroying the working man's country, the youth of the nation needed some relief from the pressure of everyday life and so they turned up in their droves for the sell-out 12 date 'Seaside Tour'.

The tour was to take in all those well known seaside resorts such as Aylesbury and Leeds! The line-up saw the Specials headlining with support from the Bodysnatchers and US female rockers the Go-Gos. With the audiences mainly there for the expected 2Tone ska sound the Go-Gos' power pop tended to be ignored and they would later leave the tour to become support to Madness. They were replaced by Coventry's Reluctant Stereotypes, featuring Paul King who would later go on to have commercial success with the group King and become a video jockey for MTV and later VH1 satellite channels. Just as the Stereotypes were about to sign a deal with WEA Records, Jerry Dammers offered to release their debut single on 2Tone. Both sides were to lose out.

"It was a pleasant change being on tour with two girl bands." said Roddy, "The coach was a beehive of conversation, with girly pop tapes as a background. They made it quite scenic!"

The original idea, conceived by Jerry, was for the group to sail around the British Isles on a boat, anchor offshore and travel to the gigs by means of a speedboat!

"That got translated by our manager into doing a tour of every seaside town in Britain." said Jerry "That sort of thing happened often with Rick Rogers. His intentions were totally right but it somehow went wrong. For too long the band doubled up in hotel rooms because that was what we did in the early days and Rick thought that I didn't want the policy changed. Of course I did!"

Prior to the tour Dammers got pre-tour nerves and the signs of stress were there for all to see: "On the first day of the tour," remembers Horace, "Jerry was going 'I don't want to do this.' Everybody else was saying 'The trucks are here, the tickets have been sold.' I suggested doing it with another keyboard player, because I could see that Jerry was at the end of his tether, but the rollercoaster had started, nobody was allowed to get off it."

On June 5th the Seaside Tour was a mere two days old when the bands played at the Sands Show Bar in Skegness and the by now obligatory stage invasion got completely out of hand. The gig descended into chaos when too many fans crowded the stage too early and the hydraulic stage suddenly weakened and folded and collapsed under the sheer weight of the stomping feet. Thankfully, nobody was injured but there could easily have been a fatality, especially if the shaking lighting rig above their heads had come down. After the gig, Jerry Dammers expressed his concern: "It's very difficult this jumping onstage business. They're not really causing any problems, its just youthful enthusiasm, they just wanna be part of it but if it goes on like it did tonight, someone's going to get badly hurt. I can't believe some weren't injured tonight. We told the audience it was too dangerous and they wouldn't have it and it ended up in a massive ruck with the bouncers."

The Seaside Tour included a special party night at Friars in Aylesbury to celebrate 2Tone's first birthday, but again the gig descended into pandemonium due to stage invasions. Frailties in the band had really started to hit home, with excess drinking at the root of most of the inter-band breakdown and the constant touring and 'man-in-a-suitcase' lifestyle also gnawing on frayed nerves. Twelve months of sheer hard graft were taking their toll on bodies and minds. Roddy had smashed his guitar over Jerry's keyboards during one gig as the frustrations and paranoia grew. There was a further spat a few days later at a photo-shoot for *Melody Maker* in Blackpool when it was decided by Jerry that the band looked inappropriate for the shoot and should go back to the hotel and change. When everyone arrived back at the shoot on the beach suitably attired, Jerry turned up in a full red tartan suit and matching trilby hat, much to the indignation of the others. As Jerry mounted the sea wall and began to jape around, Roddy pretended to push him off the wall. Dammers yelled that Rod was trying to kill him and that everyone had witnessed it. Dammers' version of events states: "Actually, Roddy give me one of those jokey little pushes, but it was a bit more dangerous than it should have been."

Roddy, in particular, had become discontent with the situation within the group: "I always rebelled against authority and Jerry started to be an authority figure to me." he said, "I saw him as the guy who was telling me what I could and couldn't do. I wasn't happy with my internal situation and I was drinking too much."

The gig that night was laden with intensity and it was here that Roddy finished up smashing his guitar over Dammers' keyboards. The crowd thought it was part of the show and were thrilled but tempers were being tested.

The temperature gauge was rising and no-one had stopped to take notice, or if they had it seemed like there was nothing they could do to prevent the build-up of heat.

After the Seaside Tour culminated in a crowd skirmish in Portsmouth, a phone call came from the States; the Specials were wanted to play on NBC's world famous television comedy programme *Saturday Night Live*. Since it was a one-off, the group agreed to appear and flew out on the ill-fated Laker Airways to New York. On arrival, Jerry again refused to stay in the hotel that had been booked by the show's producers but since the band were only due to stay in the city for a very short period, he eventually conceded and took the room. *Saturday Night Live*'s guests were always given star treatment, so it was standard procedure to send limousines to convey the band from the hotel to the studio. However, although in America the difference between the cost of hiring a limo and hiring a taxi was a few dollars, Jerry was adamant that he would not travel in executive style. So, while the rest of the band travelled in limos, Dammers made his own way via taxi.

On arrival at the studio, Jerry was not in a good mood. Lynval Golding recalled: "Jerry was thinking so far ahead of us. He said to us, 'It's a live TV show in front of millions of people, we can do anything we want.' I just thought, 'Oh my God, he's really lost it. We're dealing with racism and political problems in England and he wants to take on America as well.'"

The show was broadcast from the NBC studio in the Rockefeller Centre, and

Dammers was not at ease with the Rockefeller capitalist mentality. Nevertheless, the band went into rehearsal and ran through a sincerely lacklustre version of 'A Message To You Rudy' where they all stood still and gave off no perceptible energy or enthusiasm. When they had finished the producer, Tom Davis ordered Rick Rogers up to his office and bellowed at him: "He stood there shouting at me." said Rick, "He said that the group were just awful and wanted to know where the wild energy that he had heard so much about had gone. I tried to explain that it was only a rehearsal and that they were saving themselves for the show. How right I was! That was one of the finest performances I had ever seen to this day."

Even so, Davis was still unconvinced and threatened to pull the band if they didn't address the situation. In the end the group went on to perform 'Gangsters' and 'Too Much Too Young' and gave one of the most extraordinary performances of their career, with a display of frightening intensity and an air of pure menace. The band were on edge and strung out and there are stories that their performance was charged with an added chemical energy. Roddy Radiation's act was utterly fierce as he thrashed murderously at his guitar. It was out of this world and is still regarded as one of the best musical interludes of the programme's history. Keith Richards from the Rolling Stones had been told about the band by an impressed Jagger and when he heard they were going to appear on the show he went down to the studio to see them in action. After the show, he went backstage where local journalists and photographers wanted to snap him with Jerry. Whether he was taking the piss or not nobody knows, but as Jerry was ushered alongside Richards he turned to Rick Rogers and asked "Who is he?" Horace was equally nonplussed: "A little wizened old man with wild hair and a lived-in face went up to Jerry and gave him a hug and said something like 'I love your record man.' He handed me a spliff, which I declined 'Wow! You have got a problem.' was his reply."

After the show, all the guests and regulars Bill Murray, Chevy Chase, Dan Aykroyd and John Candy decamped to a New York club owned by the dangerously eccentric John Belushi of *Blues Brothers* fame. On arriving at the establishment, the members of the Specials' entourage who had gone along were surprised to find the bar unattended and even more surprised to find that if you wanted a drink you merely helped yourself! The place was heaving with celebrities and the free availability of drugs shocked the Specials' manager: "On that night" said Rick Rogers "I saw more drink and drugs than I've ever seen before or since."

Drugs hadn't been of massive interest to the Specials; they had been mainly alcohol and marijuana enthusiasts (another reason that the Clash had enjoyed having the band on tour in 1978 was that they could always get good dope!), with the occasional blast of speed. However, around that time cocaine had begun to creep into the circle and its destructive nature had certainly not helped the band's endeavours and relationships during a very fraught period in their career. Rico was a big user of marijuana but despite all the speculation about who was taking what it was widely observed that drink was the band's demon, as Neville Staple later observed: "When everybody got sloshed and all that crap, I used to go back to the room with my weed and women. When they were pissed that was when their inhibitions came out, that's when it all became 'I hate you'. I never thought, 'He's like that because he has been taking cocaine or amphetamines', I thought 'He is like that because he has been fucking drinking'."

After their triumphant engagement on *Saturday Night Live*, the boys flew back to the UK and immediately received some bad news. A concert to celebrate the first twelve months of the 2Tone label, pencilled to take place on Clapham Common with the

Specials, the Selecter, Madness, the Beat and the Bodysnatchers, had fallen through. It had promised to be an occasion of riotous ska magic, but sadly, local businesses and even the church protested to the Greater London Council, who consequently refused to grant the gig a licence. An alternative site in the Midlands was sought, but ultimately the idea fell by the wayside.

To add to the disquiet, the band had started receiving its royalties. It was intended for the money to be equally shared amongst the group, but when the song publishing royalties came to the actual songwriters, the equality of the group began to change. If any resentment was harboured, it was kept well in check, but all the same, some of the band were going to be better off than others. There had been talk in the media about how much money 2Tone was making, and some said that the label and groups were making a mint, but the Specials were far from being millionaires (had 2Tone occurred in the 21st century the bands would definitely have made their money!). On all sales, the Specials received 2% royalties on top of what the 2Tone artists received, and this was shared between each band member and Rick Rogers. Each member of the Specials was also paid £300 a month as a flat wage. As it turned out, being successful in the music biz didn't pay much more than a good trade job.

"The £300 a month each, for me, was a vast improvement from the dole," said Roddy later, "but try telling two teenage daughters how come you were famous but didn't get rich? I met a member of the Reluctant Stereotypes who had supported the Specials in our heyday and he was saying how wonderful it was. What with their hotels paid for, their transport provided (Specials tour bus, British school-type coach.) and 'PD's' everyday (cash per day spending money). This went for all our support acts! So with that and the huge numbers of kids, hangers on, and anyone who fancied the crack, I guess that's where some of the dosh went. Also, unlike some other socialist bands, the financial split was very uneven, although as the second major writer I didn't do as bad as some. But the money was not what the band was about."

"If a 2Tone record sells 100,000 copies, which gets it into the Top 10, I stand to make a maximum of £250." said Jerry "That doesn't even pay the costs of running the office."

The band's next assignment in their punishing itinerary was a long-haul flight to Japan where 2Tone had really taken off. The fashions, music and the memorabilia were selling like hot cakes and even 2Tone cigarettes were available! The trip was a popular idea with the dedicated tourists among the group, mainly Horace and Brad, who were often seen armed with their cameras, but although the band were well looked after, they found the experience worse than America.

"My god, Japan was horrible." said Rick Rogers, "It was like America, only ten times worse!"

"Japan, for us, was a real culture shock!" reminisced Roddy, "We didn't really take it seriously, which shows how small-minded we were then. For most of the band it was almost a holiday."

The first night's show at Konen Hall, Tokyo, made a welcome change from the antics of the UK audiences, as the reserved Japanese took their time to get into the swing of proceedings, but the night finished on a high and both band and crowd were satisfied. The second night in Kyoto followed along the same lines, but, on their third date at the Expo Hall in Osaka the mood changed. The venue was an all-seated affair, where standing and jumping were, technically, forbidden. The gig started well and as the set progressed the audience began to go wild with excitement. They began to move into the orchestra pit, but were met by a wall of security, who attempted to push the crowd back into their seats. The chaos escalated until the house lights were turned on and the group expressed their antipathy by walking off stage, wrecking microphones as they went and shouting at the management.

They later agreed to play the rest of the gig with the lights on, but the crowd, bowled over by their heroes, continued to attempt a stage invasion. Rick Rogers was standing in the wings watching the pandemonium when he was grabbed by a tearful stage manager and panicking promoter, who both pleaded with him to stop the stage invasion: "In Japan, the lower a person bows to you indicates the more respect he has for you," said Rick "but the promoter was on his hands and knees almost crying, pleading with me to get the stage invasion stopped. The whole stage was eventually cleared, but such is the weird way that the country works, the bloke didn't work anywhere in Japan for the next three years."

Because of the gig, the police arrived and dragged the despondent promoter off to the station. Once the situation had calmed down the band retreated to the hotel. The following morning Rick immediately phoned Chrysalis in the UK, begging them to bring him and the band home early. To add weight to his case he exaggerated the extent of the story and claimed that everyone was under house arrest. His exaggerated story was retold, with added spice, by the *Sun* and *Daily Mirror* newspapers and the band members consequently had to phone home to placate worried relatives and refute the tabloid 'fact' that they were 'Rude Boys in Jail' as reported! After deliberation, promises and concessions from both band and venue, the tour remained intact. The remaining gigs, including one in a discotheque and another in an outdoor theatre, were played with no further unrest. The end of the tour brought cautious optimism that some of the cracks that had appeared in the band's facade over the last few months had been repaired. The boys still had a lot of work to do before they would be able to draw breath; their unrelenting schedule saw them land in Belgium directly from Japan for a couple of festivals.

Once these dates were completed, some of the band jetted back home for some well-earned rest and relaxation. With an eye on their next big event, a jazz festival in Montreux, Switzerland, Jerry and Horace stayed on the continent for their free time. But trouble, it seemed, was waiting around every corner for the Specials. Just a day or two after arriving home, racial violence was brought to the fore again when Lynval, the easy-going and most peace-loving member of the band, attended a gig by the Mo-dettes at the Moonlight Club in London. As he left the venue in the company of two female friends, three men screaming NF slogans leapt out on him and gave him a vicious beating, which landed him briefly in hospital. The incident would later lead him to write the track 'Why?'

"I got beat up badly," he remembered. "My ribs were smashed in. It was a frightening experience. It was a racist attack; it was because I was walking down the road with two white girls."

He dosed up on painkilling injections and flew out to Switzerland for the July 11th date at the Montreux Jazz Festival. The festival was conceived in 1967 and was one of the most respected events on the European circuit. Originally, a jazz only event, it opened up to rock and reggae in the Seventies. The festival took place at the Montreux Casino, which famously burned down in 1971 during a performance by Frank Zappa, an event immortalised in the Deep Purple track 'Smoke On The Water'. The Casino was eventually rebuilt in 1975.

The Specials topped the bill over a fledgling Paul Young and his band the Q-Tips,

Jo Jo Zep and the Falcons and the Tickets. The gig was televised and has since been turned into a bootleg DVD that shows the band in fine fettle and on top form, the onstage chemistry obvious to all.

The summer of 1980 would see the 2Tone camp remain surprisingly silent, when the label was unexpectedly hit by a double whammy. Alarm bells began to ring when the Bodysnatchers' July release 'Easy Life', only reached Number 50 in the charts. The sniping critics who had waited so long to get their claws into 2Tone now had their injured prey. The media rumour machine went into overdrive; was 2Tone losing its momentum?

Whammy number two came when the Selecter dropped the bombshell that they were leaving the 2Tone label and signing direct to Chrysalis. They left with the unwelcome advice to the Specials that they should close down the 2Tone label, as they believed it had gone as far as it could go. As 2Tone consisted solely of the 14 members of the Specials and the Selecter, this was quite a hammer blow.

"We decided it was time to leave," said Selecter singer Pauline Black in 2005. "The Specials were rowing, they couldn't see eye to eye. They were always off touring, so we could never get together to plan anything. We thought we'd get more attention if we signed directly to Chrysalis."

Her counterpart in the Selecter, main man Neol Davies echoed her sentiments: "Times had changed. In the beginning, there was a real sense of belonging, but it fell to pieces so quickly, we felt there was no communication any more. I remember sitting in a London café with the Specials before the Selecter had formed, talking about the label, how we'd market the single, how everyone had an equal say. It was a real community back then, but by this time Jerry Dammers wanted to do it ALL himself which just wasn't workable."

Lynval Golding was the Specials' spokesman on the subject of the Selecter's departure: "The idea behind 2Tone to start with was to have a certain sort of music that would be identified with the label like Motown. Now, it's like the end of phase one, things have been so hectic. With the Selecter, we didn't do anything bad. They had the freedom to do anything that they wanted to do. The actual running of the label got out of hand and a lot of things that should have been looked at weren't. The Selecter wanted more control and thought to themselves that we were ignoring them. I didn't think the Selecter were right in what they did. Instead of sitting down and talking it out, they just said 'Well, that's it.' The worst thing was they got a better deal out of Chrysalis than we did."

That said, another 2Tone signing soon took place, a Coventry outfit called the Swinging Cats. The Cats were old friends of the Specials and the Selecter, well-known faces around the Coventry music scene and at one time had included Valerie, Dammers' girlfriend at the time. Valerie ultimately left the group when she found it hard to be in a band, to cope with the media attention Jerry attracted and with her father becoming ill. Although the line-up often changed, it eventually settled on Jane Bayley (vocals), John Shipley (guitar), Toby Lyons (keyboards), Paul Heskett (sax), Billy Gough (drums) Steve Vaughan (guitar) and Chris 'Rhythm Doctor' Long (percussion). They played support to the likes of Bad Manners and the Mo-dettes and had replaced the band Holly and the Italians on the Selecter's early-1980 tour. Holly and the Italians had received harsh treatment at the hands of the partisan 2Tone crowd and promptly left.

The Cats played an eclectic mix of easy-listening ska based around Latin rhythms and TV and film themes. They were definitely the most avant-garde of the 2Tone outfits, so much so that many thought their style was totally unsuited to the 2Tone genre. Chris

Long began DJ-ing at Lanchester Polytechnic (the 'Lanch') in 1976 and got to know the would-be 2Tone musicians through events there and at the Hope & Anchor pub in Coventry. After winning a Battle of the Bands at the Lanch, the Cats were offered support slots with major bands and, prior to the tour with the Selecter, were offered a single deal on 2Tone by Jerry Dammers. The result was the 7" 'Mantovani' (a tribute to king of the 'soft' orchestra sound, Italian conductor Annunzio Paolo Mantovani) with the track 'Away' as its B-side. The record was a bold move, with bossa-nova overtones, but it unfortunately became the first 2Tone release to completely miss the charts, despite the first few copies being sold at a measly 50p. Although 'Mantovani' was the official track, 'Away' was very much within the 2Tone ska style, and is often held in higher regard. Those critics waiting for the label to stutter pounced and one review of the single was a solitary line of denouncement: *Are the 2Tone quality control on holiday or what?'*

The touring time spent away from the limelight did nothing for the label's credibility, but the Specials had been far from idle; being idle simply wasn't in their makeup. The Specials had been playing more or less the same set for well over a year and they needed new material, so they had been locked away in Horizon Studios in Coventry preparing their second album, which was already behind schedule. Some band members had wanted to take a breather from their frantic timetable before recording the album, but there was little chance of that happening. Drummer John Bradbury was the most enthusiastic about calling a temporary halt: "The situation last year and so far this year has been really crazy," said Brad at the time. "I've suggested we knock the Specials on the head for a while and go off and do different jobs, just take it easier. I've lost touch with reality this last year or so, and if we do have a rest I really might go and work on a building site for a few weeks 'cos with blokes working on a building site you can get back to what reality is all about. You can really find out what's going on, you get no bullshit, just real communication."

Brad's visionary idea of a cessation of the group and a 'down tools' approach would ring true before long, but a rest was not on the cards in the foreseeable future, and so depleted energies were spent on getting material arranged for the new album.

The strain of making the second album was yet another factor that led to the band's ultimate disintegration. Too many problems had not been addressed before they went ahead with the album, but instead of pausing to tackle these head on, the Specials machine drove on, slipping its gears on the road to nowhere. No one could see the damage that was being caused and everyone was wrapped up in their own cocoon. Jerry's urge to control and oversee all the band's interests made him increasingly paranoid, which in turn fired a rebellious stand from Nev and Roddy who described it as 'rebelling against a strict dad.' There was also ill-feeling caused with other members of the band who felt their creative tendencies were being suppressed. The group was ready to detonate.

"We went from playing a lot to starting the second album and we didn't have any breaks." said Terry Hall "The management were really nice, but that's where we really could've done with someone who took a grip and said 'Look, you've gotta have a break here or else you'll do yourselves in.'"

"We were going through a rough time," said Neville Staple, "and everyone was irritable. After all the rush and panicky shit that gone on before, the idea was cool down, do the opposite."

The album was delayed as ideas were bandied about, with no one able to agree on the content. Each member had his own material and demos for the album that they had worked on while on the road. Tension mounted and arguments broke out over unimportant incidents.

"Every day someone left," noted Lynval Golding.

The band were finding the album hard to contend with, not least because Jerry unilaterally decided to bring in drum machines and synthesisers, even bypassing the ska beat that had propelled them into the public eye, leaving some band personnel worrying about the direction the group was to take. He had dropped some large hints about his growing interest in soundtrack music and a style called Muzak, a sort of sleazy instrumental background music often heard in supermarkets and elevators. As Jerry tried to convince the band about his ideas, Terry Hall tried to portray an upbeat demeanour to the media: "We've been listening to a lot of things like John Barry albums. There are so many good theme tunes around, but they just get wasted. One of my personal favourites is the film theme to *The Third Man* but all of this is just another idea. Jerry has written a song called 'International Jet Set' which stemmed from touring America and all the crap we went through and he has given this odd feel to it, it's spooky. All of this listening to old theme albums is something that kids thought dad would be into. The same thing happened when we presented ska in our way, it's been going on for years but it hadn't been presented to the British public and when it was the kids liked it."

Although Jerry's introduction of new musical ideas was a clever adaptation and a bold step forward, it could only work if all seven agreed on the policy. They didn't. Roddy, a big contributor to the songwriting, was far from happy with the direction his songs were taking under Dammers' steering hands: "He'd been right up to that point, but I started to think he was losing it a bit. He had wanted the new album to be a radical change musically, drum machines, lounge music and very little ska. He wanted to use drum machines, but I didn't want them on my songs. When questioned about this, he said he wanted to do songs that people couldn't tell whether they were good or bad!

"My first disagreement with Jerry was over my song 'Hey, Little Rich Girl'. Jerry's new sound included the use of robotic drum machines. I thought this would ruin my ska-rockabilly song, but after a long chat, and by letting Jerry admire my new 'James Dean' flick knife, he left the studio while we got on with the song. He put his part on later, along with a "sha-doobie" backing vocal, which he thought was hilarious. Then I put the lyrics to one of my other tunes, 'Why Argue With Fate', on the studio wall. I think Jerry thought the words were about him. The next thing I know it has become 'Holiday Fortnight' and had also become an instrumental."

> *"There are no perfect people, and if you're looking for revenge,*
> *Thought I'd found the answer, but it was just another dead end,*
> *But I wait and wait and wait and wait,*
> *Why argue with fate.*
>
> *There are two kinds of people, some wrong some right,*
> *Thought I'd found the answer, but all I got was sleepless nights,*
> *But I wait and wait and wait and wait,*
> *Why argue with fate.*
>
> *Thought I'd found the answer, a cause for me to fight,*
> *But you can't believe false prophets, with hearts as cold as ice."*

YOU'RE WONDERING NOW

Dammers countered with his own take on events during the recording of the album: "I wanted everyone to write songs, I didn't want to do it all myself, just trying to keep everyone happy was difficult. Roddy had a song called 'We're Only Monsters'. The lyrics went something like, 'We're not the boys next door, we're the werewolves from down your street.' It was not right for the album, so I told him to go and write something else. He came back with this song and the lyrics were essentially saying 'Jerry Dammers is a heartless bastard and he won't do any of my songs.' I was like, 'No, that's not a good one either'. Then Neville came up this idea, called 'Neville's Erotic Sounds'. It was ahead of its time, genius. It had classical music and dub reggae playing at the same time in the background and Neville arguing with some girl about having a tape recorder under the bed. I didn't like to listen much further than that."

Whoever's version of events you believe, there is no doubt that the album and Dammers' perfectionism were creating alienations within the group. A combination of the previous twelve months' tiring agenda, the band's inability to confront their demons and the simmering dissent meant the Specials were sitting on a time bomb. To make matters worse, more travelling was added to the pot as a final ingredient for disaster.

Once the album was completed, the obligatory promotional tour was organised. Two weeks of rehearsals were planned, but the internal problems continued, with Dammers showing signs of stress and, to some extent self-inflicted, pressure. He was unwilling to delegate, and his obsession with the success 2Tone and the Specials meant that his health began to suffer. He began to turn up late for the rehearsals, or not to appear at all.

The tour would not only see a change in the method of live performances, but would reaffirm the need for the group to get off the treadmill. The chances of the tour being cut short or cancelled were still very high.

The Specials managed to haul themselves together for the opening date on September 13th at The Riviera, St Austell in Cornwall. The morning was spent setting up the stage and running through the tunes that the band had chosen for the tour, primarily material from the new album with some of the favourites from the past year. Jerry was still a weary, jaded shadow of his normal self, so practice was cut short, and the group retired to a nearby pub. It was there that the heavily-drinking Jerry announced to his fellow band members that he had to return to the venue for a consultation with a local doctor. As the GP examined him, the other band members were ushered out of the pub and into an urgent meeting with Rick Rogers. For over an hour, the tour was on the verge of collapse until a weakened Jerry emerged from talks with the practitioner.

"The doctor said I'm ill from overwork," said Jerry at the time. "I thought I had glandular fever, which I've had before and it's really horrible. I knew if I had it, the tour was finished. I think I was trying to think myself into it, because I knew that if I had got it, all I could do was stay in bed."

Roddy could see Jerry was crumbling: "He was coming apart before our very eyes. I must admit I didn't help by suggesting that Paul Heskett the sax player could play keyboards. Anyway, a doctor was called, and Jerry was given medicine to help sort out his physical breakdown. I had my own, booze, which was making me more and more crazy too."

The news that Jerry was okay came as a great relief to the tour party, and again things were back on some kind of an even keel.

The tour was a week old when the first single from the new album was released, and the public got a taste of what it would sound like. It was a radical change of direction for the Specials. The energetic ska of the first album had almost vanished, ska-punk was out, and the lounge lizard had arrived. 'Stereotype' (CHS TT13), penned by Dammers, was typical of his new haunted, elevator sound with electronic rhythms and a muzak/flamenco overtone. The lyrics were a sombre and desolate jibe at the 'Lad Culture' of the era, with the protagonist catching VD, going on a drinking binge and then getting into a police car chase resulting in his death when his car is wrapped around a lamp post. The B-side was the instrumental saga of 'International Jet Set', inspired by the tiring American and Japanese tours.

At the outset, the skinheads and rude boys were left bemused by the new Specials sound, but although it may not have been a stomping track, in the fans' eyes it was the Specials, and that's what really mattered. The single reached Number 6 in the charts, but it was a wonder it managed to climb so high given its dubious lyrics. Radio stations banned the track from daytime airplay because it contained the word 'pissed' in the chorus. Tony Blackburn, then the DJ in charge of Radio 1's flagship Sunday evening chart rundown, actually had the offending word faded out, before the record came to an abrupt end just over halfway through.

As the tour entered its second week, the much-awaited second album was released. *More Specials* (CHR TT5003) proved to be a staggering new step for the band. Despite the shift in sound, the critics loved its quirky edge, and so did the public. One magazine review bore the headline 'THE SPECIALS GROW UP', and another critic branded the work 'The supermarket spook'. The picture on the cover depicts the lads and a local female Specials fan (and not Rhoda Dakar of the Bodysnatchers as is often thought) in a lounge pose. The picture was taken at a bar in Leamington Spa by Chalkie Davies and Carole Starr and was, in fact, a Polaroid shot that Dammers and Davies chose for its fuzzy, unprofessional style.

"Jerry loved that," explained 2Tone designer Dave Storey. "He wanted things to look homespun, nothing highbrow. He hated things looking clean and stiff."

Chalkie Davies recalled the photo-shoot: "I remember we had to finish photographing the sleeve for the second Specials album by 4.15pm because the soccer crowds would be out on the streets by then. People who looked like the Specials were hated in Coventry. Terry used to get chased all the time!"

The album wasn't entirely based around Jerry's newfound desire for muzak and synthesisers, and despite the musical revolution, the ska fans were catered for. The album possessed a split personality, evident on each side of the record.

"I thought we had to change." said Jerry "It's a natural process for every musician I think. You simply have to move on a little, otherwise people will get fed up of the old stuff. I suppose I'm taking a bit of a gamble with the new album because it's removed from the ska that made us what we are. I don't think that we'll lose much sleep over what people will judge it to be. We like it. It's just the next step."

It may have been the next step for Jerry, but some aspects still rankled with his associates. Despite talk of Jerry domineering the project, Terry Hall maintained that the album was a joint effort and not something that been created in essence by Mr Dammers.

"You've got seven individuals and seven sets of ideas. It's just a question of bringing them all together to represent the Specials."

The schizophrenic recording starts with a bang, opening with a cover of Prince Buster's 'Enjoy Yourself', a rasping 'knees up' track with the atmosphere of a bustling bar room. Brad's drumming hits home with the regularity of a busy cash register, and the uptempo brass provided by Rico and Dick perfectly compliments the raucous backing track and Terry Hall's somewhat camp introduction of himself. Although the song touts a good-time vibe, the Specials' tongue-in-cheek attitude recurs and leaves you to enjoy yourself now, because dark times may be ahead:'

"Hello, I'm Terry, and I'm going to enjoy myself first.
It's good to be wise when you're young,
'Cos you can only be young but the once,
Enjoy yourself and have lots of fun,
Serve God and live my friend and it will never done,
Enjoy yourself; it's later than you think,
Enjoy yourself, while you're still in the pink,
The years go by, as quickly as you wink,
Enjoy yourself, enjoy yourself, it's later than you think."

The album continues with a Terry Hall composition, 'Man At C&A', about the grim threat of nuclear war. At the time, the Cold War was at freezing point with America and Russia in a political standoff and Ayatollah Khomeini in Iran also threatening the West's stability. The track begins with Neville declaring warning of an imminent missile attack, with chilling backing from the brass section, Roddy's haunting guitar, the booming bass of Horace Panter and Terry's observant lyrics:

"Warning, warning, nuclear attack,
Atomic sounds designed to blow your mind,
World War 3 – Nuclear attack,
Rocking atomically – This third world war – Atomic sounds.

The man in black he told me the latest Moscow news,
About the storm across the red sea,
They drove their ballpoint views.

I'm the man in grey; I'm just the man at C & A,
And I don't have a say in the war games that they play,
The Mickey Mouse badge told the Ayatollah at his feet,
You drink your oil you schmuck, we'll eat our heads of wheat."

The harsh realities of life are put to one side as Roddy Byers' creation 'Hey Little Rich Girl' subsequently bursts forth with a more up-tempo tone. With rockabilly nuances and lyrics that are quintessentially Specials, Byers tells a cautionary tale of an old girlfriend of his who headed from Coventry to London to find that the good life she sought was anything but. A sweeping, screaming sax provided by Madness' Lee Thompson fits superbly around the track, giving that unique rock'n'roll sound, with a hint of ska chopping its way through.

"You left for London, when you were nineteen,
Had to pawn all your nice clothes, just living on dreams,
A man in the bright lights took all that you own,
Now he's taken your freedom, for a fate unknown,

But you were a rich girl, hardly having fun,
Your worn out dresses brought stares from everyone,
Hey, little rich girl where did you go wrong?"

Next, the album drops into the group's comfort zone, with the lilting soft reggae sounds of Lynval Golding's composition 'Do Nothing'. The song cunningly depicts the people of Margaret Thatcher's Britain who had little to look forward to and who, at that time, were living in a cultural wasteland where apathy ruled and so nothing ever changed. People talked of change but did nothing. Lynval talks of walking down an endless, lonely street, looking only for some hope at the end. He takes a nudge at racism in the police and the boozy non-culture of young white males:

"Nothing ever change, oh no,
Nothing ever change,
I walk along this same old lonely street,
Still trying to find, find a reason,
Policeman comes and smacks me in the teeth,
I don't complain, it's not my function,
Nothing ever change, oh no,
Nothing ever change,
They're just living in a life without meaning,
I walk and walk, do nothing,
They're just playing in a life without thinking,
They talk and talk, say nothing."

A tale of emotional and physical decline comes next, in the hilariously worded Dammers' tune 'Pearl's Café', a song from the band's early days, originally entitled 'Rock'n'Roll Nightmare.' It is a story of having lived and lost everything, including your looks, and a descent into oblivion. The hook comes from its glorious chorus, the legendary 'it's all a load of bollocks' sung with style by Terry Hall backed by Rhoda Dakar. The theme continuously runs through the album in one form or another, whether it refers to relationships or the state of the country:

"You tell me you think that they should lock her away,
And scrape the make-up off her skin,
Then we'd see the warts around her chin,
She tried to keep her looks,
But lost her mind when she lost her youth and grace,
Your words were just an insult to her face,
It ain't easy when there's no-one to lean on,
It ain't easy when there's nobody there,
It ain't easy when your lovers are all gone,
And bollocks to it all.
When I first met you, I really thought you were a wet dream come true,
Now I know that you don't care, about somebody else's nightmare."

The first side of the album closes with a barnstorming John Bradbury-produced gem entitled 'Sock It To 'Em, JB'. The track was a cover of a classic Stax recording by

Rex Garvin, a Sixties bandleader who specialised in foot stomping semi-instrumentals. Brad had wanted to record some Stax and soul for a while and had been toying around with the track for some time before submitting it to the *More Specials* melting pot. The JB in question is either James Bond or Bradbury himself, keeping time and leading on the track with his pinpoint rhythm on drums. This unusual number has James Bond film titles shouted out over the sax and organ. It features a fantastic toast courtesy of Neville, and sax played by Paul Heskett of the Swinging Cats.

If the first side of the album was recorded with the band's loyal ska following in mind, side two was a real voyage of discovery for them. Coated in the new Dammers cloak of electronic synth beats and muzak-styled lounge music, the show opens with 'Stereotypes (Parts 1 and 2)', the aforementioned dirge about lad and yob culture. The album version contains an extra slice with Neville showing off his toasting skills to the max as he pays homage to his girl, his stereo and the merits of marijuana over alcohol: "I did the toasting in just one take," he said. "I made it up as I went along. I can't write something like that down in advance and then read it out, that wouldn't be very natural to me so I just did it off the top of me head."

> *"The tablets are finished, the cure is complete,*
> *He hasn't had a drink now for seventeen weeks,*
> *Seventeen pints, tonight is the night,*
> *It goes straight to his head; he ends up in a fight,*
> *Police chase him home through the dark rainy night,*
> *Fluorescent jam sandwich with flashing blue light,*
> *His mum's waiting up, she hopes he's alright*
> *But he's wrapped round a lamppost on Saturday night,*
> *He's just a stereotype,*
> *He drinks his age in pints,*
> *He has girls every night,*
> *He doesn't really exist."*

This fades into the instrumental 'Holiday Fortnight', which is the perfect soundtrack to the customary British invasion of Benidorm during the 'factory fortnight', a national holiday when factories all over the country closed for two weeks and people took their holidays en-masse. Stripped of its lyrics by Dammers (remember 'Why Argue With Fate'?), the track is composed by Roddy Byers. It proved to be quite a departure for the Specials, not ska, but not layered in the new style either.

Next up is 'I Can't Stand It', a narrative of tortured love between Terry Hall and Rhoda Dakar, both commenting on their dying relationship in bitter tones. The track highlights an aspect of this album, which was emblazoned on the rear of the sleeve: 'For added enjoyment adjust stereo balance control.' and that tweak sounded superb on this track, where you can hear Terry and Rhoda bickering and sniping in opposing speakers. The tune was free-form jazz from Dammers' keyboards, and possibly pointed towards where he wanted to take the Specials at a later date:

> *"When I woke up this morning alone in my bed,*
> *In a cold room with damp sheets, and a pain in my head,*
> *I saw you last night and you drove me insane,*
> *Why must you hurt me again and again?*

I've had enough, if I don't come back for more that's tough,
'Cos I can't stand it, the way you've planned it,
No, I can't stand it any longer,
Sometimes I get so I tired I can't get no sleep,
I'm so drunk I can't stand up on my own two feet,
I'm feeling so hungry I don't want to eat,
You make me so angry I can't even speak,
I'll stay at home where I can be alone,
Because I just can't stand it, the way you've planned it,
No I can't stand it any longer."

The penetrating and equally cynical ode to air travel and all its absurdity, which the band had suffered on their America and Japanese tours, is revisited in 'International Jet Set'. This version, complete with lyrics, sees Dammers take the listener on a haunting, ghostly roller-coaster ride through the clouds. Like a bad trip, you can feel the pessimism and surrealism becoming too much for the weary traveller. The tune is the perfect embodiment of the new Specials form that Jerry wanted to unveil:

"I've seen the carpets on the walls of hotels rooms around the world,
I never want to hear the screams of the teenage girls in other people's dreams,
Spread the disease, from the South China Sea to the beach hotel Malibu,
Phone my girlfriend to ask her "How's her weekend?"
I say "Hi, Terry here", and she says "Terry, who the hell are you?"
The businessmen are having fun, are they on a different plane to me?
I've lost touch with reality, they all seem so absurd to me,
Like well dressed chimpanzees,
Spend and spend and spend and spend,
Will the muzak never end?"

The album squeaks to a close with a short reprise of 'Enjoy Yourself' in 'Bontempi' keyboard style, with more special guests in the shape of the Go-Gos (who included Jane Wiedlin and Belinda Carlisle in their ranks) on backing. The track sounds like a New Year's Eve party winding down.

There were two other tracks that were submitted for inclusion on the album, but which never made it. They became part of the marketing for the album, and were pressed as a double 'A' side project. The first was 'Braggin' And Tryin' Not To Lie' (CHS TT999), another Roddy Byers track that was credited to Roddy Radiation and the Specials. It is a pure form of rebellious rockabilly and ska, featuring Paul Heskett on saxophone.

"'Braggin' And Tryin' Not To Lie'," said Roddy, "well I thought it was going on the album but Jerry thought it didn't fit in with his master plan of lounge muzak. The 'Braggin' track was about a very early Specials gig where the band thought I'd scored with a lady but I hadn't but no-one would believe me! Anyway, so I guess as a peace offering they put it out as a free single backed by a jam session with Neville toasting that became 'Rude Boys Outa Jail Version'."

The other track is a high speed remix of 'Rude Buoys Outa Jail', credited to Neville Staple AKA Judge Roughneck. This single, complete with a free poster from the 'More Specials' photo-shoot (not dissimilar to the front cover), was given away free with the first 100,000 copies of the album. There was a rumour that Terry Hall also submitted a song that he had written a few months previously with Go-Go Jane Wiedlin. It was called 'Our Lips Are Sealed', but was deemed unsuitable at the time. However, within a year, the song would earn Terry a tidy sum of money when a version recorded by the Go-Gos went to Number 1 in the US.

The new direction of the Specials may have temporarily confused diehard fans, but they still rushed to the record shops to buy the album and helped propel it to Number 5 in the charts, and kept it in there for a further three months.

On the promotional tour, things became disorderly. Considering all that had gone before, the band and new set were outstanding, but the party mood was once again spoiled by violence which was becoming much more vicious than the sporadic outbreaks on previous tours. The stage invasions became a cause for concern and combined with the aggression, gigs were quickly degenerating into chaos. The band had never complained about fans clambering on to the stage to dance and sing with their idols because most of the invasions hadn't occurred until the end of a gig, but on the *More Specials* tour large sections of the audience unthinkingly brought performances to a halt by invading at an early juncture. This left other fans disgruntled at paying good money for disrupted shows, and not being able to even see their heroes amongst the hordes of youths on stage. The band became pissed off because they were having to stop-start their set. One solution was to build stages with different levels so that the band could climb on to the 'risers' out of the path of the marauding fans and continue to play, but it was not a permanent solution. The Specials did not want to stop the incursions totally, because they had become an important part of the Specials experience, but as a result of their reluctance things went from bad to worse.

Although the violence was perpetrated by a small faction of the crowds, it became a matter of great concern. There were serious outbreaks in Newcastle and Leeds, where Terry Hall was accused of causing a near-riot. Matters reached an all time low on October 9th when the Specials and latest 2Tone signing the Swinging Cats appeared in the city of Cambridge. The gig was held in the Midsummer Meadow Supertent, and a capacity crowd of 3,500 turned up to see Coventry's finest perform. The Swinging Cats had been onstage for quarter of an hour or so, when around 40 ticket-less youths gate-crashed the gig and began to chant 'Coventry, where are you?', obviously in a bid to provoke any Coventry City football supporters in the crowd. Fighting broke out at regular intervals during the Swinging Cats' set and, as was reported in the press, 'several short haired youths' continually bombarded the band with cans. The Cats' lead singer, Chris Long, tried to quell the crowd: 'Why do you want to fight? It's probably the last chance to see the Specials in Cambridge.'

According to the press, he then challenged the culprits to come up onstage and fight him. Long saw it differently: "The events at the Midsummer Meadow Supertent in Cambridge in 1980? Well, sometime during our set a group of about 20 to 30 Cambridge United football fans waded through the crowd chanting. I think they had played Coventry City a week or so before in a cup game. One of them jumped up on stage and was coming for me, but thankfully one of our roadies, whose name escapes me unfortunately, saved my bacon by chinning the twat, sending him flying in a reverse swallow dive back into the audience. Would love to have a pic of that! It was classic! It was a calamitous gig."

Minutes later the Swinging Cats left the stage and returned to the safety of their dressing room, cutting their set short in the process. After the tour, the Cats broke up. When the Specials took to the stage, the violent outbursts continued, forcing the group to stop their set and plead for order. Once the chaos had died down, the group resumed the concert but the violence quickly flared up again and, once more, the band called a halt to proceedings. Terry Hall told the crowds that if the fighting continued, the group would leave the stage and end the concert. In between songs, Terry became involved in a slanging match with the hooligans who were situated at the front of the stage. The yobs began to spit at the Specials, which riled Jerry Dammers: "You're not doing anything new. We've got hot and cold running gob in our showers at home."

The gig descended into further farce when some bouncers strode into the mob and tried to eject them from the Supertent. Terry, well known for his dislike of concert security, turned on the offending youths and shouted: "You blood claats [derogatory Jamaican term] have spoilt this evening for everyone. We're going down the pub."

He then directed his venom at the security: "You're just as bad!"

One of the bouncers retorted and told him, in no uncertain terms, to keep his mouth shut. Hall lost his already frayed temper and picked up a microphone stand and attacked him. Other band members managed to restrain Terry before he caused any damage. The group then left the stage, a signal for thousands of discontented fans to leave. Five minutes later the Specials returned to the stage to complete their set, but it was too late and the gig was a certified wreck. Finally backstage, all hell broke loose when a representative of the promoter approached the group and accused them of being responsible for the trouble. When the group remonstrated with him, he called the police who arrived to try to separate the warring parties. Incensed, Dammers told the boys in blue to fuck off and was promptly arrested. Whilst Dammers was being dragged off to a waiting Black Maria police van, Terry Hall voiced his disapproval and was also arrested. Both were driven to Cambridge's Parkside police station where Superintendent Murden charged them with using threatening words and behaviour. The press inundated the station with phone calls, but Murden refused to discuss the case until one journalist asked about the band he had arrested, Superintendent declared with alleged wit: "What did you call them? A band? Well they weren't a band as defined in the dictionary! I don't know how you can call that row a band."

The incident was exacerbated by a report in Cambridge's local newspaper, which quoted a council official as saying: "Shouting and swearing at the audience are all part of the group's set. They do it everywhere they go and take along a group of hecklers to excite the crowd and warm them up. They also storm off stage regularly as part of their set to excite the audience."

The statement enraged the Specials' management and Rick Rogers considered taking legal action for defamation of character. The chaotic gig hit the headlines in the national press and the music weeklies, and gave critics of the band and 2Tone more ammunition to fire in their direction. Friday 5th November 1980, traditionally Bonfire Night in England and the day for fireworks, saw Terry Hall and Jerry Dammers appear at Cambridge Magistrates Court. It was a heated session; the gig organisers gave evidence to support the theory that the Specials were the instigators of the disturbance. Prosecutor David Beale and his main witnesses, two members of the security team, maintained that Hall and Dammers had deliberately provoked the fighting for publicity. Jerry defended the band's position, corroborated by Terry and the defence witnesses, a local doctor and a local solicitor, who both backed the band and reiterated that the group had tried hard to stop the fighting. As a result of the hearing, the two Specials were each fined £400 plus £133 in costs. Outside the court, the band members were met by the paparazzi: "I would like to be able to say it's a fair cop," said Terry "but it wasn't."

Jerry Dammers was bit more forthright: "The 3,000 people at that concert will recognise the injustice of the decision. We detest violence at our gigs. We were trying to stop the fighting."

"I just didn't see the point," commented Terry a few days afterwards. "It was so stupid all that trouble at Cambridge. Everyone was out for a good time, but you'll always get your odd moron wherever you go. Those people who went home are the ones I felt sorry for. They paid their money, they were entitled to a good night out, but we couldn't give them one because all our attention was focussed on the mob that started it all. As a group, we're now thinking whether or not to carry on doing tours and stuff. We don't like the violence at our concerts; we've made that clear from the outset. We offer music as an alternative to fighting. It's easier to use your energy dancing than punching somebody in the mouth. Anyway, if the fighting doesn't stop then there's only one way to make it stop. We either stop gigging or call it a day."

Terry's statement showed just how grave the situation had become. The strife caused by the Cambridge concert and its consequences had affected the Specials a great deal more than any financial punishment handed down by the law. A couple of weeks after the Cambridge court judgement, it was announced that it would be a substantial amount of time before the Specials would go back on the road. According to a spokesman (yes, the mysterious spokesman), the incident at Cambridge brought matters to a head and the band wanted to get away from the constant treadmill of touring and releasing records, to spend more time writing new material. They would only play gigs at weekends, when they wanted to. The plan to stop touring wasn't taken lightly, but before the situation got completely out of hand, it needed to be nipped in the bud. The runaway 2Tone train had come off the rails and the Specials had been left clinging to the controls. The decision to jump off before it crashed was a wise one.

Despite the announcement, the band were booked to play at a couple of one-off gigs that promoted causes close to their hearts, but even one of these proved problematic. The first event on October 26th was for Bruce Kent and his Campaign for Nuclear Disarmament (CND) in London's Trafalgar Square. With slogans of 'Grow up or blow up' and 'Don't Cruise to oblivion', the CND had grown to be one of the biggest activist groups by 1980 and 80,000 people were expected to attend the mass rally. However, the Department of the Environment's noise abatement section refused to give permission for the use of the immense PA system, and so CND dropped the Specials. What hurt the band was that other groups, such as Killing Joke, weren't cancelled and played their sets from the backs of lorries, something that the Specials would have been more than happy to do. For their part, CND thought that the Specials were too big a band to play on the back of a lorry. The disillusionment of the last tour had left the band pining for the good old days, when they had played tightly-packed atmospheric clubs up and down the country. The urge to return to the club scene was fuelled by their two-day stint at London's Hope & Anchor pub, on behalf of the charity Blanket Coverage, who raised funds for the capital's homeless and elderly. The venue was a favourite of theirs, and they were delighted to be able to team up with old friends Madness, the Selecter, and Bad Manners, plus other artists like Ian Dury and the Blockheads, to help generate the much-needed cash.

"It was a great gig," said Lynval Golding. "Everyone was so enthusiastic and as the Specials we'd not performed better. We're definitely going to do a lot more club-like venues because in the bigger ones you can't get across to the audience as well as you can in a small place."

Despite this, the band then flew to Spain for a gig in Barcelona, where they appeared in a bullring on a makeshift stage, and played another supreme gig.

Within two months, 2Tone Records were back to square one, basically a one-band business, apart from Rico Rodriguez having released the classic 'Sea Cruise'/'Oh Carolina' single, but he was very much a part of the Specials anyway. The Swinging Cats had failed to finish the *More Specials* tour, and their single 'Mantovani' had dive-bombed out of sight. The music weeklies then announced the split of the promising Bodysnatchers because of supposed 'musical differences.'

"Live, it gelled. Offstage it was a different story," said Rhoda Dakar. "We had different lifestyles, experiences, aims. Stella's parents had a huge farm in Yorkshire and her dad had a plane. Some of the band wanted to change musically more than others. Nicky and me wanted to carry on doing reggae-influenced stuff, others wanted to develop. There were two schools, the rock'n'roll school, who wanted to make music, and the business school, who wanted wealth. It was split on class grounds really."

The loss of Nicky and Rhoda was quite a blow. The Bodysnatchers' releases had included some very promising material and hopes had been high. In the wake of the split, the remainder of the girls went on to have middling success with the commercial pop group the Belle Stars.

The Specials were left to carry to the 2Tone flag alone, which they did in their own peerless style with the release of Lynval's 'Do Nothing' (CHS TT16) on December 13th 1980, just in time for the lucrative Christmas market. Issued in the first 2Tone picture sleeve since the 'Too Much Too Young' EP, it was their sixth single and sixth direct hit, reaching a high of Number 4 in the charts. The track had been lifted from the *More Specials* LP and remixed, with the addition of Jerry's 'ice-rink strings sounds', or as the mis-pressed copies read, the 'ice rrk strg srds'! This laid-back reggae track, with its philosophical lyrics, saw a return to the band's traditional roots. The B-side featured a radical reworking of Bob Dylan's 1965 hit 'Maggie's Farm', the Specials version inevitably aimed at Margaret Thatcher. As the single climbed the charts, the group found themselves back in contention for a place on *Top Of The Pops*. With a typical two-fingers-up mocking style, Jerry ensured they all appeared on *TOTP* donned in hideous Christmas-themed chunky knitted sweaters, complete with reindeers and snowflakes, the kind you might be unfortunate enough to receive from Grandma for Christmas and be made to wear for the rest of the day. Bassist Horace Panter was replaced on bass duty by Dave 'Shuffle' Steele of the Beat. He and Horace wanted to swap groups for the evening, and so Horace took Shuffle's place in the Beat on their track 'Too Nice To Talk To' on the same programme, not that *TOTP* noticed!

"At least I wouldn't have to wear one of those dreadful Christmas jumpers that Jerry had bought us all for the occasion!"

Horace was obviously relieved at the prospect of not wearing the offensive jumpers, but it could have been much worse – Dammers' original idea had been that they all wear balaclavas!

The Specials then took a self-imposed exile for approximately six months. They were desperately in need of a break, to get things into perspective and re-align themselves musically. It was agreed that they would go their separate ways and come together when the time was right to decide on the healthiest way for 2Tone and the Specials to move forward. Although the band relished the chance of a rest, for some the start of 1981 couldn't have been busier and individual workloads increased with personal projects.

Neville Staple had been working with his girlfriend, Stella Barker, guitarist from the recently defunct Bodysnatchers, on the launch of his new label, Shack Records, from an office in Spon Street, Coventry. He signed 21 Guns, which featured two Specials roadies, Trevor Evans and Johnny Rex, as well as well-known Coventry musician Gus Chambers (who had replaced Terry Hall in the punk band Squad when Hall moved on to the Specials, and who sadly passed away in 2008), Stuart MacLean and Kevin Tanner. They released the single 'Ambition Rock', but it flopped due to lack of airplay. Shack also released 'Bobbing Up And Down Like This' by Lieutenant Pigeon (the early-Seventies band who had a UK hit with the classic 'Mouldy Old Dough' and who were once Terry Hall's neighbours). Neville had approached the group to see if they had any un-issued Lieutenant Pigeon recordings on the shelf, saying he was about to launch his own record label and he wanted to use some well known names as 'label warmers'. 'Bobbing Up And Down Like This' became the last original Lieutenant Pigeon track to be released.

When 21 Guns split, Trevor Evans and Johnny St John (alias Rex) formed the band Splashdown. Their single 'It's A Brand New Day' featured the vocal talents of sisters Kim and Debbie Shields, Lynval Golding on guitar and the magnificent horns of Leicester's Swinging Laurels, but unfortunately it was not a hit. Shack's lack of success must have been a huge disappointment to the ever-optimistic Staple, especially when he had put so much time and energy into it. Neville admitted he never expected enormous financial returns from his venture, but saw Shack as the inevitable extension of his long-standing involvement with sound systems: "I always wanted a label," he explained, "'cos when I used to run a sound system all the other DJs knew people who worked in recording studios and they were able to get special versions of records cut. I used to get frustrated 'cos I couldn't do it."

Neville also wanted to issue some of his collaborations with Stella Barker, although nothing ever came of it, and even fancied his chances in the acting world: "I'd like to have a go at films. There may be something going on at Chrysalis and if it happens, I would definitely love a part in it. I'd like to be an actor; I think I'd be good at it. I mean, I'm acting all of the time anyway!"

John Bradbury also spent valuable time establishing his own label, Race Records. Alongside him was Sean Carasov, the manager of the Mo-dettes, who had been involved with the Specials for some time through his responsibilities as a roadie and merchandise man. Brad's approach to Race was a lot more business-like than Neville's artful methodology. Brad saw Race as a further development of the 2Tone exercise. His original urge to run his own label came from way back when he worked at the Virgin Records store in Coventry, where one of his jobs was to monitor independent record sales. In the last few weeks of 1980, he developed the Race ideology. A Coventry soul and R&B band called Team 23 were to be Brad's first clients. The original line-up of Team 23 consisted of Dave Chalmers, Gray Summers, Jerome Heisler, Adrian Black and John Hewitt and they had played support to Dexys Midnight Runners. Chalmers decided the style wasn't for him so he departed. Summers added a brass section consisting of Roy Wall on sax and Lynn Thompson on trumpet and new guitarist Jim Landsbury (later of Eighties Coventry band King). Whilst signed to Race, the revised line-up would go on to support the Specials and Madness, mainly playing original songs written by Heisler and Summers.

Through Race they released the double A-side single 'Move into The Rhythm' and 'Whatever Moves You' (due to the Specials connection this is now a highly sought after collector's item). It received limited airplay, and just afterwards Team 23 disbanded and left Brad with an expensive lesson learned. Sales from the single were never likely to recoup the luxurious production he had lavished on it, as he readily confessed at the time: "I'm responsible for slipping up on the budget that I allowed initially," said Brad, "because after all, the groups have to pay for that. I don't give them money to go and record a single, win or lose. The deal is that they have to pay back, on a percentage basis, the money I loaned them to go into the studios over whatever period they need to. Of course, if the record stops selling, I don't go up to them and say 'Here, you owe me so much', we just leave it at that. I want to take all that kind of pressure off the artists. This is a musician's label."

Brad also offered high royalties to his artists and he didn't tie them to long contracts. He always insisted that, should a major company want to sign them up, he would simply tear up their contracts and let them go.

Race's next release was 'Just Enough'/'Hits And Misses' by a reggae outfit called Night Doctor, which regrettably failed to make a dent on the market. Brad's biggest hopes for success came with the People, who were no strangers to 2Tone. The group consisted of recent ex-Selecters Charley Anderson and Desmond Brown, Chris Christie, who had played with the ex-Selecter boys in the band Hard Top 22 in 1977, and John Hobley, the former drummer of Coventry band God's Toys. The single 'Musical Man', a tribute to master trombonist and honorary Special, Rico Rodriguez, was produced by Dave Jordan, and came in a sleeve designed by John 'Teflon' Sims, but despite all this, and being a great sounding record, it failed to be a hit. The last issue on the Race label came from the band the Lemons (which featured Paul Hookham from socialist band the Redskins) but it also proved unsuccessful. Afterwards, Brad closed down the label, which just wasn't viable without airplay to recoup some funds.

Terry Hall was his usual droll and witty self when asked by reporters about the other band members' aspirations: "2Tone isn't as big anywhere now. It was a very big thing at the start 'cos it was something new, just like Adam and the Ants or punk rock or futurism, but everything dies down a little, it's on a good level now, it's a record label. Brad and Neville have got a label each where they put out records by their favourite bands. I have never understood the desire myself, we created this monster and now they want to create little monsters."

Roddy Byers meanwhile, kept his hand in by inventing a new genre of music. Since November 1980, he had been involved, albeit in his rare spare time, with his band the Tearjerkers, which consisted of Roddy on guitar and lead vocals, his brother Marc on guitar and vocals, Joe Hughes on bass and vocals and Steve Young on drums. They had already played a number of gigs and Roddy began putting together songs that featured rock'n'roll, rockabilly and ska, to create a crossover style/genre which he christened as Skabilly. The style had first occurred on the track 'Braggin' And Tryin' Not To Lie'. The Specials' US tour had reinvigorated his old passion for rock'n'roll, and he had also taken the opportunity to purchase some real vintage rock'n'roll clothing: "Jerry said I'd come back looking like Marlon Brando circa *The Wild One*! I could get all the gear I wanted in American thrift shops, leathers, cowboy shirts, hats and motorbike boots, Brando, Dean. Most of the band didn't want to wear the same old suits, and this, among other things, caused disagreement. I had also gotten into rockabilly in a big way; it was a music I'd always liked, but now it became my religion."

If you look at Specials photos and videos from the period, especially post-US tour, Roddy always looks very much the rocker. He was, first and foremost, a singer and frontman, and the frustrations that brought to his time in the Specials were eased by the formation of the Tearjerkers. Roddy enjoyed going back to his roots at the mike, while playing his special brand of music. The Tearjerkers spent some time in the studio and recorded the old Ned Miller/ Jim Reeves hit 'From A Jack To A King'.

"Listen to the old rockabilly track, 'From A Jack To a King'," said Roddy, "it almost has a ska feel. It just depends on whether you're wearing a cowboy hat or a pork pie hat!"

Horace Panter, meanwhile, went on holiday in Switzerland and was involved with some clandestine recording sessions. He would not divulge any details, but said at the time: "It's something I'm doing in conjunction with some other people, just a project with some friends, and that's all I want to say about it really because it detracts from what I'm doing in the Specials."

What he was actually playing around with was a fun recording session with a few friends, which gave the world the first Yorkshire rap record! 'The Barnsley Rap' was credited to the non-existent artist Barnsley Bill, who became something of a cult figure. Horace had become a fan of the early American rappers such as Grandmaster Flash and had bought a few 12" vinyl discs on his travels with the Specials in America. In his book, Ska'd For Life, Horace commented: "I thought it would be good to have an English rap record but in an 'Oop North' style. Some old college friends and I who I had become reacquainted with had writing sessions that usually ended up in side-splitting, rolling-across-the-floor-in-laughter disarray. I had recently met a Coventry drummer Rick Medlock and together with local musicians, we cut our first comedy record over at Woodbine Studios in Leamington Spa."

On the 'Barnsley Rap' track, Horace didn't want his name on the credits for the record (Specials street-cred would have plummeted no doubt!) and it was eventually released on Mother-In-Law Records, receiving massive airplay but failing to sell. Barnsley Bill took a stand against the common mimicking of his US counterparts, choosing to deliver hard raps in a comedy Northern accent. The B-side was an instrumental version that was followed up by the 1981 12" single 'Freewheeling Rap' in which Bill is so 'hard' he can even 'eat THREE Weetabix!'

The records were produced by Ronnie Bossanova, and backed by the Daves, who supplied the heavy funk riffs. In a comedic nod to the Stiff Records phrase of 'If It Ain't Stiff, It Ain't Worth A Fuck', the label says 'If It Ain't Mother-In-Law It Ain't Worth A Stiff.' The Barnsley Bill rap records actually pre-dated any serious UK artists attempting the genre.

Panter had also become involved with a 'self-assertion' group called Exegesis. They promoted an intense, in-depth programme of group therapy sessions with like-minded converts which aimed to transform the negative forces in ones life into positives, to bring about life changes and a more assertive self. Members were then encouraged to recruit more members and then persuaded to attend more specialised courses, at a cost. The group almost achieved cult status, and at one point claimed to have over 5,000 members.

Exegesis began, along with a number of other similar groups, on the West Coast of America in the Sixties, these included organisations such as the Rev Jim Jones's People's Temple, whose followers committed mass suicide in 1978 in Guyana in South America. The leader of Exegesis was Essex born Robert D'Aubigny, who was reported to have made a lot of money through promotion of his 'therapy', which cost £200 for a three-day session to solve personal problems such as work or relationships. Their questionable methods were said to involve being screamed and shouted at, abused, and ordered not to leave the room.

By 1984, concerns about the Exegesis programme were being raised in the Commons by several MPs, who cited cases of people who had become disturbed after attending some of the courses. David Mellor, then Home Office minister, condemned the organisation as 'puerile, dangerous and profoundly wrong'. Scotland Yard went on to conduct an investigation, but no charges were brought and Exegesis collapsed shortly afterwards. Although the programme received much negative press attention, Horace maintains that it had a lasting positive effect on him.

Meanwhile, Terry Hall was telling the media that, apart from writing some material, he was not involved in anything bar the Specials.

"Outside the Specials," he said, "I'm not really interested in anything apart from watching the telly. At the moment, the Specials as a working unit are stronger than ever and I feel we've got a lot more to give yet. Things were really big last year and it was like we'd created this runaway monster thing, plus we became a little disillusioned, so we decided to end phase one and bring in phase two, which was *More Specials*. So you could say we've now moved into our third phase."

He had also laid down some potential Specials tracks as demos with Neville and Lynval; the latter had been busy with organising new band the People and assisting Nev with Shack Records. The new tracks were covers of Question Mark and the Mysterians' '96 Tears' and John Holt's 'Wear You To The Ball', plus a Lynval Golding original, 'Why?', inspired by the beating he'd received from racists outside the Moonlight Club.

Jerry Dammers had been holidaying in Scotland and returned with a new 'mad French painter' look. He had been collaborating with ex-Bodysnatcher Rhoda Dakar on what was going to be a 'disco rap' track called 'The Boiler', originally a Bodysnatchers tune that told the harrowing tale of a rape victim. The track was intended to be the next release on 2Tone, but the plans were shelved by Dammers when a bigger project arose, a film documenting 2Tone and featuring live performances by the 2Tone bands. The film would be titled *Dance Craze* and was the idea of minor American writer and director, the late Joe Massot. Massot had some experience of working with music and film, including *Wonderwall*, the 1967 film for which he employed George Harrison to compose the soundtrack, and the 1976 Led Zeppelin concert film *The Song Remains The Same*. He also wrote the script for controversial film *Universal Soldier*, which starred James Bond actor George Lazenby.

Massot's interest in 2Tone was sparked when he and his son were sitting by the side of the pool at a hotel in Los Angeles, watching a bunch of high-spirited young Brits frolicking in the water. The youngsters turned out to be Madness, taking time out on a leg of their US tour. Massot consequently saw the band perform that night and they knocked him for six with their youthful musical exuberance. He had originally wanted to make a film solely about the Nutty Boys until his son Chris pointed out that Madness were just one part of a collection of groups that were taking the British music scene by storm.

Massot eventually began to film the bands on jaunts around the country but mainly at venues in Aylesbury, Bradford, Hemel Hempstead, London, Cherry Hill, Portsmouth and Sunderland. The Specials were filmed at Liverpool's Rotters venue and at Leicester's de Montfort Hall, the Selecter were caught at halls in Leeds and Glasgow, whilst the Beat were shot during their US tour, in Philadelphia.

"I remember Massot," said Horace. "Big guy, curly hair, quite nervous, came up to Jerry's flat in Coventry to pitch his concepts to us. We had all the bands crammed into Jerry's front room and he told us about this ground-breaking technique using the latest cameras on gyroscopic harnesses so the cameramen could be onstage with the bands and there'd be no flutter or wobble in the film."

The camera system he was talking about was the Steadycam.

"I wanted to try it out with ska to see if the camera could dance." said Massot in a rare interview in the early Eighties. "It strutted its stuff."

In an interview before his death in 2002, Massot said: "Encountering the 2Tone scene I saw right away the impact the bands and their music were having. Going to Dingwall's I saw the Bodysnatchers for the first time, with the fans packed wall-to-wall dancing almost on top of each other. I went with the Beat to a photo session in Covent Garden where I met Saxa, who is the finest sax player in the world, and he told me stories of Prince Buster.

"In Leicester, I saw the amazing energy of Pauline Black and the Selecter. Pauline never stopped moving onstage, she was like a tiger. Seeing Madness at Bradford where the pounding of dancing feet made the whole building vibrate and the stage shook like it was being blown by a strong wind. I remember Jerry Dammers of the Specials being woken at nine in the morning by me and a cameraman. That's a sight I will never forget. He was wearing a dressing gown that he must have worn in school. There was the so-called '2Tone Office', which consisted of records strewn all across the floor and Jerry offering me and the cameraman a cup of tea, then discovering he didn't have any after all!

"We filmed so many gigs that I lost count, but above all I came to love this thing called 2Tone. It was the sight of seven, eight and nine year olds in the queues dressed in their 2Tone gear to see their favourite bands and I remember thinking 'this movie has to happen because the fans really want it. It was such a simple idea, all the bands together in one film, so that what would cost kids £50 if they were to go to all the gigs, they could now enjoy for the price of a movie ticket. I loved doing it and I hope the fans did too."

The bands included in the film were the Specials, the Selecter, the Beat, Madness, the Bodysnatchers and – appearing with the bands for the first time in a 2Tone project – were London lunatics Bad Manners.

Dammers became involved and was quite upbeat about the project: "My idea," said Jerry, "was to reproduce the atmosphere of a 2Tone concert in the cinema for the kids who were too young to go to the show."

In hindsight, it was probably the worst time to record the film. 2Tone was on a downward turn and the Specials were exhausted and crumbling before the media's eyes. However, the film would go on to immortalise the label on celluloid for posterity and didn't show the cracks behind the scenes. The film contained some strange imagery and was cut with old black and white Pathé newsreel about dance crazes through the years, as well as a ballet scene and a shot of bouncing, dancing, Dr Marten boots during Madness' rendition of 'Swan Lake'.

During the Selecter's 'Too Much Pressure' a realistic-looking fight takes place mid-tune between the band members. Pauline Black recalled: "The fight sequence during 'Too Much Pressure' was actually filmed in a studio in Wembley. It was more like how we really behaved a lot of the time. I wish people could have seen the outtakes of the film as this was at a time when people were still doing the punk thing of spitting at the bands. During filming Gaps, our other vocalist, got gobbed full in the face and he picked up the mike stand and was about to brain the offending skinhead when I jumped in and stopped him. But my act of kindness meant that I got my leg badly cut with the mike stand instead, so I spent the rest of the gig hopping around on one leg!"

Although the film was seen as a fantastic adventure by fans, the behind-the-scenes aura surrounding the movie was a negative one. The film was previewed at the Midem Music festival in France in January 1981 and went on national release on February 15th. The 2Tone theme was starting to wear thin and although the diehard supporters went to the cinema to catch a glimpse of silver-screen ska, it failed to register on a nationwide scale. Had it been released a mere six or seven months previously it would have played to full houses.

"The only person who had any real involvement in making it was Jerry," said Roddy Byers. "It became Jerry's baby. By the time filming started, we'd pretty much lost interest. They had the film premiere in London but most of us didn't go. There was so much bad feeling that going to the premiere was the last thing any of us wanted to do."

The film came in for some denigration for its style and approach from a small number of critics and it is widely agreed that there could have been so much more added to it. The general consensus is that it could have been an astounding tribute to 2Tone but fell well short of its potential.

"People did criticise it because there were no interviews, no little insights into what the people were like," said Pauline Black. "The image was of all these people in 2Tone bands, black and white, living and working together in total harmony but, of course, it wasn't always like that. We were angry young people."

Neville Staple was also despondent that the film failed to portray them successfully: "It was disappointing. It didn't catch the excitement of all those bands as they were onstage. We always gave 100% onstage and I didn't think that came across."

Dammers busied himself taking the live tracks from the movie and putting them down on vinyl as the ultimate soundtrack. He collaborated with Teflon Sims on all the artwork and promotion and this punishing workload began to take a toll on his health, to the point where it was rumoured that he was on the verge of a nervous breakdown, though this has never been substantiated. Once more, it appeared that he was pushing himself to the limit in his dogged determination to achieve perfection.

"To me, seeing the completed film represented the exact moment of ska overkill and exhaustion," said Jerry. "It was actually a bit boring. To a certain extent, though, it did achieve what it set out to do, because it let those kids see the shows, although I was hoping for skanking in the aisles [There had been rumours that cinemas across the UK were asked to remove their first four rows of seats to leave space for dancing] but I don't think that ever happened. The film's real value now? It's one of the very few visual records of the 2Tone phenomenon."

The movie soundtrack *Dance Craze – The Best of British Ska – LIVE!* (CHR TT5004) was released on February 14th 1981 and featured 15 live tracks out of a total of 27 on the album. The record also featured Bad Manners' first recording on the 2Tone label. The album reached Number 5 in the charts and proved that, if 2Tone was dying, the fans weren't going to let it go quietly. Although the movie wasn't nominated for any awards, the soundtrack had more success. The Specials and the Beat were so confident with their live performances that they didn't even take the opportunity to doctor their tracks in the studio. In retrospect, the album would have made a marvellous double gatefold LP to incorporate all the tracks from the movie, but sadly, it never was. The film was released on video briefly in 1988 and was followed by the release of the 30-minute video *Ska Beatz*, also titled *Joe Massot On The Road – Ska Beatz*. *Ska Beatz* contains footage that never made it into *Dance Craze*, mainly footage from Bad Manners, the Selecter, Madness and the Bodysnatchers, but it doesn't carry the kudos of the official movie.

After the pressure of compiling *Dance Craze*, Jerry went back to 2Tone to help with the release of its next effort. Rico Rodriguez had used his time away from the Specials to return to Jamaica to record his first album since the seminal *Man From Wareika*. His new recording was *That Man Is Forward* (CHS TT5005), recorded with the help of long standing friends like Sly Dunbar, Robbie Shakespeare and of course his brass partner in crime, Dick Cuthell, who also mixed the album. Other Jamaican stalwarts like Cedric Brookes, the saxophonist from Coxsone Dodd's Studio One stable (later of the Skatalites), and Jah Jerry Haynes, one of the founders of the Skatalites, also contributed. Sadly, the album just didn't strike a chord with the mass market and faded away. The placid trombone master himself felt a little let down by Chrysalis: "I got no promotion on that album, man, I don't think," said a disappointed Rico, "I don't think they promote it in any places. I didn't get much promotion with that, man, at all. Only one time I get a lickle promotion with was *Man From Wareika* after doing the tour with Bob Marley."

Now, after all their frenzied work on individual projects (and Terry Hall's compulsive TV watching) the Specials were ready to return. Whether they were ready to test their popularity after being out of sight and mind for six months, only time would tell. The unease created over the previous year had far from dissipated and indeed had festered. The band continued to perform and despite the internal tension, they flew to Ireland for a few dates with the Beat as support. It was certainly a hair-raising start for the Specials, with the first gig due to take place at the Ulster Hall in Belfast. Their arrival in the city coincided with a bomb attack, leaving the band members understandably edgy. Knowing that English accents weren't overly popular among some Belfast residents, they all decided to stay in the Europa Hotel, which was surrounded by barbed wire and armed soldiers because of the threat of terrorist attacks. Even outside the gig, the police were kitted out in their mandatory bullet-proof vests and riot gear. Nevertheless, everything went pretty well on the night, some of the proceeds were given to the 'Corry Mylee' charity that sent both Catholic and Protestant kids for summer holidays on Ireland's West Coast.

The next concert was held in Dublin at the Stardust Ballroom and seemed to go well until trouble started when the Irish fans were prevented from invading the stage during the traditional 'Skinhead Symphony'. The Irish crowd wanted to know why it had been acceptable for the English crowds to join the band onstage while they could not. Simply, it was because there were no drum-risers on the stage and it had been decided that a stage invasion from the audience would be dangerous. In frustration the crowd began to clash with the bouncers, who lashed out indiscriminately at anyone in the vicinity with coshes, lead-filled hoses and makeshift clubs. The police eventually restored order but the gig was in ruins. The authorities blamed 'greedy promoters' for the riot, accusing them of taking advantage of Ireland's 'music famine' (it was rare for big name bands to play their due to 'the troubles') and for packing the hall to twice its normal capacity.

A mere two weeks later, the ill-fated Stardust Ballroom burnt to the ground killing 48 people and injuring 214. According to the Stardust Support Group, it was Valentine's Day night 1981 and people came to the club for a disco and also a Trade Union function. When the fire was found, in a closed-off balcony area, attempts to extinguish it failed. The people at the Trade Union function were evacuated. When security staff moved a screen dividing the area it caused the fire to rush out and set light to the ceiling tiles and walls in the disco area that immediately began to produce large volumes of thick black smoke. The club-goers panicked and a stampede ensued. Some people were trampled in the rush, others collapsed unable to breathe in the noxious fumes. Because most of the fire exits were locked, people couldn't escape as horrified rescue workers attempted to save them. The Specials' gig troubles faded to insignificance when compared to this tragedy.

The following gig in Galway passed without incident, except for one extremely rude girl who approached Horace Panter after the gig and cajoled and teased him into parting with his underpants. The gig in Cork went off peacefully, even though the sound in the auditorium was poor. Despite the trouble at the ill-fated Stardust and the unease in Belfast, it was agreed that there had been fewer problems in Ireland than at most London gigs. The money accrued from the Irish gigs amounted to a princely sum of £8,000, which was looked after by tour manager Pete Hadfield. On his attempt to leave the country Hadfield was stopped at the airport by custom officials and the sum was confiscated as it was in breach of Irish currency laws to take that amount from the country. The band were left well and truly out of pocket!

As usual with the Specials, time off was limited and the band went across to Europe once more for a few uneventful dates in Holland and Norway before jetting back to the UK to rehearse and record.

Relationships between the band members were still fractious and they spent any spare time apart. They got together for rehearsals in a room at the General Wolfe in Coventry, during which the tension and mistrust had the group at arm's length from each other. As Horace Panter eloquently put it, had the room had seven corners, then each one would have been occupied by a weary Special.

The new material was ready and it was time to record some fresh tunes that would put them back in the spotlight. Terry, Neville and Lynval seemed to have the healthiest relationship and were regularly seen in deep discussion, or sitting around with facial expressions resembling the harbingers of doom, an appearance which caused the Specials' engineer Dave Jordan to christen them the Fun Boy Three. Horace Panter felt that life as a Special was losing its sparkle. His involvement with the Exegesis programme had put distance between himself and the group and infuriated old friend Jerry Dammers: "People weren't co-operating." said Jerry, "Just to add to the fun and games, Horace joins some nutty cult and starts giving them all his money. It was a nightmare. Everybody was stood in different parts of this huge room with their equipment, no-one talking."

Horace corroborated the series of events: "Jerry stormed out a couple of times, virtually in tears, and I went after him, 'Calm down, calm down.' It was hell to be around, but I just felt like I was being sucked into a black hole of depression. I was full of Exegesis and self-assertion and Jerry was dead against that. It must have been hell for him."

With this atmosphere, it is almost incomprehensible that any work at all was completed, never mind work that was to be hailed as their greatest ever, but three tracks were eventually chosen as possible singles. In a change of tack, Dammers wanted a new producer for the material as an alternative to either himself, Dave Jordan or Elvis Costello twiddling the mixing controls in the studio. Dammers' search for a fresh approach led him to reggae fan and producer John Collins who ran Local Records, a small label working with local talent who recorded in the front room of his home in Tottenham. Rumour has it that Collins had once submitted a tape to 2Tone, and Dammers remembered him and tracked him down.

"It started in March 1981 with a phone call from Jerry Dammers," recalled Collins.

"He had heard a reggae record I had made at home in Tottenham, 'At The Club' by Victor Romero Evans, and asked if I would be interested in producing the Specials. Suspicious that it was some sort of joke, I nevertheless agreed to travel up to Coventry a couple of days later to meet the band and was surprised to find that they were serious. They were surprised to find that I was white. There were clearly tensions in the band, they needed somebody to unite around and they seemed keen to work with me. Jerry was disillusioned with high-tech, expensive studios and liked my homemade approach and reggae credentials. He had found a small 8-track studio in Leamington and although it was a step down for the Specials, it was a step up from my 4-track home studio. It was decided to go there to record three songs for the band's next single. I was given a producer's contract and an advance of £1,500 which was a good deal for an unknown producer."

Rick Rogers obtained the services of Woodbine Studios in Leamington Spa for the sessions and told Collins that time wasn't a problem, the studio was relatively cheap and to take as long as was needed to get the sound right for the three tracks. The tracks were to be 'Ghost Town', 'Why?' and 'Friday Night, Saturday Morning'.

"I can remember walking out of a rehearsal in total despair because Neville would not try the ideas." said Jerry "I remember Lynval rushing into the control room while they were doing it going, 'No, no, no, it sounds wrong! Wrong! Wrong!' In the meantime, Roddy's trying to kick a hole through the wall from the control room to the studio room. It was only a little studio in Leamington and the engineer was going 'If that doesn't stop, you're going to have to leave!' I was saying, 'No! No! This is the greatest record that's ever been made in the history of anything! You can't stop now!'"

The Specials would often record together in the studio as a live band, but the new material was to be systematically recorded bit by bit, 'Ghost Town' in particular. Dammers had worked out every note and conceivable chord on the track for at least a year. The style was a combination of the first and second albums, a complete audio history of the band crystallised in one song. The tune captured the state of the country at that time under Margaret Thatcher's reign. Unemployment had risen to three million, apprenticeships for school leavers had ended, coal and steel industries had closed, tearing apart communities, and a stop and search policy was implemented by the Police in ethnic minority areas such as Brixton in London, and Handsworth in Birmingham which had resulted in minor outbreaks of violence and rioting with people and police injured. The lyrics to 'Ghost Town' were pertinent to say the least.

"The lyrics, once I got an idea, came pretty quickly," said Dammers "but it was about the whole mood of things. It was about Coventry, but not just Coventry, as I take elements from other places, so it's not about a specific town although the 'boomtown' line in the chorus was definitely aimed at Coventry as it had been a real boomtown in the Sixties and early Seventies, but we were seeing a lot of the heavy industries closing down. It wasn't just that, the country was falling apart. You travelled from town to town and what was happening was terrible. In Liverpool, all the shops were shuttered up, everything was closing down. Margaret Thatcher had apparently gone mad; she was closing down all the industries, throwing millions of people on the dole. We could actually see it by touring around. You could see that frustration and anger in the audience. In Glasgow, there were these little old ladies on the streets selling all their household goods, their cups and saucers. It was unbelievable. It was clear that something was very, very wrong."

Dammers superbly caught the whole context of the country's sad decline in a few verses.

"This town, is coming like a ghost town
All the clubs have been closed down
This place, is coming like a ghost town
Bands won't play no more
too much fighting on the dance floor
Do you remember the good old days before the ghost town?
We danced and sang, and the music played in a de boomtown
This town, is coming like a ghost town
Why must the youth fight against themselves?
Government leaving the youth on the shelf
This place, is coming like a ghost town
No job to be found in this country
Can't go on no more
The people getting angry
This town, is coming like a ghost town."

The single was released as an EP, with 'Ghost Town' as the main track and Lynval's heartfelt tale of his racist attack 'Why?' and Terry Hall's superlatively crafted story of everyday tedium in 'Friday Night Saturday Morning' as the other two tracks. John Collins told www.2-Tone.info: "Terry was professional and cooperative but didn't say very much to me. 'Friday Night, Saturday Morning' was pretty much Jerry's arrangement. I suggested the descending semi-tones and double tracking on the chorus. I liked this track a lot, particularly Terry's vocal and all the keyboard parts that Jerry played. The decision about which of the three tracks should be the A-side was made on which one would sound the best."

In the wake of the Specials' split, Terry revealed that his original idea for 'Friday Night Saturday Morning' had been for the track to consist of his vocals over a piano, to conjure the idea that he was singing in a bar.

The in depth of technique on 'Ghost Town', combined with its hard-hitting lyrics, really made this track the most prominent recording of the Specials' catalogue and gave the impression that their new choice of producer was a stroke of genius. However, 'Ghost Town' had almost fallen at the first hurdle during early work on the track at Woodbine Studios. Producer Collins had asked Jerry to perform some keyboard overdubs, a trick that Dammers wasn't familiar with, and despite the production team's reassurances, Jerry still felt they had the wrong tempo and was not happy with the way the duo of Collins and engineer John Rivers were working. Jerry had been ready to call it a day, but after Rivers had physically shown Jerry on a stopwatch that the tempo had not varied, Dammers continued with the job in hand.

"We used a new producer because we felt we wanted somebody from outside the band to pull the single together," said Terry Hall. "It gave us something a bit fresher and that's what we needed. John Collins sent a tape to Jerry and we were going to release it on 2Tone but, like a lot of recordings, it just didn't happen. After Christmas, when we were talking about doing the single, Jerry played us the tape and we asked the bloke if he'd be prepared to produce us and he did a good job I think."

It took just two weeks to record 'Ghost Town' at Woodbine, despite the troubles within the band that had affected recording. John Collins returned to London and set about creating the final mix of the would-be masterpiece. Collins takes up the technical story: "At this point, 'Ghost Town' was too long, and had just a drum lead-in at the start and no proper ending. I got Jerry to overdub a two-handed shuffle on a Hammond organ that was in the studio. The rhythm was now sounding almost Jamaican! When the backing vocals were added it still hadn't been decided exactly where they would be used so, to keep the options open, I got Jerry, Neville, Lynval and Terry to sing throughout the track, this was before samplers. This turned out to be very useful for the ending; by the time they got to the end of the track, 'this town is coming like a ghost town' had become a hypnotic chant. After the tracks were laid, I spent the following three weeks at my house in Tottenham mixing and editing. Since there was no automated desk, I mixed each section of 'Ghost Town' separately and spliced the sections of 1/4-inch tape together manually. To keep the 7" version close to three minutes long I decided to leave Rico's trombone solo for the 12" version. Other things I decided to leave out altogether included a 'toasting' Terry Hall section.

"I thought the middle section ('do you remember the good old days') featuring Terry worked brilliantly, and for me it was a case of 'less is more'. It was at this stage I sorted out the beginning and end of the track by using my kit-built synthesiser to make the ghost sound effect at the start of the final mix, fading up the Specials from Brad's drum count-in and fading down the synthesiser under Jerry's chromatic diminished chord sequence. Paul Heskett's flute was the last overdub to be added to 'Ghost Town' at Woodbine. Jerry wanted to add some congas after that, but I thought the track was better without them and they were not recorded. At the end, I muted everything apart from bass, drums and backing vocals, dub-style, and faded the ghost synth back up just before the Specials come to a halt, leaving the synth on its own again for a few seconds before the final fade."

It was the birth of a modern classic, a classic that was holding the band together... just.

The band, with new addition Rhoda Dakar, who had recently left the Bodysnatchers and was on board to participate in her *More Specials* role as a backing vocalist, flew out to Holland for a gig in Zwolle, the first of a couple of European dates, although Rhoda and Specials' bassist Horace almost missed out when Rhoda found she had no air travel ticket and Horace had forgotten his passport. From Holland, the re-united band travelled on to the Metropol in Berlin and ran through their set with a seeming lack of communication on stage. They quickly returned to the UK to participate in a concert to raise funds for the Liverpool-London March For Jobs campaign at a very successful May Day gig, which took place at the legendary Rainbow Theatre on Seven Sisters Road, Finsbury Park (the building still stands today but is now the UK headquarters of the Brazilian-based United Church of the Kingdom of God). With unemployment at a record three million, it was a cause close to the band's hearts as they had seen their beloved Coventry become a shadow of its former self. The planned march culminated in a rally in Trafalgar Square attended by over 100,000 people.

Another less publicised gig took place for the Leamington Spa Anti Racism Committee just outside of Coventry, at the Leamington Theatre. The well-known Leamington Group began in November 1977 as an immediate response to the shock number of votes for a British Movement candidate in a district council by-election earlier that month in Leamington Spa. After the war, a large number of people moved to Leamington Spa to seek work in the town's many factories, including Lockheed and Ford. The influx consisted of people from a diverse mix of cultures, amongst them Asians, Irish, Scottish, Welsh and West Indians. In response to the activities of a high-profile local fascist, Robert Relf, a local anti-racist group was founded. Relf's well publicised campaign to have the right to choose to sell his house only to a white family had caused bitter divisions in the town and given a green light for racist views to be aired in the pubs, workplaces and local press, under the guise of free speech and individuality.

It also helped to foster an atmosphere in which racist attacks and, in one instance, murder was committed. That murder occurred in Coventry in April 1981, where the National Front and the British Movement had been leafleting the city centre on a regular basis. With high unemployment, racial tension was likely to explode and sure enough it spilled over when 19-year-old Satnam Gill, an Asian student, was stabbed to death in the city centre by a white youth. There was a massive outcry and anti-racist groups across the Midlands and nationwide rallied together. A march through Coventry was organised on May 23rd to fight the extremists. An estimated 10,000 white and Asian people attended, only to be met by a counter-demonstration of neo-fascists from the National Front and the British Movement. The situation was dire. The Specials, in their battle to change hearts and minds and unite black and white, found that the success at unification they had enjoyed on the road had fallen on deaf ears in their home town. It was a frightening state of affairs.

"Racism has crept back," said Jerry Dammers at the time. "There's so many foolish people around that put on things like Union Jacks just to impress people. It's got very serious. I've noticed it in Coventry, the place was great last year but all of a sudden, it's gone mad. There are British Movement, or whatever they call themselves, handing out leaflets in the city centre every Saturday now, and there was the murder of the Asian youth a few weeks back. Got stabbed, it's just unbelievable."

Terry Hall was equally concerned as those around him of the effect that the incidents were having: "Actions speak louder than words and it's no use saying you believe in something in a music paper and doing nothing about it at the gig. We've never faced a thousand people sieg-heiling at any of our gigs and we're not likely to either, but if anybody does then we just stop the show and get them out. We just won't play while they are there."

The Specials responded to the murder and the city's grave mood in their own style and swiftly organised a concert using the banner 'Peaceful Protest Against Racism' with local acts Hazel O'Connor and the Reluctant Stereotypes. The concert was to raise funds for local anti-racist organisations and Satnam Gil's family and was held at the Butts Athletic Stadium in Coventry on June 20th. The day was also the release date for 'Ghost Town', which was certainly apt. In retaliation, the far right organised another march in the city on the same day, affecting attendance at the gig as some people stayed away wary of any possible clashes; thankfully, there were none.

A week after the Coventry fundraiser, the band were the headliners at a free concert at the Herring Thorpe playing fields in Rotherham, South Yorkshire where, unfortunately, intense fighting between mods and skinheads interrupted the concert. This was followed on June 28th by an appearance in Norway at the Horten Festival, where they played alongside the likes of Ian Dury and the Blockheads and UB40. According to the band's contract, along with a hefty rider that included lunch for 12 people, a hot three-course meal for 20 and a large amount of alcoholic and non-alcoholic drinks, they accrued a tidy sum of £5,800 for their performance. Interestingly, perhaps uniquely, the contract stated: "Management shall guarantee no interference by security in the event that the audience or any part thereof should wish to dance in the auditorium or in the event of persons being invited on to the stage by the artiste."

In addition, in a reflection of the band's inclusive sensibilities, the contract stated:

"Management agrees that no person shall be refused admission to the venue on the grounds of dress, hairstyle or appearance."

'Ghost Town', meanwhile, was selling in its thousands. On its day of release it went straight into the charts at Number 21, and by the time the group had completed their set in Rotherham it had jumped 15 places to Number 6. The media were hailing it as 'one of the best records ever made'. It was certainly something to live up to. The band were whisked down to London to shoot the promotional video to accompany the single, filmed on the deserted streets of the capital in the early hours. The video depicts the band peering morosely from a black saloon car (a Vauxhall Cresta), driving aimlessly around depressing scenes of dilapidated back streets, and through the Blackwall Tunnel. At one stage, a camera strapped to the bonnet fell off, but the resultant effect fitted and the shot was left in the video.

The video perfectly encapsulates the dark hinterland of the Specials' 'Ghost Town.' The ominous mood of the song and the accompanying video seemed to summarise society's collapse. The success of the record resulted in the band being booked for what would be their last *Top Of The Pops* appearance. Sartorially, they looked a peculiar bunch compared to their earlier appearances. Gone was the sleek, sharp rude-boy image, replaced by a 'wear what you like' policy of baggy zoot suits and trendy shirts (a style made popular by early-Eighties British pop group Blue Rondo A La Turk). The band had grown into an 11-piece ensemble with the inclusion of Rhoda Dakar and Paul Heskett, but even then the members were finding it difficult to talk to each other and afterwards in the dressing room there was a wall of silence. Terry Hall later recalled: "It was very traumatic, so much arguing. Once we'd done it though ['Ghost Town'] it was like, this is really fantastic, it really felt like the country was falling apart. I must admit it was very painful to go on *Top Of The Pops*. It didn't feel right, but it felt great as well because of the nature of the record. We were at each others throats, but you look at us on that programme and the tension between the band was fantastic. It wasn't at the time, but that's why we made a great record, that tension. In a subversive way, it felt like it should all go wrong at this point."

The prophetic nature of 'Ghost Town' was about to be seen and as it climbed the charts, the country exploded into inner city war with riots all over the land. As Britain's major cities burned, 'Ghost Town' was to provide a haunting soundtrack. This timeline depicts the state of affairs that led up to the most major episodes of civil unrest on the British mainland in the 20th century and which climaxed as the worst of the violence erupted and 'Ghost Town' hit Number 1 in the charts.

In March and April 1981, as part of a city-wide campaign against burglary and robbery, the London Metropolitan Police launched Operation Swamp '81 in Brixton. The Operation took its name from remarks made by Margaret Thatcher in January 1978, when she said: "People are really rather afraid that this country might be rather swamped by people with a different culture. The British character has done so much for democracy, for law, and done so much throughout the world, that if there is any fear that it might be swamped, people are going to react and be rather hostile to those coming in."

Using the so-called 'Sus' law, police were given the right to stop and search, or even arrest, anyone on grounds of suspicion that they *may* commit an arrestable offence, and over the course of six days in Brixton over 100 plain-clothes officers stopped nearly a thousand people, the vast majority of them black, and arrested 118. The local CID (Criminal Investigation Department) labelled the drive a 'massive success'. Police later justified the operation on the basis that the Brixton area had seen a 138% increase in robberies during 1976-80, compared with 38% across London as a whole. The problem was that hundreds of law-abiding black people were among those stopped, and complaints of harassment and racism multiplied. Among those arrested were three employees of the Lambeth Community Relations Council, leaving relations between the black community and the police plumbing new depths.

Directly after the Brixton fiasco a 600-strong street party was held in the St Paul's area of Bristol, in the South West of England, to commemorate the first anniversary of a notorious police raid on the legendary 'Black and White café'. The Caribbean café, which served popular Jamaican dishes, was said to have been a problem to authorities ever since it was allegedly set up as an illegal drinking den in the early Seventies. Up until its closure in 2004 the police had dubbed it the country's most raided drugs den. In 1980, when a Detective Constable emerged from the café with a bag of cannabis, he was confronted by a group of black youths and one of the most serious riots in Britain since the Second World War broke out. During the riot a bank and post office were attacked, and a row of shops and a warehouse were set ablaze. Twelve police cars and several fire engines were damaged and dozens of people were injured. The party, which passed off peacefully, was billed as a celebration of 'triumph over an oppressive establishment'. In the week prior to the party the last four of 16 people charged over the riot were freed from jail when the jury hearing their cases failed to reach a verdict. There were 12 others; four had the charges against them dropped before they came to trial, three were found not guilty on the judge's instructions and a further five were acquitted by the jury.

Later in April more strife occurred in Brixton as a result of the mistrust between the police and the black community fuelled by Operation Swamp '81. The police, who claimed to be treating a black stabbing victim, were surrounded by about 50 black youths who then 'rescued' the victim. Police reinforcements were called but were driven back and tension remained high all day, with sporadic confrontations between black youths and the police. The speed of events was startling and more fuel was added to the fire with the arrest of a black youth outside a taxi office in Atlantic Road, Brixton following a scuffle with a plain-clothes police officer. The arrest triggered even more violent confrontations, and by early evening a police car had been set alight and petrol bombs thrown as clashes escalated between the police and local youths (both black and white). The fire brigade were unable to get through to deal with fires that were raging in several locations and to make matters worse a fire engine was hijacked. By the end of the night 14 properties and 22 vehicles had been destroyed by fire. The Metropolitan Police commissioner at the time, Sir David McNee, declared: "I have this message for the people of Brixton. We will uphold and enforce law. Brixton is not a no-go area, nor will it be."

Later, Home Secretary William Whitelaw toured Brixton with the Metropolitan Police Commissioner to taunts of 'sieg heil' and 'Why haven't you been here before?' That night saw yet more clashes and an outbreak of looting. Over 7,000 police officers were deployed in Brixton before civil order was eventually restored. Whitelaw announced the appointment of Lord Scarman to conduct a public enquiry into the disturbances in Brixton. Scarman had previously headed an enquiry into the violent clashes in London in 1975, when student Kevin Gateley was killed during protests against a National Front rally. Prime Minister Margaret Thatcher dismissed suggestions that unemployment and racism lay behind the Brixton disturbances, even though figures show that half of Brixton's black population were without jobs at the time: "Nothing, but

YOU'RE WONDERING NOW

nothing, justifies what happened," she said. She also denied that increased investment in Britain's inner cities would help: "Money can not buy either trust or racial harmony."

When a local council leader complained that the police presence 'amounted to an army of occupation' and had indeed provoked the riots, Thatcher responded with: "What absolute nonsense and what an appalling remark. No-one should condone violence. No-one should condone the events. They were criminal, criminal."

With racial tension mounting, the country wasn't helped by anti-immigration veteran Enoch Powell (infamous for his 1968 'Rivers of Blood' speech against immigration) who threw his hat into the ring with a renewed warning that Britain 'had seen nothing yet'.

Thatcher then went to India on an overseas mission and defended the government's Nationality Bill, which would further limit the rights of people from black Commonwealth countries to come to Britain, and would make Britain the only country in the world where being born within its borders did not automatically confer nationality. She told the gathered masses that immigration needed to be limited, prompting the *Times of India* newspaper to print its unimpressed views, declaring that Thatcher had 'done more harm to race relations in Britain than any other post-war leader there.'

At the end of April, more than 100 people were arrested and 15 police officers injured in clashes with mainly black youths at fairs in the London Boroughs of Finsbury Park, Forest Gate and Ealing. A further 350 were arrested in incidents outside London. Most went unreported by the press, but they offered a hint of how widespread the potential for violent confrontation actually was.

In early June in Manchester's Moss Side area, following the use of 16 police vehicles and 28 officers to arrest one youth who had gone into a library carrying a two-foot-long bamboo cane, the Black Parents Association said that Moss Side police station had 'long been regarded by the black community as the operational base of a racist army in occupation.' They accused the police of 'SAS-style raids and brutality, violence, intimidation and racial abuse.' The youth was later released without charge. Local minister, the Reverend Alex Mitchell, said Moss Side was a 'tinderbox', but feared that talk of a riot would become a self-fulfilling prophecy.

In mid June over 70 arrests were made during clashes between racist skinheads and black people in Coventry. The National Front had planned a march later that month on the 20th, the same day as the 'Peaceful Protest Against Racism' concert by the Specials at the Butts Stadium. Shortly afterwards, Lord Scarman's enquiry into the Brixton riots opened and was followed by a wave of neo-Nazi extremist attacks on the premises of black, multi-racial and left-wing organisations. Several bookshops and a North London community centre were targeted in arson attacks, while in Walthamstow, also in North London, four members of an Asian family, the Khans, including three children, were killed in an arson attack on their home.

Between 1976 and 1981, 31 racist murders of black people were recorded in Britain, including in 1981 a disabled Sikh woman killed in Leeds after a petrol bomb attack on her home, and an elderly Asian woman who died in Leamington Spa, set alight by racists who doused her in petrol. These truly shocking statistics showed how quickly Britain had descended into anarchy, but matters were to get worse.

In July, in Southall, London, (one of Britain's biggest Asian communities) the Hamborough Tavern was the venue for a concert by Oi! Band, the 4Skins. Several hundred skinheads, many of them sporting National Front banners and badges, were bussed in from outside the area. The pub then came under attack from Asian youths after an Asian woman was assaulted. Rioting ensued in the surrounding streets and the pub was eventually firebombed and burnt out. Barricades went up and the area was sealed off. The police seemed completely unprepared and unaware of the trouble that such a concert might have caused, even though a National Front meeting in Southall in 1979 had led to the death of anti-racist protester Blair Peach after he was struck on the head with a police truncheon. The next day's *Guardian* newspaper printed: "At the very least this is incompetence on a pretty grand scale."

On July 4th the Specials travelled up to Potter Newton Park in Leeds for the 'Carnival Against Racism' and arrived as the National Front marched through the city. By their own standards they gave a lacklustre performance, but the audience was appreciative and the gig was a success for race relations. Neville Staple told the crowd: "It's like a zebra crossing, black and white, black and white as far as you can see."

The rifts in the band, though, had grown to epic proportions and some members travelled back separately.

That weekend in Toxteth, a deprived area of inner-city Liverpool, trouble flared up when the police, again using the 'Sus' laws, arrested Leroy Alphonse Cooper. An angry crowd watched the arrest and perceived it to be unjust and heavy-handed. The disturbance erupted into full-scale rioting. Battles were pitched between youths and the police, petrol bombs and paving stones were thrown, and the police used CS gas for the first time in the UK outside Northern Ireland. The riots lasted for nine days, and police accounts record that 468 police officers were injured, 500 people arrested and at least 70 buildings destroyed. However, later estimates suggest that actual numbers were double those presented officially. Toxteth residents were enraged by comments made by the Merseyside Chief Constable Kenneth Oxford, who attacked 'irresponsible parents' for letting out their children to become involved. He went on to accuse around a hundred 'thieves and vagabonds' living in Toxteth of being ringleaders of the violence, and further inflamed local feeling with his description of black Liverpudlians as the 'product of liaisons between white prostitutes and black sailors.' Hardly diplomatic or likely to defuse the situation! The preconception that the riots in England at that time were 'race riots' was widespread, but there are many reports of similarly frustrated white youths travelling in from other areas of Liverpool to fight alongside Toxteth residents against the police. Taking advantage of prevailing prejudices to blame the country's black population allowed people to ignore the broader social issues, such as poverty and deprivation, that lay at the heart of the unrest.

Meanwhile, with every MP and political analyst having their voice heard, MP Teddy Taylor MP called for the police to be issued with water cannons, and his fellow Tory Michael Brown demanded an end to all immigration. The Liberal leader of Liverpool City Council, Trevor Jones, demanded that the army be put on standby, and senior Social Democrat politician Shirley Williams accused the left-wing Militant Tendency of training people for riots and including factions from the anti-establishment extremist group 'Class War' in attempts to stir up feeling in the affected areas. Others pointed to police racism and unemployment as an underlying cause of what was becoming known among black activists as an 'uprising'.

In Toxteth unemployment had risen to 37%, reaching 60% among young blacks, with 81,000 people chasing 1,019 jobs in Liverpool as a whole. It was admitted that at the end of the school term, the local careers office had information on just 12 vacancies to offer school leavers throughout the city.

On July 8th more incidents were reported as 250 youths, both black and white, clashed with police in Wood Green, North London and 43 were charged with theft and violence. More than a thousand young people laid siege to the local police station in Moss Side, Manchester. This provoked Manchester's Chief Constable, James Anderton, to abandon the 'softly softly' approach, and he announced that he would deal with rioters 'his way.' The police moved in on the area in force with a zero-tolerance stance.

On July 9th, 300 police were needed to quell street disturbances in Woolwich, South London, and new riots in Brixton were accompanied by a wave of disturbances the length and breadth of Britain. Southall, Battersea, Dalston, Streatham and Walthamstow in London, Handsworth in Birmingham, Chapeltown in Leeds, Highfields in Leicester, and the towns of Ellesmere Port, Luton, Leicester, Sheffield, Portsmouth, Preston, Newcastle, Derby, Southampton, Nottingham, High Wycombe, Bedford, Edinburgh, Wolverhampton, Stockport, Blackburn, Huddersfield, Reading, Chester, Aldershot, York, amongst others, all experienced 'riots' of varying magnitude over the next few days. Some of the unrest was dismissed as 'copycat' behaviour used as an excuse to cause damage and vandalism, although whether this was the case or not will probably never be known.

Prime Minister Thatcher cancelled a planned visit to Toxteth because she was told that her safety could not be guaranteed, and in London all demonstrations and marches, including one planned by the National Front in Chelsea, and a counter protest by the Anti-Nazi League, were banned for a month. A funeral procession for Mrs Khan and her three children, killed in the arson attack at the end of June, was called off due to fears of disorder.

By July 11th the Specials sat at the top of the charts with 'Ghost Town', capturing perfectly the distress of the nation. Two days after the Specials hit the top spot, Margaret Thatcher eventually paid an 8am visit to Toxteth. Merseyside Chief Constable Kenneth Oxford called for armoured cars for the police, while government spokesmen suggested that army camps might be used to detain rioters if need be. Early morning raids in search of petrol bombs triggered new clashes in Brixton, but no bombs were found. A media blackout was imposed in an attempt to avoid potential flashpoints and prevent so-called copycat behaviour. Huge numbers of police were deployed to counter any possible disturbances, and it seemed at last that the troubles had abated. Environment Secretary Michael Heseltine was appointed 'Minister for Liverpool' in an attempt to reverse the decline of the once wealthy port. However, no extra Government money was made available to areas that had been affected by the riots.

At the end of July, the Specials' 'Ghost Town' enjoyed its third week at Number 1 as a thousand motorcyclists clashed with police in the Lake District town of Keswick, perhaps the last large-scale confrontation of the summer, although isolated clashes between young people and the police continued on a much smaller scale into the autumn.

The Scarman enquiry eventually found that discrimination, unemployment and poverty were the primary underlying causes of the riots. But while accepting that there may have been individual cases of racism within the police and other institutions of British society, Scarman rejected the notion of 'institutional racism' within the police. (In 1999 another enquiry, this time into the murder of black teenager Stephen Lawrence and the subsequent failure of the police to gather enough evidence to prosecute the charged suspects, found that the recommendations of the Scarman Report had been ignored and famously concluded that the police force was indeed 'institutionally racist.') Scarman also found unquestionable evidence of the indiscriminate use of 'stop and search' powers by the police against black people, and those laws were subsequently dropped. In 2008, David Cameron, leader of the Conservative Party announced in Parliament his intentions to restore similar powers to the police as part of anti-terror laws should he get into power. Peter Hain, at the time a candidate for Labour's deputy leadership, said: "We cannot have a reincarnation of the old 'sus' laws under which mostly black people, ethnic minorities, were literally stopped on sight. That created a really bad atmosphere and an erosion of civil liberties."

To quote Lynval Golding: "Nothing ever change."

As the riots subsided and Britain returned to an uneasy peace, Prince Charles and Lady Diana Spencer were married at St Paul's Cathedral. Paradoxically, the event united the whole nation, and the Specials slipped from the top spot (although they remained in the charts for another 14 weeks) to be replaced by the somewhat less politically-motivated 'Green Door' by Shakin' Stevens. This bizarre switch from darkness to light heralded the end of the summer of discontent.

With the band almost at breaking point, they still had professional commitments to fulfil. These included a couple of dates, one in England at the plush art deco Royal Court, Liverpool, and the other at Dalymount Park, Dublin, a stadium belonging to Irish football side Bohemians FC. The Liverpool gig passed off peacefully, except when, as if to rub salt into the band's wounds, they were treated to 'sieg heils' from a member of the crowd during the song 'Why?' (Lynval's anti racism track). The Specials were left wondering if all their efforts had managed to change anything at all. The Liverpool crowd were unaware that they would be the last to see the original Specials play as a unit on British soil. The Dalymount Park gig, billed as 'The Garden Party', was due to take place on July 26th. Everything had seemed to be going to plan; promoter Pat Egan had hired the football stadium at a cost of £8,000, the contract was signed, the official fee payable to the band set at £9,000. The tickets were even printed and on sale when, out of the blue, the band cancelled the gig. Egan ran a record shop in Dublin, one of the first 'underground' stores, and had brought some massive names in music to play in Dublin. The city, and Ireland as a whole, weren't at that time popular haunts for touring musicians, and Egan had pulled off a massive coup in 1980 by having reggae superstar Bob Marley play at Dalymount Park to great acclaim. He had wanted a suitably big name to carry on the tradition and he saw the Specials as that band. He had also booked the Selecter and the Beat as support acts and it promised to be a 2Tone extravaganza.

When the band cancelled Egan was livid and immediately took action to sue and recoup the money spent on hiring the stadium: "We booked the Specials in advance of them hitting Number 1 with 'Ghost Town'," said Pat, "and we were negotiating with the promoter Steve Hedges of Aragorn Promotions and he was a nightmare to deal with. We had posters and tickets printed when, out of the blue, the show was cancelled. We immediately sought High Court proceedings against all seven members of the band and their management. I was furious! Nothing ever came of the proceedings, especially once the group had split, and I never ever received compensation. It took me over a year to get my deposit back. I never received an official reason as to the group cancelling, but was later told by a reliable source that they simply had better offers and that was bad business."

Theories on the reasons for the cancellation are varied, the most popular being that the band were still concerned about the previous brush with the currency law, and feared arrest when re-entering Eire (an unlikely scenario as they would have been arrested on the day of the original offence). Other grounds cited in the press ranged from illness within the band to the unlikely theory that the Specials did not want to play Ireland due to the success of 'Ghost Town' (ie they had been given better offers to play elsewhere). There was, of course, talk that the band were on the verge of a split.

Once the furore of the cancellation had subsided, and attempts had been made to get the band to communicate again, a short six-date tour of America was inexplicably booked. To those close to the group it was obvious that relations were at an all time low, with Jerry's health in question, Roddy past caring, and the clique that comprised Terry, Neville and Lynval strengthening. Notwithstanding all the problems the band did indeed fly out to the US. The tour had been postponed once already at short notice because of Jerry's failing health, but there was no get-out clause this time. America had given the boys a taste of the music business that had left a bitter taste and sown the seeds that had fractured their friendships. To go back was an insane step but nevertheless a commercial one that had to be undertaken. Chrysalis wanted their money's worth out of the Specials.

"It was too much pressure man," said Neville Staple. "You know, we used to do two shows a day! What we needed wasn't another American tour, not another UK tour! We needed good management to say 'Ok, guys, you've been working a long time, take a year off.' That's how it should have been done, but instead of blaming management, people were blaming different members of the band, which was ridiculous. We were knackered. People have to remember that we were also touring two years before we became big, it was non stop. In the end it killed us."

The band's repertoire not only now incorporated Rico's tracks 'Sea Cruise' and 'Chang Kai Shek', they were also to include the old Bodysnatchers rape story 'The Boiler' with vocals by Rhoda Dakar. Alongside the recently-introduced 'Why?' in the set were the other two numbers from their most recent release, 'Ghost Town', and 'Friday Night Saturday Morning', although not every audience was lucky enough to hear 'Ghost Town'.

One of the tour's highlights was a small festival at the Liberty Bell Racecourse in Philadelphia, with 16,000 in attendance, and the Police, the Coasters and Oingo Boingo also on the bill. The tour continued with some high tension but quality performances, although on August 21st, the show at the Paramount Theatre in Staten Island, New York was held up for 15 minutes by crowd trouble and crushing incidents. Despite pleas from Terry, Neville and Jerry, the trouble did not die down and the crowd spilled over into the orchestra pit at the front of the stage. Jerry made a plea to the unconcerned arena: "Listen, please, please move back. This is very dangerous. If you could please get out of the orchestra pit because if you don't it might collapse and then you'll all be killed. We don't care, anyway if we'd have our way you'd be up onstage and we'd be down there in the pit."

Lynval tried a change of tack: "Listen, move back. If you don't then this next tune is the last in the set. You can join in when we do 'Nite Klub' at the end of the show. Everybody can come nite klubbin' at the end of the set."

Terry Hall's impatience surfaced as the fray continued: "There are people down the front getting really fed up. Sort it out! Move back and you'll be in for a treat as we will play you our fantastic British Top 10 hit that made us so famous," he said sarcastically.

Jerry Dammers, hands in pockets, turned to Hall and replied: "What it is, is that these people find us so wonderful they want to join us," and then with a final shot of venomous derision, "We're so special…"

Hall's final exclamation came at the end of the set, during 'Enjoy Yourself': "My name's Terry, and you've left me speechless."

They may have held it together for the show, but afterwards in the dressing room, there was complete silence.

The most notable performance of the tour was to be at the 'Police Picnic' at the Grove, Oakville, Canada, just outside Toronto, where the Police were the headline band. The show started early in the afternoon on a sweltering Sunday. The Grove venue was actually a 70-acre farm field that had never hosted a concert before. The gig was promoted as 'Oakville's Woodstock' and most appropriately, given the 'Police Picnic' title, there were 200 police officers monitoring the show. The reported marijuana cloud over the audience throughout the afternoon led to three arrests. In addition, the cops began confiscating the watermelons that were for sale because people were spiking them with alcohol.

The band were part of the support roster, along with the Go-Gos, John Otway, the Payolas, Nash The Slash, Oingo Boingo, Killing Joke and the legendary Iggy Pop. The huge crowd of 29,000 saw the Specials put on a virtuoso display, out-shining everyone on the bill, presumably much to Sting's annoyance, and by the time the Police came on at 11pm the crowd had dwindled considerably. Keith Dawes, owner of Recordings record store in Oakville, who had sold the majority of the Police Picnic tickets, was a relatively new music-store owner at the time and attended on his complimentary tickets out of curiosity.

"I didn't really like the Police," said Dawes. "They had some good grooves during the show, when Sting shut his mouth for a few minutes, but I thought the Specials were great."

But, despite being on a professional high, the pressure brewing amongst the band members was still growing, and after the Police Picnic, it exploded. Jerry Dammers refused to travel to the gig in the provided limousine, although apparently it was a battered older model, and made his way to the gig via the road crew truck. To some, his behaviour was becoming more and more unreasonable, and the fact that he was constantly grating against Roddy and Neville was unsettling matters. Back at the hotel after the gig a heated discussion between Jerry and the management developed into an argument: "That night in Toronto," said Rick Rogers, "Jerry walked into my hotel room and told me straight out that I was sacked. I couldn't really say much because there was never any contracts between myself and the Specials. I just took an equal share of the profits. I think I saw it coming anyway."

Jerry had big plans to transform the Specials and wanted Rhoda Dakar and Paul Heskett to become full-time members of the group. He also planned to keep the 2Tone Label solely for use by the Specials, decelerating the issue of records to two singles a year only. Rick Rogers tried to dissuade Jerry, but the General was adamant: "I think if Jerry hadn't stuck to his guns there would have never been his greatest moment with the 'Nelson Mandela' single." said Rick.

After being sacked by Dammers, Rick was approached by another band member.

"I heard a knock on my door and in walked Terry Hall. He just said to me that Neville, Lynval and himself were thinking of leaving the band and asked me if I would like to go along with them as their manager. I said yes and that was the birth of the Fun Boy Three."

So, unbeknown to Jerry Dammers, the band was undoubtedly headed for a calamitous split. The completion of the US mini tour was carried out, with two further dates, one in Long Island and one at the Bradford Hotel Ballroom in Boston, Massachusetts, the historical final appearance of the Magnificent Seven (or the Enigmatic Eleven?). Horace Panter, in his book *Ska'd For Life*, summed up the gut-wrenching period in which the light went out in one of the most dazzling supernovas in music history: "Neville would not get on the coach to go to the gig and stayed up in his room." said Horace, "I went up to talk to him and he went on about how nobody wanted him in the band. He knew it was finished too. I persuaded him to come and play this one last show."

Most of the Specials flew back to the UK, but Jerry opted to take time out and stayed in New York. Once home, the majority of the other members again took up the reins of their fledgling sideline projects and there was a distinct lull in Specials activity. In October there was a flurry of press and music industry rumours regarding the Specials and a possible spilt. Around that time Terry, Neville and Lynval paid a visit to Jerry and revealed their intentions, and shortly after, despite initial denials, the three publicly announced their split from the group.

The headlines read "BREAKAWAY TRIO BURST COVENTRY'S FINEST INTO FRAGMENTS" and "SPECIALS IMPLODE!" Ultimately it was left to the jilted leader Jerry Dammers to give a press statement to officially announce that the trio had left the Specials: "As the official spokesman for the Specials, all I can offer at this stage is no comment. The fact is that, at present, those of us remaining are considering our future."

During the weekend in which the split was announced, emergency meetings were quickly held at Chrysalis Records. The splinter group, the Fun Boy Three, had landed a deal with the 2Tone parent label and taken with them Rick Rogers and Specials engineer Dave Jordan. Roddy Byers, breathing a sigh of relief that the madness had come to an end, had been given a somewhat limited four days to record some new material to convince Chrysalis that he would be worth keeping on their register. Locking himself away in the studio with his brother Marc and two Coventry friends, Joe Hughes and Steve Young, he employed the services of Dave Jordan to work the controls for him, but Jordan, battling with a drug habit that he would ultimately lose, failed to show for two of the days and so Dick Cuthell filled in as producer.

"I had plenty of new songs, but so little time," said Roddy. "Chrysalis dropped me saying they weren't interested in my rock'n'roll stuff. I heard Jerry was angry that I had been dropped, so I asked him if he would put my 'Skabilly' out on 2Tone. This was at a student party in Coventry just after the split. He turned around and headbutted the wall. I was relieved that we had broken up then. If I'd carried on in the band I'd have ended up dead or someone would have got hurt. I wish I'd drunk less and not argued so much, but you can't change the way you are."

The news of the split had hit Jerry like a missile. The group had had their fair share of problems, but the tension behind the scenes had always added electricity to their live performances. However, the band's incessant touring had caused further stress and had ultimately destroyed the members themselves. Nonetheless, the break-up had come like a bolt from the blue as far as Jerry was concerned. He hadn't known about the conversation between Rogers and Hall in Toronto, and was livid that the planning and execution of the Fun Boy Three's departure had been taking place behind his back. He knew the trio had been working on material, but he had presumed it to be new demos for the Specials (in hindsight, they were probably just that) but the idea that all the developments had been arranged in secrecy left him scarred: "Everyone in the band was involved with their own thing," said Jerry "but that didn't bother me, because no matter what we were all doing, the idea was to return to the Specials and pick up where we left off. I think the Fun Boy Three could have been a sideline to the Specials, but I guess it wasn't to be."

The killer blow was dealt when the Fun Boy Three and Chrysalis released their debut single a mere seven weeks after 'Ghost Town' had slipped out of the charts. Jerry decided not to make any further comment and spent some time taking stock of the situation. Chrysalis still wanted their money's worth out of the Specials as they were still a Chrysalis act. After the split, and with Roddy gone to perform with his band the Tearjerkers, Jerry, Horace and Brad decided to carry on in some form and until it could be figured out which way they would turn. They flew out to Germany to perform as backing musicians for Rico Rodriguez's tour, no doubt a much welcomed distraction from the Specials crisis.

Jerry believed the American tours had contributed massively to the bands demise: "America was a waste of time," he said. "It was exhausting, and the Americans hardly knew what reggae was and they had no retro culture. Maybe ten years later we could have broken America, but at that time we might as well have been from another planet. Then there was the wisdom that the Fun Boy Three weren't able to do their songs in the Specials. As far I remember we did every song that they wrote and brought to the band. I helped them with arrangements and writing and contributed some lyrics to some songs, un-credited. I actively encouraged them and at the time of the split the idea was for everyone to have a break and go and write some songs for the Specials. I think Neville wanted to do more toasting and solo singing and I was happy with that, but I don't think Terry was. I thought some of Roddy's songs were excellent, and some just weren't good enough, and I don't remember anyone disagreeing with me. When the band split, Roddy wasn't in either camp. I've never really seen a proper explanation for why the Fun Boys left. Maybe it had something to do with Terry being so young and not having been singing for long when he joined the Specials, and Neville had gone straight from being a roadie on to *Top Of The Pops*, that they didn't fully appreciate what we had. I don't know. I do know that something which I planned and worked towards for 16 years was over."

Jerry's driving force and his craving for professionalism and perfection had perhaps allowed him to get caught up in the Specials machinery and painted him as dictator, although it was never a case of 'my way or the highway'. The job of organising a successful record label and band were far too much for one man, and, even with managerial help, the pressure eventually told.

With Jerry swimming against the tidal wave created by the Fun Boy Three, he still believed that after all the struggles, the distinct lack of money, and the battle for recognition, it was worth keeping the Specials alive in one form or another. There were seven individual perspectives and points of view on the split. Terry Hall felt that there was no way back for him once the meltdown has started: "I found it very difficult to express to the rest of the band how I felt. I just felt like I had to get away from it for a bit, and Lynval and Neville felt the same way. I didn't think it was a permanent thing, I just didn't feel that there was any way of us grabbing control of it again, so the natural thing was to leave it. I didn't want to battle with people who I had so much affection for. I'd rather walk away and see it as mission accomplished. I had no idea where it could have gone after 'Ghost Town' because that captured everything we were trying to say. It felt very awkward leaving and two-thirds of the group despised me for doing it at the time."

Roddy Byers felt that Jerry had been too domineering: "The Specials were a unit with seven sets of ideas. I for one wanted my songs performing how I had written them and that was the same for others. Jerry tried to do it all himself and he took too much on. It affected relationships within the band and it affected relationships with other people in 2Tone."

Neville Staple was critical of the stance taken by the record company and felt that instead of backing the band and the label all the way, they were always on the look out for the 'next big thing' from day one: "Spandau Ballet were on the same label as us, so they were like the new stuff happening. Chrysalis started spending more time with them, because it was the newer thing coming in. We wasn't commercial enough for them, because Jerry's concept wasn't driving around in limousines and stuff like that. It was like 'Give these kids cheaper records' and I guess the record companies weren't into that. Plus we wasn't, like, lovey-dovey. We were totally different with the lyrics as well. So it depended on the record company and promoters and people. They're the people who killed ska."

Drummer John Bradbury had his own take on the crash of the group: "Jerry was basically the leader of the Specials, the main songwriter and the best. But when you have a bunch of egos like ours, particularly with singers, there's bound to be a bit of 'I want my own songs in' tension, but it got so bad all round that no one could deal with each other in the end."

As already documented, any examination of the group' s exploits makes it clear that the never-ending round of record-tour-record-tour was a huge factor in the break up. The Specials were the ultimate live experience, but they were rarely off the road, and the travel, forever hanging around venues and hotels and the excessive drinking fuelled by boredom all contributed to killing the band off. Rick Rogers later admitted that he wished he could have guided the group with more experience: "What made the Specials so very special (or is it, as they put it 'nobody is special'?) was the fact they contained very different personalities, each with differing tastes in music; punk, rockabilly, soul, ska and reggae (no wonder they were once called the Hybrids!) and it was never going to be a "til death do us part' undertaking, but while it lasted it was incredible. The Specials kicked arse and stomped over the murky waters that were the music industry. They didn't cause ripples, they caused a flood! Wherever they went, in an exhilarating four-year blast, they made people think, they made people dance. Their influential legacy is still felt today."

PART 2

MORE SPECIALS

"Take away my right to choose, take away my point of view."
The Fun Boy Three 1981

THE FUN BOY THREE

*t*HE SPLIT of the Specials shocked the music world. Their demise so soon after the career high of their Number 1 single 'Ghost Town', left it as the perfect epitaph for the group. The music hacks were unrelenting in their quest to track down the various band members for an explanation as to why the Specials had really split, but they all maintained their silence. In his rare interviews Terry Hall had not given any outward hint of trouble within the band around the 'Ghost Town' period, nor had he mentioned any collaborations with Neville and Lynval. The three had all agreed to return to the Specials base when the time came, and it seemed that they had indeed wanted to make the band work, but then found themselves in such a situation that they felt compelled to leave. Unfortunately, the split led to a painful and anguished 20-year media battle between both sides in the Specials camp.

It started almost directly after the 1981 split, in a no-holds-barred fashion, when the Fun Boy Three were established as a band in their own right. With the echoes of the 'Ghost Town' fade-out still whistling in their ears, the group, with a comfortable Chrysalis contract under their belt, released their debut single 'The Lunatics (Have Taken Over The Asylum)'on November 7th. The picture on the cover maintained Terry's reputation as pop's 'Mr Misery'. The trio hardly looked like Fun Boys in their glum monochrome pose, but the band name was a great bit of sarcasm. It was very difficult for the group to talk constructively about the Fun Boy Three, their aspirations and future, without being grilled as to why the Specials had split. Terry Hall led the media on a merry dance over the Specials saga, but eventually capitulated and offered some insight into why one of the country's most exciting bands had dissolved: "The split was planned in advance," said Terry, "but there was no real point in telling the others when we first started thinking about breaking away. It would have only caused more friction. Some of them knew it was on the cards anyway. Originally, our last gig was going to be the Campaign For Jobs at the Rainbow Theatre but me, Lynval and Neville decided to stay on for 'Ghost Town' and an American tour to see if there was any way we could hold on to the group, but we felt there wasn't."

The trio were confident that they had done their utmost to keep the Specials in one piece, but also that their eventual break away had saved the sanity of those involved.

Lynval Golding recalled: "We all tried very hard to keep the Specials intact, but the politics within the group just weren't right. We just couldn't communicate with each other any more and that upset and annoyed me the most."

Neville Staple had been one of the members at loggerheads with Jerry Dammers towards the end, and had his own view on matters: "It got to the stage where we didn't have a say. I helped write some of the lyrics for 'Ghost Town' but got no credit for it."

As a result of Neville's comment, Jerry went as far as seeking legal advice and the early fallout from the Specials became acrimonious.

"It was really weird," said a shocked Neville. "I was travelling down to London on the train with Lynval, and Jerry happened to be heading from the same destination so he sat with us. I knew he was considering taking me to court over 'Ghost Town' but nothing was mentioned. We just sat there. Thing is, as soon as we reached London, he only went and told his solicitor that I was going to be at Chrysalis so that his solicitor could come down there with a summons."

Obviously, the recriminations were beginning to mount. There were rumours that Hall and Golding had been a little unhappy with the production of the other two tracks on the 'Ghost Town' EP. Terry Hall said at the time: "I think as a rule we all thought 'Ghost Town' was as good as it was going to be. I got a little pissed off with the track I wrote on the B-side. 'Friday Night Saturday Morning' was written by me about my life, and I wanted the song to be performed with myself on vocals and just a piano as musical accompaniment, like it was being sung in a pub, but Jerry wanted it jazzed up, which is what he did. It sounded ok."

Lynval had the same sort of problem with the other track on the EP: "I was far from happy with the way 'Why?' turned out. The production was lousy, particularly as we'd done some demos of the same song as an early Fun Boy Three demo back in January [1981] before 'Ghost Town.'"

After a few weeks the media virtually gave up their constant barrage of questions about the Specials, and instead concentrated on the Fun Boys and the reason why they were making music.

'The Lunatics (Have Taken Over The Asylum)', backed by the bizarre 'Faith, Hope And Charity', eventually climbed to a high of Number 20 in the British charts. The single made use of deep chanting and monotone vocals with a heavy, driving African drum influence. Lyrically, it seemed to carry on where 'Ghost Town' left off.

"The song is about the lunatics who are voted in to take control of a country," said Terry, "If you had the same ideas as politicians and went around shouting them on the streets, you'd get locked up. It's about the things that people tend to ignore like poverty. It doesn't affect Ronald Reagan (the cowboy in the lyrics) in his White House. It's got 26 rooms and his wife has a bullet-proof petticoat."

The record was, at the time, one of the most emotionally apt political songs reflecting the dread and near-despair of the Reagan/Thatcher era. The song's title and controversial lyrics so enraged the eccentric Irish MP Padraig Flynn, then Minister for Trade and Commerce in Ireland, that he told the Irish parliament: "This record should be outlawed. It is an insult to patients and staff in mental hospitals, and it is politically subversive."

"I see a clinic full of cynics
Who want to twist the peoples' wrist
They're watching every move we make
We're all included on the list
The lunatics have taken over the asylum
The lunatics have taken over the asylum
Go nuclear the cowboy told us
And who am I to disagree
'Cos when the madman flips the switch'
The nuclear will go for me
The lunatics have taken over the asylum
The lunatics have taken over the asylum
I've seen the faces of starvation

> *But I just cannot see the points*
> *'Cos there's so much food here today*
> *That no-one wants to take away."*

The track was also issued in a special 12" format disc. As any vinyl buff and collector will testify, the 12" versions often contained slight remixes and overdubs of the original track or extra added tracks, a great marketing ploy and one which the Fun Boys would use throughout their career. The invention of the 'picture disc' provided another way to get fans to part with their pocket money; a photo or design was pressed into the vinyl of the record. The Fun Boy Three's record label (along with many others at the time) took full advantage of the new technology and issued a picture disc with each new release (except 'The Lunatics'). These limited editions would later become collector's items and have commanded some amazing price tags over the years. Chrysalis would have most certainly been rubbing their hands together.

The formation of the Fun Boy Three, whether people liked it or not, was a quick cure for the personal problems that had increased in the Specials pressure cooker. The demands away from the feverish 2Tone scene were far fewer, and for the first time in many months they began to relax. Terry Hall, used to playing on stages crowded with band and fans, felt exposed on stage, a sensation of being amputated from the Specials: "It was really funny at first." he said, "It felt like half the Specials had left us and when we did *Top Of The Pops* for the first time, we'd turn around and expect to see the Specials there, but of course they weren't."

Lynval Golding recalled the revelation of a constraint-free recording career: "The freedom we had to express ourselves was very liberating and creatively very much needed. To say what we wanted and how we wanted it to sound. The first Specials album we were all throwing ideas in. The second was very much Jerry's vision of where we should be going. Fun Boy Three was Terry and myself really having room to experiment and we loved that. It was an incredibly creative time. Terry is a extremely talented lyricist. It was wonderful working with Terry and Neville. Neville is a great showman. He thrives on the stage, wonderful to watch. We made some great pop songs, but also tackled important things. 'The Lunatics (Have Taken Over The Asylum)' was a brilliant debut single for us. Spot-on lyrics and production. Spot-on introduction to what we wanted to say and how we wanted to sound."

To further distance themselves from the Specials they created a strange new image for the group. It wasn't quite as snappy as the standardised 2Tone uniform of pork pie hats and tonic suits, but it was very new wave. The group formed a relationship with a company called Roots Clothing who provided clothes to promote their line of attire, which consisted of white T-shirts, sweatshirts, jogging pants and moccasin shoes. Terry Hall created the symbolic Fun Boy trademark, the 'spiky pineapple' haircut that became instantly recognisable all over the world. The image couldn't have been further from that of the Specials.

"I go to this bloke in Coventry," said Terry, explaining his interesting new tresses. "He always cuts it pretty badly. When he does it, he keeps the top brushed back and then shaves the sides and back. When I get outside, I just brush the top forward again, but if he could see me walking around like this he'd probably have a nervous breakdown!"

Interest in the Fun Boy Three gathered momentum and they soon appeared all over the music press and were regular guests on the ITV's manic Saturday morning children's show *Tiswas* and its adult version *OTT*.

Ten weeks after the initial success of 'The Lunatics (Have Taken Over The Asylum)', their follow-up single was issued, a jazz number called "T'Ain't What You Do (It's The Way That You Do It)'. The track was first recorded in 1939 by Ella Fitzgerald, and was written by Melvin 'Sy' Oliver and James 'Trummy' Young, trumpeters with the world famous Tommy Dorsey Jazz Band. Terry unearthed it on an old 78rpm record and the Fun Boys decided to give it the Eighties treatment. To give the track a commercial feel they recruited Siobhan Fahey, Keren Woodward and Sarah Dallin, better known as the all-girl trio Bananarama, to perform as guest vocalists on the new record. The girls' image bore an uncanny likeness to that of the Fun Boys and the match was perfect. The girls were living above the rehearsal room used by ex-Sex Pistols members Steve Jones and Paul Cook, at that time known as the Professionals. The punks helped Bananarama record the demo 'Aie A Mwana', (sung in Swahili) which became a hit on the underground music scene. This was heard by Demon Records and they signed the group to record and release it. Terry Hall bought the single and liked the African influences on the record. When music and style magazine *The Face* ran a feature on Bananarama, Hall contacted them to collaborate on the new Fun Boy project.

"We were looking for people doing stuff like us," said Neville. "We were concentrating on vocals and so were Bananarama. They were more or less in the same boat as us."

The single was Hall's first serious attempt at playing a musical instrument, keyboards, and Neville played a xylophone, which he proudly announced 'cost £21 from Habitat!' They began to experiment with new instruments and techniques and revelled in their creative freedom. Their style was based around the driving rhythms and African influences they had worked on since their Specials days.

"T'Ain't What You Do (It's The Way That You Do It)' was finally released on February 13th 1982 and became the group's biggest hit. The track's irritatingly catchy chorus propelled it to a UK chart high of Number 4, and their success brought them three *Top Of The Pops* appearances, including one on the Christmas Day edition of the show later in the year. The B-side was the 'Funrama Theme', a chaotic instrumental celebrating the FB3/Bananarma union. The single made the Fun Boy Three a household name, catapulting them into the pop-star bracket, and it also helped to launch Bananarama on their way to pop superstardom. The partnership was reaffirmed on vinyl again just eight weeks later when the Bananarama single 'Really Saying Something' was released with the FB3 on backing vocals. This hit Number 5 and was to be the first of an impressive 42 chart hits for the girl band (in various forms) between April 1982 and the end of 2005.

After the success of both singles, the Fun Boy Three retired to work on their debut album. A lot of the embryonic material had been initially drafted during the final few months of the Specials. The eponymous *Fun Boy Three* was released by Chrysalis on March 5th 1982. The hyperactive ska beat of the Specials was replaced by moody pop music with a hint of reggae. With infectious harmonies and beats it was clear that the Fun Boy Three had fully embraced the generic sound of the Eighties. The 11-track album had an African influence combined with an excellent use of Jamaican vocal harmonies. According to Neville, each song was built up from a rhythm box machine base (a contraption that hosts drum and bass sounds) and then recorded and mixed by ex-Specials producer Dave Jordan in just one take. The Specials connection continued across the album with Dick Cuthell employed to appear on French horn and Sean Carasov, who was in charge of merchandise at Specials gigs and had helped John Bradbury at Race Records, credited as the 'man on the telephone' in the introduction to the track 'The Telephone Always Rings'. The album was issued with a free poster of the album cover and the chance to purchase Fun Boy Three signed photos and other merchandise. It received a fair amount of critical acclaim and proved popular with the public, who sent it to Number 7 in the album charts.

The Fun Boys were in rehearsals for their promotional tour of the UK, due to commence at the end of March, when an incident occurred that almost brought a premature end to the group and to the life of peace-loving Lynval Golding. As part of the promotion for the new collection, Lynval and Neville went on a night out around Coventry with the intention of distributing free copies of "T'Ain't What You Do (It's The Way That You Do It)' to customers at the Shades discotheque/night club in Coventry city centre.

After a night of well-intended socialising and well-worked publicity the two friends left for home, but as Lynval walked out of the club he was savagely attacked. The assailants left him for dead with horrendous knife wounds down the right side of his face and neck, narrowly missing his jugular vein. Lynval recalled the knife attack and its aftermath in frightening detail: "I was conscious all the way through it. I remember just staggering around, it was like walking across a tightrope, trying to balance yourself. I could feel myself going, falling over, but I just kept thinking that I had to pull myself together. At first I didn't realise how badly I'd been cut up. It wasn't until I tried to get a drink of water and couldn't hold the glass that it hit me. My nerves were dead down the right side of my body. I couldn't do a thing. I was like a baby.

"I suddenly realised that I was pretty badly injured. I was in intensive care and all I could hear was the bloke in the next bed coughing all night long. The worst thing I have ever experienced was thinking I was going to die. The morning after it all happened I just couldn't get to sleep because I had this real fear of dying. Even at six in the morning after I'd been stitched up and was starting to nod off, I just had to pull myself together and stay awake. It was just awful. I'd never been in hospital before and it totally freaked me out. When they started to ask about my religion and next of kin and everything I began to think 'Bloody hell, I am going to die!' I'd never felt anything like it before."

Lynval spent a few more days in hospital and needed to see a specialist to determine whether or not he had suffered any lasting nerve damage. It was the second time he had been the victim of an assault. The first was a year and a half previously outside the Moonlight Club when he was a part of the Specials: "If it happens a third time," said Lynval, "I'll just go down on my hands and knees and plead with that person because I just can't handle it anymore!"

Lynval's mental scars would take far longer to heal than the physical ones. Three men were eventually charged for the assault, but Lynval's bad luck continued as The Sun newspaper published his address in an article on the attack, and while he lay recumbent in his hospital bed his home was burgled. Neville was also in shock over the callous attack: "One of them tried to have a go at me as they walked into the club, but I just jumped out of the way 'cos it didn't have anything to do with me, but I didn't know that Lynval had been done over outside 'cos if I had I would have got stuck in. Once I got out I just couldn't believe it."

The Fun Boys curse struck again shortly afterwards when the planned UK tour had to be cancelled after Neville was admitted to hospital for an operation on his vocal chords. Like so many singers before and since, he'd damaged his vocal chords, and the resulting nodes had to be removed. The op rendered Neville speechless for a full nine days, after which he was instructed to rest his voice for at least two months before undertaking special voice therapy and singing lessons to ensure it didn't happen again. The band apologised through the media to the disappointed fans and promised to be on the road as soon it was possible. In fact, it would be a year before they went on the gig circuit for the first time as the Fun Boy Three.

To go some way to compensate for the lack of a tour, a new single was released on May 18th. It was a remixed version of 'The Telephone Always Rings' from the debut album, featuring the horns of Leicester's Swinging Laurels (who would later session for minor and short-lived 2Tone signing the Apollinaires) The B-side, 'The Alibi', was considered by many to be a better recording and could have easily have replaced the main track. The by now almost obligatory 12" release featured two extended versions, and two picture discs were released, each carrying a different print and limited to 10,000 copies. The single became the band's third chart hit in a row and reached Number 17. The Fun Boy Three were now one of Britain's top pop groups in their own right even though the dust from the Specials' split was still to settle. Terry Hall's new-found freedom gave him confidence and made him more amiable and approachable: "We sing about things that affect us," he said. "We make mood music, we play according to what mood we are in. Music is work, being in a group is work, but we do realise that we're lucky to have jobs, especially the ones we've got. All of what we do is a job, buts it's a joke as well. It'd be funnier still if we weren't successful, then we'd be real idiots."

The band appeared in many mags aimed at teenage girls, such as My Guy, Jackie and Just 17, and Terry Hall in particular became a reluctant pin-up. On July 31st 1982 they released another single, 'Summertime', a radical reworking of the song from the George Gershwin musical Porgy And Bess. The group's sound had progressed to a smoother style, but the African drum rhythm was still prevalent. They were also joined by an all-female backing group. The Fun Girls were 'the Sly & Robbie of British brass', Annie Whitehead on trombone (who recorded with a host of top artists and went on to front her own band), ex-Ravishing Beauties main woman Nicky Holland on keyboards (she would go on to record, write and tour with Tears For Fears, as well as recording as a solo artist) and Caroline Lavelle on cello (who would also play with artists such as Massive Attack, Radiohead and Peter Gabriel, and who continues to sing, record and tour in her own right to this day). 'Summertime' finally reached Number 18, despite the critics slamming the track as 'dour'. The video featured a Terry Hall smile, unseen in any promotional video until then! T

The band increased in size over the next few months, with more female session players – Ingrid Schroeder on backing vocals (who went on to record with acts like the Silent Poets and in her own right as a solo artist), Bethan Peters on bass guitar (who had been a member of Leeds band Delta 5, vanguards of the Rock Against Racism stable who had two bass players who played at the same time) and finally, June Miles-Kingston on drums (an assistant to director Julien Temple on the Sex Pistols flick Great Rock'n'Roll Swindle who later bought Paul Cook's drum kit and formed the Mo-Dettes, who toured with the Specials. Later she would appear with the Communards and Everything But The Girl, and currently plies her trade as a jazz singer).

With no concert tour on the horizon, the FB3 went to play live in the studio on the BBC2 cult youth programme Something Else, where they performed 'The Telephone Always Rings' and 'The Alibi' before being grilled by a host of pimply teenagers whose questions ranged from the music business to racism. From there they headed back to the studio, and for the next five months worked on their second album.

As 1983 breezed in, a taster of the new material was heard when, on January 15th,

YOU'RE WONDERING NOW

'The More I See (The Less I Believe)' was released as a single. The Fun Boy Three had previously dabbled in the field of politics with 'The Lunatics (Have Taken Over The Asylum)', and the theme for this new song was the troubles in Northern Ireland. Their blunt approach meant that it fell foul of the radio stations airplay terms and conditions and charted badly, peaking at Number 68. The only DJ who afforded the song any air time was John Peel, but it was left largely untouched by the mainstream. The accompanying video was rarely aired either, apart from on Channel 4's radical new music show *The Tube*.

The video was hardly controversial, and the subject matter in the lyrics was counteracted by a comedic angle which depicted Terry as a newsreader, with a backdrop of images of village life and Morris dancers instead of bombs and riots. Neville was the weatherman and Lynval played the part of an on-the-spot reporter. The idea for the song had stemmed from their visit to Belfast with the Specials: "I thought the whole set up was disgusting," said Terry Hall, "and the whole place was like a B-movie. Everything was so false. When we were over with the Specials we stopped in a hotel that was surrounded with barbed wire and soldiers ringing the building. At the gig they had Catholics upstairs and Protestants in the stalls. Everywhere else we played people had clapped but in Belfast they waved Union Jacks. It was definitely a bit off."

The failure of the record to get any decent airplay didn't surprise Hall: "That's to be expected in our society." he explained, "Things like Ireland get rejected while stuff like *ET* is accepted. We had to fight the record company all the way to get it released. They said 'Simon Bates wouldn't play it' so we said 'we don't write songs for Simon Bates'. We told them how much money we'd made them throughout '82 with such 'beautiful' songs and then they didn't have much choice."

As a result of the virtually blanket airtime ban, a mere 35,000 copies were sold nationwide.

Events soon returned to the 'beautiful' when at the end of January the long-awaited second album hit the market. The introduction of Talking Heads supremo David Byrne as the producer was a surprise to everyone, but it was a move that was felt necessary to help the group to progress. Byrne's production skills gave the group a far more sophisticated sound that supported their burgeoning pop career. *Waiting*, as the new album was titled, was a smoothly produced, sleek-sounding record, filled with tales of life's tribulations, told in the band's familiar blend of snide sarcasm and lyrical wit. The album delivered a potent mixture of styles and song structures, with socio-political concerns always close to the Fun Boys' lyrical hearts. It opens with the quirky foot-tapping instrumental of 'Murder She Said', the theme from the 1961 Miss Marple movie of the same name, which starred Margaret Rutherford. The track fades into the snarl and shriek of the Irish comment single 'The More I See (The Less I Believe)'. The following tune, 'Going Home', discusses the subject of institutionalised racism, with undertones of the Specials interwoven through the song:

> *"Racist politicians call for repatriation,*
> *White bureaucrats ask for black deportation -*
> *'This is my home, this is my home, this is where I'm from,*
> *Is this home? Is this home? For this is where I belong?"*

The fun and frolics of pop star life were ridiculed in the self-mocking track 'We're Having All The Fun'. The song pointed out that being a pop star wasn't all glitzy parties, photo shoots and being on *Top Of The Pops*, at least for the Fun Boys, whose life was pretty much ordinary. Terry Hall told it in song:

> *"I live in a flat, I like Manchester United,*
> *I live with my girlfriend and my cat, we're really happy,*
> *I like watching television, wearing duffle coats and moccasins,*
> *Eating crispy pancakes and having Monday haircuts, that's me done!"*

"People think being a pop star is really glamorous," said Terry at the time. "It might be for Duran Duran. I don't class myself as a pop star, that's other people that do that. I keep clear of these parties where the same people always attend. They are all idiots really. Music is my job. I love doing normal stuff, I like playing with the cat, I'm a normal bloke. We all are."

The worldwide drugs trade and the inanities of the supposed war on drugs were covered in the punchy 'Farmyard Connection' before the ghost of the Specials materializes once more in the thumping anti-marriage song 'Tunnel Of Love', the Fun Boy Three's very own version of 'Too Much Too Young':

> *"So consequences, altered cases,*
> *You tried honeymoons in far away places,*
> *But the trial separation worked,*
> *And ended up in a divorce case.*
> *You gave up your friends for a new way of life,*
> *And both ended up as ex husband and wife,*
> *There were twenty two catches when you struck your matches,*
> *And threw away your life in the tunnel of love"*

Next on the track list came 'Our Lips Are Sealed', a romantic song that tells the listener of a clandestine relationship. The subject matter of the song was close to true for Terry Hall, who co-wrote the track with Go-Gos guitarist Jane Wiedlin. When they met on the Specials' 1980 US tour whispers abounded about the amount of time the couple spent in each other's company. Jane Wiedlin tells the story: "In 1980 we were playing at the Whisky on Sunset Strip, and the Specials were in town from England, and they came to see us, and they really liked us and asked us if we would be their opening act on their tour. I met Terry Hall, the singer of the Specials, and ended up having a kind of a romance. He sent me the lyrics to 'Our Lips Are Sealed' later in the mail, and it was kind of about our relationship, because he had a girlfriend at home and all this other stuff. So it was all very dramatic. I really liked the lyrics, so I finished the lyrics and wrote the music to it, and the rest is history, his band, the Fun Boy Three, ended up recording it too. They did a really great version of it also. It was like a lot gloomier than the Go-Gos version."

Speaking years later about her relationship with Terry Hall, Wiedlin went on to add: "Like I said, he had a girlfriend in England, and they were talking about getting married and all this stuff. So I don't know how I got in the picture. And, you know, that's something that I did as a teenager, or maybe I was 20. That's something I would never do now, knowingly enter into a relationship with someone who was with someone else. I mean, it was completely screwed on my part. Although I think when people do that, you really have to look at the person who's in the relationship, and they have to take the burden of the responsibility as well. Anyways, it was one of those things with the tragic letters, 'I just can't do this.' You know, 'I'm betrothed to another.' All that kind of stuff."

The song notched a US Number 1 for the Go-Gos:

"Can you hear them, Talking about us?
Telling lies, Well that's no surprise,
Can you see them, see right through them,
They have no shield, nothing will be revealed,
It doesn't matter what they say, in the jealous games people play,
Our lips are sealed"

The Fun Boys' ability to capture a microcosm of British culture in a three-minute yarn was highlighted again with the bouncy track 'Things We Do', which teemed with observations of idiosyncratic Britain, the life of the nation captured on vinyl:

"Do middle-aged women wear cameo brooches?
Do young office lechers drive clapped out old Porsches?
Do sales girls at Tesco's wear Boots Number Seven?
Do you eat digestives at half past eleven?
Do you act your age, or the size of your shoes?
Has a man got to do, what a man's got to do?
The things we do, the things we do."

"That song," said Neville Staple, "is all about what we all do, everyday, every week. We all do those sorts of things. It's about the monotony of life and about routine, the things we do. We like to write about what we experience, I mean, we've all eaten biscuits in bed haven't we?"

The increasing tumult of life and the stress and strains it could bring are aired in the high- pitched, brass laden 'The Pressure Of Life (Takes Weight Off The Body)'.

"Still dreaming of living without problems?
Is that your idea of heaven?
You're eating but your body just rejects it,
Slow down, the death rate's one in seven,
The pressure of life takes weight off the body."

"Life can do strange things to you, stress can do strange things to you. It's well known it can kill you. It was a statement to say don't let the bastards grind you down basically," said Terry Hall. "Modern-day worries about not having a job, not having any money to clothe and feed your kids, about not having even the money for a night at the bingo. Being so stressed that you're off your food, you're spewing up. Its real life worries, not the type of life advocated by the likes of Wham!"

The closing track was a poignant number for Terry. 'Well Fancy That' was based on his true-life experiences of childhood sexual abuse, which he suffered as a 12-year-old at the hands of his school teacher. A school trip to France was turned into the worst nightmare imaginable as Terry was subjected to repeated attacks, and these continued on his return to England. In the end he suffered a nervous breakdown, and whether or not the abuse caused the depression that was set to dog him for the rest of his life remains unknown. Terry found that expressing his personal turmoil rid him of some inner demons and used the song as a cathartic experience. The lyrics perfectly spit venom as the whole sorry tale unwinds in front of the listener:

"We found the hotel, checked in to a room, and unpacked,
It had been a long day, you said let's hit the sack,
As I changed, I could feel your eyes watching me,
I crept into bed, you pretended to read,
The lights went out, I fell asleep,
Woke up with a shock, with your hands on me,
I couldn't shout, I couldn't scream,
Let me out, let me dream, I turned on to my side,
I laid there and cried on my first night in France.
Well fancy that.
You terrified me I just wanted to sleep,
Well fancy that."

It was a chilling end to the album, which on the whole was well received by the music media. It was described in the *NME* as 'Their true debut LP' and others stated 'Rude boys don't get older, just more articulate.' Despite the album being more sophisticated than the debut release, it failed to chart higher, but still reached a respectable Number 12.

Once everyone was fit and raring to go, the Fun Boys arranged a short UK tour to promote *Waiting* in early February 1983. Prior to this the band were invited to perform live on *The Tube* TV programme, and it was here that the trio, along with their female session players, strutted their stuff live for the first time. Terry Hall, it seemed, had tried to learn the guitar on his musical journey and he attempted to perform with it on a couple of the tracks, dropping chords all over the place: "God, I felt so powerful behind my axe!" Terry commented about his less than successful attempts to strum. It was however, a disjointed performance, and the trio seemed distant from each other. Terry's rhetoric was set to 'fully cynical', especially when he introduced the latest track 'Tunnel Of Love': "This song actually sold 330 copies last Tuesday."

The tour was to be the group's first live experience since they left the Specials, and they threw themselves enthusiastically into major rehearsals, only to be set back by health problems yet again. Neville and Lynval developed influenza and Terry caused alarm when physicians diagnosed him with nervous and physical exhaustion and prescribed total rest for a fortnight. Rehearsals were cancelled and manager Rick Rogers hesitatingly rescheduled the tour's debut gig for March 5th at Leeds University. 'Tunnel Of Love' was issued on February 20th and its meaty rhythm and topic of youthful marital disharmony struck a chord with the general public, who sent the record, and the band, back into the Top 10, proving that the failure of 'The More I See (The Less I Believe)' had not affected their top pop status. The B-side was entitled 'The Lunacy Legacy', an eerie acappella version of 'The Lunatics (Have Taken Over The Asylum)'.

With the group's spirits lifted by the success of the single, the long-awaited tour finally got underway. A capacity audience greeted the band at Leeds, complete with some quite obvious Specials' fans who turned up in 2Tone regalia. The gig was a fantastic accomplishment, with the early Fun Boy Three material improvised into a rhumba style. But, whether the band liked it or not, the tunes which received the loudest

130

cheers were two Specials' tracks, 'Gangsters', and their unique acapella version of 'You're Wondering Now'. Terry's new role as a pin up and teen-idol, was emphasised by the screams of hordes of girls: "I'd like to thank the girls at the front for making me feel like Simon Le Bon," he said at the encore, whilst Neville, still the embodiment of energy itself onstage, became the target of female attention as they repeatedly screamed instructions to him to expose his genitalia to them!

The Leeds gig was great morale booster for the Fun Boys, and as the tour progressed the venues were packed. While they were on the road, another track was lifted from the *Waiting* album and remixed for the next single. On April 30th 'Our Lips Are Sealed' was released. The track had technically been on standby for about three years, and after The Go-Gos' massive hit with the track it was now the Fun Boy Three's turn. The 12" version featured the compulsory extended remix and an Urdu version of the track, complete with Middle Eastern influences. The single was issued as a picture disc and a limited edition collector's item double pack which contained a free single with two live tracks, 'We're Having All The Fun' and 'Going Home', recorded at the Regal Theatre, Hitchin for the BBC's *Old Grey Whistle Test*. The programme would later be broadcast on a Thursday evening in July 1983 on BBC2 and repeated three days later on BBC1. In 1994 the broadcast became available as a live CD recording when the Windsong International label released *Fun Boy Three – Live At The Test*.

'Our Lips Are Sealed' climbed to Number 7 in the charts and earned the boys an appearance alongside former 2Tone stablemates the Beat on the 1,000th edition of *Top Of The Pops*. Back on the road, the group performed a two-night sell-out stint at the Hammersmith Palais, where Bananarama joined them onstage for a rousing version of "T'Ain't What You Do (It's The Way That You Do It)'. The tour had been an incredible accomplishment, but one blot on the landscape occurred when they appeared at Tiffany's in Glasgow. The group had just completed 'Gangsters' when an over-zealous bouncer began to punch members of the crowd for no apparent reason. Terry Hall saw the commotion, and as visions of many wrecked Specials gigs flooded back, he launched himself towards the edge of the stage, microphone in hand and burst into a tirade of abuse in the offender's direction: "This isn't the days of fuckin' skinheads now big boy!" Hall screamed.

His stirring invective sent the crowd wild in agreement, despite the presence of a few skinheads in the audience. Hall faced the crowd and pointed an accusing finger at the slightly embarrassed bouncer and continued the stream of venom: "I don't know how you put up with this? Every time we play this fuckin' city we get fuckin' bouncers who think they are God's gift. Just pack it in or we fuck off now," and then turned back to the excited multitude. "Anyway, let's try to forget about the arsehole and enjoy ourselves."

The next night was incident-free and they played a fantastic show at the Playhouse in Edinburgh. After four encores, Neville conducted the heaving crowd in a rendition of 'Happy Birthday' for Terry Hall, who almost refused to come back on stage due to embarrassment. That night he had also attempted to play the guitar again: "That was only the third time I'd played the guitar live," said Hall, "and I got all the chords wrong and I was really happy, because if I started to get it right all the time, I'd get bored. I kept getting my fingers caught in the strings! And besides, I'm selling my guitar after the tour."

Not surprisingly, Terry's guitar skills were the subject of some mirth within the band and he was often the reason for much of Lynval's onstage hysterics. The Boys all agreed that their first live experience since the Specials had been brilliant. Despite the tour's success, there was trouble in the camp. Not so much the personality clashes of the Specials, but a lethargy and apathy pervaded and it was as if the group were running out of steam. What would, startlingly, be the trio's final performance in the UK was at the 1983 Glastonbury Festival. It was noticeable, even to the untrained eye, that communication within the group was poor. They ended with a strangely clairvoyant (or was it?) rendition of the old Doors classic 'The End', Jim Morrison's ode to a doomed relationship.

The band's next task was to cross the Atlantic to try and break into the American charts with a tour. With the memories of the soul-destroying Specials US tour still fresh, the FB3 spent two months fine-tuning their set list and flew out for eight dates spread over two weeks. The Americans quickly warmed to the quirky-looking outfit, but they caused some waves when, in a televised show in San Francisco, the band burned an American flag in protest at America's invasion of Grenada. There was talk about work permits being revoked, but Terry was unrepentant: "I got this flag out and said to the crowd 'You can stick this up your arse.' We got bottled so heavily it was untrue. But it was just to wind everyone up."

Meanwhile, back in England, rumours gathered about the future of the line-up, but talk of a split was denied. After the last gig of their US excursion took place in San Francisco, and just when it seemed they were going to make a dent in the US market, Terry Hall returned home to England. Neville and Lynval jetted to Jamaica for a much-needed and well-earned holiday. On their return to the UK they discovered Terry had pulled the plug on the Fun Boy Three, but they were not overly surprised. It seemed the American tour had, after all, had a negative effect on Terry: "After the second LP, I thought that was enough but I was prepared to try and save the group by trying out some live work. Outside, the band seemed OK but inside is always dodgier. Some people said I had developed a habit of breaking groups up after doing American tours, well, the Fun Boy Three American tour I thought was really pathetic. I couldn't work out what I was doing there, corporate record-company bollocks made us do it. I just wanted to come home. In some ways I enjoyed it because I saw it as our farewell tour, but after the first gig it felt like I was going mental.

"We'd been rehearsing for eight weeks, checking every chord in every song and when we got there people were so wrecked we might as well have not bothered. One of the worst things was we played a town in New Jersey called Wildwood. It was the sort of place where all the houses have white picket fences and when we turned up it was July 4th, American Independence Day, so everything was decked out in the stars and stripes. The promoters threw this gig in when it was supposed to be our day off. God, it was terrible. It was all rednecks, beer guts and check shirts waving American flags, it wasn't the sort of thing we needed at that time."

According to Hall, he had mentioned to Neville and Lynval that he wasn't happy and wanted to talk about the group's future, but had received no response. The situation deteriorated and 'Hello' and 'Goodbye' were the only words the trio could manage to say to each other. Neville and Lynval went to ground and remained very tight-lipped about the whole Fun Boy Three experience. Terry's explanations were eerily similar to those he had given at the end of the Specials a mere two years earlier: "You see," he explained, "I thought that being in a group meant that you all took decisions. That's how we set out to be, but by the end it had got to the stage where if I said "Let's do a cover of 'Jingle Bells'", the others would have said "Oh, alright then". I remember when we played Nottingham on the Fun Boy Three's '83 Tour, I went out and bought six American flags and got to the gig early and hung them up on stage very badly. Not one person questioned them, nobody was bothered that they were playing under American flags. I was just testing what everybody else in the group was thinking. They weren't thinking at all. We couldn't do anything else but split up after that."

THE SPECIAL AKA

THE DESERTION of Terry, Neville and Lynval to form the Fun Boy Three had left Specials supremo Jerry Dammers with a bitter taste in his mouth, not least because he felt that the Specials still had far more to give. His initial reaction to the formation of the Fun Boy Three was: "They decided their own demos were good enough so why need the rest of the band?"

He obviously felt hurt and betrayed over the implosion of the Specials, his brainchild of some ten years. The change of direction in the progressive sound of *More Specials* from the original raw ska roots, was part of Jerry's masterplan for the development of the Specials: "Ska was part of the launching point for the band," he said, "not the be-all and end-all. I didn't want us to end up like Bad Manners. I wanted to refine our sound, to move on, still using the ska background as a crutch, but I didn't want us to sound like we did on the first LP, so *More Specials* was brought in and the rest, as they say, is history."

Stunned but determined to carry on, Jerry took the decision to trudge on through the post-Specials mire with Horace and Brad. To help heal the wounds, Jerry threw himself into the next single to be released on 2Tone Records, 'The Boiler'. The track was originally pencilled in for a 1981 release, and Dammers had wanted the Bodysnatchers to record it, but at the time they were on the verge of their own split. For some months previously he worked on together on the track with ex-Bodysnatchers vocalist Rhoda Dakar and bassist Nicky Summers. With Summers on bass there was no place for Horace Panter, who in his own words saw the session as a 'retaliatory statement' from Dakar and Summers towards the other girls in the Bodysnatchers who had asked them to leave. Summers had to suffer the indignity of being booted out of a band she had created! Dammers recruited John Shipley of the defunct Swinging Cats to play guitar, Dick Cuthell provided the brass, Jerry maintained the keyboards and John Bradbury forwent his traditional drumsticks and replaced them with his new drum simulation machine.

'The Boiler' (CHS TT18) hit the shops and radio stations during the first week of January 1982, under the collective group title of Rhoda and the Special AKA, Dammers' reference to the original name of the Specials. The song was to be the most controversial 2Tone release ever, its baleful soundtrack and Rhoda's bloodcurdling screams as she spoke in graphic detail about being raped, chilled the blood. It was the sort of radical record that would never be released now. Dammers reflected: "We paid a price for that, career-wise. But I thought that track was important. I never really considered the career implications of anything. It was a total fluke that the Specials ever got as famous as they did."

Not surprisingly, the track received a lot of media coverage, and reaffirmed the 2Tone tradition of highlighting controversial subjects more likely to be brushed under the carpet. The ever-confident Dakar handled the media interest with flair. She found herself inundated with requests for interviews and radio station phone-ins. On the BBC2 arts programme *Oxford Roadshow*, she gave an inspirational solo performance of the track to the instrumental version from the 7" B-side, then answered questions from the audience. Within days however, its content being deemed too graphic for daytime airplay, the majority of radio stations banned the record and placed it on an airplay blacklist. The fact that the record managed to reach a very respectable Number 35 in the charts with little or no airplay was indeed a remarkable feat.

"The first song we did really as the Special AKA was 'The Boiler'." said Rhoda "It was a song I had written in the Bodysnatchers about rape. We'd split up because the others didn't want to rock the boat politically while I did. When you're working class, you don't have much to lose. Jerry wanted to release it as he said there'd never been a song about rape before. The week of its release there was a rape trial where a guy got a slap on the wrist and people said we had timed it that way, which of course we couldn't have."

'The Boiler' and its controversial subject material still failed to distract the media's attention from Dammers and the breakup of the Specials. To escape the hordes of music journalists picking at the bones of the Specials' carcass, Jerry, Horace and Brad took up the offer to play as rhythm section for Rico Rodriguez on his short tour of small clubs in Germany. For the three Specials it was ideal, and they enjoyed the smooth run of the tour. It proved the perfect tonic and they had time to realign their relationships, although Horace's involvement with Exegesis still caused locked horns psychologically with Jerry. After the German expedition, it was agreed that Rico should record a selection of tracks from the tour and issue them via 2Tone. The first was a variation of the Stevie Wonder track 'Watcha Talking 'Bout (Say You Don't Like The Reggae Beat)' which was re-titled and rearranged to become 'Jungle Music' (CHS TT19). Released in February 1982, and billed as Rico and the Special AKA, it held the rare treat of the master musician on lead vocals. The record was bouncy, up-tempo blend of good old fashioned reggae-cum-ska. The single featured the return of some of Rico's friends from the band that toured Germany, such as Dick Cuthell, Satch Dixon (who appeared on *Man From Warieka*) Anthony Wymshurst and Island Records' percussionist Tony 'Groco' Utah, not to mention the three remaining Specials. The B-side was another tour favourite, 'Rasta Call You', and as an added bonus for the 12" version, an extra track entitled 'Easter Island' was provided as a teaser of a planned forthcoming album.

Despite 'Jungle Music' being a truly delightful, jaunty track that received generous airplay, the record failed to sell. The rapid rise of the New Romantics meant that this latest fashion, complete with its accompanying soundtrack, was splashed across the music papers, the TV and the charts, and Rico and his music were suddenly out of step. Unperturbed, the collective musicians held themselves together and returned to the studio, or rather studios, as five tracks were recorded at the Joe Gibbs Studio in Kingston, Jamaica and the remaining four at the Town House in London. The album was mixed by Dick Cuthell and Jerry Dammers and 2Tone designer Dave Storey created the distinctive African mask cover, which Storey claimed represented both the album's sound and Rico's weathered features! The album, Rico's second on 2Tone, was called *Jama* (CHS TT5008), and was crammed with legendary Jamaican stars of ska such as Tommy McCook (The Skatalites), Winston Wright (who worked exclusively with Jackie Mittoo), Ansell Collins (of Dave and Ansell Collins fame), with reggae pioneers Sly and Robbie, and legendary sessionist Felix 'Deadley Headley' Bennett and, of course, the Specials trio. The album teemed with the cream of vintage and modern ska and it is unbelievable that it made almost no impression on the public. Ignored by most, except diehard 2Tone fans, it remains a lost gem.

Armed with demos from 1981 and a sense of determination to carry on the Specials' work, Dammers single-mindedly began to form a new incarnation under the name of the

Special AKA, with former Specials tour manager Pete Hadfield in the manager's role. However, Jerry's increased annoyance at Horace Panter's involvement with the Exegesis movement, and Panter's resultant change of persona and renewed confidence, brought matters between the two once-close friends to an all-time low. Relations between the two became so strained that Horace would go on to leave the group, at the same time Dammers' health began to suffer. Times were not good: "Jerry had ideas for the third Specials album," said Horace "but not finished songs, and so recording was extremely painful. I'd got into the Exegesis programme and was unbearable to be around, acting like, 'Results now! Come on!' And Jerry was in the process of falling to bits by this stage, trying to run the record label on top of everything else. I said he should take time off but he said 'No, my frustrations have to come out in the music'. We were a nightmare to be around and it got so bad I couldn't do anything else than leave."

Rehearsals turned into a farce as Brad now lived in London and had to commute to Leamington every day, adding to the many other niggles that contributed to the sour mood: "I would arrive in good time for our sessions" recalled Horace, "Brad would arrive by half past twelve, Jerry would appear at about three o'clock and want to go for breakfast. We'd start work around five. It was unbearable, like going to a funeral every day. I tried to get the sessions stopped so that we could somehow change the atmosphere in the studio. It was to no avail, Jerry's determination to continue had turned into tunnel vision."

Soon afterwards Panter made the decision to quit the group.

Rhoda Dakar was made a full-time member, as was guitarist John Shipley (Roddy Byers was amused that he had originally taught Shipley to play guitar and now he would be the one to replace him in the newly-reshaped Specials), while Egidio Newton, a former vocalist with jazz funksters Animal Nightlife was recruited alongside Coventry soul singer Stan Campbell, who had briefly auditioned for a spot with the Selecter. To replace Horace on bass, in came Gary McManus, who had been in the Leamington Spa band the Defendants (a band on friendly terms with the original Specials from their Automatics days), and outfits such as the Rent Boys, Toucan and Three Amazing Cats. Like a dog with a bone, Dammers ignored any health worries and problems with the insurrection in the Special AKA and turned his attention back to the 2Tone record label itself. He returned to the original remit of the label, to launch new up-and-coming bands, and the first band that caught his attention was a six-piece (later up to 11-piece) funk band from Leicester called the Apollinaires.

Their debut single on 2Tone, 'The Feeling's Gone', was not the usual 2Tone fare, but a brassy, funky, very mid-Eighties tune. The record had some tenuous links to the original 2Tone, with Rhoda Dakar drafted in to guest on backing vocals, and the brass sessionists from the Swinging Laurels, (who had also just finished their brass participation on the Fun Boy Three's 'The Telephone Always Rings' single), and Dammers in the production chair. Swinging Laurels' main man John Barrow said: "The Fun Boy Three single happened at roughly the same time that we appeared with the Apollinaires, who were mates of ours from Leicester. As the Swinging Laurels we had played live with them on several occasions, including the one where Jerry Dammers came along to check them out with a view to signing them to 2Tone.We had worked out the brass lines to 'The Feeling's Gone', so when Dammers eventually signed them, they asked us to do the honours on the record. Jerry produced it at Woodbine studios in Leamington Spa. Specials' vocalist Rhoda Dakar sang backing on the track. Dammers was a perfectionist and had us playing the same phrases over and over, our lips were dragging on the floor after that session. But it was a great experience to have anything to do with 2Tone, even on a session basis."

The single was released in 12" format which featured a 'dance mix' of 'The Feeling's Gone', the B-side 'The Feeling's Back' and a bongo medley version of the main track. Unfortunately the track was not mainstream enough and suffered the same fate as Rico's release before it. Some felt that the 2Tone deal flattered the band, but it was argued that the Apollinaires were much better live and the record had failed to capture their true aura: "I was a bit pissed off the way The Apollinaires single was received," said Jerry. "I thought my production on it was okay. People automatically assumed the new stuff would be ska, ska, ska, but I was more interested in new up-and-coming bands who were dedicated and could make music that would make people dance."

Unfortunately for Jerry, the Apollinaires couldn't make people dance their way to the record stores.

Jerry's next assignment were a well known indie band called the Higsons. Their lead singer was Charlie Higson, nicknamed 'Switch', who later enjoyed much success as a novelist, comedian and comic actor, made famous by his work on the BBC's *Fast Show*, while their sax player, Terry Edwards, would go on to form the band Butterfield 8 with Madness's Mark Bedford. Like the Apollinaires, they played funk and jazz, but were a bit more heavyweight. The band had formed in Norwich in 1980 and had released five singles before the 2Tone deal came along. They released their 2Tone debut, 'Tear The Whole Thing Down' in October 1982, with Dammers at the production controls once more. Again, the single suffered exactly the same fate as the Apollinaires', with funk simply too unfashionable to make any impact at the time. Whether or not the 2Tone connection was a hindrance remains unknown, but in some respects it seems likely.

The label that brought ska to the fore suffered because of its past glories and became, in the public's eye, inextricably linked with that genre. The powers that be in the music industry regarded the 2Tone label as a spent force, and to break the mould any 2Tone release would have to be both innovative and extremely strong. Both bands released follow-up singles on 2Tone, the Apollinaires issuing 'Envy The Love' in November '82 and The Higsons unleashing the superior 'Run Me Down' in early '83, but both flopped and the two bands left the label within a year. the Apollinaires split directly afterwards while the Higsons went on to have some chart success before calling it a day in 1986. Jerry had remained true to the 2Tone doctrine of assisting young bands in the cut-throat world of the British music industry. The failure of the bands and their material saddened him, but he remained philosophical: "I guess deep down, I knew what was going to happen," he confessed. "It's a bit of a shame but I will always stand by those records and the groups."

In December 1982, the Special AKA resurfaced as a fully formed outfit. A press conference was announced to introduce the band to the media. The Special AKA were suddenly back in some kind of vogue and appeared in the staple music rags, *NME* and *Sounds*, and even in the now very infantile *Smash Hits*. Their hard-hitting, politically charged single 'War Crimes (The Crime Remains The Same)' (CHS TT23) ensured they were greeted with great interest when it was released in January 1983. At long last, as the Fun Boy Three were in and out of the charts, Dammers was back with a solid group with himself at the forefront. 'War Crimes' saw Horace Panter's final work on a Specials single, but in John Taylor's controversial promotional video, which depicted bodies being buried and shots of bombings, it was his replacement, Gary McManus, who stared solemnly at the camera. Also appearing in the video was York University student

Nick Parker, who had been brought in to play violin on the single. The record itself was not for the faint-hearted and proved Dammers' commitment to his convictions. He could have easily recorded a sure-fire pop hit, but his political and social commitment meant that Beirut bombs and the Nazi atrocities of Belsen were thrown at an unwitting public: "If you're going to put across the truth as you see it," said Dammers, "it's not necessarily the most popular thing to say. Take 'War Crimes' and its lyrics, I felt the need to tell people about the fact that what is happening in Beirut is just the same as what happened in Belsen with the Germans. I needed to say that bombs were being dropped on innocent people. I think people need to be told these things, so if you're going to say unpopular things and try and sell records, it's going to be a bit difficult if not impossible. I mean, Margaret Thatcher is supposed to be pretty popular at the moment and that doesn't say much for the population does it? 'Too Much Too Young' reached Number 1, but I didn't sit down and write it for that reason. I don't write songs to be popular."

The single was issued in a special 10" format. Due to its content, however, the single went down the same road as 'The Boiler', into the blacklist bin and, apart from John Peel, received little airplay. The heavy promotion it received failed to encourage sales and its highest chart place was Number 84. Amazingly, in a move that left Dammers dumbstruck, it was voted the best single of 1983 by former Special Terry Hall in a celebrity poll.

"I really don't know how to take that." was all Jerry could manage to say on the matter.

The Special AKA's dour image and serious approach to life caught the attention of the readers of *Smash Hits* magazine whose end of year poll voted the band 'The Most Miserable Group Of The Year'. That said, any magazine that highly values information on the colour of pop stars' underpants is probably not to be taken seriously, at least for those over the age of 11.

The political and social awareness of the original Specials had come of age within the Special AKA, who possessed a much darker, mysterious edge most prevalent in their lyrics, always controversial and close to the bone. They had a knack of making people feel uneasy.

After 'War Crimes' the group entered the studio to complete their album. As with *More Specials*, which had been a drawn out nightmare, Jerry's tunnel vision for perfection tested the group members to the limit, with re-recordings, overdubs and repetition of lines worked over and over until they were perfect. Some of the work they managed to complete saw the light of day in September 1983 when the double A-side of 'Racist Friend'/'Bright Lights' (CHS TT25) was launched. On the list of credits people were surprised to see the name of Roddy Radiation on guitar for 'Racist Friend'. Any vain hopes that there had been a reconciliation were dashed when it was made clear that Roddy appeared by default, as his part had been recorded as part of an old Specials demo from 1981. It was released in 7" and 12" formats and also, for the first time on the 2Tone label, a picture disc with the front cover of the single pressed into clear vinyl with lyrics on the reverse.

The lyrics behind 'Racist Friend' occurred to Dammers as the original Specials made the big time. He had realised that he had become a magnet for hangers-on who maintained that they were his friends: "I woke up one day to the fact that I needed to sort out my life drastically," said Jerry. "I knew that I'd attracted hangers-on, but so much was going on around me that in the end I was devoting less time to the people who meant the most to me. I decided to get rid of those who had racist tendencies for a start, so I opened my address book and begun to scribble names out. It was what I needed to do and I felt much better as a result. You've got to make a stand against racism in any form."

The track 'Bright Lights' criticised the way that bands like Wham! and Duran Duran portrayed life as one big party in London. The Special AKA warned that the streets were not all paved with gold, and attempted to deter the many young people who headed for the capital each year in search of fame and fortune, a good number of whom ended up living on the streets. The song was also a sideways swipe at singer Stan Campbell, who was impatient with the lack of success in the group. He found life in the Special AKA tough going, as he had originally joined in light of the 2Tone legacy and things were not going as he had planned: "I thought it would be great stuff," said the moody Campbell, seen by some as a black Terry Hall. "Get on the road, have fun, go to parties and make lots of money. Y'know, you don't think about any problems you might have in the studio and things like that. I thought it was going to be on the road to America, Europe, having hit songs because I was working with this guy who wrote 'Too Much Too Young' and 'Ghost Town', this guy who started the whole 2Tone thing. The whole concept was 'Oh, I'll join the Specials 'cos they're politically motivated' and I was an out-of-work musician, and to me it looked like a good move."

'Bright Lights' also covered the Colin Roach controversy. Colin was a young black man who died in police custody from a gunshot wound received at Stoke Newington police station in 1983. The song lyrics 'demanding that Colin Roach's family demand an enquiry' hoped to raise awareness of the facts. The police claimed that Roach committed suicide, but many believed that Roach was murdered by the police. The police surgeon who examined Roach's body said that the body's position was inconsistent with suicide. The shotgun he was killed with didn't fit into the sports bag that Roach had with him; no fibres from the bag were found on the gun, and no oil from the gun was found in the bag. Medical experts stated that when a shotgun is used for suicide the recoil would damage or break the trigger thumb and no injury was found on Roach's hand. It was also shown that a gun's recoil would normally cause it to hit a wall or floor very hard, but no marks were found. Two police officers who were believed to have been present at the police station claimed not to have been there, and there were inconsistencies in the records for who was present. On the other side of the argument, there were no marks on Roach's mouth consistent with a gun being forced into it. Roach's death incited protests and demands for an independent public inquiry, and the Special AKA added their weight to the campaign.

The single spent three weeks in the chart and peaked at a disappointing Number 60, slipping by almost completely unnoticed by the record-buying public, their minds awash with glitzy pop and New Romantic ideals. People weren't interested in life's darker side, they were too busy 'having fun on the dole' as advocated by George Michael and Wham!

Elsewhere, as well as being the musical backbone for the Special AKA, drummer John Bradbury had his musical fingers in other pies. He turned his hand to more production work, and as a sideline to the Special AKA, he formed a soul revue band called JB's Allstars, which at its height contained 15 members. Its main line up consisted of the irrepressible Brad on drums, Dee Sharp on vocals, Mark Hughes on harmonica, Jason Votier on trumpet, Robert Awahi on guitar, Steve Nieve (from Elvis Costello's backing band the Attractions) on keyboards, and 'Big' George Webley on bass. Webley went on to become a session musician, record producer, songwriter, award-winning broadcaster and freelance journalist, working with many household and international names. His claims to fame are numerous, but the ones that stand out are that he composed the theme tune to the TV programme *Have I Got News For You* and arranged, produced and recorded a version of 'Handbags and Gladrags' for the theme to the hit TV series *The Office*. With Rick Rogers as manager and Dave Storey on board to sort out the artwork, the group were signed by RCA Victor and in October 1983 released 'One Minute Every Hour', a cover of the 1973 northern soul classic by John Miles. It was good quality tuneful soul, with a track composed by Brad called 'Theme From 903' as the B-side. The single made it to Number 78 in the UK charts, but the project was more a labour of love for Bradbury and should not be measured by much money it made. Brad spread himself between his own creation and the Special AKA for a further two years.

No sooner had he completed studio work with the Allstars than he found himself back there again for work on the new Special AKA album, which was fast becoming Dammers' own personal albatross. The General's overarching desire for flawlessness was beginning to alienate those around him, which in turn increased the pressure upon himself: "Recording that album was the final madness," recalled Rhoda Dakar. "Two whole years stuck in the studio overdubbing, singing the same thing 50 times in a row. I think that production is a skill best not learned in a 24-track studio. On my last visit I was sitting on the floor of the vocal booth, sobbing. A cab was called for me. Going back in a studio was something that filled me with horror for a very long time."

Simply getting everyone into the studio at the same time proved extremely difficult because band members were spread around London, Coventry and Leicester. Stan Campbell tweaked the unrest up a notch with his daily threats to quit the group if any situations arose that he could not handle. The fact the album was ever finished was a miracle and despite the shared lead vocals Rhoda Dakar reckoned she only met the temperamental Campbell a handful of times: "Stan had the wrong approach," she said, "He hated hold-ups in the studio, and if we had any problems he would just moan and groan. He expected instant success and loads of money but the rest of us knew it wasn't going to be like that. We were committed to that at the beginning, Jerry more than anyone, but Stan did not make life easy."

Chrysalis Records executives had started to drum their fingers on desktops and check their watches as the completed album failed to materialise. Costs on the record began to soar and the recordings that had already been released far from offset any outlay. Company alarm bells were ringing. While Jerry plodded on with the project, and tried to hold the band together, 2Tone's parent company, Chrysalis, opted to compile an album of 2Tone tracks called *This Are TwoTone* (CHR TT5007) in order to recoup some of their money. Despite a concerted promotional push by Chrysalis to refresh the memory of the nation, and the addition of a free poster of the bands to tempt the public, the plan was unsuccessful and the album only creaked to Number 51 in the charts. It was a decent enough collection but the diehards were the only people interested in purchasing a copy. To many, the lack of success with the compilation album and the 2Tone label's recent run of misses were seen as the label's final death throes, and the Special AKA were the final mast of the sinking ship visible above the waves.

Dammers remained unflustered, he was originally going to release the track 'Lonely Crowd' as a follow up to 'Racist Friend', but instead he had composed a tune that could restore the bands fortunes, all he needed was some lyrics. He was due to attend a concert at Alexandra Palace in London, organised by the Anti-Apartheid Movement to celebrate the 65th birthday of black South African Nelson Rolihlahla Mandela, jailed as a terrorist by the South African Government because of his fight against Apartheid. Eager to learn more about this man and his plight, Jerry was set on the road towards his finest moment.

John Bradbury, meanwhile, was back working intensively with his JB's Allstars. 1984 saw the meaty, beaty ensemble release a further three soul boomers on the RCA Victor label. The first on February 11th was a great cover of the Mel and Tim soul classic 'Backfield In Motion' backed by Brad's latest instrumental composition 'Theme From A Beam'. The single did very well and received a vast amount of airplay, managing to reach a credible Number 48 and giving Brad his own, individual chart hit. The follow up was 'Sign On The Dotted Line', with the B-side yet another Brad instrumental 'And He Was Gone', but this only scraped to Number 97. The band also appeared on a special 'dance' edition of Channel 4's innovative rock/pop programme *The Tube* with the band expanded to 15 members. Along with Brad, bassist 'Big' George Webley, keyboardist Seamus Beaghan, pianist Wix, guitarists Chris Parks and Earl Grey Pointer, lead vocalist Drew Barfield, singers Bill Hurley and Dee Sharpe, backing vocalists Molly and Polly Jackson and brass section the Rumour Horns all crammed on to the stage and performed a high-octane ten-minute medley of 'One Minute Every Hour', 'Sign On The Dotted Line' and 'Backfield In Motion'. It was a fantastic display from this underrated band.

Jerry Dammers returned from his jaunt to celebrate Nelson Mandela's 65th birthday with a purpose. To fit the tune he had already composed, he created lyrics designed to highlight Mandela's predicament. The end result would prove to be his magnum opus, and also reunite him with original Specials' producer Elvis Costello.

"I went to a concert to celebrate Mandela's 65th brthday," said Jerry, "and I realised I didn't know much about him. Subsequently I got the idea for the lyrics, I had no idea how much impact it would have, it was just a song to me. Ironically, I'd been reduced to begging the band to sing the track, as I had been before with 'Ghost Town'. I'd lost any influence over the band because they'd lost respect for me, so it was helpful to get Elvis Costello back in. I'd been producing everything lately it seemed and I was getting a bit stale. I needed a new outlook on things and since Elvis did a good job with the first Specials LP, I thought why not? So he did, and I was pleased as a result."

Costello was eager to help his friend out: "The Special AKA were taking so long in the studio that I got called in to produce 'Nelson Mandela'. It was important Jerry got the track out so that people could think about the issue. He had a definite idea of the music in his head, but it was somehow elusive, which is why I think it took so long for him to record anything. He was always trying to capture the feeling he wanted which he'd hear on other records."

Rhoda Dakar saw the situation very differently from Costello: "There was a whiff of mental illness in the air with the Special AKA. We were spending five days a week in the studio, in the dark. Singing is connected to your mental state, so when you've been made to do something over and over from noon 'til 5am...People interpreted that as you giving up. We were all in a catatonic heap, babbling, it was a nightmare."

No matter how dark and complicated the studio atmosphere was, Dammers persuaded the other sceptical band members to record the track. With Costello on

140

board, the song was eventually recorded in only four days, a remarkable feat for anyone, never mind the Special AKA!

'Nelson Mandela' (CHS TT26) reunited Jerry and Co. with a number of old friends, and they were joined on the single by the former Special, and now ex-Fun Boy, Lynval Golding. Dave Wakeling and Ranking Roger, previously of the Beat and now in the band General Public also featured, as did Afrodiziak, an all-female trio of session singers who at that time consisted of Claudia Fontaine, Naomi Thompson and Soul II Soul's Caron Wheeler (who had just guested on Madness's 'Michael Caine'), providing the backing vocals. Brass accompaniment came from former Specials legend Dick Cuthell on trumpet, and three new faces; Andy Aderinto (sax), Dave Heath (flute) and Paul Speare (penny whistle). The uptempo track bristled with fervent energy and followed in the Specials' tradition of social comment allied to great dance beats. The record was the first of its kind and highlighted Mandela's plight to a nation mostly ignorant of his situation, opening up the Mandela story to the world at large. Anti-Apartheid groups adopted the track as an anthem, and the snowball effect was monumental, ensuring 'Nelson Mandela' would become a classic.

Although the track did not secure Mandela's eventual release, it ignited the global fuse that eventually led to the events which finally saw him released from captivity after 27 years. The record, backed by 'Break Down The Door', hit the shops in March 1984 and the jubilant, almost celebratory, bouncy melody made sure that the radio stations would sit up, listen, and play the single. Radio 1 took the track to their hearts, and DJ Simon Bates declared the single Record Of The Week. The flood of airtime propelled the song to reach Number 9 in the charts, which enabled the group to perform on *Top Of The Pops* for the first time in three years. Stan Campbell had already made his daily threats to quit a reality and had to be persuaded to briefly rejoin and finally get the taste of commercial success that he had craved so badly.

The momentum that followed the 'Nelson Mandela' release was immense. Dammers was highly sought after by the media and he appeared on the distinguished ITV documentary series *World In Action* to talk about Mandela's situation and the work of the Anti Apartheid Movement. The record caused a huge panic in South Africa, and the Chrysalis office there contacted its London headquarters to tell them not to send any copies over as they were liable to be prosecuted. On hearing of the release, PW Botha and his racist government immediately had it banned, but this did not stop it from becoming an anthem for thousands of black Africans who chanted it on the streets of Soweto and other shanty towns.

In April, the Special AKA made what was their one and only live appearance on *The Tube*. For ten minutes at the end of the show, 'Nelson Mandela' was performed on a packed stage by all the individuals on the record, bar Stan Campbell who had finally departed, leaving Elvis Costello to sing lead vocals with zest.

In August, after two years of work, the long-awaited album from the Special AKA was unleashed. The aptly titled *In The Studio* (CHS TT5008) was a treasure trove of jazz, soul and reggae and was quite an eye-opener. The amount of cash spent on the album by a nervous Chrysalis was in the region of half a million pounds, which made it the most expensive album in history. They eagerly awaited the chance to stick their claws into it – after so much time and money being spent on recording it, they wondered what could be so 'special' about it – but were silenced by the excellent production quality and the equally excellent music. It was a pity that five of the ten tracks included were already known as 7" releases and a sixth single was soon to be released in the shape of '(What I Like Most About You Is Your) Girlfriend'.

The album had links to the original 2Tone, recorded as it was at John 'Ghost Town' Rivers' Woodbine Studios in Leamington Spa, being produced by Dammers and Dick Cuthell, including appearances from Rico Rodriguez, Horace Panter and Roddy Radiation, and having artwork by stalwarts Chalkie Davies and Carole Starr. It was full of gloomy but brilliant and thought-provoking material. The music retained some of the atmosphere of the torturous recording sessions that had brought it forth, and the anguish suffered in the studio by its creators. The collection began life with the anti-celebrity 'Bright Lights':

> *"I thought I might move down to London Town,*
> *I could get in a band, have fun all the year round,*
> *The living down there must be pretty easy,*
> *I could rip up my jeans deliberately,*
> *The streets really must be paved with gold,*
> *If everybody goes WHAM! and has fun on the dole,*
> *Imagine what it would be like for me,*
> *I've seen the pictures in the magazines."*

This was followed up by a Dammers/John Shipley creation 'Lonely Crowd', originally intended as a single release, that depicted the hollow falseness of night clubs and their posing patrons, with direct lyrics and an eerie piano intro:

> *"Put out my cigarette and switch off the TV set,*
> *This is not the life for me, I'm going out tonight,*
> *Put on my trendy clothes and head for where the in crowd goes,*
> *Might find true love who knows, Tonight might be the night,*
> *Will you be there? Will you see me?*
> *In the lonely crowd,*
> *I can hear you, can you hear me? Everybody's talking so loud,*
> *I want some freedom from the tedium,*
> *I've got no where to go tonight,*
> *I'm in the lonely crowd."*

On the tail of that track came 'Girlfriend', with the rarity of Jerry Dammers on lead vocals, complete with hilarious falsetto voice. It is a wickedly comic track, soaked in jazz, covered live by Elvis Costello later in the year and later appearing on his 2004 album *Goodbye Cruel World – Deluxe Edition*:

> *"Hello and how are you, and how do you do?*
> *And who is that girl standing right next to you?*
> *And what is her name, and what does she do?*
> *I'm looking at her, while I'm talking to you,*
> *Her love must be sweeter than candy,*
> *Must be stronger than brandy,*
> *Why does she like you not me?*
> *Can I buy you a drink, you seem a decent chap,*
> *I'm friendly to your face but behind your back,*
> *What I like most about you is your girlfriend, it's true"*

The quirky, claustrophobic 'Housebound' was next on the list. With its disconcerting rhythms and oddball ambience, it was aimed, by Dammers, at Terry Hall, who had felt agoraphobic since the demise of the Specials and Fun Boy Three. He had felt unable to leave his home, avoiding the limelight as paranoia of being recognised and mania set in:

> *"Looking at the world, through lace curtains,*
> *Would they like you out there? You're not certain,*
> *Scared of walking down the street,*
> *You never know who you might meet,*
> *Or who you might bump into,*
> *They're out there waiting for you, Housebound,*
> *You daren't go out, Because you're housebound,*
> *You don't want to go out, Because you're housebound,*
> *There's no way out, Because you're housebound,*
> *You daren't go out!"*

The first side of the album closed with the jaunty 'Night On The Tiles', another Dammers/Shipley composition, which featured Lynval Golding on backing vocals. Its content encompasses a fly on the wall look at an overbearing and controlling relationship:

> *"This is a life sentence, what did you expect?*
> *What you want is not always quite what you're gonna get.*
> *You say you'll never love me, so you can't lock me away,*
> *I promise I'll come back, let me go for just one day,*
> *Free me from this prison, just for a while,*
> *Let me out if only for one night on the tiles,*
> *You hold the key, please don't throw it away,*
> *I promise to come back, let me out for just one day."*

The second side begins in style with the anthemic 'Nelson Mandela', Dammers' tribute to the caged ANC freedom campaigner, which bursts forth and showcases social and political comment in music at its finest:

> *"Twenty-one years in captivity, his shoes too small to fit his feet,*
> *His body abused but his mind is still free,*
> *Are you so blind that you cannot see,*
> *I say free Nelson Mandela, I'm begging you,*
> *Free Nelson Mandela,*
> *He pleaded the causes of the ANC,*
> *Only one man in a large army,*
> *Are you so blind that you cannot see,*
> *Are you so deaf that you cannot hear his plea,*
> *Free Nelson Mandela, I'm begging you,*
> *Free Nelson Mandela."*

The political and social themes feature heavily in the next track, the militant and roughly Middle Eastern-sounding 'War Crimes', which, as mentioned previously, was the

Special AKA's debut single. The anti-war song, with its cold rhythms and emotional lyrics, went for the listener's throat:

> *"Bombs to settle arguments, the order of the boot,*
> *Can you hear them crying in the rubble of Beirut?*
> *I can still see people dying, now who takes the blame?*
> *The numbers are different, the crime is still the same,*
> *From the graves of Belsen, where the innocent were burned,*
> *To the genocide in Beirut, Israel was nothing learned?*
> *I can still hear people crying, now who takes the blame?*
> *The numbers are different, the crime is still the same."*

Another single, and the drumbeats of 'Racist Friend', Dammers' tale of taking a personal stance against racism, even against friends and family:

> *"If you have a racist friend,*
> *Now is the time, now is the time for your friendship to end,*
> *Be it your best friend, Or any other,*
> *Is it your husband or your father or your mother?*
> *Tell them to change their views, or change their friends,*
> *Now is the time, now is the time, for your friendship to end,*
> *So if you know a racist who thinks he is your friend,*
> *Now is the time, now is the time for your friendship to end,*
> *Call yourself my friend?*
> *Now is the time to make up your mind, don't try to pretend,*
> *Be it your sister, be it your brother,*
> *Be it your cousin or your uncle or your lover."*

Subsequently there is 'Alcohol', a tremendously well-crafted song that was written about Jerry's experiences with drink and about friends' drug habits and the damage it causes: "'Alcohol' is straight from the heart," said Dammers. "I saw what drink did to people, especially at first hand when the Specials were on the road. It made me very ill at one time, I was skipping meals but the drinking never stopped."

> *"An icy wind blows through the door,*
> *You feel like you've been here before,*
> *You tremble and you start to sweat,*
> *The symptoms of withdrawal,*
> *Alcohol.*
> *Why do you do it?*
> *Why do you keep beating me?*
> *You give some people a real good time,*
> *But you cause some untold misery,*
> *Heroin.*
> *Why do you do it?*
> *I don't like what I've seen,*
> *You promise someone a real good time,*
> *And then you take them from their family,*

> *You tremble and you start to sweat,*
> *You don't want to withdraw,*
> *And when your flesh begins to crawl,*
> *You'd rather not be here at all."*

The album closes with the soul flavours, and ambiguous (possibly autobiographical?) lyrics of the song 'Break Down The Door', which was the B-side of the 'Nelson Mandela' single:

> *"For too long, I have lived in a trap built of lies,*
> *But one day I'm gonna break out because at last I've realised,*
> *Break down the door of the trap that you're in,*
> *You've got to breakout before the four walls have closed in,*
> *Break down the door,*
> *Do it you've gotta,*
> *You've gotta do what?*
> *You've gotta do what you wanna,*
> *You've gotta get out,*
> *But you can't because you're up to your neck,*
> *And there's no turning back so you try to forget,*
> *The cracks have started to appear,*
> *You want to get away,*
> *Before the fun turns into tears,*
> *You wish that you could,*
> *Break down the door."*

On *In The Studio* Dammers' world view had grown darker, and his lyrics reflected this. The humour and sarcasm of the Specials' lyrics was replaced with a black and white condemnation of the world's ills. 'Nelson Mandela' comes as something of a shock smack-bang in the middle of the set, as its glorious melody and jubilant atmosphere stand out so starkly against the other intense and shady songs. The contrast between 'Nelson Mandela' and 'War Crimes' directly after was, like everything else on the album, a deliberate ploy. At a time when Wham!, Frankie Goes to Hollywood, Spandau Ballet and Duran Duran reigned with empty optimism, *In the Studio* offered something distinctly different, which explains its popularity even to this day. The album reached a respectable Number 36 in the charts, but it had not done as well as Chrysalis or the Special AKA needed it to, and sales in no way covered the production costs. Specials' photographer Chalkie Davies said: "'Nelson Mandela' was a hit, and the third album was an incredible record, but it arrived four years after the second album, which is more like Led Zeppelin behaviour. Timing is everything in Britain and basically, it was too late. 2Tone's influence was swiftly curtailed: Madness had become a pop band, albeit a fantastic one, the Beat had split up and Jerry wanted to move on musically. By that time, people weren't listening because they had moved on themselves."

After the original band split, Jerry still had contractual duties to fulfil for Chrysalis, who had wanted five albums from him, but rather than shelve *In The Studio* and rework the concept of the band to accommodate live appearances, he traipsed on. As the months went by and the finances clocked up, he must have realised the futility of it all. He was suffering ill-health, relationships with the other band members were at rock bottom and they had doubts about the future of what was really only a studio band: "I don't want to go through the experience that I had with *In The Studio* ever again," said Jerry. "I was glad to see it completed and out but it was such a nightmare period. It was a nightmare band created in a nightmare situation."

Whilst being hand in glove with Jerry on the album, Brad was also with his Allstars and their last release of the year, the excellent 'Ready, Willing And Able' which featured guest vocalist Shezwae Powell from California (who would later record for Pete Waterman and went on to become an actress). The B-side was entitled 'Chance Meeting' and the single was produced entirely by Brad (prior to this, production duties had been handled by the team of Willi Morrison and Ian Guenther) but unfortunately the soul genre was by now exclusively underground on the music circuit and the record failed to chart entirely.

In a further attempt to recover finances, Chrysalis issued yet another album track as a single, the Jerry Dammers vocal track '(What I Like Most About You Is Your) Girlfriend' (CHS TT27). The record company were hoping that the success of 'Nelson Mandela' and some of the critical acclaim afforded to *In The Studio* might mean that this tongue-in-cheek, uptempo, jazz tune would become a hit. Chrysalis pulled out all the stops to promote the single and released the customary 12" extended version that included a Rhoda Dakar rap-style piece, 'Can't Get A Break', on the B-side, and which came with a free poster of Dammers clad in a space suit, a still taken from the bizarre promo video. Also issued was a limited edition double pack, with a free single of the 'War Crimes' track. To complete the collection there was the 'Girlfriend' picture disc. Despite a good promotional push by Chrysalis, 'Girlfriend' spent five weeks on the UK chart, but only reached a high of 51, hardly a total failure but certainly not the success that Chrysalis had hoped for. The lack of live work was the group's undoing, as they weren't in the public eye enough. To try and compensate, they made a number of TV appearances on shows like *Switch*, and videotaped a performance that was shown on *Black On Black*, former Selecter singer turned TV presenter Pauline Black's flagship programme, where the political stance of the Special AKA was used to initiate a studio debate amongst the audience.

A Channel 4 programme entitled *The Special AKA – Play At Home* was an hour-long feature devoted to the band which consisted of videos from the songs on the album (scenes of mass burials and of drugs being injected were the lowlights here, but necessary) alongside interviews with band members, Brad being particularly humorous, and shots of actual studio rehearsals. One of these practices, in which the whole band were together, even Stan Campbell, was their first ever attempt at the song 'Nelson Mandela'. Jerry stared nervously into the camera and said: "Please remember, it's only a rehearsal!"

All the Special AKA footage taken from *Play At Home* was made available to the public through a video release called *The Special AKA – On Film* (Chrysalis CVIM15). All the album and 7" tracks were included, except for 'Night On The Tiles'. The band seem to have taken a leaf out of Madness's book by making low-budget promo videos featuring some hilarious moments, the best being from the 'Girlfriend' video where Dammers plays an alien who arrives on Earth in what can only be described as a *Blue Peter* style papier-maché spaceship (I suppose the album had emptied the coffers!). The image of Dammers in his sparkling space suit and Roman sandals is side-splitting material and definitely a sight to behold.

1985 arrived and the band were to release a track called 'You Can't Take Love

Seriously', but Chrysalis decided enough was enough and, along with other tracks 'Female Chauvinist Pig' and 'Photo Love' it never materialised. *In The Studio* had used up all the funds intended to finance the further three albums the record company had expected from the Specials camp. With Stan Campbell gone, Jerry's search for a permanent replacement had come to nought and shortly afterwards the Special AKA simply disappeared into vinyl and public obscurity without ever officially or openly declaring that they had ceased to be. Reflecting on Special AKA life, Jerry said: "Because we had such a big debt at the end of it all, I couldn't get any new musicians involved, because any money would have gone straight to the record company. That's when I got involved in Artists Against Apartheid."

So, to take his mind off all things studio, and get off the treadmill and depression of being in the Special AKA, Jerry set out to become more involved with the Anti-Apartheid Movement's British contingent. The organisation was originally founded in America by Steve Van Zandt, guitarist in Bruce Springsteen's E-Street Band who left at the height of their success to travel to South Africa to research his next record. He was interested in South Africa because he had read that the Apartheid system was actually modelled on America's system of Indian reservations, an issue that was his major passion. While in South Africa, he was distressed by a place called Sun City, a gambling resort located in a Bantustan, black African homeland, which was territory set aside for black inhabitants of South Africa as part of the policy of Apartheid. Artists Against Apartheid UK was formed by home-grown artists, and chapters appeared in countries all over the world.

After attending the Mandela 65th birthday concert, Dammers had found a new project he could get his teeth into. He then pulled off a massive coup when he staged a huge event on Clapham Common. The origins of the concert dated back two years, to 1984, with the formation in Britain of Artists Against Apartheid. The organisers, Jerry Dammers and Dali Tambo, son of African National Congress (ANC) main man Oliver Tambo, invited a host of artists to take part in a Freedom Festival on Clapham Common, in London. The concert was preceded by a march to the Common which was attended by 100,000 people representative of most sections of British society. At the height of the afternoon, 250,000 were gathered to listen to the artists express their solidarity with the people of Namibia and South Africa through their words and music, and to listen to representatives of the ANC, SWAPO and the British Anti-Apartheid Movement. The Freedom Festival took place shortly after a state of emergency was imposed in South Africa. It was a new high point in mobilising public opinion in Britain. In spite of this, it was not a financial success. The Anti-Apartheid Movement, always short of funds, lost £80,000. It was only saved from bankruptcy by an emergency appeal, and was therefore hampered at a time when maximum activity was required. For a couple of years, throughout the Anti-Apartheid campaign, Dammers became an unpaid charity worker. This work put his musical creativity on the back burner, but he saw the ultimate realisation of the 2Tone dream that day in South London: "I organised several Artists Against Apartheid events with the help of the Anti-Apartheid Movement. These culminated in a huge concert of a quarter of a million people on Clapham Common featuring Peter Gabriel, Sting, Boy George, Hugh Masekela, Maxi Priest and many more."

As for some of the Special AKA players who were not members of the original Specials, Stan Campbell eventually signed to the WEA label as a solo artist, where he released a critically acclaimed self-titled soul/jazz-orientated album and the singles

'Crawfish' and 'Years Gone By', which climbed to Number 65 in the charts, but he never achieved the success and fame he craved. His career soon faltered and the failure of the album and singles saw the start of a downward spiral. His mental health began to take a turn for the worse and whilst in London, he was involved in a couple of sexual harassment cases. He returned to Coventry where he began to sleep rough. He became a well-known, if quirky, character around the town, and told anyone who wanted to listen (or didn't want to listen) that he was once in the Specials, becoming the unfortunate butt of many a local joke in the process.

He was arrested for his involvement in a sex crime against a woman he had followed around, and was later convicted of the kidnap and sexual assault of a young girl he had met in a newsagent's. He followed her, abducted her, took her down to a railway line and attempted to rape her but she managed to get away. The police had a big dossier on Campbell, who for some reason had developed an underlying hatred of women. Stan was sent to a secure psychiatric hospital for an indefinite period, but it is rumoured that he was subsequently released. Stan may have never set the world alight, but he did grace the 2Tone label and appeared on the historic 'Nelson Mandela' single. His is a sorry tale of a man who tried to achieve his 15 minutes of fame, but was ultimately left with a life of sadness.

Gary McManus tinkered around in the music business and then became a house husband to his two young children Finn and Ry. It came as a massive shock to hear of his sad and untimely death on February 10th 1999 from peritonitis due to a perforated bowel at the early age of 44. His legacy in the music world would live on through the Special AKA association and simply because he also played on 'Nelson Mandela'. On hearing of his death, Mandela himself sent Gary's partner Deanne a fax thanking Gary for his 'unique contribution to the international campaign for the release of South African political prisoners.' His funeral was a fantastic celebration of his life as Deanne told the News Of The World: "We all wanted to decorate Gary's coffin ourselves so that it reflected his bright, colourful character. So it was delivered to the family home and sat on our coffee table for five days. We covered his coffin with the Specials' magazine covers, newspaper cuttings, Newcastle United memorabilia (Gary was a big fan), family photos, drawings and paintings. On the day of the funeral, I saw the coffin covered in our handiwork as a symbol of our love for Gary. When it arrived at the church everyone gathered around reminiscing. On the end of the coffin was an 'Access All Areas' backstage pass to Gary's 'Last Gig' which I designed to complement his brother Kevin's 'End-of-tour' invites to the party after the funeral. The journey home in the funeral car was filled with shrieks of delight as the children pretended to be pop stars. Their enthusiasm continued through the party afterwards and was a great leveller, very life-affirming. We all felt that Gary, ever the party lover, was enjoying it all, too, somewhere."

John Shipley continued to work with local musicians in Coventry. He still writes and records, and at the time of writing is rumoured to be back with his old friends from the Swinging Cats.

Vocalist Egidio Newton would go on to dramatically exploit her talents, being both socially and politically engaged as an artist, musician and photographer. She was the founder and director of the children's interactive music company Young Music Explorers, which offers music workshops for children. She also worked in creative partnerships with schools, nurseries and local community projects in London where she delivered 'creative thinking packages' and music/arts workshops designed to 'inspire children to aspire', and encourage creative growth. She became a passionate children's champion, which led her to work for their human rights. As well as being an ex-member of Animal Nightlife, Big Balls and Great White Idiot, Egidio has worked with many artists including Chrissie Hynde, Captain Sensible, the Pogues' Shane McGowan, Gil Scott-Heron, lovers-rocker Dennis Bovell, Amii Stewart, political satirist Mark Thomas and the late Caron Keating. She has worked as a music programmer and researcher/reporter for World and European music on Radio Five, and her diverse career has also included work as an actress, including playing the lead role in the acclaimed *Mass Carib*, the highly-praised play by Felix Cross that told the story of the Europeans in the Caribbean slave trade.

She is also now a renowned photographer whose portfolio includes images of the Reverend Jessie Jackson, singer Kelis, black historian Dr Tony Martin, designer Jeff Banks and actor Jude Law to name but a few. Her political aspirations have continued as she successfully created an Albanian Shoe Project for Romany Children denied access to education and school due to not owning shoes, and was also involved in the outer reaches of Artists Against Apartheid. Of late she has been involved in the promotion of God's Golden Acre, a charity set up to support African children who have been orphaned or abandoned through AIDS/HIV or violence. Also, she is involved in the theatrical dance company the Young Zulu Warriors, a group of teenagers from Kwa-Zulu Natal, South Africa, who have been raised by God's Golden Acre and who tour the world performing a cultural showcase of vibrant traditional African music and dance, consisting of foot-stomping performances suitable for all ages. She is due to release a solo album and mount an exhibition of her photographic work.

Meanwhile Rhoda Dakar, scarred from her Special AKA studio experiences, did her utmost to stay clear of recording. Her thoughts on her experiences with the Special AKA and the *In The Studio* debacle have already been documented. Unlike others who were involved however, evidence of her moment in history with the 'Nelson Mandela' track seems to have been erased and her input remains uncredited: "Well, on 'Mandela', originally, I wrote a verse, which you can see on the *Play At Home* TV show we did. The lyrics were changed in the studio but there's only a couple of lines left, I think."

In 1985-86 she resurfaced with the band Happy House, which featured Leicester musicians Gaz Birtles (now promoter at the Donkey venue in Leicester), Phil Birtles and John Barrow of the Swinging Laurels. They performed live on a number of occasions and recorded the track 'The Shelter' with Culture Club producer Steve Levine, but unfortunately the record was never released. She lay low for a while before her next vinyl appearance in 1993, on Palm Skin Productions' track 'Sunlight In The Garden'/'In A Silent Way', which was based on a 1938 poem by British poet and playwright Louis MacNeice. Palm Skin Productions was essentially Simon Richmond, who also recorded for Mo' Wax Records under the name Bubbatunes. He played on the record along with saxophonist Chris Bowden, and the single was released on Mo'Wax. Rhoda's distinctive and unique vocal talents are in evidence on the recording, which was described by one reviewer thus: "The garden comes into view with a skittering rhythm, a deep and thoughtful bass line, and a shooting flash of kingfisher colour across the established sombre shades as Rhoda Dakar, who also graced the Special AKA's '(What I Like Most About You Is Your) Girlfriend', sings the opening verses of MacNeice's poem. In its easeful intricacy it manages to be both thanksgiving and ominous."

The single failed to cause a ripple and it would be another three years before Rhoda ventured back into the studio. In 1996 she collaborated with friend and former lead singer of the Blow Monkeys, Bruce Robert Howard, better known as Dr Robert. He had maintained a healthy following over the years since the Blow Monkeys had split (they re-formed in 2007) and had released a number of albums. Rhoda guest-starred on backing vocals on the single 'The Coming Of Grace'. It was in this year that she met someone who would later have a profound effect on her career. He was singer/bassist/songwriter Nick Welsh, an ex-member of Bad Manners and then lynchpin in the re-formed Selecter with Pauline Black: "At that time, if you said the word 'ska' to me, I would run screaming in the other direction," said Rhoda. "In fact I met Nick at the Shepherds Bush Empire, backstage at the Sex Pistols in '96. A friend introduced us and I remember thinking, 'well, I'll never see him again.' I was seven or eight months pregnant and in the wrong sort of shoes to run away!"

Nick and Rhoda had met years before when they had both been 'faces' around the London punk scene in the mid to late Seventies. There was another three-year gap before she appeared on the track 'Getting High On Your Own Supply' for Liverpudlian electronic big-beaters Apollo 440 in 1999, by which time Rhoda was a doting mother. Her real return to form was in 2002 when Jennie Matthias, former lead vocalist with the Belle Stars and ska punkers Big 5 (another band formed by Nick Welsh that for some time ran alongside his Selecter duties) contacted Rhoda and asked her if she would like to participate in a collaboration with herself and Pauline Black. The plan was to play a series of ten gigs where they would sing a selection of Belle Stars, Bodysnatchers and Selecter hits in front of a backing band that consisted of Nick Welsh, ex-Bad Manners and Selecter keyboardist Martin Stewart and a brass section, under the title of 'The Ska Divas'.

The gigs were well received and Dakar rediscovered a taste for ska music, a genre that she had purposefully avoided for the previous 20 years. As part of her ska rehabilitation she was asked to play some gigs with the Selecter as a special guest, which gave the gigs a real 2Tone theme. This developed into a stint that covered at least 30 concerts with the band all over the UK. Nick Welsh said: "Just around the time she was gigging with us, I was approached by Pauline Black who said why don't I write some songs for Rhoda and help her out, so to speak. I did just that and it was the start of a great working relationship."

On December 16th 2006, Welsh and Stewart gave notice and left the Selecter after 15 years in the group and re-materialised with a new outfit called Skaville UK, which also featured drummer Al Fletcher and another former Bad Manners stalwart Louis 'Alphonso' Cook. As part of the Skaville UK set up, the band undertook a virtual non-stop tour of the UK for many months, and received great reviews as they went. Rhoda Dakar was commandeered and appeared as a special guest at many gigs to perform her Bodysnatchers numbers alongside a sultry cover of Dawn Penn's rocksteady classic 'You Don't Love Me (No, No, No)'. Skaville UK signed to MoonSka World Records and in August 2007 released their highly-lauded debut album *1973*, on which Rhoda appeared on many of the tracks, either as lead vocal ('Brixton Cat' and '0-900-LUV') or as co-vocalist and backing singer. She accompanied the band on the *1973* promotional tour and appeared in the promo video.

At that time she and Welsh began to record what would be her comeback album, on which Welsh played all the instruments. She signed to MoonSka World Records and her album was released in November 2007 to confirm her comeback as an artist in her own right. *Cleaning In Another Woman's Kitchen* is an 11-track mix of soulful, acoustic ska-orientated tunes. She performed some tracks when she appeared as guest artist at the Skaville UK shows and her association with Welsh spawned another side project.

150

They concentrated their energies on acoustic aspirations and performed up and down the country with a mix of both their own material and new tracks written as a team.

Rhoda's political nous was required for the BBC TV programme, *Soul Britannia*, a series that examined the dynamic impact of black American and Caribbean sounds on British music and the fabric of UK society, where she spoke on the subject of racism. Rhoda's political commentator role was in demand again when she appeared on BBC's Sunday morning programme *The Politics Show* in 2008 discussing Rock Against Racism and whether or not it actually achieved anything. She was pitched against outspoken journalist Toby Young who forced the argument that Rock Against Racism had done nothing to help race relations in the country. He was brought down to earth with a bump as Rhoda verbally savaged him to great effect in front of millions on live TV. '

July 2008 saw her take lead vocals on 'The Alternate' and ' Backfoot', two tracks on the second Skaville UK album *Decadent*, again issued by Moonska, and once more she guested with the band on the lengthy tour to promote *Decadent* as well as teaming up with Welsh for more acoustic dates. As if her endless travel around the country to gig is not enough to keep her active, in between all her work since 2002, Rhoda has managed to stay exceptionally fit through her membership of the Herne Hill Harriers Athletics club, an organisation that boasts top UK Olympic long jumper Jade Johnson in their ranks. Rhoda said: "I do 5k and 10k cross country and 800 metres and 1500 metres on the track. I have tried 3000metres on the track once and it nearly killed me!"

At the time of writing this book, Rhoda and Nick Welsh are still performing as an acoustic duo but have changed angles again with their new electric guitar-driven material which will see the light of day on the album *Back To The Garage* in 2009.

JERRY DAMMERS

JERRY WAS still in debt to Chrysalis, who were determined to have some sort of reimbursement for the cash they had spent on *In The Studio*. But he didn't sit around and let it get him down, he flung himself into a project that had been brought to his attention by his old friends at Madness. During 1984-85, Ethiopia and nearby countries had undergone a prolonged drought, which led to severe food shortages and mass starvation. Fighting between the rulers of the countries and well-armed rebels meant that donated aid did not always get through to those who were in desperate need of help. Supplies were regularly hijacked or simply destroyed. Ethiopia was on the verge of collapse and people were dying in their thousands. Something had to be done.

Although it was on a small scale, a young Madness fan called Mick Toohig walked into the band's Camden office and suggested that the band record the Pioneers' 1970 hit 'Starvation' to raise money for the Ethiopian Aid charities. After much consultation, the project was thrown open and Jerry Dammers was contacted to help out. Soon, Liquidator Studios (owned by Madness) was brimming with old acquaintants from the 2Tone era, as well as a few from the original ska era in the Sixties, all getting involved in Starvation, a project that predated Band Aid by several months and that only came to be released after Band Aid because it took so long to coordinate people between hectic tour schedules. Madness were asked to play on the Band Aid single, but were already committed to Starvation. Mark 'Bedders' Bedford said: "We've had to blow a lot of studio time. There were days when our own studio was booked up so we had to go and mix the track elsewhere."

Ali and Robin Campbell, along with bassist Earl Falconer represented UB40, the Specials were in attendance via Jerry, Brad and Lynval Golding, Woody and Bedders appeared as the Madness connection, whilst the Beat/General Public were there courtesy of Dave Wakeling and Ranking Roger. Jackie Robinson, George Agard and Sydney Crooks, better known as the Pioneers, were there to help spread the message across the world, and the brass section came in the form of the ever-reliable Dick Cuthell and former Fun Boy Three trombonist Annie Whitehead. It was the first time that people like the Pioneers met the artists who had cited them as their original influences. Vocalist Jackie Robinson said at the time: "We met Madness four years ago at the Lewisham Odeon when we were singing backing vocals for Desmond Dekker. The Specials and the Beat all recorded our songs, but we'd never met them before, so it was good to finally meet them."

Lynval was extremely pleased to be back amongst friends for such a prestigious assignment after the dissolution of the Fun Boy Three, and the Starvation project had rekindled his love for being in a band: "I was up in Coventry writing songs," he said. "I'm a sort of a free agent, I suppose. I've got one little band that I've been helping for the last two years. They're called After Tonight. I've got an eight-track studio at home, which they use to write and record their stuff on. The stuff I am writing now is quite close to 'Starvation', the feel 'n' that, 'cos that's my sort of roots music. That's where I'm really from, the reggae and soul thing. That's what I enjoy playing the best. The 'Starvation' record has made me want to play again properly. I'd love to go and play again. I'd love to work in a band situation again, 'cos I haven't done it for two years y'know. It was really good, everyone getting together."

On March 9th 1985 the single 'Starvation' was released on Madness' very own Zarjazz label and climbed to a chart high of 33, which earned a respectable sum of money for the Ethiopian appeal. The B-side had a track called 'Tam Tam Pour L'Ethiopie' which was performed by the cream of black African music, legends such as King Sunny Ade, Hugh Masekela and Manu Dibango. The 12" version featured a lightly extended version of the title track and included an extra bonus track, written by Dick Cuthell, entitled 'Haunted' and featurin the vocal trio Afrodiziak who had appeared on the 'Nelson Mandela' single. The money raised from sales was to be distributed to famine-hit areas of Ethiopia and Sudan by well-known charities such as Oxfam and War On Want. Dammers was asked if working with his old friends had brought back memories: "Sort of, though none of the people on it had worked with me before, apart from Brad and Lynval. But yeah, obviously it's that connection 'cos it's an old ska record. I'd love to do it again though, get lots of different people together specifically to make one record, raising money for a good cause. It's like the Band Aid record, I thought it was great as a fund raising exercise. I think it was especially good that Sting put ten grand of his own money into it. Otherwise it's just like everyone congratulating themselves when really it's the public that's giving the money."

Jerry had started to feel a little more relaxed again with his old 2Tone compatriots, and he thoroughly enjoyed the production element, which he carried on into his next project, an up-and-coming American ska/soul/mod revival band who hailed from Silver Lake, Los Angeles. They had brought the old 2Tone sound, with a flavour of Eighties Britain, back mixed with a US flavour. They went by the name of the Untouchables, formerly known as The UTs. In their sharp suits and pork-pie hats, they were heavily influenced by 2Tone and had come to England to promote themselves. Stiff Records, once home of Madness, were quick to sign them up after a newspaper item and a report in Smash Hits talked of a renewed interest in the Specials and Madness. The Untouchables' appearance in the UK did go some way towards reviving the ska sound,

152

and there was further evidence of this when their UK debut single 'Free Yourself' reached Number 26 in the UK listings in April 1985. Their follow up was to be a cover of the Jamo Thomas song 'I Spy For The FBI' and the group wanted Dammers to produce it. To them it was like working with the Messiah: "We wanted Jerry from the start of our career," said lead vocalist Jerry Miller, "but he was unavailable, so we just kept on pushing the guy until he said yes and he produced a great record."

The polished song reached a somewhat disappointing Number 59 in July 1985, the same month the band's debut album *Wild Child* made it to Number 51 in the album charts. 'I Spy For The FBI' was to be Dammers' only involvement with the LA ska revivalists.

Jerry kept himself busy and toured clubs, partook in a spot of DJing here and there on his travels, and attended various gigs. At one of these nights out, he came across a band that had come to London from their native Scarborough to try their luck. He was impressed enough with the group, called the Friday Club, to offer them the chance to record and release some material on the 2Tone label. The group, which consisted of Andy Brookes on vocals/guitar, Michael Hodges on vocals/percussion, Adele Winter on vocals, Terry Bateman on sax, Eddie Eve on keyboards, Graham Whitby on bass and Anton Hilton on drums, had a big soul influence to their sound. Dammers produced their one and only 2Tone single 'Window Shopping' (CHS TT28), with the B-side an instrumental version of the title track, and the 12" featuring an extended version. It was a credible start for the Friday Club and could have easily found its way into the charts, but it wasn't to be. The group gained the support slot on the lucrative *Mad Not Mad* tour, on which former 2Tone band Madness were about to embark. As a result, Chrysalis wanted to release the record to tie in with the tour, which was around October/November, but unfortunately that meant the single vanished amongst the year's pre-Christmas releases. Despite the overall disappointment with the record, it received a fair amount of airplay and Simon Bates placed the track on his Radio 1 breakfast show playlist, but this still couldn't help it break into the charts. The group disbanded shortly after the Madness tour.

1985 continued to be a whirlwind year for Jerry. As well as the Starvation endeavour, he became involved with a similar collection of artists, mainly from the African continent. 'Wind Of Change', released on the Rough Trade label and credited to the distinguished singer Robert Wyatt and the SWAPO Singers, was a very classy track that could have easily come from the 2Tone stable itself. Using an up-tempo approach, they told the plight of the inhabitants of Namibia, a country occupied illegally by the Apartheid regime of South Africa. SWAPO (South West Africa People's Organization) was the national liberation movement for Namibia, who had fought for the country's independence since 1960. The brutal administration in South Africa had forced over 70,000 Namibians into exile, where they had to live in tiny SWAPO settlements in other countries such as Angola and Zambia.

The British-based Namibia Support Committee was set up in conjunction with the SWAPO group to further their campaign. Robert Wyatt was attracted to their cause, became involved, and contacted Jerry Dammers, and the rest, as they say, is history. Wyatt and Dammers, both political pitbulls, were vociferous in their condemnation of South Africa and in support of SWAPO: "Personally," said Wyatt, "I shall not be convinced that freedom has come to Namibia until Namibian artists themselves have a secure platform from which to speak directly to the world, their own record companies, publishing houses, film and TV industry, independent from the whims and

Jerry in funny hat backstage 1979. Photo by R.Byers

Jerry & infamous jumper on tour bus 1979. Photo by R.Byers

154

fashions of the neo-colonialist power communication centres that currently dominate and shape world thought."

Dammers was in full agreement with Wyatt's stance and added: "Namibian and South African collaborators with Apartheid should not be granted asylum in Britain or any other country when their racist regime is eventually overthrown."

The 'Wind Of Change' record was a new arrangement of a song from an original SWAPO Singers LP One Namibia, One Nation, and all the proceeds from sales of 'Wind Of Change' went to the SWAPO cause. The track was backed by the song 'Namibia', an interpretation of a poem called 'When I Think About My Country', and an old SWAPO song, 'Namibia Inkanda Vetu'. Alongside the throng of artists from SWAPO on the record were Lynval Golding on rhythm guitar, Dick Cuthell on cornet, Annie Whitehead on trombone and Dammers, who as well as production and arrangement of the track, played keyboards and guitar(!). The video to the song was filmed in a dance hall, but one shot showed the musicians performing the track outside the South African embassy in London, where the attachés called in the police to keep a check on the group and the gawping bystanders that had crowded around. Both Dammers and Wyatt were asked to appear on the Old Grey Whistle Test to promote the single, and, while viewers listened to host David Hepworth, Jerry raised the cover of the single at many angles for the camera and mimed the words 'Buy It!' The record, definitely up there with 'Nelson Mandela', failed to have the same impact and only spent two weeks in the chart, stalling at Number 86. By 1990, Namibia was granted independence and SWAPO would go on to be the dominant political party in the country.

Dammers, who revelled in his new role as a free agent, remained fully booked after the SWAPO single and went back to guest DJing in London. He often worked with Lynval Golding before he returned to Liquidator Studios to make a brief appearance on keyboards for Madness (for anchorman Mike Barson who had left the group to live in Amsterdam) and their long-awaited return to the charts with the laid-back single 'Yesterday's Men'. The session at Liquidator produced a moment of hilarity when an old Hammond organ, which Dammers had especially ordered for the track, would not fit through the studio doors and he was eventually forced to play in the freezing corridor.

Around this time, Jerry also became quite engrossed in the UK hip-hop scene, and his keen ability to spot young, talented bands was now brought into play as he took up the role of unpaid publicity agent whilst he worked the club scene. Towards the end of 1985 Jerry donned his socialist hat and joined another political venture, the Labour Party-affiliated Red Wedge project. Red Wedge was a musician-based pressure group that attempted to influence the national debate and to politicise the nation's youth through rock and ska music. The collective included a host of well-known British musicians who put together the revue to tour the country with the overall aim of publicising the policies of the Labour Party in an attempt to help to oust Margaret Thatcher at the forthcoming 1987 General Election. Initially, Red Wedge was led by the respected and overtly political artist Billy Bragg: "We were committed to ousting the Conservative Government with the formation of Red Wedge," said Bragg. "We formed it in order to focus in on the '87 election, to use the opportunity that we had in the [youth-oriented music] papers to have a debate about what we were voting for. We did not go out and say, 'People, vote Labour.' We went out and said, 'People, look at the issues, who is going to make a better society?'"

Red Wedge held its launch party at The House Of Commons on November 21st 1985, with the backing of the musicians, trade unionists and politicians like Labour leader Neil Kinnock and Robin Cook. The creation of the official organisation magazine *Well Red* was also announced. At the launch, Dammers said: "We hope Red Wedge is like a party atmosphere, we just want to be part of the massive anti-Thatcher popular movement. Red Wedge aims to create, through the world of the arts, a fresh and direct approach to politics which will ultimately affect and involve the youth out there."

The list of musicians included Dammers, Bragg, Paul Weller and the Style Council, Jimmy Somerville and the Communards, Junior Giscombe, Madness, the Smiths, Prefab Sprout, Tom Robinson and Lloyd Cole. They toured the country and charged low admission prices. On the day of a gig, the artists and politicians would visit the town where they were due to perform and seek out youth training schemes and various photo opportunities. Before the main concert, local bands in the town would perform their own Red Wedge support gig. At the main event, the politicians and their crew would mingle with the audience and distribute Labour Party material and other political paraphernalia. The first music tours took place in January and February 1986, and later in the year these was followed by a comedy tour, featuring stand-up comics such as Ben Elton, Lenny Henry, Craig Charles, Harry Enfield and Phill Jupitus: "In the early Eighties, I got involved with Red Wedge," said Jupitus, "in which Neil Kinnock got various bands to stage concerts for Labour. The reason I got involved was 20 percent because I believed in the cause, 30 percent because I loved Billy Bragg, and 50 percent because I wanted to meet Paul Weller. I still have a Red Wedge backstage pass, which reminds me of how optimistic I was about socialism. I was also at the Red Wedge launch that Jerry Dammers was at, and did do a couple of gigs with him too. I recall him playing with a little Casio keyboard I used at the time, and him handing it back to me with the words 'I fucking hate music!'"

Despite all the hard work, many miles travelled and many a song sung, Red Wedge failed in their attempts to get more youth policies in the Labour manifesto, these ideas eventually being lost in the small print of the party programme. After the 1987 election, when Labour's failure to convince the nation produced a third consecutive Conservative victory, many of the musical collective drifted away. Further gigs were organised and the group's magazine *Well Red* continued to appear, but funds eventually ran out and Red Wedge was formally disbanded in 1990.

On the cessation of his Red Wedge duties, Jerry was approached to write some music for director Julien Temple's film *Absolute Beginners*, an adaptation of Colin MacInnes' 1959 novel, which depicts teenage life in swinging London. The movie follows the young narrator, a photographer played by Eddie O'Connell, and his opinions on the newly emerging youth culture, the mods and his love for his ex-girlfriend Crêpe Suzette, played by Patsy Kensit, in the summer of the Notting Hill race riots. The film also starred David Bowie, the Kinks' Ray Davies and Ed Tudor-Pole, then known as Tenpole Tudor. Dammers submitted a nine-minute instrumental called 'Riot City' which became track 10 on the eventual soundtrack album.

Jerry then focussed on his Anti-Apartheid commitments for a year or so and, after the success of the Freedom Festival and his visit to the Nelson Mandela 65th birthday bash a few years earlier, Dammers drove forward with what was to be the definitive 2Tone dream, a 70th birthday concert for Nelson Mandela to be held at Wembley Stadium. Jerry had worked in conjunction with impresario Tony Hollingsworth in an attempt to bring the grandiose plan to fruition: "I was," said Jerry, "involved in the early stages of getting the 70th birthday concert off the ground, with all the planning and contacting artists. It got a bit sad later when the powers that be eventually took over, it

Jerry & Neville on tour bus 1979. Photo by R.Byers

Roddy & Jerry play up on tour 1979. Photo by R.Byers

The SPECIALS – from conception to reunion

Jerry & Terry in back of van 1979. Photo by R.Byers

was inevitable really but it worked real well, which is the main thing."

The idea to make Nelson Mandela a focal point, standing out from all the other political prisoners caged in South Africa, was originally opposed by members of the ANC and the Anti-Apartheid Movement. Furthermore, Dammers' and Hollingsworth's plan to make the event a positive, upbeat birthday tribute to Mandela that would simply call for his freedom was very different from the normal campaign communications of the ANC and the Anti-Apartheid movement, who called for sanctions. The eminent Anglican Archbishop Trevor Huddleston and Anti-Apartheid Movement General Secretary Mike Terry got the idea of a change in campaign direction pushed through. The event finally took place on June 11th 1988 at a packed Wembley Stadium, crammed with 72,000 well-wishers. The event was seen by a TV audience of 600,000,000 across 67 countries, topping Live Aid as the most successful televised musical event of the Eighties. The highlight was Jerry Dammers and Friends' version of the Special AKA's 'Nelson Mandela' where Jerry was joined onstage by the other musicians for a rousing rendition, but it was hastily assembled and suffered from terrible sound quality: "That was a bit of a disaster," admitted Jerry. "Everyone seemed to forget what we'd done in rehearsals. So many musicians wanted to be involved. Someone came up behind me and started trying to play my piano around me, doggy style!"

The artists who played that day included Whitney Houston, Stevie Wonder, George Michael, Phil Collins, Sting, Peter Gabriel, Tears For Fears and Bryan Adams. Some thought that Houston's contribution was not in the spirit of the day, but Dammers thought otherwise: "It was felt to be very important to get a massive black artist on board to give the whole thing credibility and viability. Whitney Houston was that artist and it has to be said that it was a very bold move for such a massive middle-of-the-road American artist to do that at that time. She must have been under a hell of a lot of pressure not to."

The concert was a great triumph, and although it was never broadcast in South Africa, as the Apartheid Government controlled the media, and the scale of the international event went largely unnoticed in Mandela's home country, news of the event *did* reach Mandela and the other political prisoners in South Africa. Much to Dammers' satisfaction, even Margaret Thatcher, who had previously declared Mandela 'a terrorist', joined in the international condemnation both of his imprisonment and the imprisonment of hundreds like him in South Africa. The global broadcast created a tidal wave within the international community and, within two years, Nelson Mandela was released from prison after 27 years of incarceration.

After the adrenaline rush of the Mandela concert, and some valuable time off, Jerry continued his hectic schedule with more session work, this time for The Madness, a splinter from the original band formed by Suggs, Chrissy Boy and Chas Smash (or Carl Smyth as he was addressing himself now) after Madness called it a day in 1986. The self-titled album *The Madness*, was the group's one and only vinyl album offering and was recorded at the Town House and Liquidator studios. The guest line-up featured Jerry on keyboards for the tracks 'Nightmare Nightmare' and 'Beat The Bride'. The other guests were Earl Falconer from UB40, Steve Nieve of the Attractions and JB's Allstars, and a ska band causing a few ripples in the late Eighties called the Potato Five. The album was not a commercial success and Jerry found himself back DJing again. He also kept himself busy and composed new material with a view to recording it, but at the time he found interest in him as a recording artist somewhat lacking. He went to Chrysalis Records about the possible release of his new material but they had decided he was no longer viable and suggested that he went elsewhere, a real shame considering his past achievements.

"The work on the Nelson Mandela event took me four years to organise," said Dammers, "by which time I'd lost the thread of my music and by then Chrysalis had lost interest in me."

However, Chrysalis soon knocked on his door for a favour. They asked him to choose a number of tracks from the 2Tone vault so that they could create a double album to commemorate the tenth anniversary of 'Gangsters' and 2Tone in 1989. *The 2Tone Story* (CHS TT5009) was a delightful mix of studio and live cuts with the welcome addition of something brand new, a never-before-released live version of the Specials' 'Stereotype'. The live cuts were a rehashed 'Dance Craze' collection, and the album did not include either the Apollinaires or the Higsons, sticking instead to the traditional original ska/reggae 2Tone fare. It was in the same vein as *This Are 2Tone* and some tracks, including the live version of 'Stereotype' were dropped for the compact-disc release of the album, the omissions no doubt instigated by Chrysalis to save money. The finances raised from the album sales were ploughed into the coffers drained by the recording of *In The Studio*.

Around this time, a ska and 2Tone-influenced scene began to surface and threatened to go mainstream. All across the UK, Europe and America new outfits popped up and *The Sun* newspaper ran an article on rude boys, the style and the music.

It featured an Aylesbury band, the Riffs, and the fashions of its lead singer, Aidan Sterling. the Specials and 2Tone suddenly found themselves back in vogue and a burst of new ska bands extolled them as their influence, such as the Loafers (John Bradbury would produce many of their records), the Hotknives, Maroon Town, SkaBoom, the Skanxters, the Skadows, the Deltones, the Potato Five and the Trojans to name but a few. Bigger names such as Laurel Aitken, Prince Buster, Derrick Morgan and Desmond Dekker found themselves in demand for live shows, and Bad Manners (who had remained active throughout the Eighties) topped bills up and down the country. A huge concert with the cream of the current bands took place at London's Astoria on 23rd March 1989 and was packed to the rafters. Although it threatened a national explosion, the late-Eighties ska revival remained underground and simmered for a few years, and despite the renewed interest and the odd record making it into the charts, it has remained so until the present day. Even the reformation of 2Tone bands such as Madness and the Selecter has failed to revitalise the scene on a national level.

With the Specials and 2Tone experience behind him, his sleepless nights over with the end of the turbulent Special AKA, and with all other ventures done and dusted, Jerry decided to return to Coventry to recuperate and renew his energy levels. He took up a DJ residency at the newly refurbished Tic Toc Club in Primrose Hill Street, Coventry, where he teamed up with Lynval Golding on a number of occasions. After a few months, he returned to London with a new enterprise, a club where he could show off his DJing skills without having to travel. He teamed up with Dermot Smyth, brother of Madness' Carl (aka Chas Smash), to run and DJ at a dance club at Covent Garden's Rock Garden venue, where they played hip hop and house music. He was still very active on the PR front, and encouraged companies to sign up new bands that he promoted at his various club ventures:

"I'm having a good time at the moment. At the club I run with Dermot we're currently promoting house music, hip-hop, rap and ragga and I'm doing some DJing and hopefully I'm helping to get further recognition for black British outfits like Dominant Force [who went on to be respected UK hip hop group], the Demon Boys [who went on to record on the Mango label, an offshoot of Island Records] and the London Posse [who released an album on Big Life Records produced by Tim Westwood]. Anyway, things are okay at the moment but they have to be don't they? Although I haven't really earned any money in the last seven years. I've sort of lived off old Specials royalties, but that's coming to and end now so I'd better pull my finger out. I want to get back into music and I still write and play but nobody is interested in putting it out these days."

The attitude adopted by the music industry towards Dammers enraged Lynval Golding, who said about his long-time friend and colleague: "Jerry's exile from the music scene is really disgusting. They show more respect for style and fashion than good singers and writers here in the UK."

Over the ensuing years, into the Nineties, Dammers fell away from public glare and was quiet on the music scene. He kept active and wrote and recorded personal material alongside intermittent production work for other artists, but he also remained heavily involved on the political stage supporting anti-racist and other causes, such as the Global Poverty Group and War On Want. He was also instrumental in trying to save the Tic Toc Club in Coventry after it closed in the early Nineties. The closure of one of Coventry's best venues, where the re-formed Selecter recorded their live comeback album *Out On The Streets*, caused an outcry and a benefit gig was arranged. The gig featured a reggae band called the Cosmics who were joined onstage for some pure

160

2Tone pandemonium by the likes of Dammers, Golding, Roddy Byers, Neol Davies, and Charlie 'H' Bembridge. The venue eventually closed, despite all the protestations, but soon reopened under a number of different owners. The live experience still exists for the locals and is now known as the Kasbah.

By the late Nineties Jerry was in demand on the production front, now pretty much his forte, and he remixed the track 'Black And White' for drum-and-bass outfit the Asian Dub Foundation. His DJing skills were increasingly in demand, and he made guest appearances all over the UK and Ireland. By the millennium, finally released from the concrete boots of his Chrysalis contract, Jerry formed a band called Jazz Odyssey, a bizarre jazz/trance outfit that occasionally played live. Unfortunately Jerry developed a case of tinnitus that meant live work had to be curtailed, which left him to concentrate on the DJ side of his career: "My DJ stuff has always been ignored really," said Jerry. "It's funny. Once, a rock journalist came up to me while I was actually DJing, and said, 'When are you going to do something, Jerry?' 'I'm doing it, as you actually speak to me!' I said through clenched teeth!"

The 25th Anniversary of 2Tone arrived in 2004, and although there were rumours of big plans to celebrate this landmark in Coventry, nothing happened. Dammers, meanwhile, was back in the studio for the electronic abstract jazz band Akasha on their track 'Attack Of The Invisible Robots From Planet US' which he remixed and also played a small synthesiser part on.

Yet another proud moment in his illustrious career arrived when recognition for all his work over the years came from Coventry University. He was nominated by Coventry journalist Pete Chambers and was chosen to receive an honorary Doctorate in Letters for his outstanding contribution to the international music industry. On Monday 20th November 2006, with support from his family and Lynval Golding, he was honoured in the ornate surroundings of Coventry Cathedral. Professor Michael Tovey presented the degree and referred to the influence of his music on society, dealing with issues of teenage pregnancy, rape, social decay and the incarceration of Nelson Mandela. Professor Tovey told the audience: "There were powerful themes, powerful lyrics but still excellent music. It came as a surprise to many hearing it for the first time that protest songs could be such great music. Coventry has become a better place for his contribution and music has become a better art form for his creativity."

The genuinely astounded Dammers, who still wore the customary graduate regalia of gown topped off with a Tudor bonnet, said: "That was fantastic. What he said was amazing! I didn't really think of it that way. I couldn't believe it. I wasn't really prepared for that. I would like to thank those who nominated me for this, and everyone from the Specials and the Selecter and all the other bands that were involved, because none of this would have happened without them. It's just incredible."

That evening Dammers launched the Coventry Anti-Racist Campaign's own division of Love Music Hate Racism at Coventry's Dogma in Fairfax Street. He spent the night DJing a selection of Jamaican-influenced music, ranging from the Sixties to the Jungle sounds of the present day (and threw a bit of 2Tone in for good measure!).

After taking some time out, Jerry returned to the public eye in an eccentric live experience with his new creation, the Cosmic Engineers. Known for being experimental, Dammers' described his new project as 'A journey into space music, electronic images, distressed signals and robot moods.' His partner, Kodwo Eshun, was a UK-born writer and musician, who focussed on black identity and diffusion of African culture. He spread his ideas through conceptual use of electronic music and its interface with art, science fiction, technology and 'machine' culture. One show featured a special screening of Romanian cult director Andrei Ujica's space film *Out Of The Present* which told the story of cosmonaut Sergei Krikalev who spent ten months aboard the space station *Mir* while, on earth, the Soviet Union ceased to exist. On the night, as the film was aired, a new soundtrack to the film was DJed live by Dammers and Eshun.

Dammers then moved on, in spectacular style, to his first major group since the Special AKA. With a nod and a wink (and maybe two fingers) to his former bandmates, he put together the big-band trance jazz collective the Spatial AKA Orchestra (a fantastic play on words). The 15- to 18-strong troupe, which features prominent contemporary jazz artists like pianist Zoe Rahman (who played on the Terry Hall & Mushtaq album *The Hour Of Two Lights*), MOBO award winner Denys Baptiste and Larry Stabbins on saxes, and Alice Coltrane, wife of the jazz legend John Coltrane. They played a tribute to experimental jazz artist Sun Ra and also some radical re-works of Dammers' own material, including 'Ghost Town'. The Orchestra came as a musical and conceptual surprise to many Specials fans, with the band dressed in masks and Egyptian-themed costumes.

Jerry's influence, Sun Ra, was originally known as Herman Poole Blount and was born in Birmingham, Alabama in 1914. By the time he was 11 he could play the piano and write songs. He was heavily influenced by musicians such as Duke Ellington and Fats Waller. By his student days Blount claimed that, in the throes of deep meditation, a bright light had engulfed him and that he was 'teleported' to an interplanetary audience on the planet of Saturn: "My whole body changed into something else. I could see through myself. And I went up, I wasn't in human form. I landed on a planet that I identified as Saturn. They teleported me and I was down on a stage with them. They wanted to talk with me. They had one little antenna on each ear, a little antenna over each eye. They talked to me. They told me to stop attending college because there was going to be great trouble in schools, the world was going into complete chaos, I would speak through music, and the world would listen. That's what they told me.'

In Chicago in the Fifties, when he renamed himself 'Le Sony'r Ra' his interplanetary experiences began to stamp their mark on his music and he began to create the 'cosmic' jazz for which he is best known. As Sun Ra and his Arkestra (you see the origins of Jerry's clever play on words) moved to New York and then Philadelphia during the Sixties and Seventies, Sun Ra cemented his reputation as an innovator and was one of the first musicians to employ electric synthesisers and tape delay systems to achieve his cosmic landscape. His ever-changing band of musicians toured regularly and continued to do so after his death in 1993. This outlandish, free-form style of jazz found an avid fan in the innovative Jerry Dammers who, as he did with ska, brought it to the attention of the British public: "When the US government was going to the moon," explained Jerry, "Sun Ra was saying that, for black people in America, they could still travel through space mentally, without all the expense of rockets. So his ideas were political. We're playing versions of the funkier, groove-based, African end of Sun Ra from the Seventies; hip-hop-influenced, modern versions, very much my arrangements. It's visual and theatrical on stage too, there are mannequins and masks and helmets. Half the band aren't jazz musicians, they're more reggae or rock. They're the best young musicians in Britain. It's a new kind of jazz band. I don't want them to be compared to Jerry Dammers or the Specials, they're so special themselves."

The Spatial AKA is quite possibly what the Specials would have developed into, given that Dammers had wanted to increase the size of the original band, and taking into

162

account the jazz influences clearly audible on *In The Studio*. This new band is a fundamental creation based loosely on the grand plans for the Specials that he hatched many years ago.

Dammers' political passions fired him to use music to get his views across. His hatred of any form of racism is the force that drove him through his career and he still felt he had more to give: "There are still things I need to say," he explained, "But it's much, much harder to say 'em now. If you're talking about political stuff, I think there's a real problem with making those statements that we made at that time, without it sounding like a cliché from that era. I think it's one of the surrealists who said that revolutionary art has to be revolutionary in form. Unless you can shock people with the way you say it, they're not going to take any notice. And it just seemed anyway that music had changed. All the best music till recently was instrumental black hip-hop, dancehall and jungle that I could only play on vinyl. The punk era created a whole group of people working together, throwing their twopence worth in to a much larger movement. Music gets political when there are new ideas in music. Punk was innovative, so was ska, and that was why bands such as the Specials and the Clash could be political, but that era's gone. I still try and write songs. It's not all over yet. Probably. Hopefully. But I have to find new ways to say it."

Ironically, Rock Against Racism ceased to be after the 1981 concert at Potter Newton Park in Leeds, where the Specials, going through their death throes, had headlined. Back in 2002 the organisation re-emerged as Love Music Hate Racism (LMHR) and Dammers got on board immediately to help the group in any way he could. He was concerned with the rise of the British National Party across the UK, with the boneheads of the Seventies replaced by suits, ties and smart haircuts. Dammers set about creating an agenda to spread the word against the 'Devils in Saville Row suits'. The Anti-Nazi League that had battled the National Front and British Movement in the Seventies and Eighties was also reborn in the Nineties, and along with the National Assembly Against Racism, the TUC and other smaller groups, helped to form the current Unite Against Fascism assembly.

"The BNP are like the Daleks; no matter how many times they're defeated they don't get the message. But they're not from a fantasy and we can't be complacent and relax in the struggle against them. It's when they're at their most boring and tedious that they are at their most dangerous. Everyone should do everything they can to counteract them."

A concert was arranged by LMHR at London's Victoria Park for Sunday April 27th 2008 and Jerry Dammers was instrumental in its organisation. He pulled off a coup when he enticed Damon Albarn and Paul Simonon's studio band The Good, The Bad and The Queen to play the headline slot and his new acquaintances, London band Hard-Fi, were also recruited to the cause. Dammers essentially became the face of the LMHR, and with a track record such as his, was well qualified for the job: "Love Music Hate Racism," said Dammers. "I always say that you don't have to love music, it's the second part that's important! Hating racism should be as natural as liking music, or breathing air for that matter. Anti-racism is not 'political' it's normal. I hope everyone will please support Love Music Hate Racism and help correct the hysterical lies and distortions of the BNP. Its worth noting that the BNP don't march any more, but they give the appearance of being more respectable, by wearing suits, and in some ways they are more dangerous. They have this veneer of respectability and as mainstream politicians they are quite successful at stirring up a lot of hysteria about immigration in the media."

On the day 100,000 people attended the free concert, and a racially diverse audience celebrated the LMHR ethos together. More than 40 artists appeared, along with some who had been at the first RAR concert in 1978, such as Sham 69's Jimmy Pursey, Clash collaborator and film producer Don Letts and Poly Styrene from X-Ray Spex. Throughout the day, the crowd were addressed by the likes of the original founders of Rock Against Racism, Roger Huddle and Red Saunders, and the Mayor of London, Ken Livingstone. Jerry Dammers took on the role of compère and had his moment when Damon Albarn introduced him onstage: "And now someone else who, especially for me, had a massive influence on opening my mind to things. Mr Jerry Dammers."

Dammers was applauded by the crowd before he addressed the multitude with a heartfelt tirade at the BNP: "The BNP are like weeds in the garden," Jerry told the gathered thousands, "unfortunately, they keep coming back. They are also like mouth ulcers, and what we do with mouth ulcers is to take a bit of Listerine and we have a gargle, so I want you all to gargle against the BNP!"

He then introduced 'Ghost Town' and told the crowd that it 'was a bit of a weird version 'cos its arranged for my orchestra, I got an orchestra now.' The Jerry Dammers Allstars, which featured Damon Albarn on keyboards were joined on stage by the Hypnotic Brass Ensemble, which included the legendary Rico on trombone, and Jerry played the role of conductor. The event ended with the spine-tingling ambient version of 'Ghost Town' with added live vocals from electronic dub band the Space Ape. The success of the event led to more LMHR concerts being planned to take place all over the UK.

Dammers found himself back in demand on the music scene and he began to appear at shows all over London and the length and breadth of the UK as a DJ (including a stint at the two day Boss Sounds reggae festival in Newcastle). Suddenly, rumours abounded that a reformation of the Specials was imminent, fuelled by Terry Hall and Lynval Golding making many appearances together and Jerry joining Neville Staple onstage when Neville was playing London as part of his tour. The rumours were vehemently denied and ignored by Dammers.

He was then called upon to take part in a massive national event, the 90th Birthday celebrations of Nelson Mandela. The venue was to be Hyde Park, London on June 27th 2008. Although Mandela was officially retired and quite frail, he agreed to attend the concert as all the money raised from the occasion would go to the 46664 AIDS charity set up by Mandela. 46664 had had raised money over the last few years with concerts in countries like South Africa, Norway and Spain. The significance of 46664 stems from Mandela's time imprisoned on Robben Island, where he was the 466th prisoner to arrive in 1964, and so the prison's scheme for numbering prisoners bestowed him the number 46664. The Nelson Mandela Foundation's own website is 46664.com.

Around 50,000 people attended the concert which was broadcast on ITV to millions of others. The event was opened by US actor/musician Will Smith and the finale saw artists such as Razorlight, Annie Lennox, the current incarnation of Queen, reggae legend Eddy Grant, Simple Minds, the Sugababes and Leona Lewis join headliner Amy Winehouse and Jerry Dammers onstage for a raucous rendition of the Special AKA classic 'Nelson Mandela'. Dammers seemed to enjoy himself immensely as his 2Tone ideology lived on in front of millions.

At the time of writing in early 2009 Dammers is still touring as a DJ and with his eclectic Spatial AKA Orchestra and is fending off questions about the Specials. The last word must go to the man himself. In an interview with Coventry journalist Pete Chambers, he was asked if he and 2Tone should be commemorated in the city, and in typical Dammers self-deprecating style he answered: "Renaming one of the multi storey car parks 'Ghost Town Park' would do me, but seriously, if it's true anyone really wanted to do anything like your suggestion, it would be brilliant, it's not really for me to say though. Maybe because 2Tone was against racism I should also really say I hope there's something in the city to commemorate people who've been killed in racist attacks, like Satnam Singh Gil who was 20 when he got killed in 1981. Doctor Amal Dharri got stabbed in the chip shop off Albany Road in the same year, it was supposedly for a 50p bet. I think they deserve to be remembered more than we do, really."

TERRY HALL

WHEN TERRY returned from the Fun Boy Three's American tour he was disillusioned and it was reputed that he was suffering ill-health. He used his spare time to recuperate and realign himself mentally and physically. He reappeared in the public domain in January 1984, just four months after the split of the Fun Boy Three, with yet another three piece band, the Colour Field. The line up consisted of Terry on vocals and, occasionally, the guitar (clearly he wasn't daunted by his failure to become the next Eddie Van Halen while in the FB3), Toby Lyons, once of 2Tone band the Swinging Cats on guitar/vocals, and an unknown bass guitarist, Karl Shale. Both of Hall's new recruits came from the 2Tone city, but by this time Terry had relocated himself and his partner Jeanette Powell to the wilds of glamorous Stockport in Greater Manchester, which gave him an excuse to go and see his favourite football team, Manchester United, although he was wary about going along at first: "I thought there'd be pressure on me," said Terry, "but once I got there it was great. You're just there amongst 40,000 people and nobody gives a toss who you are."

Terry Hall in France 1979. Photo by R.Byers

The SPECIALS – from conception to reunion

Manchester United was a calming influence during the turbulence that followed the Fun Boy Three split, and football-mad Hall relished his new found freedom. When asked if he would rather play a gig in front of thousands, or watch Manchester United win a European Cup Final, the convivial Hall replied: "European Cup. Without a doubt. I've done the pinnacle of gigging with the Specials with crowds of about 10,000 in America, which is pretty big, but it really doesn't compare to the European Cup does it?"

Hall's fascination with the Red Devils started at an early age and became a love affair that would stretch across the years: "It was definitely the '68 Euro Cup final that got me into United. I was nine and up until then my Dad used to go and watch Coventry, he used to try and get me to go but I used to hate it. Even post crawling stage I knew I shouldn't be going to that crap! He took me to a couple of games but that night, when I watched United v Benfica, that was like real football and it left such a massive impression. My very first game I went to Old Trafford. We had an Auntie in Bolton and her son had moved down to Coventry and he watched them and he took me up to see United v Coventry. I'm trying to think of the date and it has always bugged me, but it was around 1970-71. We sat at the back of the Stretford End. From that point, it's been said many times before over the years, but you get the bug, it's beyond football, you get the bug! I had to wait a couple of years before I started getting part-time jobs and going more."

He had tried to go to matches during his stints with the Specials and Fun Boy Three but wasn't always able to for obvious reasons: "Going during the Specials was difficult. I had to drop off going to games for about a year or two because I just used to get so much hassle. I just couldn't really do it. When we started Fun Boy Three I made sure that we would never work around a game, we just wouldn't work, and they were cool with that because there were only three of us then, so I got a season ticket back at the start of the Fun Boy Three. Just so I knew where I would be every Saturday."

The many sabbaticals spent at Manchester United helped him manage his life and brought an element of normality which de-stressed him after hectic years of being on the road which left him overwhelmed and disenchanted. After the Fun Boy Three, Terry contemplated quitting the music scene altogether. He felt that he had lost touch with his true self and his 'ordinariness'. He hated being singled out as the face of the Fun Boy Three and he hated doing all the talking: "I think I would have stopped if I had no contract. I thought the whole music business was crap. It had got to the point where I didn't trust anybody and I thought seriously about packing it all in, it had affected me that much. It was Jeanette who pushed me on, I really liked writing songs and stuff, I just need that little shove and encouragement."

In the Colour Field, Terry developed a new style of writing with his fellow composer Lyons, and between them they wrote all of the group's songs. Terry emphasised the difference between his associates in the band and his cohorts in the Specials and Fun Boy Three: "We are friends first and foremost but we are also in a band. When I was with the Specials and Fun Boy Three, yes we were friends, but more of a working unit than anything else."

The group first took shape when the FB3 started going under. Toby Lyons had gone to America with the Fun Boys as part of their backing band and witnessed the tensions as they mounted: "Why the Fun Boy Three ever bothered going to the States, I'll never know." said Toby. When Toby and Terry returned they began talks in earnest: "I was talking to Toby for quite a while," explained Hall, "Trying to sort out ideas to go into the studio with. We were just talking, there was never a group in mind at that stage."

When the time felt right to put a band together and make their ideas more substantial, Toby contacted his friend, bassist Karl Shale, who had been in bands such as Solid Action and Aching Tongue before playing with Toby in a Coventry garage band called the Zander System. With Shale on board they made the joint decision to have no leader within the trio, but predictably, Hall was in constant demand with the media. The group eventually came up with two compositions that they deemed worthy of release and, with Terry still under contract to Chrysalis, the idea was embraced by the label as an outlet for his work. Terry Hall recalled: "The coming of the band only really happened because we had to think of a name so we could release a single. I never said to the others 'Will you join MY group?' It's just built on friendship, which is why this group is so much stronger."

On January 21st 1984 the Colour Field released their debut single. The name was borrowed from an American expressionist art movement which had emerged in the Fifties after the Abstract Expressionist art revolution led by people like Jackson Pollock. Colour Field painting was largely characterised by abstract canvases painted primarily with large areas of solid colour, but the connection ended there between the band and the name. The single, itself simply entitled 'The Colour Field', had a political edge and sound not too dissimilar to Echo and The Bunnymen, one of Hall's favourite artists of that time. The reverse side of the record was the sombre acoustic 'Sorry', a tale of divorce and soured relationships. The Chrysalis marketing team persisted and a 12" single was also issued with a remixed version of the title track.

Hall enlightened the world on the roots and basis of the track: "The song is about the state of mind you get in about things. The first verse is about wanting or hoping for things while trying to escape from something else. The second verse just describes the sort of stuff you're up against and the third admits that it's there, that is how things are and you either accept it or not. Either way you're fucked. I'm not interested in stupid arty words, its pointless singing words that nobody else understands. I mean, if you're going to release a record then show people some respect by letting them in on what you're on about. Why keep it in the group? For God's sake, what the hell was 'Karma Chameleon' about anyway?"

The release proved that there was promise in the new band and that Hall's social and political attitudes were still very much intact. The single fell short of being their first hit, but reached Number 43 and spent four weeks in the chart. The resurrection of Terry Hall and the appearance of his latest project generated a mass of interest. He made the cover of both *Melody Maker* and *Record Mirror* and the group were interviewed by Radio 1 DJ Mark Page on TV-AM, the ITV early-morning entertainment show, at the ridiculous time of 6.45am. On January 25th they got a big Radio 1 slot on the Richard Skinner-hosted *Saturday Live* where they announced their intention to play live and revealed that they were recording material for a debut album. The next few weeks were spent on the promotion of the single and recording of the aforementioned album. When asked about its progress, all Hall would say to curious journalists was: "Well, every couple of days, we go into the studio, mess about, come out, smile at each other and then go home."

The group performed live for the very first time on February 10th on Channel 4's *The Tube*. There was no glitzy presentation, just Hall seated on a stool, guitar in hand, with the versatile Lyons on drums and Shale on his bass. It was Terry's first appearance with the guitar since he strummed out of tune with the FB3 only a few months before on the same show, but this time around he played it very competently and with some aplomb. They opened with 'Sorry' and when the crowd applauded in appreciation, Hall sneered Johnny Rotten style into the camera and said: "My god. We are SO privileged."

They performed 'The Colour Field' and a strange, almost psychedelic track, with equally mind-boggling lyrics, called 'Lets Take A Trip'; although there was no mention of it being about LSD, you couldn't help but draw that conclusion. Overall it wasn't a bad live debut, and was better in many respects than the Fun Boy Three appearance.

Terry's attitude towards the Specials, especially after the split, was varied to say the least. One minute he was full of praise, the next he made sideways swipes at the band in the media, but he grew a little wiser and to some extent, less cynical: "I'm genuinely surprised at the legacy left by the Specials. You can still get Specials ties in Carnaby Street and I'm still receiving cheques from the sales of the first album."

He may have become more philosophical about his former colleagues, but it was at this period in the Colour Field's existence that Terry sparked a minor controversy that angered his former Specials mentor, Jerry Dammers. In an interview with the *NME*, Hall said that racist skinheads did not exist in Coventry until the Specials started talking about it: "There wasn't a racial problem with the skinheads before the Specials started singing about one. There used to be, years back in the late Sixties and early Seventies, but I never saw anything on the streets back in 1977 when the group started. Then we told people with short hair not to hate Pakistanis, then it all began. All of a sudden, Paki-bashing was back in fashion."

This moved Jerry to release a statement which fervently denied what Terry had said. He countered with a quote that Hall had 'simply taken to forgetting about it for some reason.' It must have been a tough time for Pete Hadfield, former Specials tour manager, who now managed both Terry and Jerry. Hall found himself hounded by the music media, some of whom still wanted to know why he had dissolved the FB3 and helped to finish off the Specials. He dodged any questions he could on the Fun Boy Three, but freely discussed the Specials. He told Radio 1 DJ Peter Powell: "You know, in the beginning it was great. I was enjoying myself a lot just getting on with being in a group and strutting our stuff onstage. I was never bothered about being an idol to people or being in the papers at all. Anyway, it was Jerry who got most of the headlines, but what did bother me was that Jerry didn't deserve a lot of the flak he got. I got on with Jerry brilliantly.

"The first year was great, we all had a lot in common and it was fun sitting around Horace's house stamping the sleeve for the first thousand copies of 'Gangsters' for Rough Trade. I thought the whole 2Tone thing was fantastic when bands like Madness, the Beat and the Selecter came along. We were like one big happy family for a year or so and then things slowly began to fall apart. Pressure and money changed people's attitudes drastically and it affected me so much that I had to leave the group taking Neville and Lynval with me because at that time, we all felt closest to each other and something had to be done. After a few months we had decided to quit the Specials and go it alone. Some might think it was a stab in the back, but we did it for the other Specials' sake as well as ours."

Meanwhile, the Colour Field were still writing and recording numbers to be included on the album. Six months after their debut single, its follow up was released on July 28th 1984. 'Take' was a bittersweet view of a failed relationship (an area that Hall would visit for inspiration a number of times), which culminated when the girl left for pastures new:

"I'm desperately lonely,
And certainly homely,
With nothing to do,
'Cos the lads and the match,
And the Friday night stags,
Were just some of the things that I gave up for you."

The single featured the percussion talents of Echo and the Bunnymen's Pete De Freitas (who sadly died in a motorbike accident on June 14th 1989). Hall's tastes in music changed to take in influences from easy listening, and the likes of Jack Jones, Andy Williams, Simon & Garfunkel, Bobby Goldsboro and Burt Bacharach indicated a direction that he would go on to master. Some thought he had suffered a blow to the head and were surprised to find these influences in the mix that shaped the early Colour Field sound. The band's penchant for the writers of the big hits of the Sixties came to light on the 12" edition of 'Take' with an acoustic cover of the 1968 Academy Award-winning Noel Harrison classic 'Windmills Of Your Mind', which had originally been the theme to the Steve McQueen movie *The Thomas Crown Affair*. The sound suited the Colour Field's new musical direction perfectly. Also on the 12" was the sublime 'Pushing Up The Daisies', which in fact was a completely revised and re-recorded version of the bizarre 'Lets Take A Trip' track that had been played live on *The Tube*. Regrettably, the single made no real impact on the UK charts, and only clambered to Number 70. It had been widely tipped to be a hit for the band, and is still critically acclaimed as one of Terry's best ever compositions.

As the tunes on the record showed, the raw political edge of the debut single had evaporated to be replaced by Sixties organs and acoustic guitars. The sound of the group was far more important to Terry than any commercial success, they wanted to create a distinctive Colour Field timbre, so that as soon as the listener heard the opening bar of a tune, they would instantly recognise it as the band's. Their ideology was simple, if they had any commercial success it would merely be a by-product of their art. The lack of achievement with the first two singles might have demoralised any other artist or would be pop star, but not the unpredictable Hall and his merry men: "The first single was just a test for us on how well we would work together," explained Terry. "It was the first time we went into the studio and tried to write together so I didn't care where the record reached in the charts. 'Take' was a bit more disappointing, but even so, the failure of the records really helped me a lot, not on a business and financial level but on a personal level. It allowed me to get things into perspective."

For the next couple of months, the Colour Field went to ground, mainly to add the spit and polish to the album, and nothing more was heard of the group as 1984 drew to a close. But they didn't waste any time once the new year was rung in, and on January 11th they released next single 'Thinking Of You'. This track became an immediate pop classic with its upbeat tempo, acoustic guitars, and sweeping strings, plus the addition of real life singing strip-a-gram girl, Katrina Philips, whose vocals complimented Terry's plaintive nasal crooning. The record flew up the charts and peaked at Number 12. The band found themselves all over the media, and top of Radio 2 DJ Jimmy Young's, Record Of The Week list (it's worth noting that Radio 2 back in 1985 was very much an easy-listening MOR channel that your parents would listen to and didn't have the kudos it has in the present day).

They made two appearances on *Top Of The Pops*, which made Terry something of

A rare smile from Terry as Horace catches up on the news 1979. Photo by R.Byers

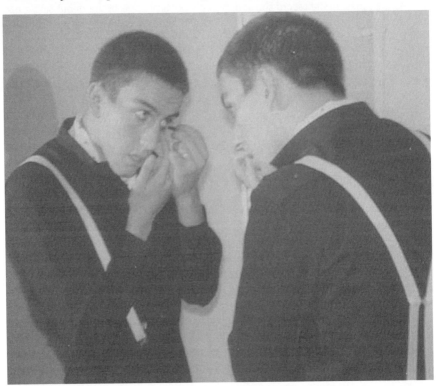

Great Terry Hall applying eye liner shot backstage 1979. Photo by R.Byers

Terry off duty 1979. Photo by R.Byers

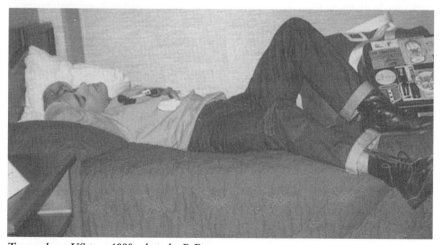

Terry asleep, US tour 1980. photo by R.Byers

The SPECIALS – from conception to reunion

a *TOTP* record holder for having hit singles with his last three bands. There was even an in-depth piece on the BBC's *Oxford Roadshow* in which the Colour Field took over with interviews and video inserts. The song may have gained the band a major hit, but Terry later explained that the track wasn't always destined for chart success: "When we wrote 'Thinking Of You', it was very gloomy, but we took a conscious decision to make it more upbeat. The single took four weeks to make because we wanted it to sound like a pop record. We really needed this one to sound right and that's why we got Katrina in. It all gets a bit obvious, but it works. I mean, I enjoyed singing about being by a graveside and everybody thinking it sounds nice but basically we needed this to chart well because we have to keep the group running. If it wasn't for that I couldn't care less, but we needed to sell singles to sell LPs to survive just like any other group does."

The 12" limited edition release boasted the single plus its 'Sing-A-Long' version (essentially an instrumental) and the reverse contained the track 'My Wild Flame', an eccentric overhaul of the debut single. All record companies now released their records in every format known to man in a cynical attempt to make more money and achieve higher chart positions. In conjunction with the 12", Chrysalis issued a double-pack single which was all the 12" tracks and an added bonus track over two vinyl singles in a gatefold sleeve. The bonus was a version of Dave Berry's 1965 hit 'Little Things'. The final cut is a studio session which went horribly wrong, with hilarious results and captures Terry's maniacal laughter which has to be heard to be believed.

With 'Thinking Of You', the Colour Field had now established themselves on the music scene and felt the time was right to show the public what the group were likely to be like as a live experience. On January 22nd they appeared as an eight-piece unit on the *Old Grey Whistle Test*, where they performed the hit and a taster from the album entitled 'Faint Hearts'. This was followed up by hastily arranged Radio 1 sessions, firstly on Bruno Brookes' drivetime slot and then another on Janice Long's evening show. To prove how easy-listening the Colour Field were, they even appeared on the relaxed BBC daytime flagship programme *Pebble Mill* to the ridicule of the critics. Hall retorted: "What the hell is wrong with being on *Pebble Mill* anyway?"

With the group now in full swing, and to try and build on the success of the last single, Chrysalis issued a follow up in the form of the elegant Latino tinged 'Castles In The Air', complete with its big orchestrated sound which created a very atmospheric backdrop to Hall's morbid vocal. Alas, the new release failed to have the impact of 'Thinking Of You', the synthesiser-riddled Eighties pop charts not exactly suited to psychedelia-flecked acoustic folk-rock, but that's what the Colour Field were producing. Their sound fell to the wayside when pitted against the likes of Duran Duran, Bronski Beat, Prince and Frankie Goes to Hollywood. The public's imagination had been captured by the new breed of pop bands, and the Colour Field's middle-of-the road quality just didn't make the grade. Undeterred, the band carried on, and had soon built their hand-picked in-house backing band who would play with them live over the next four months. They enlisted the talents of Pete Barratt on keyboards, Jim Morrison on guitar, Preston Heyman, one of the most respected session musicians in the UK on percussion and the reliable Pete De Freitas on drums.

With rehearsals well under way, the start of the tour was announced as May 2nd 1985. The one and only outing before the tour commenced was on Gary Crowley's show on Manchester's Piccadilly Radio, where the band performed numbers from their album which hit the shops on April 26th. Titled *Virgins And Philistines*, the album sold steadily and climbed to Number 12. The critics didn't know what to make of the material, or indeed the whole package. To them, the record had a lousy cover, a lousy title and it was played by a plain looking trio (Hall had forsaken his Sta-prest and Roots jogging suits for the 'Man at Austin Reed' look) but those who looked beyond image found it to be a fantastic debut album, which brimmed with Hall's trademark lyrical invention and melodic sparkle. One critic signed off his gracious review with 'Smile, Terry. You've finally arrived.'

In line with the subject-matter of the last three singles, the album was a rollercoaster ride of emotion, the theme of doomed relationships used in no fewer than eight tracks. For a record with such 'hippy' flair and dainty sixties keyboards, there was not a lot of peace and love on *Virgins and Philistines*. Terry Hall was already a renowned 'grumpy old man' and the album ensured he held on to his media nickname 'Mr Misery'. He purposefully soured the flowery sound in lyrics to former lovers; *So I'll say sorry, I hope it will do,'* and with vicious backhanders, like his description of hunters in the anti-hunting song 'Cruel Circus','*within a sport that's legal, within the minds of the mentally ill'*. Even in the made-for-pop jollity of the classic 'Thinking Of You', many reviewers couldn't help feel that Terry Hall was cackling sarcastically between the lines. The album included a superb cover of the Roches' 'Hammond Song', with ear-catching harmonies and lush acoustic guitars. The sorrowful cello in 'Castles In The Air' calls to mind the bittersweet loss of the lyrics. The ideals of the Sixties were dismissed off hand in 'Faint Hearts' which had the sounds of an acid-pop song. Katrina Phillips, who, after the Colour Field, went on to join West Yorkshire gothic rock band the Skeletal Family and sign to Chrysalis Records, gained praise from the critics for her backing vocals. Everyone thought that the album had Terry Hall's personality stamped all over it.

The album was relatively free from politics, apart from 'Cruel Circus', which had stemmed from Hall's turn towards vegetarianism: "I felt I wanted to write about animal abuse, but I didn't want to go to the extent of Morrissey and call all humans bastards. I just wanted to point out the ignorance. That's why we called the LP *Virgins And Philistines*, how to be naïve and ignorant at the same time."

When asked about his other political views, compared to his earlier overtly political deportment with the Specials, he said: "Lets face it. I really don't know what's happening in Russia. I don't know what's been happening in Northern Ireland. I don't know what's happening in Stockport! I know what time the shops shut. That's about as political I am. I'm ignorant to a lot of the political stuff, I suppose I've got to dedicate more time to them. When I did Rock Against Racism with the Specials I didn't bother to find out where the money was going. I think that's a bit crap and now I want to avoid these sorts of festivals unless I know the full facts."

The *Virgins And Philistines* tour kicked into life on May 2nd at Coasters in Edinburgh. The band were very good live and they always brought the house down with 'Thinking Of You'. They toured the length and breadth of the country over 13 dates, playing smaller venues rather than big-city halls, a detail that the band were adamant about: "We want to go out at weekends," said Terry, "and not have to be in Scunthorpe on a Monday night when we played some godforsaken hole at the other end of the country the night before. We want to work it so we can enjoy ourselves as well. We want to go to clubs and the like where people go on a Friday and Saturday night, where I would go on a Friday and a Saturday, and just play."

The tour was a reasonable success, but the group, Terry in particular, were given a rough ride by hecklers. One of the worst episodes, which brought the gig to a halt, occurred at Rock City in Nottingham, where Terry was cascaded with abuse from certain areas of the crowd. After years of similar treatment with the Specials and the Fun Boy Three, he had mastered the classic retort. At one point, when one heckler called him a 'fat bastard', he replied angrily: "And just what's wrong with being fat? Anyway, you're only upset 'cos Man Utd kicked the shit out of Nottingham Forest last night."

The same happened at Liverpool University on May 17th, when one crowd member in particular tried to make the band's life a misery. As they were about to perform 'Castles In The Air' as an encore, the perpetrator began to spit at Terry Hall. Terry shot the heckler down with typical assurance and managed to irk any Liverpool FC supporters in the crowd in the process as he introduced 'Thinking Of You' with: "This one is called 'Ian Rush is a skinny twat'!" with reference to Liverpool's (and the country's) top football striker at the time.

It was also noticeable at the gigs that many diehard rude boys and skinheads attended to watch their old hero. Hall may have moved on, but he was still seen as a key figure in the Specials and 2Tone, and there was no way that that connection would be broken over the years, no matter how much he tried to distance himself from it. His audiences would always be peppered with reminders of his chequered past.

After the tour, the Colour Field took time out for holidays and some well earned R&R. They waited a month before their next live appearance, at the famous Glastonbury Festival on June 22nd. It had rained badly before the festival got underway (doesn't it always?) and by the time the festival goers had arrived, the once-green fields had become a quagmire. The band were again on top form musically, and despite a serious spat with hecklers (Hall's responses were, as always, delivered with the speed of a bullet and the subtlety of a brick), the crowd received the band well, even when Hall made references to the state of the arena by changing lines during songs. However, the peace-loving revellers didn't smile much when Terry told them that they reminded him of extras from *Apocalypse Now*!

The band's last gig before the end of a very hectic 1985 was back in their home town of Coventry. They appeared with 14 other bands, mostly local outfits, for 'Cov Aid', a fund-raiser to help the people of drought-stricken Ethiopia. The Colour Field headlined the event, which also featured a dance band called the Supernaturals, led by ex-Selecter singer Pauline Black, with former Special AKA guitarist John Shipley in its line-up. The Colour Field helped to make the show a hit, and even Terry smiled when he was joined onstage for an encore by his favourite contemporary artist, Ian McCulloch from Echo and the Bunnymen.

Despite all the frenetic live work, the Colour Field had also managed to compose enough material in readiness for a second album. Terry Hall had wanted for some time to try his hand at mainstream pop, something which Toby Lyons was a little wary of as it seemed to betray the group's initial intentions. The result appeared with the new single 'Things Could Be Beautiful', a mix of pure pop and indie which sounded a touch like Echo and the Bunnymen (no surprises there then). The B-side 'Frosty Mornings' had a country and western tinge with Red Indian war cries that would have made Johnny Cash proud, and it was felt by some to be the better track than the A-side release. The 12" featured both tracks from the single, but the bonus live tracks of 'Pushing Up The Daisies' and 'Yours Sincerely', recorded at the Hammersmith Palais on their recent tour, were an inspired inclusion. The cover of the record also gave away the news that the group had grown to encompass a new recruit in the shape of Gary Dwyer, former drummer of the Teardrop Explodes who had just split up. This record also saw the first association for Terry Hall with Ian Broudie, a talented writer, musician and producer who would later have massive worldwide success with his band the Lightning Seeds.

In Broudie, Hall had found a comrade, sharing personality traits, musical direction and more importantly, a love of football: "I first met Ian in a field in Somerset in 1982 or 1983." said Terry, "It was the WOMAD Festival. I was friends with Mac (Ian McCulloch) from Echo and the Bunnymen, who were playing. Ian had produced some of the Bunnymen's albums, so he'd gone down there to see them, too. We were introduced in their dressing-room, and I remember Ian was very polite and warm. That was good, because I find meeting new people quite an awkward thing. I'm always thinking, 'Is this a possible friendship or not?' At that time I was in Manchester and Ian was in Liverpool. Every Sunday, I'd go over there to play football in Sefton Park with him and a crowd of other musicians. Ian's actually a fantastic player. He's a midfield grafter, but I'm more concerned about my hair. I suppose you could say that I'm David Beckham to his David Batty. Six or seven years ago, we played our first game together for ages, and I just couldn't run any more. Ian could, but he was in trouble as well. We realised that our bodies were falling apart, and that was another thing we had in common.

"Football's a massive one for us, especially as Ian's a Liverpool fan and I'm Manchester United. There's a deep hatred of each other's team, but we never go into that, which is weird. In the past five years, that's been particularly true, because we've been beating Liverpool. I've noticed Ian goes quiet for a couple of days after those matches. For a while, our families were quite intertwined. A few years back, we all went on holiday to Malaga together. Our kids would be running around the pool screaming, and Ian and I would be sitting under an umbrella moaning about the sun or the Spanish food. Aside from music and football, moaning is one of the biggest things we've got in common!"

Broudie had been a little wary of Hall at the beginning, but later professed that it was just the image that he gave: "I vaguely recall seeing Terry at WOMAD," he said, "but I'd met him before that, too. In 1979, I was working as a DJ at a venue in Liverpool called Eric's, and the owner would give me an extra tenner to help the bands load their gear in and out. At that time, the Specials were called the Coventry Automatics, and they turned up one night to support the Clash. I remember being nervous about meeting Terry, because he was Terry Hall and I was a bit of a fan. We started to get together for a kick-about in Sefton Park in Liverpool. It would be us, Mac from the Bunnymen, and some other guys. Not long after that, Terry was doing some stuff with Colour Field, and he asked me to produce him.

"Everybody had told me he was awkward to work with, but I thought he was focused and straightforward. I think we're both moody bastards, and my friendship with Terry gives me the rare opportunity to go out with somebody who's gloomier than me. Initially, we bonded around music, but now we'll go out and drink and chat about all kinds of things. One passion we share is football, but he's into Man United, which is odd. Liverpool was dominant over United for ages, but now their positions are reversed. When United won the European Champions League against Bayern Munich, I remember Terry saying, 'We were dead lucky' and me going, 'If it was just luck, you wouldn't have got to the final, would you?' I'm sure we were both thinking the complete opposite, though. We are a bit like peas in a pod."

Unfortunately, Broudie's touch on this release failed to propel it into public favour and the record bombed at Number 83. Not only was this the band's last vinyl offering of 1985, but it also marked the end of phase one of the Colour Field, who did not re-materialise for another 12 months. As previously mentioned, there had been some unrest within the ranks about the direction the band were going to take. Whether this caused major problems is unknown, but a seed was definitely planted that would affect the group's future. As it started to germinate, and away from the media glare, the Colour Field went into the studio to record the new album with some misgivings. The only public activity in the 'year out' period came courtesy of Chrysalis Records USA who issued the mini album *The Colour Field*, which was made available in the UK on import. It contained only six tracks taken from *Virgins And Philistines* and the 'Things Could Be Beautiful' 12", and it went on to become collectable.

The band undertook a short two-week tour at the end of 1986 to take in a number of cities that they had omitted from the 1985 tour. Their set had more of a rock edge to it and proved that the group had indeed changed their musical bearing. With a full electric guitar accompaniment, the set consisted of an amalgam of old material, cover versions and new compositions which tended to focus on God and happiness: "The new stuff is very light." said Terry "I mean some of the songs deal with God, that's a phase I'm going through at the moment. I'm feeling more at one with myself, yeah, I'm finding some happiness. I don't feel bitter about anything in 1986, nothing affects me much now."

Indeed, some of the new material was unashamedly religious, as Hall explained: "I think that everyone has a God-shaped hole in their lives."

Their new live set saw a rousing cover of the Monkees' 'She', and thrown into appease his fans were covers of his work with the Specials and Fun Boy Three. The heckling of the previous tour had vanished and the tour coasted along trouble-free, but attendances were low, which could probably be blamed on the group's lengthy absence from the public eye and the fact that the tour was not widely publicised.

With the tour complete, the Colour Field went back into hiding to write and record the forthcoming album. 1986 had been a disappointment for the band and Chrysalis began to get nervous. They had spent a lot of money on what were essentially flop records, and had put together the tours, but had seen little reimbursement besides the brief flirtation with success that had followed the release of the single 'Thinking Of You' and the debut album. They expressed the need to see some results, clearly still mindful of their experience with the Special AKA.

Terry Hall was now convinced that the direction the band should take was towards making precision pop, and their next single set about putting his ideas into action. In February 1987 they released 'Running Away', a cover of the 1972 hit by Sly and the Family Stone. The new sound was truly run of the mill pop and featured rasping saxophones and heavy percussion. The B-side 'Digging It Deep' was a track from the new collection and provided a further taste of the new Colour Field. The single, despite its pop-laden sound and production by Blondie's producer Richard Gottehrer, panted heavily as it reached Number 84 in the charts. Not the comeback they had all hoped for, given that all aspects had been thought through to make the group more attractive to the record-buying public. The sound had changed, moody studio publicity photos had been taken and the name of the group had been altered slightly to Colourfield, but the biggest transformation of all was within the group itself.

The four-man line up had been cut to two. Drummer Gary Dwyer had departed and more surprisingly, founder Karl Shale was gone. Despite the fact he had recorded material for the new album, *Deception*, the change of direction for the group may have caused Shale to leave, although the reasons for his departure have never been disclosed. The

YOU'RE WONDERING NOW

progression to the group's current style had taken much creative wrangling, and a month or so later, Lyons, too, decided enough was enough. With the band (I use the term loosely) reduced to one, Terry was left to conclude the album on his own, which proved tough and eventually made him ill: "*Deception's* failure is all my fault because I didn't want to do anything with it. I should have split the group up before we started to record it. I was listening to A & R men and managing directors who were saying 'you should go to New York and do this or do that.' But I was really ill, mentally ill."

It seemed that Terry was losing ground in his long battle with depression, which had deepened due to the stress of completing the album by himself: "I was totally mentally ill. I didn't know that, but I know that now. I just flipped, that happens sometimes. So we went to New York for six weeks to record that album and I didn't go into the studio. I walked through the park, that was great, better than being in a studio with lots of people that I didn't know or want to record with. You should stop it but you can't sometimes, but you leave all these people in the shit so you see it through, even though you hate every second of it."

On April 4th 1987, *Deception* was released. Those critics that bothered to review it gave the record a mixed reception. One *NME* review was particularly scathing: "*This lot have absolutely nothing going for them. No sense of humour. No glamour. No good melodies. No danceable rhythms. No excitement. No controversy. No emotion. Nothing whatsoever. They are, in short, ruddy awful.*"

The album was given little or no promotion as it was obvious that Chrysalis had lost hope and interest in the the Colourfield. It was very apt that the grim black and white cover shot depicted a large close up of Terry Hall's face bearing a very worried look. The album proved to be a complete lame duck and spent just one week in the charts at Number 95. In all fairness, there were some highlights in the shape of 'From Dawn To Distraction', and 'Confession' and although it was the Colourfield coming of age so to speak, no one, bar the diehards, was interested in it. Hall was simply glad to see it off his back and he was left to contemplate his future yet again. While he did so, Chrysalis issued a tympani-drum remix of 'She' with another track from 'Deception' entitled 'Monkey In Winter' (which featured the vocal talents of Sinead O'Connor before she hit the big time) on the B-side. As with previous Colourfield singles, all the remixes in the world could not save it from fading away unnoticed, and it failed to even register in the Top 100. In late 1987 the Colourfield door was closed by Terry.

Karl Shale continued in the music industry, first with the band Vagabond Joy before gaining recognition for his work with the Candyskins. He later moved on to the electronic experimental band Ausgang, and later still was part of Zero Zero, who released the track 'Ava', a tribute to actress Ava Gardner, on Redhead Records. Toby Lyons abandoned music and re-trained as a graphic designer in the late Eighties. He worked as a designer in consultancies in London and the Northwest and taught graphic design at Stockport College. He then expanded his design talents and took up the challenge of digital media within the graphic design field and went on to gain a Masters Degree in Multimedia Arts from Liverpool's John Moores University. He is currently part of the graphic design tutor team at Sheffield's Hallam University. Drummer Gary Dwyer joined forces again with Teardrop Explodes singer Julian Cope.

Chrysalis demanded one more album from Terry, who re-appeared from virtually nowhere in late 1988 with yet another band imaginatively called Terry, Blair and Anouchka. The line up featured American actress-cum-singer Blair Booth and designer Anouchka Groce. Booth had come to the UK in 1981 and formed the band The Rest Is History, and she wrote the song 'Heaven Knows' that was covered by Robert Plant, and gave him a big hit. She also went on to supply vocals on the *Copy Cats* LP for one-time New York Dolls guitarist Johnny Thunders before she teamed up with Terry Hall. Groce, born in Sydney, Australia, had made jewellery, and performed in a transvestite metal band!

The trio formed with a shared love of kitsch conventional pop music and Sixties tracks and used their influences to further Hall's drive to create the perfect pop song. They began to write songs immediately and passionately but it took them a year to refine their style which resulted in their single, 'Missing', issued by Chrysalis on November 11th 1989. Although the cover portrayed the trio, the record was credited solely to Terry Hall. The track was a typical Hall concoction, the story of a broken marriage wrapped up in an upbeat melody. The lyrics showed that despite being a married man and father (to Felix, born in 1988 – Terry had had to help with the birth due to a shortage of doctors and nurses caused by several premature babies born the same day – and later Theo, who would follow his dad's footsteps in music as guitarist with the band Le Volume Courbe) he still preferred the trials and tribulations of relationships to spur his songwriting. Was 'Missing', with its tale of divorce and separation, taken from his real-life experiences?

"Well, in relationships," he said, "that's what might happen or could happen. I'm trying to avoid that happening. I have tried to get a good balance between my family and my work."

The reverse was another sombre look at life, sugar coated in a colourful tune, called 'Happy Families'. The record received reasonable airplay, even on Radio 1, but it was another flop, rising no higher than Number 75. The new group initiated minor media curiosity, and Hall was still happy to divulge his thoughts and feelings to any one who wanted to hear them: "I was quite disappointed with the last Colourfield album." said Terry, "not necessarily the record but everyone I was working with. I got fed up of working with men. I'm not that keen on male company, I find it a bit boring. I find women much easier to work with and there's no bullshit, and besides Anouchka has a good-shaped head that looks really good on the sleeve of the record."

The group quickly followed up the debut single in early 1990 with the far superior 'Ultra Modern Nursery Rhymes', a cut that sounded very much like the Colourfield meets the Lightning Seeds meets the Mamas and Papas. Controversial stand-up comedian Jerry Sadowitz was recruited to appear in the promotional video. His management initially demanded £10,000 for his three-minute appearance, but this was refused and he eventually did the shoot for £400. Despite everything, this eclectic mix only spent a week in the charts and reached a poor Number 77. It deserved better, although it did notch up a Top 5 spot in the Danish listings. The charts at that time would have been livened up by characters like Terry Hall every now and then, to prove that music hadn't been reduced to a collection of electro beats conjured up in a studio, or endless teeny-pop manufactured by the ubiquitous Stock, Aitken and Waterman. Hall and the girls gave it one final go, and in February released their one and only album, also entitled *Ultra Modern Nursery Rhymes*. Hall explained: "The songs all have something in common and a lot of it has something to do with me. If you tend to write ten songs over a period of a year, that's what comes out, yourself. I can only write about me, really, I can't write about anything else. I don't know what pop music is really nowadays. People say Jason Donovan, that's what people say pop music should be. Disposable. I disagree; it shouldn't be disposable, it should be memorable. Pop should last forever, it shouldn't be a Kylie Minogue record. I think it's pretty desperate at the

178

Terry & Brad at the Moonlight Club, 1979. Photo by R.Byers

Terry with young kid fan backstage 1979, photo by R.Byers

The SPECIALS – from conception to reunion

moment, it's nothingness. What is dance music? I don't understand. I don't understand how thousands of people can listen to a bass drum, it bothers me. It bothers me that people can actually dance to drums. That leaves a lot to talk about with your friends doesn't it? 'Do you like that drum?'"

Hall had crafted the album he craved, full of pure pop. One track, 'Three Cool Catz', a cover of the 1958 Coasters song and later famously recorded by the Beatles on their audition tape for Decca Records in 1962, echoed a not too distant past with the Fun Boy Three with its hints of "T'Ain't What You Do (It's The Way That You Do It)'. Unfortunately, the album followed its predecessors into vinyl obscurity and would also signal the end for the short-lived Terry, Blair and Anouchka. The album is regarded as one of Terry's best works and is now highly sought-after.

Booth moved on to record with the Associates, Marc Almond and the band Oui 3. In 2001, she formed the company Peach Productions which established itself as an 'outstanding provider of music services to the creative industries'. Anouchka Groce went back to jewellery design, lampshade production, did a stint as a muralist and later became an accomplished writer of books aimed at teenagers. Hall's least successful venture to date had come to a close after a year and a half and his 13-year association with Chrysalis ended with the demise of the trio.

He withdrew from the music scene to concentrate on his family duties. In 1992, Terry found himself part of a chart hit for the band the Lightning Seeds when he worked again with former Colour Field producer, and long-time friend, Ian Broudie. One Lightning Seeds track, 'Sense', that featured Hall on backing vocals became a Top 30 hit. Terry also appeared on the Lightning Seeds album of the same name that was released after the single. Ian Broudie said of their alliance: "There was a period after I produced Colourfield when I didn't see Terry for a while, but I still thought of him as a mate. Then he phoned up out of the blue and we decided to do a bit of writing together. People always think my stuff's really happy and Terry's is glum, but he's got this wry sense of humour and an odd take on life which makes you chuckle. The truth is that some of the Lightning Seeds' most positive and uptempo songs are the ones Terry and I co-wrote."

Later he went on to an unlikely collaboration with former Eurythmics main man Dave Stewart. Buoyed up by his success with the Lightning Seeds, Hall threw himself whole-heartedly into his new project with the multi-talented Stewart: "I was walking down the street when I bumped into Dave. We started talking and decided to do some work together. It's as simple as that," recalled Terry.

The partnership was never meant to be long-lasting and was essentially a couple of friends who tinkered in the studio. Their efforts needed an outlet and so they created the band Vegas, Terry Hall's fifth group. Dave Stewart was signed to the Sony BMG label, a giant in the music industry, and they agreed to be the outlet for Vegas. So, now with a co-writer of some stature, Hall was possibly on to something big. News of the collaboration spread through the media, although they unfairly dubbed Terry as the 'erstwhile Eighties star' and Piers Morgan of The Sun branded him 'a has-been who last had something decent in the charts back in 1982'. So the project was given a mixed reception, although the general consensus was that the duo were leagues above Wet Wet Wet or Right Said Fred. Hall and Stewart pooled their writing resources and got Olle Romo, formerly of Eurythmics, to drum for them. On September 19th 1992 the track 'Possessed' silenced the mocking journalists and came in at Number 35. The Stewart influence of electro-pop was obvious on the record and dominated the style of the group, and it proved to be an effective approach as the modernist/futurist approach was popular in the UK at the time. Two CD singles were released, the first containing an extra Dave Stewart composition 'Lying Barefoot In Bed' and the second a Terry Hall track, 'Infectious'.

Hall and Stewart were suddenly in demand and appeared across the media in glossy magazines, newspapers and on TV. They were interviewed on GM-TV by Lorraine Kelly, although Hall only spoke four words, all about Manchester United. The success of 'Possessed' was followed up by news of a tour in November which turned out to be only a handful of dates, one at London's Town & Country Club where they were quite brilliant. The release of their debut album was imminent, but before the album was issued Chrysalis Records decided to try and milk the cash cow that was Terry Hall. They released a compact disc compilation called *The Collection*, featuring cuts from the whole of Terry's musical career including tracks by the Specials, Fun Boy Three, the Colour Field and Terry, Blair and Anouchka. The CD proved to be a collector's item only and any thoughts Chrysalis had of making a mint fell by the wayside.

To keep the momentum going BMG released another single 'She' (not be confused with the Colourfield track of the same name), a cover version of the Charles Aznavour classic. The video, shot in the South of France, actually featured the diminutive Gallic legend. 'She' was very heavily promoted, including a huge TV advertising campaign, and it became a minor hit, reaching Number 43. Almost immediately, *Vegas*, the self-titled album, was issued and proved to be a mixed bag, with Hall's work easily distinguishable from Stewart's more progressive contributions. Terry's quintessentially English style of song-writing was in total contrast to Stewart's baffling abstract ditties. Terry's ongoing theme of unrequited love appeared on a number of tracks, but they never made a dent on the charts: "With Vegas we wrote this fantastic song on the album called 'The Trouble With Lovers'" said Terry "and met up with Barry Manilow and played it to him to see if he wanted to sing it. Such a fantastic fucking highlight. I saw him the night before at the Albert Hall with all his fans and it was like Jesus. He's got a big nose, y'know, but he doesn't write shit songs."

The duo played 'She' live on the ITV programme *This Morning*, and Stewart took the opportunity to unveil his hidden talents as a painter. He showed off a number of paintings he had done of people he had worked with over the years, one of which was an unusually posed picture of Terry Hall in front of stained glass, which raised a few eyebrows. In a final throw of the dice, another track was lifted from the album, 'Walk Into The Wind', featuring the vocal talents of Mrs Dave Stewart, Terry's old friend from Bananarama, Siobhan Fahey. Despite a decent promotional push, including a live appearance on Jonathan Ross' *Saturday Zoo* show, the public remained unimpressed and the record limped to Number 65. Its failure effectively brought an end to a promising partnership. Terry's plans to 'to make lots of money from Vegas and fuck off forever' never came close to fruition.

In early 1994, Terry proved he was not one to rest on his laurels, and began quietly playing low-key shows in Camden, London, to test the waters for a career as Terry Hall, solo artist. He had a new troupe of backing musicians who could boast a wealth of musical experience, and the sound was very contemporary and very Brit-Pop. The musicians included former Smiths guitarist Craig Gannon and ex-Bunnymen bassist Les Pattinson, while drums came courtesy of Chris Sharrock, once of World Party and The La's, and at this point sticksman for the Lightning Seeds. The Seeds connection did not end there and Hall drafted in friend Ian Broudie again. Hall, Broudie and Gannon established a very strong writing team and a collaboration with Nick Heyward, formerly of Haircut 100, was planned for the upcoming album.

The group retired to Liverpool to record, and within weeks the album was cut. Dave Stewart helped out by signing Terry to his own label, Anxious Records. The next step was to try out the new collection on unsuspecting gig-goers. A five-date tour was organised to take in Newcastle, Leeds, Liverpool and London with a finale at the Phoenix Festival in Stratford, where they delivered a perfect set. The new Hall persona and style received great reviews and brought critical acclaim, most commentators declaring it to be his best work since the Specials. The evolution of Terry Hall as an all-round musical chameleon had reached its conclusion. This is he what he had been searching for through his regeneration and reinvention with all of his previous bands, and he could afford a wry smile. In August 1994, with TV appearances on *Music Box* and *The Big Breakfast* under his belt, he released his first major solo single, 'Forever J', the story of a 30-something couple based on his long term relationship with wife Jeanette. It should have had major chart impact, but sadly it only appealed to his fans and reached Number 67. However, hot on its heels came the album *Home*, an apt title, as he was now back living in his native Midlands, in Kenilworth near Coventry.

Home was a stunning ten-song collection that showed new depths, inspired by the recent death of his father (Hall would dedicate the album to him). On the album were 'Forever J', and the track 'Sense', which was to be his next single. 'Sense' was the same song that Hall and Ian Broudie had written and which had been a Lightning Seeds' hit two years before. Terry's version, commercial as it was, failed to hit the mark, but surpassed 'Forever J' and reached Number 54. The track's Radio 1 exposure proved futile, but Hall was having the time of his life, he was making great music and he knew it. He was rejuvenated and back in demand and found himself back on Radio 1 reciting poetry to DJ Mark Radcliffe. He then played a refined set on the BBC's *Later...with Jools Holland* before taking off on a small tour as part of the backing for the Lightning Seeds. Another track from *Home* called 'No No No' was slated for release as a single, but for reasons unknown the record was withdrawn before it was issued.

Terry then caused a stir in an interview with *Record Collector* magazine when he said that, if the reasons were true and just, he would consider playing again with a re-formed Specials: "You know, looking back, after everything that had gone on, it was fun," said Terry, "I wouldn't have missed it. At the end it was a case of growing apart from each other. I still like to hear Specials records every couple of months."

During this period, Terry forged a long-lasting friendship with Damon Albarn, who was then the lead singer of Blur, one the UK's biggest bands. The Specials had had a huge influence on Albarn's career. Albarn had spent his early youth listening to the Specials ('Fade Away' on the Blur album *The Great Escape* reeked of the Specials) and Madness (their influence can be heard all over the track 'Parklife') and it was this hard-edged music from the streets that would pave his way over the ensuing years: "Ska and 2Tone," Albarn explained, "was the music of my teenage years. To me, the most influential pop music was when I was a kid. It had a lasting effect."

Terry had also his children to thank for keeping him up to date with the latest recording fads and artists while he had been estranged from the music industry: "My five-year-old bought 'Parklife', which I told Damon about and I think he was worried for about a second that a five-year-old likes Blur!"

He added: "I bought *Modern Life Is Rubbish* when Blur were unpopular, but I met Alex James later on at some do, and he was like Bambi, so pissed and fragile. Through

182

him came Damon. I knew he'd said he liked what I did, so it was pointless talking about the records we'd made, so we just tried to write some songs. He'd finished writing for this new Blur album and he still had a lot of ideas left. Someone else might have worried whether it was a good career move, but he didn't. His style of writing's one that I recognised. Funny, isn't it, British music? It's always been there."

The Hall/Albarn partnership spawned a fantastic version of the Specials' 'Nite Klub', which they sang live on French TV, with Terry on lead vocals. Around the same time, Hall was asked by UK trip-hop artist Tricky to join him in a recording session. Hall was suddenly very much in vogue with the younger generation of bold, new artists. They were seeking inspiration and not afraid to stretch the boundaries of music, they were in a position that the Specials had found themselves in, able to politicise their work and spread a message. Tricky said: "I've been listening to Terry's stuff for years, since I was 15. I've got more in common with him than I have with most. He's very real, and there's not many real artists out there, is there? He relies mostly on talent and he'll only prostitute himself so much. I respect that."

The duo almost never made it past their first encounter after Tricky had cited him as one of his favourite singers, as Hall explained: "I read this thing where Tricky put three or four singers down that he liked, saying I was nowhere near as good as Martina [British vocalist Martina Topley-Bird]. So he rang me and we went to Bournemouth. We said nothing for about two hours until we found something funny to talk about. It was a real release, like when we used to record in the Fun Boy Three when we didn't really understand what we were doing and held it back for B-sides because we were embarrassed. I'd seen this film with three poets saying your initial thoughts should be your last thought, which coincided with Tricky's way of working; I did one vocal where I went out of tune and he said, 'That's alright'. It was good for someone to say that again. Tricky gets caught up in this thing where, maybe it's because he's black, but a lot of stuff he plays is like Nirvana or something. He's got a very odd slant to what he does and what he listens to. We can get very caught-up in this dance-rap whatever it is thing, but he's got a weird, really typically English slant which I quite like. Certain Specials songs were influential on him, too, but I don't know why, he just thought we were pretty honest. We've become friends, really, and we go off on these funny ideas that go nowhere fast, but we share a 'clueless' approach of not really thinking about things. And he takes the piss. Bristol and Coventry are very similar places; you're really nowhere and with nothing great to draw on, so you have to make these things happen yourself."

The friendships and working relationships that Hall shared with Albarn, Tricky and Ian Broudie came to fruition in 1995 with the *Chasing Rainbows* EP. Broudie produced the EP, which was released in a twin CD set and featured a mix of studio and live cuts. CD number one contained 'Chasing Rainbows' which was written by Albarn and Hall, and 'Mistakes', written by Hall and Broudie, 'See No Evil', a live cover of the song by US rock band Television and a totally unrecognisable 'Ghost Town', recorded live with Tricky at the Shepherds Bush Empire. The second CD featured the title track and the live version of 'Ghost Town', but there was an unexpected bonus of two further live tracks taken from Hall's prolific past, 'Our Lips Are Sealed' and 'Thinking Of You', both recorded at Manchester University the year before. The 'Ghost Town' track with Tricky caused the most interest. the Specials classic had been stripped completely and cleverly amended: "It would have been impossible to stick to the original of 'Ghost Town,'" said Terry. "It would have been like a cabaret thing, just sad, so I got Tricky to rip it apart and not keep anything of it. We did a version of 'Little Drummer Boy' as well, which is fucking mad!"

The *Chasing Rainbows* EP crawled to Number 62 in the charts, but Hall remained unflustered. He had even considered opening a sandwich shop for his own personal sanity, and to help keep afloat in the quieter times! He remained focused enough to help work on a musical with Vegas cohort Dave Stewart, based loosely around the secret life of Queen Victoria: "Dave has been working on it for ten years, it goes through changes. I have no idea when that could end up on a stage but, like lots of these things you work on for years, it's so complicated to launch a musical."

A few months later, and Terry returned the favour to Tricky by appearing as guest backing vocalist for the Bristol trip-hopper's Top 30 single release 'Pumpkin'. Terry would appear on a number of different tracks over the coming months as a guest vocalist, but one of the more important was on behalf of the charity War Child. The organisation was founded by British filmmakers Bill Leeson and David Wilson in 1993. It focussed on providing assistance and care to children in areas of conflict and post-conflict. Shocked by the plight of children in the former Yugoslavia, they decided to use their film and entertainment background to raise money for aid agencies operating there. They then decided to expand their work to a worldwide scale. The album was the brainchild of Tony Crean, International Marketing Manager at record label Go! Discs. He had been at home, nursing himself through a bout of 'flu and watched the fighting in and around the Bosnian capital of Sarajevo on TV, when the Balkan War was at its height. The conflict had cost 250,000 lives and had displaced over 2,000,000 people. Hundreds of thousands of families were left with nothing as a result. When he returned to work, he couldn't stop thinking about what he had witnessed: "Everyone was aware of it, but no one knew what to do." he said, "I was reading a quote from a charity worker who said 'We need £200,000 to feed and clothe these children, and it's £200,000 we haven't got.' And I thought, 'If *Melody Maker* and *NME* readers just gave a pound each that would do the trick'."

Crean bumped into Anton Brookes, who was managing ex-Happy Mondays vocalist Shaun Ryder's new band Black Grape, and persuaded him to get involved. That night Brookes talked to the band about doing something and they agreed. Another phone secured the services of the Stone Roses: "The initial idea was a big gig with the Stone Roses and Black Grape," said the Stone Roses' PR officer (the ironically named Terri Hall, who would later come to work on the Specials' reunion), "but the venue, Old Trafford Cricket Ground, fell through."

Crean, Brookes and Hall knew every British rock and dance act worth their salt and, with Black Grape and the Stone Roses on board, thought that other acts might follow. They formulated the idea to put together an album to raise funds, and just days after this first meeting, Crean turned to the charity War Child with a list of artists who would contribute to the record. They included Portishead, Suede, the Chemical Brothers, Paul Weller, and of course the new Brit-Pop favourite, Terry Hall. Crean had a plan to get all of the acts into studios in record time: "The idea was to get some of the laziest people you could think of to do something as quickly as possible," said Crean. "That a band like the Stone Roses, who took five years to record one album, could actually turn round a track in a day sends out a signal that anything is possible."

Crean's plan was to record and release the album within a week, making it the fastest album ever recorded. The album, to be called *Help*, would be recorded on Monday, mastered on Tuesday, pressed on Wednesday, released on Saturday and be Number 1 by Sunday. When the clock hit one minute past midnight on Monday September 4th 1995 there was no going back and the recording sessions started.

Initially, the non-stop 32-hour production process ran six hours over schedule, but on Wednesday, finished copies of the album began to arrive at Go! Discs and by Friday, a convoy of Securicor vans had delivered over 300,000 copies to record stores the length and breadth of the country. The War Child charity was thrilled when the record entirely sold out on the Saturday and did indeed reach Number 1 on Sunday. *Help* raised a staggering £1.25 million, which began to help the children of Bosnia immediately.

On the day of recording at the Metropolis Studios in London, it was arranged for Terry Hall to perform with Marijne Van Der Vlugt, the Dutch vocalist of UK band Salad, on 'Dream A Little Dream Of Me', a 1931 song made famous by Mama Cass Elliot of the Mamas and the Papas in 1968. Although it was all short notice and the track needed to be recorded within the day, Hall said: "You usually get more time than that but the Beatles did it in minutes."

Marijne explained how relaxed the day turned out to be: "We hooked up with Terry to record 'Dream A Little Dream Of Me' for the *Help* album. Like all bands on the album we had to have our song recorded and mixed by midnight. Producer Stephen Street came up with the goods. TV crews, a string quartet, a dog and a baby and many others waltzed in and out all day, there was no room for egos or tantrums, and a warm-belly experience was had by all. Terry had wanted Eric Cantona to do the spoken intro but Man Utd wouldn't let him come out to play, so a passing journalist from *The Times* did it instead."

Terry was still in demand, and Tricky came again to harness his vocals skills on his latest endeavour, *Nearly God*. Tricky was once more delighted to be working with his musical hero, and continued to emphasise the importance of a band like the Specials: "Terry grew up with Jamaican culture as well as English culture, that's the only way the Specials could have happened. It couldn't have been Jamaican music on one side, and English music on the other, then you'd just have had reggae and punk rock. They bled into each other. In America I know guys who've got Jamaican parents and they can't understand a Jamaican guy talking, but Terry can, and his parents are white. No other place on earth could have produced the Specials, unless a whole group of white English people did a mass migration to Jamaica, and they mixed. If you listen to American ska bands, they don't sound authentic, it's like surf music with reggae mixed with it."

The *Nearly God* collection was a bizarre but innovative recording on which Terry co-wrote two of the tracks. Lyrically it covered lullabies, sex, humour, and some darker insights into the warped world of Tricky. The most outstanding and extraordinary track was 'Poems', which featured three brooding soliloquies by Tricky, Terry and Martina Topley-Bird, tied together by the phrase 'you promised me poems'. It was released as a single and resulted in the trio appearing on Channel 4's music show *The White Room* to perform the track. On the same show, Hall and Tricky also played their stripped-down version of 'Ghost Town'.

In 1996 the Lightning Seeds had a hit with 'What If?' which was co-written by Hall. A few months later the Hall/Broudie collaboration produced another Lightning Seeds hit when they re-issued 'Lucky You', a flop when originally released the year before, on which Hall provided backing vocals. At the beginning of 1997 Hall started work on his second solo album under new label The South Sea Bubble Company. A taster from the album came with the release of single, 'Ballad Of A Landlord', which was not far removed musically from the sound of the *Home* album. It secured a minor hit, reaching Number 50. Widely regarded as one of his finest moments, 'Landlord' was the precursor of the new album, ironically entitled *Laugh*, as Terry didn't have much to laugh about.

Young Terry Hall in Jerry's flat 1978

Young Terry Hall at rehearsals in flat 1978. Photo by R.Byers

The recording and writing of the work took place as his marriage of 22 years crumbled and he found himself divorced.

He sought solace in friends like Ian Broudie: "Recently, I went through a horrible divorce," he said. "You need someone to help you work things through, and Ian's one of two friends who have been there for me. It'll be Sunday evening, and after I've dropped my kids back up North, I'll ask Ian if he fancies meeting up. Even though he knows that he'll be listening to me banging on about my troubles for an hour, he'll come, and that's OK, because it's a mutual thing. Ideally, you want that with your partner, but it's good when you have it with a mate and you can throw in the odd comment about football. I think that bonding around sport or music is a fantastic part of male friendships."

Broudie didn't appear on the new album, but Lightning Seeds drummer Chris Sharrock and bassist Martin Campbell were part of the backing band. The album overflowed with a mix of tracks describing the pain, hurt and anguish of his relationship breakdown, along with tales of suburban frustration, archetypal Terry Hall material. It is a great collection of tunes, especially a cover of Todd Rundgren's 'I Saw The Light'. Many of Hall's friends got in on the act, with Damon Albarn co-writing on two numbers, an unlikely collaboration with Stephen 'Tin Tin' Duffy, Nick Heyward on vocal duties and even a blast from the past in Caroline Lavelle, the former Fun Boy Three cellist. Hall also took the producer's chair for the very first time, along with his right hand man Craig Gannon and future Kaiser Chiefs producer Cenzo Townshend. It was well received in the music industry, but fell short in the public domain again.

Music magazine reviewer Mark Luffman said: "'I'm Terry, and I'm going to enjoy myself first,' he once sang. It seems that the only honest reaction to living today is despair, that man's natural condition is misery. Or maybe I've been reading too many interviews with Terry Hall. Say it loud and proud, Terry Hall is a miserable sod. Laugh is a delicious sulking grouch of an album and far from assuring you that there's actually quite a lot of humour in Terry Hall's new record, I'd like to make it clear that Laugh is unremittingly glum, intermittently suicidal, and absolutely brilliant. Thank goodness misery loves company. He who enjoys himself last enjoys himself longest."

Some other reviews dubbed the album 'distilled sunshine' and 'one of the richest and most satisfying pop albums of the year', while another said 'at a time when you can hardly move without stumbling into some Eighties comeback artist, this is the most welcome return.' The promo video to 'Ballad Of A Landlord' saw American ska-pop band No Doubt (who were carving a successful niche for themselves on a global level) make a cameo appearance. The band had long cited the Specials as a major influence in their career and incorporated covers of 'A Message To You Rudy' and 'Gangsters' in their set. Terry had appeared as a special guest at one of the band's concerts in Paris, where he joined the band for 'Gangsters'. Their appearance in the 'Landlord' video shoot was to repay a favour from Hall, who, a year previously, had appeared in the video for No Doubt's ska-orientated release 'Sunday Morning'.

With his divorce weighing heavily on his mind, Terry felt no motivation to do much promotion on the Laugh album. His priorities in life had changed: "I was in the middle of a divorce as I was trying to promote the album, so it was pretty impossible. I just allowed myself to fall apart I think. Just let it go. Doing a solo record, you try to write about who you are and what you know, and if life's overtaken that it's very difficult to explain it. It becomes such a painful process. I thought, 'Why am I putting myself through this? I'm talking about divorce and loss and all this shit. It doesn't make any sense. I mean, I can avoid doing this.'"

It was then he realised that the *Laugh* album was to be his requiem as a solo artist. He drifted out of the music industry to take some time for himself. There had always been considerable gaps between his projects, but Hall was dismissive of the idea that it was a case of 'slowness' being a problem: "It's just about being honest, and not bothering about brand-names and making the same album over and over. Sometimes it seems like there's a huge gap between records. To me it seems like ten minutes, because I'm spending that time listening to music, doing my homework. It's like an architect drawing up plans for a building. It can take years, it isn't a race. I've never bought into being part of that pop-music, disposable thing."

Such an approach was fundamentally at odds with the music industry and it would be almost two years before he resurfaced as a guest vocalist for Japanese electronic duo Michiharu Shimoda and Takahiro Haruno, better known as the Silent Poets, on their single 'Sugar Man'. He then quickly moved on to appear with Sinead O'Connor on the album *A Song For Eurotrash*. *Eurotrash*, the Channel 4 TV programme presented by Antoine De Caunes, managed to get a variety of acts to do new versions of Eurovision 'classics'. They were very tongue-in-cheek and they weren't averse to tackling some of the most dire examples. Hall and O'Connor maintained their downbeat personae and did a hangdog version of Dana's Eurovision winner 'All Kinds Of Everything' for the collection. The sales and reviews reflected the absurdity of the album.

By 2000, Terry had met the band the Dub Pistols, a London-based dub/bigbeat outfit founded by ex-club promoter Barry Ashworth in 1996. Along with Jason O'Bryan and a host of other musicians and vocalists, Ashworth and his Dub Pistols had become a major force in dance music and had crossed over into the mainstream with their unique collaborations with names such as Hall and reggae singer Horace Andy. Jason O'Bryan recalled their first meeting with Terry: "We first met Terry briefly at a Lightning Seeds gig at Warwick University, and later were introduced to Terry professionally through Barry Ashworth's publisher at the time, BMG. We had presented BMG with a wish list of people we would like to work with, Terry was first on the list and, as ridiculous as it seemed at the time, it actually happened!

"It was a big deal to be working with him for both me and Barry and I remember having to psych myself up to be able to deal with it on the way to the studio. We recorded the vocals in Barry's front room in Ilbert Street, Kensal Rise. Terry was instantly likeable, with his dry sense of humour and old-man style rolling tobacco, 'Problem Is' is still my favourite Dub Pistols song to date. Since those days Terry has been lucky enough to work with us pretty consistently, he sang on five songs on our third album *Speakers & Tweeters* and has been a regular guest vocalist for us on tour, usually coming on for the last three songs to close the set."

It was a case of 'living the dream' for band member Barry Ashworth: "To get someone like Terry Hall to come over to your house is unbelievable! When you have them ringing on your door and standing there, well! Know what I mean? We used to spend a lot of time, when I was in school, down Petticoat Lane market, buying loads of roots, reggae and dub and then that led on to 2Tone and Specials and all that stuff. These bands, to us, were like, the fucking nuts! We were just really into it, I guess, and if you make music you can do what you like. The idea behind the Dub Pistols was that you could throw everything into the pot and that there were no rules. In essence we adopted the Sex Pistols' punk-rock ethic of anything goes. Obviously, being into dub, there were a hell of a lot of old-school influences, such as Tommy McCook, Roland Alphonso, as well as all the Eighties producers and current artists such as Cutty Ranks,

188

Sizzla and Pressure Drop. The track that we've done with Terry is very like Specials' stuff. I think that it is probably the first time that he has done that [kind of material] in years. The reaction we are getting from people is really good."

It wasn't long before Terry and Damon Albarn were reunited in Albarn's new project, Gorillaz. The virtual cartoon alternative/rock/hip-hop band, created by Albarn and *Tank Girl* comic originator Jamie Hewlett, had taken the music scene by storm and their first single 'Clint Eastwood' had gone straight to the top of the charts. Albarn and Hewlett created Gorillaz in 1998 when they were sharing a flat on Westbourne Grove in London. The idea to create the band came about when the two were watching MTV: "If you watch MTV for too long, it's a bit like hell, there's nothing of substance there," said Hewlett, "so we got this idea for a cartoon band, something that would be a comment on that."

Later that year the first association for Hall and the Gorillaz came in what had to be the most bizarre pop pairing ever – Gorillaz and D12, the US rap band with infamous mentor Eminem (who didn't take part on this track), with Terry Hall on guest vocals. They got together at the Gorillaz Kong Studios in London to record '911', a track about the terrorist atrocities in New York on September 11th 2001. Damon Albarn said: "We had organized the collaboration beforehand, and the terrorist attacks added a different context, to say the least, to what we did together. We're trying to work out how to put that track out on the Internet for everyone. It's quite a political song, and it needs to be out there now. When I was in my early teens, I was really lucky because I had bands such as the Specials, who had that fusion of different types of music with politics. In a way, the Gorillaz is inspired by their ground-breaking attitude. Terry Hall, who I have worked with a lot and still intend to, sent me a text message the other day wishing us luck, which was nice."

Hall would re-appear on the Gorillaz track 'Lil Dub Chefin' from their dub album *Laika Come Home*.

In another milestone in musical diversity, Hall was then invited by Damon Albarn to record an album with MC Mushtaq on Albarn's Honest Jon's record label. Mushtaq's background as part of the British multi-ethnic world fusion techno band Fun-Da-Mental gave him the right credentials for the job. The album *The Hour Of Two Lights* was to be a heavily multi-cultural exploration. The recording featured a blind Algerian rapper, a 12-year-old Lebanese singer called Natasha, a Syrian flautist, a 70-year-old Jewish clarinettist (Eddie Morden, famous for playing the *Pink Panther* theme) and a bunch of Polish gypsy asylum seekers called Romany Rad. Added to the cocktail was a dash of Jewish German heritage in the shape of Terry Hall, a splash of Sufi Muslim from Mushtaq, and a pinch of the quintessentially English with the vocals of Damon Albarn. Hall jokingly commented: "Well we couldn't really keep Damon and his melodica off, could we? It is his label!"

The album was chock-a-block with Eastern European rhythms blended in with hip-hop, Middle Eastern percussion and Arabic vocals to reflect the diverse backgrounds of the artists who had been assembled to perform. *The Hour of Two Lights* needed a long period of groundwork and research in order to realise the music fully. Hall spent the best part of a year planning the record with Mushtaq before they started to look for their astonishing cast of musicians, most of whom had not recorded before. Hall was feeling strong and quite fervent about the venture: "A lot of shit was going on at the same time as us recording this album and that's going to come through. With Romany Rad, we were playing with people who had been firebombed out of their houses in Poland. The stories are very, very upsetting. Things like they don't like bank holidays because their solicitor might go away at the weekend and that's when they swoop and get deported. When I was growing up, bank holidays were about ice cream and going to the river. We also wanted to take influences from everywhere, but it's not a bish-bosh of other people's cultures. Everybody had a sense of something in common in their minority and oppression and struggle. In the end, it felt more like we were editing a film than making a record."

Terry also stressed that the album was in fact, a public forum, with some of the content focusing on the 'war on terrorism' and other conflicts, and it showed that he was still keeping abreast of matters on a socio-political level: "There was a huge political statement being made with the Specials," he said, "You just had to look at a photo and you got it. That's exactly what we feel about this. If you have Arabic and Hebrew on the same record you've made a political statement. I've been through the whole standing-on-a-box thing and it's great, but it gets sort of dangerous. The idea of suggestion sometimes is good."

His partner Mushtaq, a Muslim born in London to a Bangladeshi father and Iranian mother, had spent much of his childhood in both countries and this tangled heritage was appreciated by Hall: "I was presented with a Star of David when I was a kid and, ten years on, I found out that my grandfather was a German Jewish watchmaker. I'm still searching, but there are different stories. I grew up in an environment where you didn't really know where you were from. Coventry was built on immigrants because it was an industrial city looking for cheap labour. I don't think it's an accident that a group like the Specials came out of that."

The album received massive critical acclaim, especially the quasi-ska-driven 'Ten Eleven', and it was said that *The Hour Of Two Lights* was a 'powerful and brave piece of music that benefited and reflected the multi-cultural times of the modern era.' It spawned the 10" single 'They Gotta Quit Kicking My Dog Around' and the 12" 'Baby G' remixes of the track 'Grow'. The last lyrics on the album were: 'The word is love.' Terry summarised: "I used to believe that argument, that we're all the same under the skin. Well we're not, but it's about recognising that we're not *and* what we are. Yeah, it is obvious, but it still needs to be said. It really is about that, isn't it?"

Terry's penchant for wacky collaborations continued with the track 'Never Alone' for Dutch DJ and producer Tom Holkenborg, also known as Junkie XL. Holkenborg was famous for his remix of the Elvis Presley song 'A Little Less Conversation', which topped the UK charts. Tom had asked a number of Eighties names such as Depeche Mode's Dave Gahan, the Cure's Robert Smith and Terry if they would like to participate on his album of high-paced dance music: "I asked Terry if he was up for doing some work," said Holkenborg. "I didn't once think he would get back to me!" The track, with its chugging dance/ska feel, was well-suited to Hall and his laconic, plaintive vocal.

Terry's agreement to perform on an album by ska and reggae legends Toots and the Maytals caused massive ripples in the ska community. The album *True Love*, released on the V2 label, saw Toots Hibbert duet on songs such as 'Reggae Got Soul', 'Monkey Man', '54-46 Was My Number' and 'Pressure Drop' with a host of his favourite hand-picked artists. Keith Richards, Eric Clapton, Willie Nelson, No Doubt and of course Terry Hall, were just some of the illustrious names to appear on the album, which went on to win a Grammy Award. The track 'Never Grow Old' was a ska fan's dream as, along with the Maytals, it featured the horns of the fathers of ska music the Skatalites, the unique toasting talents of Jamaican legend U-Roy and the vocals of Terry Hall. The track proved to be one of the highlights of the recording. Toots had had no problem in rounding up so many musicians to perform on the album. On Terry Hall's inclusion he said: "No, man, it was easy. He's a fan of mine, and I'm a fan of his. We just asked him to pick one of my songs that he liked, and he listened to my catalogue and picked. It was very easy. He'd been listening to my music for years, played my music for years, just like I've been listening to his music for years."

The robust 17 tracks gained Hibbert his highest accolade, although winning the Grammy was just a by-product of what he did best; making feelgood music: "The people are my Grammy," professed Hibbert. "I maybe should have won a lot more of these awards over the years, but I take my accolades from Jah. That's enough for me."

The Dub Pistols connection brought more guest vocal work to Hall and he appeared on the single 'Things' for UK hip-hop music act Lautrec on the Distinctive Records label. He then began some serious recording for the Dubs on their *Speakers & Tweeters* album. He contributed to four of the thirteen tracks, the highlights being the Dub Pistols' version of 'Gangsters', a unique cover of the Stranglers' 'Peaches' and the sublime Blondie track 'Rapture', which became Terry's second single with the Pistols in 2007. He had really settled in with the band and made guest appearances on their various UK dates.

Terry then hit the festival trail and had the time of his life on the Pyramid Stage at the world-renowned Glastonbury festival, where he and Lynval Golding were reunited to play part of a televised set by Lily Allen which incorporated 'Gangsters' and 'Blank Expression'. Allen was another modern-day artist who cited the Specials as a major influence, her track 'Friday Night' especially resonant of their style. Allen's approach is a contemporary take on artists from a bygone era: "I was very lucky really," she said, "growing up in our house, listening to a great collection of singers and bands such as the Specials, the Kinks, the Clash, the Stylistics, Marvin Gaye, Janet Kay, the Slits, Neneh Cherry, Althea and Donna, the Stranglers, Van Morrison and Otis Redding. I prefer my ska to be like the Specials and I love the old stuff. I'm not interested in any modern ska. Most of it is rubbish."

At the same festival, Terry was reunited with Damon Albarn on the Park Stage. Albarn was honoured to present his own stage at the Glastonbury Festival and he filled the evening with a number of collaborations between his favourite African artists and some well-known British bands. He invited a host of artists including Hard-Fi, Terry Hall, Fatboy Slim and the Magic Numbers. Albarn got behind the piano himself and performed 'A Message To You Rudy' with Terry. A month later, Terry performed again with Lynval, and also the Dub Pistols at Guilfest, held at Guildford, in Surrey.

Aside from his many guest appearances, Terry was carving a name for himself as a DJ. He originally played mainly around London, but later diplayed his new-found talent all round the country. His DJing career had started after he had met Sean Rowley, a BBC London DJ who had put together the Guilty Pleasures events at the Koko Club in London. The idea was to reclaim quality pop songs that had come to be classed as slightly shameful and somewhat cheesy. His club spawned two compilation albums, a Sunday-afternoon radio show on BBC London and a television show on ITV, where established performers would perform cover versions of Guilty Pleasures favourites. Terry's tastes in music were well-defined and well-known so the Guilty Pleasures format suited him to the ground. Rowley declared him 'the Patron Saint of Guilty Pleasures'.

At a show at the Hackney Empire, Hall and former Catatonia lead singer Cerys Matthews wooed the crowd with a rendition of 'Islands In The Stream'. Terry has also appeared with Rowley on Guilty Pleasures' internet podcasts where he has revealed his liking for Seventies star David Cassidy, and a bedroom shrine dedicated to him when Hall was younger: "I remember playing Cassidy's 'Daydreamer' track on the Specials tour bus, and I was being laughed at and heckled. I said to the band 'Listen to it. Listen what he's trying to do there,' but it didn't work. In fact I blame David Cassidy for breaking up the Specials!"

Hall went on to be a DJ in his own right and was signed up by the Brave Music Agency who handle his DJ portfolio, an area he is still exploring.

In 2008 Terry was championed by fashion design house Fred Perry as their virtual 'King Of Sub-Culture'. With talk of a Specials reunion reaching fever pitch, and with the release of a combined CD/DVD The Best Of The Specials imminent, the designer stable issued a new piece of clothing in his honour. In the Specials' heyday, Hall had been an avid wearer of a black V-necked Fred Perry sweater, which can be seen in a TV performance of 'Monkey Man' for the Concerts for the People of Kampuchea in 1979. The Fred Perry re-launch publicity shots showed Terry modelling the sweater in 1979 and 2008. It has to be said, however, that at a retail price of £100 it was hardly designed for the kid on the street.

One aspect of Terry's involvement with Fred Perry was that, as part of the promotional push, the firm organised a gig at the 100 Club in London. A small but appreciative crowd, made up of Hall's acquaintances and Fred Perry competition winners, were treated to a smooth, laid-back set delivered in familiar style. He was joined onstage by his son Theo and his band Le Volume Courbe to perform an acoustic version of 'Sense' and even ultimate guilty pleasure David Cassidy was honoured. Later, Hall was joined onstage by three members of the The Dead Sixties and Lynval Golding who then played a set that included classic Specials tracks 'Gangsters', 'A Message To You Rudy', 'Friday Night Saturday Morning', 'Do Nothing' and some Fun Boy Three numbers.

Hall's new-found confidence had also made him more approachable to answering questions on the Specials. His almost complete change of heart on the subject had been brought about by dramatic events in his personal life that had made him take account of things in his life that really mattered. Terry had suffered another bout of the heavy depression that had dogged his life for years, with serious consequences. He had always worn his heart on his sleeve and told the world some of his innermost thoughts, but there were times when he had kept grave matters to himself, including the abuse he'd suffered at the hands of a school teacher, eventually documented in the Fun Boy Three track 'Well Fancy That'. Talking Heads supreme David Byrne, who produced the track, summed up the dichotomy of Hall when he said: "Take the track 'Well Fancy That'. He never told his Mum, he never told his Dad, but he was going to tell everybody with that."

In a candid interview in London with the controversial American musician and writer Ian Svenonius, Hall talked openly about his troubles and subsequent revelation: "Three years ago I tried to kill myself, but I didn't do it. I got sectioned and as a result of that I got diagnosed with bi-polar disorder. At last it all made sense and that was cool. I hadn't really noticed it before. I kept getting arrested. I got arrested for trying to steal a six-foot teddy bear from Hamleys toy shop. But I woke up to myself, things suddenly dawned on me. Life was brilliant, really brilliant. I didn't find a religion, I just found myself. I have a passion for all things eBay at the moment. I love it when the parcels arrive and the postman comes every day. I can hear his trolley coming up the road. It's a real guilty pleasure in itself. I'm into buying records and stuff that I once owned. I was told it's me trying to recapture my life by my psychiatrist, who I see once a week.

"I lost everything at 38, everything I ever owned. Well, not lost it but destroyed it all. So she thinks I am trying to piece it all back together, and she thinks I am up to about 19 years old. I remember getting a 1974 Man United pillowcase come through and it meant the world to me! So, maybe she's right. I can spend nine or ten hours a day doing this eBay thing. I've just found MySpace as well. I was amazed I could actually find a female to date in Afghanistan if I wanted. You know, you get stuck on medication and you get a certain amount of clarity. Yeah, it was a pretty much near-death thing. It was quite funny because afterwards I started being more outgoing and sociable. People were very wary; I revisited everyone, school friends and whatever. There was this big hole, which took up four years of my life. The thing I became aware of more than anything else was that I'd really like to see these people [the Specials] again."

In 2008, the opportunity finally arose, and Hall found himself sitting in a room with all the members of the Specials. For the first time in 27 years, they all started talking and the scenario had come full circle. The last words have to go to the man himself: "The Specials? It was absolutely fantastic, because it was so chaotic. It felt really good and really powerful. It felt like you were part of something important, like we could take on the world. You can be cynical and I've been through it loads of times thinking, yeah, but what does music actually change? But the Specials were a case where music really did change things."

RODDY 'RADIATION' BYERS

AFTER THE announcement that the Specials were no more, and having been told by Lynval that Jerry had been on the verge of sacking him anyway, Roddy Byers knew what direction he was going to take. He had already tentatively formed a new band, the Tearjerkers, who specialised in the crossover style created when he mixed the Specials' ska with his real first musical love, rock'n'roll. Roddy still needed the backing of a record company to help see his plans through and he spent a chaotic four days at Chrysalis, trying to record a handful of tracks to impress the board of directors. Despite his efforts he was unceremoniously dropped from the label, even though there was proof that rock'n'roll acts could still sell records in the shape of chart acts Shakin' Stevens and the Stray Cats. A short-term contract would at least have given Roddy a chance to prove himself; after all, he had been a part of the band that had had Chrysalis' coffers going 'ker-ching!'

"The break up of the band was a tremendous relief to me," said Rod. "The future suddenly seemed so much brighter and happier, but as I wasn't a front-line vocalist or a creative genius band leader, life would not be a breeze. The Fun Boys got a record deal. I was given four days to record something Chrysalis Records could sell. I asked Dave Jordan who was now with the Fun Boy camp to produce, and Rick Rogers, now the Fun Boys' manager, agreed to help me."

So with Rick Rogers' guiding hand, the Tearjerkers became Roddy's full-time concern. He revelled in his artistic freedom and could play to his heart's content without Jerry rearranging his material, or Terry singing it. The Tearjerkers included Roddy's brother Marc on guitar and vocals, Joe Hughes on bass guitar and vocals, and Steve Young on drums. The band, along with the Mo-dettes and the Bureau, immediately hit the road on the 'The Good, The Bad and The Ugly Tour 1981' and played dates across the country at small clubs and other venues.

The tracks that Rod had recorded for Chrysalis were made into the sardonically titled *The Dodgy Demos* EP, which featured 'Dreamworld', 'Nothing Lasts Forever', 'Tears In My Beer' and 'Western Song'. The EP was never officially released but was on sale as part of the merchandise for the tour. The group had plenty of material to play due to Roddy's penchant for songwriting, and, as well as a few rockabilly covers, they also played the songs Rod had written for the Specials: 'Concrete Jungle', 'Rat Race' and 'Hey, Little Rich Girl'.

"Unfortunately, the Tearjerkers had to play 'Concrete Jungle' and 'Rat Race'," Roddy explained, "because people came to hear those songs and since I'd written them, I had to play them. Also, I didn't want to use the name Roddy Radiation, but the manager disagreed. So, we went along with it. Even after the Specials split, you could say the 2Tone aspect has had held me back doing my own stuff. I've always written a lot of songs. That's the main reason why I played in local bands or my own groups. Unfortunately, my own projects never got the same kind of distribution as the Specials did. But I'm not very pushy, I don't like dealing with the suits. Some people are good at it and will do anything to get their own way. But I don't find it very pleasant, because I automatically dislike those people, which is not very helpful."

The band were soon signed by Britain's 'first true indie label', Chiswick Records, home of acts like Motörhead, the Damned and Dr Feelgood. In 1982 they issued the single 'Desire', with the B-side 'Western Song' to which a violin part was added. The fiddle was played by a Scottish folkie type, an acquaintance of the drummer, and Roddy gave him £50 and bought him several pints of Guinness for doing the session. The single failed to chart, (although 'Desire' appeared later in 1992 on the *Best Of Chiswick Records* set) but Roddy was busy having fun. However, he couldn't shake the spectre of the Specials. He was still being hounded for an explanation as to the real reason the Specials had split:

"I didn't want to drastically change the musical direction of the Specials, neither did the others. When Jerry announced he was going to put drum machines on everything for the second album, that's when things really started to go wrong, especially for me. Towards the end, I knew he was wanting me out. When the Specials stopped gigging that was it for me. Funny thing is, after the split and everything that went on, I got on with Jerry better than I had done in the Specials."

In 1983, the Tearjerkers were invited to play a live session at the BBC for Radio 1 as support to the Wilko Johnson Band. By this time there had been a change in personnel with Roddy and Marc and Joe being joined by Big Slim Pain on keyboards and former UK Subs man Pete Davies on drums. Their BBC performance perfectly encapsulated the pure Tearjerkers sound. The band gained a lot of respect over the course of their career from 1981-87, but couldn't gain enough to make them a viable commercial success. It was certainly not for the want of trying:

"The Tearjerkers split after about six years, with three line-ups in all that time. We released one single, 'Desire', and an EP on Chiswick Records, mostly of my songs. The main reason we split was, after six years, there was no major recording success, plus the taxman wanted a lot of money off me. I had wanted to do something completely different, which was the reason why I formed the Tearjerkers in '81. It was what I'd always been into and I thought I could do it. I spent six years with that band and failed miserably, but we had a lot of fun. Unfortunately, we were in competition with the likes of Duran Duran and if you didn't have brilliant production then you didn't do so well. So me, trying to turn the clock back to the early days of rock'n'roll, didn't work.

"We had quite a following and our gigs were always packed, but the kids who'd been into 2Tone weren't particularly into it and anyway the New Romantics came along and made us all redundant! I played the rockabilly scene, and if you weren't playing a certain sound, or wearing the right clothes, or playing the right instrument, the crowds were pretty unforgiving. Everything had to be authentic, so if you had a bit of punk in there they wouldn't have been too keen. It's not quite so bad now, not as purist maybe. That's good, 'cos you should do your own thing with the music, that's what originators like Elvis Presley did. Music works on your emotions, you make people happy, sad or whatever, as long as they can relate to the song."

After the Tearjerkers experience, with a young family to look after, he formed his own painting and decorating firm and fell back on his original skills as a tradesman. But it wasn't long before he was back into on the music scene with Leamington-based band the Bonediggers. Roddy was on guitar and vocals, Sam Smith on bass, Gary Muldoon on drums and Dave West on guitar and vocals. Roddy described their rock/blues sound as 'sort of Hank Williams meets the Clash', although some tracks verged on psychobilly (a blend of punk and rockabilly). Band member Dave West seemed to enjoy himself:

"Life was hectic and during the lifespan of the band and we experienced 'what rock'n'roll is all about', gigging up and down the UK and around Europe and releasing an album, which proved to be quite popular."

The album was released on the Rimshot label in 1989 and was entitled *For Those Who Died Trying*. It was well received, but soon afterwards the the Bonediggers disbanded.

In the Nineties, 2Tone was suddenly enthusiastically embraced over in the US, and a huge crop of American ska and punk bands acknowledged the Coventry-based phenomenon as an inspiration. To capitalise, the 2Tone supergroup Special Beat was formed with various members of the Specials and the Beat. The intention was to hit the festival circuit in the US, and Roddy was approached to join their ranks but declined: "To me, it felt like a Sixties cabaret tour around the working men's clubs, but I guess someone needed the money."

He continued with his painting and decorating, which enabled him to stay rooted and keep a roof over his family's head. He also joined another outfit, the Raiders: "Lads think it's funny when I was buying my guitar strings in my overalls, but when you have a couple of kids to feed I'm not that proud."

The Raiders were a heavy rock'n'roll band that featured Sam Smith and Gary Muldoon from the Bonediggers and Rod's brother Marc. The quartet played a danceable mix of vintage rock'n'roll. They recorded a demo that featured covers of the Kinks' track 'All Day And All Of The Night' and The Beatles' track 'Back In The USSR' alongside Roddy's own creations 'Heartbreak City', 'Doldrums' and the outstanding 'Man With No Name'. The band played locally, and went through three line-up changes before disbanding after a year.

In 1992, Roddy's career path changed yet again. Former Selecter and Bad Manners producer Roger Lomas takes up the story:

"I was asked by Trojan Records to record an album with Desmond Dekker, but not his band, so I thought it would be a good idea to team him up with as many members of the Specials as possible. The four members who played on the record (Lynval Golding, Roddy Radiation, Neville Staple and Horace Panter) were the only members of the Specials, at that time, who were prepared to work with each other. As they were the majority, four out of seven members of a band that equally own the name, they were legally entitled to use the name the Specials alongside Desmond Dekker. There was criticism regarding the use of the name, but I don't believe it was deserved, as they only did what thousands of other bands do to help maintain their careers...they worked for it!"

In essence, the idea to put two major ska legends together was mouth watering, but it proved to be a mis-match. The album, *King Of Kings*, was definitely one of those ideas which looked fantastic on paper, but disappointed in reality. The concept of pairing the Jamaican singing legend with the Specials was indeed brilliant, but unfortunately, it occurred around a dozen years too late. The album was not the power-packed, punk-fuelled 2Tone experience of yesteryear, but a more sedate version, better suited to Dekker's style than that of the Specials. *King Of Kings* was not a total ruin, but thoughts of what might have been weighed heavily on the final result. The album was followed up by a video release but this also missed the mark and lacked any real invention, as all the tracks were performed on a stage. The album did have the benefit of kick-starting the idea that maybe the four band members could actually work together again as the Specials. Roddy said:

"We were asked to back Desmond Dekker on an album and to get together as many of the original band as possible. That line-up became the re-formed Specials. Then we were offered two weeks in Japan, and the money was really good. It was the first time we'd been back on stage for 15 years and it didn't seem that different. It was still working well, even though some members weren't there. Then we were offered more work in America, but at that particular time, nobody had decided to make it an on-going thing. After the tour of the US, it all started looking like it might be a second chance. I thought it was a chance to get some more of my songs out. Most of the rest of the band were thinking 'let's just play the old stuff and make a living.'"

This incarnation were initially called the Coventry Specials and recruited drummer Charlie 'H' Bembridge, keyboard player Mark Adams and trombonist Adam Birch to complete the line-up. They toured Japan and were a huge success. At a signing session in Tokyo the band members, and in particular Roddy, were mobbed by manic Japanese girl fans!

"Well, they went crazy for us!" he said gleefully. "It was a bit of a shock really. During a signing at a music shop, they rushed us and a plate-glass window completely shattered! Another day, I was even recognised on the street and asked for an autograph. It has to be said that we were not trying to pretend that we had recreated the old Specials, but we were more than happy that there were plenty of the original ingredients, the energy and ideals, in the mix."

Rod found himself on lead vocals for a lot of the tracks and revelled in giving a voice to his Specials creations. The air was one of optimism and, on their return from Japan, they decided that it might be feasible to have one more crack at playing professionally as the Specials. They announced to the world that the Specials were back and the *NME* gave up space for a small article. The band prepared themselves for questions as to why Hall, Dammers and Bradbury were absent:

"Me and Horace wanted to call the band 'Specials2'" professed Roddy, "but obviously record companies and promoters wanted us to use the name of the Specials, because it would be stronger business-wise. That didn't make Jerry very happy. At first, he said he didn't mind us doing it, but when we got offered a record deal he changed his mind. He phoned me up to moan about it. He was just afraid that we might do well without him. Anyway, he didn't want to do it. He hated touring and hated America and so it wouldn't have been possible for him to do it. Also, Terry Hall was doing so well in his own career at the time that he didn't want to do it either. I enjoyed it because it gave me a chance to sing, which was quite nice."

Despite the record company's misgivings, to differentiate between the original

Specials and this new incarnation, the band came to be referred to as the Specials Mk2. This reunion, of sorts, is often overlooked, but a great amount of work went into making this a viable project and they undertook a hectic four-year touring schedule. Within a few weeks of proclaiming their return to business, UB40s Ali Campbell signed the band to his Kuff Records label, with a distribution deal through Virgin. A fan club was set up in Leicester and it looked like things were on the up. The comeback album was released as *Today's Specials* and consisted of a collection of cover versions, a move that Roddy had warned against. There wasn't a black and white check or Walt Jabsco in sight. The critics completely savaged it, and its empty, flat sound left fans bemused. Roddy was not impressed with the final result:

"I was about to leave. I was totally disgusted with it. I was totally pissed off with the whole *Today's Specials* situation! I thought the idea of reforming and doing covers was a bunch of crap, but I was the only one with any songs and I guess they didn't want to play 'Hey Little Rich Girl' type songs. The idea was that it was supposed to be like UB40s *Labour Of Love* album. Half the band thought it was a good idea, but I said at the start that to come out with a covers album and call ourselves the Specials was a bad move. I was proved right afterwards, because the press completely slagged us."

Neville had another slant on the *Today's Specials* story:

"*Today's Specials*, was supposed to be my solo album... Most of that album was done with myself and Tom Lowry, and was supposed to be my solo album, but when we were reforming the Specials, we got it so other members of the Specials got their stuff on it. So basically, that's how that was. I was gonna do a cover songs album to give me time to write my other stuff."

Nevertheless, the band soldiered on and, as ska was becoming big news in the States, they jetted out for a number of dates on the festival circuit. To their surprise, the band got a rousing reception wherever they went, which increased their enthusiasm no end:

"The tour of the States was brilliant," said Lynval Golding. "We were selling out three- and four-thousand seaters every night, and the crowds were so enthusiastic. The majority of them were too young to remember us the first time around, but the 2Tone scene had grown and become far more than just a cult."

Horace Panter was equally overawed and felt the impetus to carry the band forward despite the UK public's misgivings:

"We came back revitalized. On the tour, we had been talking about our favourite tunes and ideas of songs that we could cover in our own style. The Specials were always about bringing disparate influences together, and some of the ideas were pretty wild. We thought it would be a good idea for an album. We laid down some demos when we got back to Coventry. The city was vital to us, and the band couldn't have come together anywhere else. It was still at the centre of our creative energy."

Two singles emerged from the *Today's Specials* compilation, but neither of them charted. The first was a cover of Bob Marley's 'Hypocrite', complete with a Monty Python-esque promo video, and the second was a cover of the Maytals' 'Pressure Drop', which was the superior track. In America, the singles were released along with a third track, (not available in the UK) a cover of the Monkees' 'A Little Bit Me, A Little Bit You', which became part of the soundtrack to the Michael Keaton movie *Multiplicity*. The initial burst of new Specials activity received valuable exposure via the satellite channels such as VH1, as well as some good coverage on Channel 4 programme *The Big Breakfast*, who held a '2Tone Day'. Despite that, the recordings failed to fire the imagination of the public.

Roddy & Horace relax 1979.
Photo by R.Byers

Roddy was still the most prolific songwriter in the group and he put forward re-vamped versions of some old numbers he had originally played with the Tearjerkers and the Bonediggers, as well as new compositions. Meanwhile, the rest of the band were also creating material of their own. They continued with a number of impressive dates in Europe and gained some great live reviews. On July 8th 1995, they returned to the Montreux Jazz Festival and played a scintillating 21-song set that included a cover of the Fun Boy Three's 'Farmyard Connection'. The performance was recorded and later released on Receiver Records as *Ghost Town Live At The Montreux Jazz Festival*. Their dates in London, Bristol and Ireland went down a storm but after that, the band would never again grace a British stage:

"We should have done more UK shows," said Roddy, "but after the slagging we got from the press after 'Today's Bollocks' we decided to try and crack the US. In the US they didn't seem to mind us not being the entire original band and ska was happening big-time in the land of the flea."

So, they returned to America to tour and whilst they were there they finalised the tracks for the second album. After the debacle with Kuff Records, which folded just afterwards, the group found themselves signed to Way Cool, an arm of the mighty MCA company.

"All the songs I wrote on that album were written before we re-formed," said Roddy. "I wrote 'Bonediggin', 'Tears In My Beer' and 'Man With No Name'. The rest of the material was written between us. It took about four weeks to record it in Van Nuys, which is a rough area of Los Angeles. It was weird having to live with each other for all that time. Neville had got in with the manager of Way Cool Records at MCA, who had very definite ideas about what we should be doing, so that was always a battle. He was very bossy, we had a few problems with him, and that's why the album never got worldwide distribution. It only came out in America and Japan. Everyone in the business knows that a band is continually battling against record companies, because they always think they know better than you do. But Neville went along with the record-company guys because he thought they were right."

The recording of the album, to be titled *Guilty 'Til Proved Innocent*, didn't go to plan. After the band had had their stints in the studio, the record company insisted on studio 'tweaks' behind the backs of the group, as Roddy explained:

"We had a lot of problems with Way Cool. I caught the producer trying to match up drum sounds and stuff on the new album with the first Specials LP! I went mad, but he said he was only obeying record-company orders. Nothing ever change! Mixes were done of certain tracks over which we had no control. Lynval's guitar was actually deleted from a couple of tracks! The Specials without Lynval Golding is like faggots without mushy peas. There were also problems with me and Neville, who sang joint lead vocals,

Roddy & Lynval backstage 1979. Photo by R.Byers

being replaced by Prince Beaver [Adam Birch] the trombone player, who did a passable Terry Hall. Record-company politics again."

The album was released but had to be bought on import in the UK. The reviews were mixed, but the overall consensus was that it was a more realistic Specials album, and quite a credible attempt at fresh material. Some of the album sounded distinctly like *More Specials*, in particular 'Fantasize', which echoed 'Stereotype' and 'All Gone Wrong', where the ghostly guitar work smacked of 'Man At C&A'. Lars Frederiksen and Tim Armstrong of successful US punk outfit Rancid, who were big Specials fans, contributed to the track 'Fearful'. At that time Rancid were busy recording and wanted some members of the Specials to add a ska feel to their album. Roddy recalled:

"Lynval and Neville were invited to sing on their album and I only found out by luck. I think someone didn't want me there… But I insisted as I was bored and being an ex-punk thought I'd meet some like-minded mates. However, I was surprised they weren't drinking 'n' stuff, but I suppose their success had made them tighten up ship before they fell apart due to excess. It was Tim who suggested I played, which I don't think Lars was keen on as he was the lead player. I'd had a few and, when I was passed a battered Epiphone guitar, I complained as a joke, not knowing it was Lars' guitar. I think, after having to have another guitarist play on his stuff, my joke went down none too well. Sorry, Lars! Tim played the bit I'd done when I saw them do it on the Warped tour so I guess that says it all. Great band, though."

The band then signed up to the hectic 1998 Warped tour. This was a summer-long music and extreme sports festival held in venues such as parking lots or fields on which the stages and skateboarding structures were erected, and had originally started out as a showcase for punk rock music. Appearing with the Specials were a host of American ska-punk bands like Rancid, NOFX, Less Than Jake, Save Ferris and the Pietasters, to name but a few. Calling it chaotic was something of an understatement:

"It was hard work, the Warped tour." said Roddy, "It was all open-air gigs. I don't like playing outside very much, especially at midday in hot temperatures in Arizona or somewhere like that. Rancid were on that tour and had been influenced by us having grown up listening to us, and I used to play with them onstage sometimes. We were getting worn out, because we were twice the age of most of the other bands. Most of the other bands had flash luxury buses and loads of tour support, whereas we had the worst tour bus and no money back-up from the record company. That was a bit strange. But we still went down a storm and mostly ended up headlining the shows, because none of the other bands could follow us, but it takes it out of you. It was basically the Specials and Rancid that ruled the tour."

They released 'It's You' from the *Guilty 'Til Proved Innocent* album as a single and, although it fell on deaf ears, it did achieve the accolade of being the soundtrack to an advert for Solero ice-lollies in the UK. A follow up release, 'Bonedigging', was planned but never materialised. The band gigged non-stop around the States and won over the crowds, but the punishing schedule, just as with the original Specials, meant they struggled to keep up the pace.

They then toured Japan, but Horace had become quite ill so he was not present. The tour proved to be this version of the Specials' undoing. Tired and weary, the band completed their Japanese dates and returned to England:

"The end of the Specials Mk2 was a long story," Roddy explained. "The first couple of years were successful money-wise, and most of the time it was like being kids again, but even though we were older we were not any wiser! Everyone in the group had a different view on how we should proceed. When we first started rehearsing, I mentioned I had a few songs, which would work great. All I got was pained expressions from the older guys! I think most of them thought it would be an extension of Special Beat, a sort of tribute. Anyway, our business was bollocks; management came and went 'til we couldn't get off the treadmill and the '98 Warped tour just burned us senior citizens out. We did six weeks in the States, followed by three or four dates in Europe, with an Australian tour to follow which we bailed out from. Horace was very ill, Neville's legs were in a bad way and me and Lynval were knackered. We did Japan and just stopped after that without discussing it. Why? Because the new members were flat broke but we still had old royalties coming through and the old albums were selling more than the new album at most of our gigs."

The band basically fizzled out without splitting in the normal way, and yet another line was drawn under the Specials.

While taking some time out, Roddy kept his hand in by making the occasional live appearance with local Midlands ska bands such as the irrepressible Ska-Boom and the Splitters, from Leicester. He was later persuaded to collaborate with some former stablemates in a travelling revue that celebrated the 2Tone sound. In 1999, Coventry-based producer Roger Lomas had put together the unit, which was known as the 2Tone Collective. The main line-up included Roddy, Pauline Black from the Selecter and Ranking Roger from the Beat. Neville Staple of the Specials, Gaps Hendrickson of the Selecter, and ska legend Dave Barker would often make appearances. Lomas kept the Selecter connection by drafting in Nick Welsh as musical director and part of the backing band. There were never any recordings from this line-up and they played only a handful of mainland gigs, including a couple in Coventry (one a New Year's Eve bash, the other at Highfield Road football ground) and one at a festival in Wales where they were on the same bill as heavy-metal band Motörhead.

In Europe, where the band were billed as the Stars Of Ska, they shared a bill with Status Quo in Belguim, and also played at the Roskilde Festival in Denmark, where, on June 30th 2000, Pearl Jam headlined and nine people died in an accident at the front of the main stage. The tragedy was attributed to problems with the sound at the gig, causing the audience of 50,000 to push forward in an attempt to get closer to the stage. After playing for 45 minutes, Pearl Jam brought the performance to a standstill to tell the crowd to move back. However, with the ground muddy from torrential rain, nine people were trampled to death and 30 others injured.

Roddy's next project, the Starlight Junkies, was a short lived affair that came to him via Lynval Golding. He played a few shows, but it would only ever be a quick job for a friend:

"A few years ago when Lynval's wife was expecting," said Roddy, "he couldn't do the tour with them, so volunteered me! It was nothing to write home about as such, but I really enjoyed working with singer Finny [ex-Loafers/Special Beat]; he did a damned good Terry Hall voice!"

After that, Rod guested on the album *Wise Up* for Devon-based ska outfit Too Hot. Then came his first album, *Skabilly Rebel – The Roddy Radiation Anthology*, released through the American independent Fiend Music.

"I sent out a compilation tape to some folks in Ireland," said Roddy, "who really loved it and wanted to get it out. They did up some artwork and just released a few copies on a shoestring. One of them ended up with a bloke called Kevin at Fiend Records in Los Angeles who liked it and gave it a proper release."

The album was a collection of his work with the Tearjerkers, the Bonediggers, the Raiders and some home-spun solo work. The album rolled with typical Byers free flowing song-writing style and it received rave reviews all over the world. *Now Wave* magazine said:

"As a whole, this collection harkens back to the days when rockabilly crooners were skinny, pretty, heartbroken troubadours rather than intellectually-challenged glorified he-men trying too hard to get laid. It's damn nice to hear a tried-and-true musical formula regurgitated not only with reverence, but also with such first-rate musical gusto and well-honed song writing chops. For those of you jumping on the rockabilly bandwagon, why not let Roddy Radiation show ya how it's done?"

Immediately afterwards, Roddy decided to have another go at being in a band:

"A mate of mine suggested I give it another go. I knew a few musicians in and around Coventry, so I thought why not? I just like to play."

His first port of call was his old friend and musical sparring partner Sam Smith, who returned to bass and double bass duties, with Ian Howard on rhythm guitar and Paul Raggerty on drums. In a nod towards the title of his compilation, the Skabilly Rebels were born.

"I'd played with Sam on and off since 1990 in the Bonediggers. Ian was a buddy of mine for ten years or more, and Paul I met through a Dutch punk girl I knew. She gave me his number after I mentioned I needed a drummer."

The band began to play dates around the local area, playing the trademark Byers fusion of punky rock'n'roll and ska. The Skabilly logo was a Confederate flag shown in the colours of the Jamaican flag, which summed up Roddy and his career. In another nod to his roots, Walt Jabsco was given a facelift to become 'Hank Jabsco' with the trademark trilby replaced by a rockabilly quiff. The band quickly started playing gigs all over the UK, and soon headed into the studio to lay down demos. There were personnel changes in the form of a new drummer, Whippet, and the addition of keyboard player Jez Edwards. Roddy continued to write prolifically:

"People keep saying to me 'what's skabilly?' They don't seem to get it. All music comes from the same place anyway, so to me, to mix up things doesn't seem that unusual. It all comes from the Mississippi delta and New Orleans. People tend to forget that even in the Specials, when I was feeling a bit down, I would listen to Hank Williams, early Presley, Sun recordings and Johnny Cash. I write when I'm pissed off. When you are happy you don't tend to put pen to paper. Sometimes it's something that's happened to me a few years before and I sort of drag up the memory, but quite often I tend to get a title first, then a riff and then I fill in the gaps. I write the chorus line then the first verse, then try to work out how it's all going to evolve or stick a middle eight in. Some songs I spend ages on, others come very quickly."

The band did small tours of Ireland and undertook a tour of Europe called the Lily Marlene Tour, although the trip almost cost them a band member at the hands of the police. Skabilly guitarist Sam Smith was the man at the centre of the action:

"I lost my passport a couple of days before we were off to Berlin," Sam recalled, "so our tour manager said 'Let's just go and be straight with them when we get to the port', so we did. What the port said to me was, 'When you get to Holland, show them your old passport and some ID,' (I had a telephone bill and a gas and electric bill as I thought I'd better be prepared) 'that should do it, but if they don't like the look of you then you'll be referred back to us. Then we get billed £1000, which we pass on to you, and you get banned from travelling into Europe for 18 months.' I was so relieved to get on that ferry that I celebrated with a couple of drinks – well, seven actually. Then we approached customs on arrival to explain my plight.

"They looked out at us and asked us why we were there. 'To explain', I said. 'No, why are you here?' he replied. As I tried to explain, his partner said 'Who has been drinking alcohol?' 'Me,' I said. 'Why?' he said. Then, I had an idea: 'A birthday party on the ferry,' I said. As he looked me in the eye, he still had my old passport in his hand. 'Your birthday?' he asked. (my birthday is January, this was July!) 'Noooo!' (panic, panic, flap, flap) 'A friend from school, I just met her on the ferry and had been drinking.' In the end they just said 'Go away and stop bothering us.' Pheeeew!

"We got to Holland then off to Frankfurt. What we didn't know was, there are actually three Frankfurts, and then realised we were heading towards the Polish border, 70 miles the wrong way! We were stopped by armed police; they looked at every one of us and took our passports. Because they were so intent on seeing the driver's documents, they had neglected the fact we handed over eight passports, but there were nine of us. I hid convincingly behind a coat hanger as they checked the passport photos. One officer looked straight at me and smiled, the he turned to the driver to say 'everything in order, on your way.' I breathed a sigh of relief as we pulled the van round. Our drummer at the time, Whippet, then shouted at them 'Excuse me mate, you don't know which way the real Frankfurt is?' Nooo, Whippet! Bad dog! And the moral of the story is, shut it, keep on learning!"

After they returned home, the band went to the studio for their first serious attempt at what was to be their debut album, *Blues Attack*, named after the song by the Bonediggers:

"The title refers to teen angst," said Roddy. "Teenagers that think that everything is the end of the world and want to top themselves. It's saying 'get up and fight back.' It's like any blues song really. Talking about your problems might not solve them but will make you feel better. I'm really pleased with what I've got so far. I've added some saxophone, as I wanted brass, but not the usual ska trombone and trumpet; I wanted the more Stax soul sound. I'm gonna put down a couple of acoustic things and a cajun song. I've also got this song I've done called 'Lonesome No More', it's the only song I've written for my wife, so basically it's an apology! That's like a mix of Buddy Holly with ska with a bit of power pop thrown in. I have this song called 'Black Zodiac', about the Sixties car. I thought it was a bit of a throwaway song, I didn't think it was great writing, but it always goes down well. It's a rock'n'roll song set in Camden Town, London rather than Memphis. The Americans have always had it easier when it comes to rock songs with places names in, Memphis and Route 66 in particular, whereas if you sing about places with British names like Neasden or Scunthorpe, it doesn't quite have the same ring to it!"

Whilst keeping the Rebels as his main concern, Roddy found himself in massive demand for guest appearances. His best came in the form of a six-track contribution to Stoke ska outfit the Rough Kutz. This highly original group had been in existence for ten years and had a reputation for quality recordings and live shows. They were signed to the Dutch label Skanky Lil, and had already released two albums that had received excellent reviews. Their third album *Another Week, Another War* was hailed as the ska album of 2006, and the main track from the album 'Chell Heath' is regarded as a modern classic. The band are led by keyboardist Dean 'Hazza' Harrison, who said:

"Roddy has that sort of sound that you would recognise on any recording. The sound of his guitar and the way he plays his riffs always stood out for us as young Specials fans. So, when we recorded our third album we thought why not ask him do a song or two, he can only say no. Luckily for us he agreed and came in the studio with us and did about six or so songs on the album. He was a great laugh and totally blew us away with his playing in the studio, especially his riff on 'Chell Heath'. We would never have believed when we started the band that Roddy would play on our songs, so we were made up to say the least! To top it all he refused any payment for playing, which says a lot about him as a person. The only payment he would accept was a night on the town and a short European tour with the Kutz."

So, Roddy travelled with the Rough Kutz on a ground-breaking tour of Germany, the Czech Republic and Austria to play as part of their live show. He thoroughly enjoyed the jaunt with his new friends.

When he returned, he got straight back into action with the Skabilly Rebels, with more recording and many more live shows including the Rebellion festival in the UK. Over the next few months, Roddy would update the band with new recruits, and each time it became a tighter outfit. He added saxophone player Leigh Malin, known on the circuit as Spitty, and the sax gave a real rockabilly feel to the skabilly style. Roddy replaced the keyboard player with Jay 'Genie' Jones and the Rebels moved forward again. There was to be a major change in personnel when rhythm guitarist Ian 'H' Howard left the band and left Sam Smith to take up the rhythm guitar. Lee Pellington was drafted in to cover bass duties, but his time with the band was somewhat short-lived.

Around this time, sax player Spitty defected to play for Ranking Roger's then-current version of the Beat, which left the group without brass. Before long El Pussycat sax-man Drew Stansall started making appearances at Skabilly Rebels gigs around the Midlands and was soon a full-time member. With the arrival of outstanding drummer Paul 'Bear' Ayriss and new bassman Mac, the line up that takes us to the present day was completed. At the time of writing, the Skabilly Rebels are in the process of completing their long-awaited debut album.

The only doubt Roddy has about his aspirations is that somewhere in the realms of the splintered British music scene, with its tribute bands and manufactured pop, people have lost touch with what he is trying to achieve:

"I do my shows and, you know, I still get the old mods and skinheads coming up to me demanding Specials stuff. They can't see what I'm aiming for. It's only lately that I think I'm starting to get through to people! Its only taken 20-odd years!"

Roddy is the eternal rebel, with fire and passion in his music, his stance and styles. His attitude was and is an essential component of the melting pot that made up the Specials. The last word must go to him:

"I try and play and sing the best I can and if people like it, I'm happy. If they don't, fuck 'em!"

JOHN BRADBURY

GOING BACK to the early Eighties, John Bradbury had always wanted to record some of his favourite soul and Stax classics. After the release of 'Gangsters' there had been talk of the Specials moving in a Northern Soul direction, but such was the success of their brand of ska that it proved impossible. Brad's penchant for soul did eventually give rise to the reconstituted version of 'Sock It To 'Em, JB' that appeared on the *More Specials* album, and also a spectacularly rare French import 7" single, which saw the track as the headline cut, with the reverse being 'Do Nothing'. It was not enough to satisfy his craving, and after the demise of the original Specials, he decided the time was right to go and do his own thing.

He was still an essential part of the Special AKA as he set the wheels in motion to form his own soul revue band. He explained his ideas to Chrysalis, who surprisingly weren't interested, but around the corner from their offices was another label, RCA. Brad took the notion to Jack Stephens in the RCA A&R department and a deal was struck. RCA owned the world famous RCA Victor label and it was here that JB's Allstars, as the band were to be known, released their material. This gave them the distinction of being the first artist to appear on that branch of the RCA network since Elvis Presley himself. The band would go on to release four singles on RCA Victor. Their fifth and final offering was, technically, the last 'proper' 2Tone record release. 'Alphabet Army' (CHS TT29), released in January 1986, and gave Brad the honour of bookending the 2Tone label, being on both the first and final releases. The song, composed by Brad, who was once a teacher himself, depicts the struggle of 'the overworked, underpaid teachers who were the 'Alphabet Army' of the song's title. The lyrics were penetrating and straight to the point, making it the only Allstars release to venture anywhere close to politics, despite Brad's personal political beliefs:

"My political attitude is a socialist attitude; it's something I believe in totally. I've got no clichés to explain what the lyrics in 'Alphabet Army' are like. They're just what they are. Anybody can see that."

The standard 12" format featured three different versions of the title track but suffered a lack of airplay and,as a result, fell by the wayside. It still remains a fitting parting shot from one of the label's big contributors. After the single, Chrysalis closed down the 2Tone label in respect of new material.

JB's Allstars drifted apart after 1985, as did Brad's other interest, the Special AKA. He took a well-earned sabbatical and then went into production work with the famous PWL stable. PWL was owned by the former Coventry Automatics manager Peter Waterman. Brad worked at the company for five years.

When the late-Eighties UK ska boom exploded, he was an early advocate of one of the big bands at that time, the Loafers. They were at the forefront, with the likes of the Hotknives, of the underground upsurge that developed into a burgeoning new scene. The new wave almost broke on to a larger, national, scale but was mainly confined to the southern half of the UK. To celebrate the scene, the cream of the new wave's crop, including the Loafers, appeared at London's Astoria in the famed Ska Explosion gig. The band also often backed legendary Godfather of ska Laurel Aitken. Brad produced their second album, *Contagious* which was released in 1989 on the Staccato label.

A year later, Brad was back at the controls to produce the groundbreaking debut album *High And Dry* for Brixton ska/rap/break-beaters Maroon Town. The band made history when they were sponsored to the tune of £100,000 by Doctor Martens, the boot manufacturers. It was Britain's largest ever deal between an unsigned act and a major corporate sponsor.

Brad then teamed up with ex-Stranglers and JB's Allstars horn player Jason Votier to try his hand at a complete change of musical direction. They formed the electro duo 2 To The Power and recorded the tracks 'Flasher' and 'Make My Body Groove (The Groove Beat Mix Ft Lou and Naz)' and issued it on the UK Hi-NRG label, Lisson Records.

However, he missed the thrill of playing live and hadn't been on the road for five years, so he hit on the idea of trying to get the Specials back together. He tracked down the former band members and approached them with the proposal. He soon realised that it was not going to happen, but during his enquiries he had spoken to Ian Copeland, the brother of Police drummer Stewart, and owner of the FBI (Frontier Booking

International) Entertainments agency. Copeland had been the agent for the original Specials during their US jaunts and made a promising suggestion to Brad. With a huge interest in ska and 2Tone in the US at the time, where numerous ska clubs were opening on the west coast, Copeland felt that, if Brad got together some old faces from the 2Tone era, it would go down a storm. The idea greatly appealed to Brad and he set about recruiting a band. First on his hit list was Specials bass man Horace Panter who, after much cajoling, agreed to sign up. Roddy Byers sniffed at the opportunity, but Neville Staple and Lynval Golding joined the band. He also managed to rope in Ranking Roger, Charley and Saxa from the Beat, vocalist Anthony 'Finny' Finn and keyboardist Sean Flowerdew, who had both been in the now-defunct Loafers, plus a couple of new faces, Anthony Harty and Wayne Lothian:

"Finny was an obvious choice for me," said Brad. "When I worked with the Loafers, he would often mess around doing fantastic impressions of Terry Hall and Johnny Rotten. These qualities made him a valuable member of the band."

The group took the name the Special Beat, a natural choice when you consider it was virtually an amalgamation of half of the Specials and half of the Beat. Originally, it was planned for the group to do one large tour of the US and then go back home and disband, but it almost never happened. The night before the outfit flew to America, Brad returned home from an evening out with wife Emily, only to be told by his child-minder that Lynval Golding could not make it after all and would send a replacement around in the morning!

Keyboardist Sean Flowerdew recalled his time with Special Beat on the *Music Is Our Occupation* website:

"Special Beat was brilliant. I was 19 and not doing anything, sitting in a pub with Brad, and we came up with an idea of doing a band together and getting other Specials involved. I'd done two writing sessions with Ranking Roger and suggested him as well. Three weeks later, we were in rehearsals, three weeks after that (Halloween 1990) we landed in Atlanta, Georgia for the first seven-week tour. I toured with them for three years and had some great shows. Supported Sting and Steel Pulse, we played Red Rocks and Madison Square Garden and went to Japan twice.

"I always thought Special Beat was an awful name, though. It was Ian Copeland's idea and I guess it helped sell tickets. In my naivety, I thought we'd write a new album and be huge, not just go round like a glorified cabaret show. I think we were a great live band, just a shame there were no real songwriters in the band (including myself). We did a few new things, but not very good. One tune, 'Rainy Days', Roger released with a re-formed General Public. The potential was incredible. We were really taking the 2Tone sound to the masses, bigger shows than the Specials or the Beat ever did in the US. We introduced a lot of new people to the music; shame we didn't have anything to back it up."

The group initially played a selection of tracks once performed by the Specials and the Beat, but between the key members of the band they also attempted to write fresh material. The tour was a raving success, gigs sold out and ska fever carried them on the crest of a wave. As hundreds of like-minded bands sprung up around the country, the renewed interest encouraged the supergroup to remain together. Special Beat was a flexible unit and the door remained open all the time, allowing members to come and go so they could pursue other commitments:

"We let people drift in and out," said Brad, "it seemed to work well. It gave shows something new, a fresh approach, you know, sort of a change is as good as a rest? Well that's it. It works."

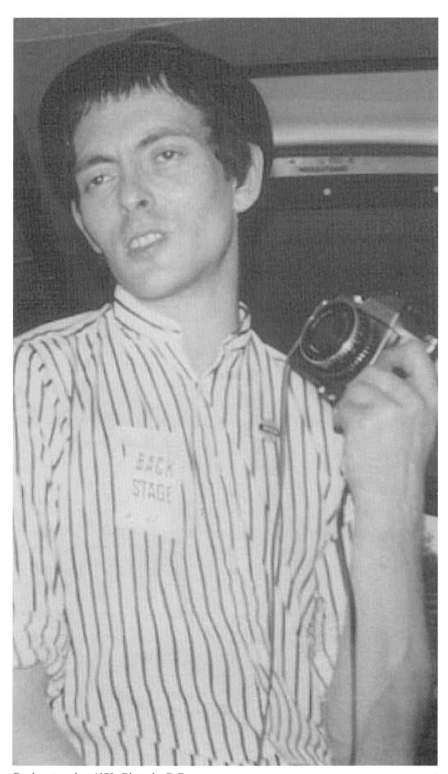

Brad on tour bus 1979. Photo by R Byers

The SPECIALS – from conception to reunion

There were frequent changes in personnel, and new recruits always brought fresh enthusiasm. Lynval Golding did eventually join up. One reason for the Special Beat's appeal was their professionalism, which was reflected in their sound, their appearance and their exuberance onstage. They became one of the leading forces in the resurgence of ska in the music world. Their main aim was to be the ultimate live experience, but they did manage to record a few tracks. One, 'Rainy Days', was destined to be a 7" single release and, although that never happened, it did find its way into the public domain when some of the material became available as a poor-quality bootleg.

One of the tracks – 'Hypocrite', a cover of the Bob Marley song – made its way on to *The Shack – Volume One*, a 1993 CD compilation on Dojo Records. The band's manager was none other than former Specials and Fun Boy Three supervisor Rick Rogers. He felt that the group had a future if they worked as a proper functioning unit, laid down demos and moved towards recording. Rogers' American contacts guaranteed that work was plentiful and the Special Beat completed three full US tours. They spent a month supporting Sting, who must still have had painful memories of the days when the original Specials upstaged the Police. They then completed a triumphant tour of Japan. The band were also huge in Europe, where they frequently played to full houses, especially in Germany, the home of a massive ska scene to this day. They returned in style to play a handful of dates in the UK and Ireland, calling at Coventry on their way. The Coventry gig took place at the Tic Toc Club (these days known as the Kasbah) and the energetic performance found its way on to an official CD release when Receiver Records issued the 14-track *Special Beat – Live*. The CD showed the band at its explosive best in front of an ecstatic Coventry crowd.

In December 1992, their trip to Japan, particularly a show in Tokyo where they loved the razor-edged sounds of 2Tone, was broadcast on a satellite TV programme called *Shibuya On Air* produced by the company Space Shower TV. The group performed a catalogue of Specials and Beat classics, and a recording was later made available on a 19-track video released by Visionary, also entitled *Shibuya On Air*. An accompanying CD entitled *Live In Japan*, which included three extra tracks, appeared on Dojo. Gigs came thick and fast, and next stop was the WOMAD festival at Reading on June 18th 1993, quickly followed by a charity event in Bristol a week later. Most of the group's British performances took place in the South and the Midlands:

"Its was often easier and more profitable to play Europe than the North of England and Scotland," said Brad. "It's harsh but true."

After a manic schedule, the band started to lose its momentum: "It was great to see the crowd having a good time," explained Brad, "but no-one was coming backstage to say what a good night they had had. It's the little things like that that keep you going, knowing that people appreciate what you're doing. Swaying to the music is all well and good but it's the feedback that really counts and anyway, I felt that some people were becoming a bit star-struck by it all."

The group were now without Lynval Golding and Sean Flowerdew, so it was decided that the band should bow out in style. In October 1993, the Special Beat joined one of the biggest ska tours ever to be undertaken in the States. Dubbed the Skavoovie tour, it took in 21 cities and featured an impressive line up of groups, including the Special Beat, the Skatalites, the Selecter (who had just re-formed with a new line up), leading US ska outfit the Toasters and a host of other American ska bands. The tour played to packed houses everywhere it went. In Prova, Utah, 1,300 people crammed into a rodeo barn to see the cream of the current ska explosion in concert. As a special treat, Dave

Wakeling of the Beat and General Public joined the Special Beat for two shows in Los Angeles. It was there that the group announced that it was to be their last tour. As a result of the tour's success, Ranking Roger and Dave Wakeling re-formed General Public, who had originally been huge in America in the mid Eighties.

John Bradbury did not remain idle for long on his return to England. After discussions with Nick Welsh and Pauline Black during the Skavoovie tour, when a drumming vacancy arose in the newly revitalised Selecter, Brad immediately stepped in. He joined forces with his former 2Tone comrade Pauline, along with other original member Gappa Hendrickson. The move saw Brad come full circle, as he had appeared on drums on 'The Selecter', the B-side of the first 2Tone release. Brad joined the band just after the departure from the re-formed outfit of Selecter creator Neol Davies. To confuse matters even more, Davies set up his own band, the Selecter Instrumental, complete with a large brass section, playing ska classics.

"I'd known Brad for years," said Nick Welsh. "We used to see each other around the clubs in London and were drinking buddies. He was wanting to get back to do more live work and our drummer in the Selecter was leaving, so as Brad had mentioned he would like to work with me a few times before, the time was right and he came on board. He was, and still is, a phenomenal drummer. I think he is one of the best."

Welsh was also in the process of setting up a sideline band to the Selecter, Big 5, where he could ply his more punky, glam-guitar edged style of ska. The band consisted of Martin Stewart on keyboards, Welsh on bass and fiery vocalist Jennie Matthias, aka Jennie BelleStar from the Eighties all-girl pop band the Belle Stars (which in turn had risen from the ashes of 2Tone group the Bodysnatchers). Brad completed the band by joining to play drums.

He stayed with both bands for a period of three years, and took in three big American tours with the Selecter. Although this incarnation of the Selecter released albums, Brad did not appear on them. He did, however, appear on the Big 5 albums *Popskatic* and *Live Jive*.

Brad was then approached by Frank Lea from Trojan Records to join his former Specials band mates Horace, Roddy, Neville and Lynval to play as part of the backing band for Desmond Dekker on the *King Of Kings* album but turned it down flat.

It turned out to be a wise move, as the album was slated in both the mainstream and underground press. When the album resulted in Neville, Roddy, Lynval and Horace re-forming their version of the Specials, Brad was approached by the media for his thoughts:

"It's a bit sad really," Brad replied. "Most people are going to gigs in Japan where I believe they are now, expecting to see the original Specials. It's the name that sells the tickets, but there's only four of the original group. The actual Specials name is still well respected in the music world, and I think it demeans what we were about."

After his stint with the Selecter, Brad contemplated a return to his first love, soul music:

"At the moment, I'm thinking seriously about getting JB's Allstars back, get it up and running. It was a great experience and I wanted to do more. I personally think the country needs a soul revue band; they are very popular in the States. It's definitely an area I would like to work in again."

Brad's plans for the Allstars didn't materialise, a shame as they were a fine band, and within months Brad seemed to have gone to ground, during which time he worked in the IT industry and in property development. Out of the blue, in the mid to late Nineties, and unknown to many fans, he re-appeared in an altogether different capacity.

Brad and Terry stay over at house after gig 1979. Photo by R.Byers

When the BBC launched *Changing Rooms*, a home makeover programme that would quickly spawn dozens of equally dreadful imitators, Brad, along with partner Emily, took part in the debut episode. In the show, two sets of people each set about re-decorating a room in the others' houses. The BBC's description of that bewildering appearance reads as follows:

"This episode brings us to Belsize Park in London. Buster and his mum Carol-Anne Turner have lived at the house for six years. Buster's room will be made over by his Aunt and Uncle [Brad and Emily]. His room currently has a lot of colour going on and a very bad need for some storage assistance. Brad and Emily Bradbury have lived in their house for six years also. Brad is a musician and Emily runs a fashion business. Linda Barker assists Buster and Carol-Anne with Brad & Emily's space. They create a layered fresco effect on the walls and then accentuate it by tracing out some old style calligraphy. They also use a part of tree to create a new lighting fixture. Andy creates some screens to cover the television and speakers. Laurence Llewelyn-Bowen helps Brad and Emily with the disarray that is Buster's room. They are going to use a bit of the existing colours on the walls by taping off squares and painting a lighter shade around them. The effect ends up with random squares of colour around the room. In a way to save space, they put the bed on a raised platform, allowing for storage underneath. They also create some interesting celebrity hangers for Buster's clothes."

Brad relaxing backstage 1979. Photo R.Byers

The look on Brad's face as he viewed the results in his room, especially the 'part of a tree used to create a new lighting fixture' was priceless.

Brad still held the Specials close to his heart and when asked if he would consider a return or comeback with the band he said:

"A full comeback? It would have to depend what the other guys were thinking. I've tried hard at it. There's a lot of interest in it. I'd like to see us get together for a big grand finale and probably play a couple of charity gigs to top it off."

Many musicians have praised John Bradbury over the years for his characteristic straight-backed style of playing. He is still a well-respected musician, and his skill with the sticks is a Specials trademark, but there is a lot more to the man than just drumming. He possesses a keen musical mind on all fronts from composition through to production, and away from the Specials is a proven artist in his own right.

He certainly does 'sock it to 'em', does old JB.

HORACE PANTER

WITH THE Specials up in smoke and the fires of their split smouldering away, it is well documented here that Horace Panter stayed loyal to his Specials' compatriots and went to Germany on tour with Jerry Dammers and John Bradbury as part of Rico Rodriguez's band. On return, Horace was convinced that his deteriorating relationship with Dammers was beyond repair, as Dammers increasingly blamed Panter's involvement with the Exegesis programme for causing creative and personal differences. However, Horace put his head down and got stuck into the band's work on the *In The Studio* album, where he appeared on three tracks, one being the 'War Crimes' single. He ultimately found the recording process too much to bear:

"Jerry and I weren't getting on after the fallout from the Specials," said Horace, "so I did the only thing I could to preserve my sanity, I left."

Whatever the reason, Panter was now a free agent and his interest in religion led him to become a born-again Christian.

Horace attempted to stay involved in music by playing and jamming with some friends in a band from Leamington Spa called the Mosquitoes, but all in all, he was played out and demoralised. He turned to helping his wife, Clare, run her clothing business, Nerve, in Coventry. Horace found re-learning his design skills in screen-printing therapeutic, and it helped him to get the stresses and strains of the Specials out of his system. He told Pete Chambers in *The 2Tone Trail*:

"The shop was started by my wife Clare in 1981. I joined her as part of my 'rock'n'roll decompression' strategy after being totally fed up with music after I had left the Specials in the spring of 1982. We went from just a small lock-up to manufacturing as well. We created our own logo brand clothes and accessories and ended up employing three people in a council-sponsored industrial unit in Alderman's Green, as well as one full-time shop assistant. Nerve clothes were sold all over the country for a while back in 1983-84. Clare eventually sold the shop to Chris Long [of the Swinging Cats] in 1984."

Working a 14-hour day while the business was thriving helped replenish Horace's worn out psyche and boosted his confidence to a level where he was prepared to get back to music again. By coincidence – or perhaps it was fate? – the Beat had just announced their split, and the two front men, Dave Wakeling and Ranking Roger, had broken away to form the pop outfit General Public. Horace contacted Wakeling and informed him that, whether he was searching for a bass player or not, Panter was his man! Wakeling agreed and so another 2Tone supergroup was created. Wakeling, Roger and Horace were joined by ex-Dexys Midnight Runners Andy Growcutt, aka 'Stoker', on drums and Micky Billingham on keyboards, and, surprisingly, Clash member Mick Jones.

Jones' membership was soon revealed to be a guest spot, as he was replaced by guitarist Kevin White when the band's line-up was officially announced. Decked out in green army jumpsuits, and having secured a deal with Virgin, the group's first effort was the self-titled single 'General Public' which appeared in March 1984. Despite the media coverage which followed the band's formation, the single only scraped its way to Number 60 in the UK charts. From the off, the group were very conscientious and went into the studio to record some tracks for a planned debut album. The album didn't surface until after the release of the group's second single, the very mainstream pop tune 'Tenderness', which fared less well thatn its predecessor, just squeezing into the UK Top 100. The second single, however, caused ripples in America, where its American 'bubble-gum pop' sound brought a hit for the group. As a result, the single was re-released in the UK, but again it flopped.

Unperturbed, they embarked on a tour of the British Isles and were very well received. They issued the album *All The Rage* (with a guest appearance by Mick Jones), a blend of pop, reggae and political comment. Disappointingly, it wasn't 'all the rage' with UK record-buyers, but proved popular in America. Across the pond, General Public took off in a big way, and a couple of the group's recordings appeared on the soundtracks for the films *Ferris Bueller's Day Off* and *Weird Science*. Since America seemed to be responsive, they spent almost two years touring there and became regulars on MTV. Their subsequent record releases also made a great impression.

They returned to the UK for a tour in 1985 and played the WOMAD festival. The highlight of that year came when they played a couple of support slots to the giants of rock, Queen. After one show, Freddie Mercury and Brian May came backstage to tell them how much they had enjoyed the General Public performance and asked if they wanted to join the *Kind Of Magic* tour full-time. In the end the band turned down the chance to appear alongside the likes of Status Quo and INXS because they had other UK commitments and another trip to America in the pipeline. They returned to Birmingham in 1986 to record their second album, *Hand To Mouth*, described by Horace as 'rather sterile'. Despite the album's pop ambience, it made little impact this side of the Atlantic, but they continued to have great success in America. It is surprising that the group came to a halt as they were on the verge of making it big in the US, but by Christmas 1987, Wakeling had pulled the plug on the band. Horace remained nonchalant. In his book *Ska'd For Life*, he said:

"I was ok about this. My son, Laurence, had arrived the previous April and life priorities had instantly changed."

Dave Wakeling, now successfully touring the US with his own version of the Beat, recalled his time with Horace:

"Horace always liked to play the role of the normal one in the band, which most of the time he did very well. Ranking Roger had wanted to play bass in General Public, but when I got Horace in, and Roger heard what he could do with the songs, he went along with my idea. Always reliable, solid as a rock on stage, we had great fun together, especially when he stopped pretending to be so normal!"

Wakeling stayed on in America, eventually working for Greenpeace, while Roger went solo, but sadly didn't achieve any commercial success. Horace played bass on Roger's 1988 album *Radical Departure*, but afterwards returned to the job he was doing before the Specials made it, that of a van driver for a transport firm. When Brad told him of his plans to form a 2Tone super-group, Horace agreed to join for what was planned as one tour. It was a chance to earn a little bit of extra money; after all, they all had mortgages to meet:

"The Special Beat," said Horace, "was a one-off that made good and then became a 'two-off', but you knew it wouldn't last. My own personal highlight was when, during 1991, we spent a month supporting Sting on tour in America. He invited us up on stage for the last number, bang a tambourine, stand at the back sort of thing. I purchased a blow-up Stratocaster and jumped on stage during 'Message In A Bottle'. While everyone else banged tambourines, I played air guitar to 12,000 people at the Spectrum in Philadelphia. I don't think it was what Gordon had in mind, but I enjoyed myself to the max!"

Horace later worked at the National Exhibition Centre in Birmingham, where he was a general assistant, or as he put it, a 'go-fer'. He enjoyed the job: "To be honest, that was fun. I bought stuff like postcards for the use of Bryan Adams, and had to find things like black material to decorate the Cult's dressing room with."

After this spell, he decided to do something constructive for his long-term future and went to college to become a primary school teacher:

"I looked at it this way..." he explained, "I figured that spending 13 years working with musicians couldn't be much different to working with children!"

Horace on tour bus 1979. Photo by R.Byers

Horace in relaxed mood. Photo by R.Byers

YOU'RE WONDERING NOW

His religious sensibilities still featured strongly in his life and he played bass at his local church on Sunday mornings:

"I play reggae and other funky stuff. We have a rocking time of it!"

In 1993, his recording career was resurrected when he was contacted by Trojan Records' Frank Lea and producer Roger Lomas to play as part of the backing band for Desmond Dekker on the *King of Kings* project. Since described by Lomas as 'a bad idea', the album spawned a CD single that featured the tracks 'Jamaica Ska' and 'Wings Of A Dove'. Once the Dekker album was finished, Horace became one of the four original band members in the partial reformation of the band that toured as the Specials, despite some criticism of their use of the name. That being said, other well-known bands such as the Selecter and Bad Manners play and perform with even fewer originals and there are no quibbles. Perhaps the fact that the Specials had always been significant and influential for so many people meant that the name was more revered than many others.

As already seen, the re-formed Specials, with a recording contract under their belts, toured in America and Europe, and played a few dates in Ireland and the UK. They released the covers album *Today's Specials*, which was torn apart by the critics, and a second collection, *Guilty 'Til Proved Innocent* that was better received but seemed to suffer because of the name of the group. However muted the response might have been at home, the huge mid-Nineties ska explosion in the US took the band on to far greater success there. Horace said:

"When we got back together in 1993, we played the old stuff, because that's what people wanted to hear, because there was the ska thing going on in America. We thought since we were out there, why didn't we get some songs together and make a real record. America though, it was about a lot of travelling on buses, a fair amount of jumping around on stage and making a loud noise. Our record went out towards the end of March 1998, so we had been pretty much constantly touring. We played a lot of radio promotion tours. We did the snowboard season, which was quite interesting if you liked playing in the teeth of a blizzard to a lot of people dressed a lot warmer than we were! We then got the Warped tour, which started at the end of June. And we did that for six weeks. So basically, the record was out, so there we were, promote, promote, play shows, play shows."

Life on the road was tough, and a bout of hypertension ended Horace's renewed Specials experience. The band eventually fizzled out after a tour of Japan.

After his bout of ill health, Horace wanted to play again. He kept things local and took on a couple of projects, the first being the formation of the Coventry Ska-Jazz Orchestra (which Horace nicknamed the Coventry Semi-Automatics) with his son Laurence on keyboards. They played in Coventry City Centre as part of the Coventry Music Festival, treating the shoppers to some cracking ska instrumental classics. In his second project, he teamed up with former Selecter supremo Neol Davies to create the group Box Of Blues, who gigged in and around Coventry. The partnership produced an album, the self-titled *Box Of Blues* which was released in 2000. It was a collection of original blues songs and one instrumental. According to Neol Davies:

"It's a mutual love of guitar, bass, drums. Bands like Free and the Who led to the recording philosophy of the album, which was to keep it simple and raw, but with snappy arrangements learnt from the 2Tone experience."

Former Paul Weller sidekick Anthony Harty defined a new style on the drums and *Box Of Blues* was highly praised throughout the blues scene in the UK and internationally. The band toured extensively as a result. In 2007, Horace published his biographical account of life in the Specials, *Ska'd For Life – A Personal Journey With The Specials*, becoming the first band member to document the trials and tribulations of the group. It was a humorous yarn and there was much excitement about the insights it gave into the band through his diary anecdotes.

Also in 2007, he issued the limited edition vinyl single 'Goa Blues' which was backed by the psychedelic organ swirl of the track 'Depleted Uranium Dub', performed under the name Sir Horace. It was released and distributed through the Rockers Revolt label, home of the band Pama International, who Horace had played with recently as a guest both live and in the studio. In doing so, he became the latest 2Tone member Pama International had recruited to join them on their campaign to bring some unique dub reggae and ska to the land, following in the footsteps of Lynval Golding, Rico Rodriguez, Lee Thompson and Paul Heskatt.

At the time of writing, Horace is still very much a part of the Coventry music network, and he gigs around the town with his current four-piece outfit, Blues To Go. Keeping his feet well and truly on the ground, he also continues to teach art to children with special needs.

NEVILLE STAPLE

AFTER THE Fun Boy Three fizzled into oblivion, Neville Staple and Lynval Golding both jetted off to Jamaica to recuperate and visit family and friends. On their return to the UK, they got wind of Terry Hall's official decision to call it a day a far as the FB3 were concerned. They did not rest on their laurels for too long, and they soon collaborated on a new project. Still signed to Chrysalis Records, they formed Sunday Best and recruited former 2Tone pal Pauline Black as guest vocalist. They also employed the rhythm section After Tonight who consisted of Jeremy Edwards on guitar, Phil Graham on drums and Wayne Lothian on bass (Lothian would later play for the Special Beat, and at the time of writing is playing with Dave Wakeling's English Beat around the US.) Pauline Black said:

"It was so long ago I actually can't remember how we hooked up, but it was fun working with them in Air Studios – we even met Macca [Paul McCartney]. They had been doing producing and this was their first main project."

Their first release was the single 'Pirates On The Airwaves'. As the title implies, the song paid homage to and supported pirate radio stations, which caused the record to be banned by the 'legitimate' radio stations, except for a few brave independents. Oddly, the record was given a public airing by the BBC children's show *Cheggers Plays Pop*. The single sank without trace and that was the last anyone heard of Sunday Best.

Neville recorded some solo work, but none of it was released. To his considerable annoyance and frustration, both he and Lynval were subsequently dropped from the Chrysalis roster:

"Most labels weren't interested in my work. I reckoned that if I'd had some white guys with me, it would have been easier. Chrysalis kept Terry and in the end didn't want to know us, which came as a bit of a blow considering our record."

Neville then moved into management, but his penchant for making music ultimately led him to the Asian Bhangra scene, where he began to do some production work and sang on a few tracks:

"I saw an opening there and at least I knew what I was talking about. I only want to make music. That's all I can do, or I wouldn't be happy otherwise. I love to work."

With activity during the Eighties at a low for Neville, he briefly appeared a host of

216

other artists, including Suggs and Chas from Madness, in the video to the posthumous release of Bob Marley's 'One Love'.

His first high-profile venture occurred in 1989, when he drifted slowly back into the ska scene. Producer Roger Lomas had been dabbling with Sixties music and working with the men responsible for the Jive Bunny phenomenon. He hit on the idea of creating something similar to the chart topping Jive Bunny mixes using 2Tone stars. Lomas initially recruited Buster Bloodvessel, Martin Stewart, Alan Sayag and Nick Welsh from Bad Manners (Welsh was also billed on the record as Prince Nutty, and provided vocals for 'Baggy Trousers' and 'Night Boat To Cairo'), but then decided to expand the ranks with other 2Tone personalities. In came Neville from the Specials, Ranking Roger, Saxa and Tony Beet from various incarnations of the Beat, while Pauline Black and Neol Davies made up the Selecter contingent. A 16-track album, *The Sound Of Ska*, was recorded at the BBC Central studios with the Jive Bunny team on production duties, and the record was issued on their Music Factory label. It was followed up by a 12" vinyl record under the name of Buster's Allstars which failed to register. Neville was responsible for the Specials' contribution on the mega-mix which was 'Gangsters'.

He then began to approach record companies with an old demo tape he still possessed of the Specials' trip to London with Pete Waterman back in 1978. This was soon snapped up and released by Receiver as the CD *Dawning Of A New Era – The Coventry Automatics AKA The Specials*.

Staple was soon recruited by Brad as vocalist and frontman for the Special Beat. One of the main draws for Neville was working with long-standing friend Ranking Roger:

"It was brilliant working with Roger in Special Beat. I got on great with him on the road. I guess I wanted to work with Roger anyway, and we were at loose ends, so, when I was asked I said 'yeah, fine'. Plus, I wanted to go out touring anyway, I wasn't working, so I wanted to work. I liked the songs and I liked Roger, so to do the songs together was fine."

He went on the US tour with the supergroup, and, following its success, decided to stay on with the band. He was glad to be out playing live and his performances were one of the main highlights of Special Beat. His onstage antics and firebrand approach to getting the audience involved rolled back the years:

"I was dying to get back on the road. I enjoyed being back onstage and travelling, but I don't think it took off as well as most thought it did."

Whilst working with Special Beat, one of his own tracks ended up on the Dojo modern ska compilation *The Shack -Volume One*, a liberal reworking of Desmond Dekker's '007 (Shanty Town)' under the title of 'Rude Boy De Ponporbation (007)', which was credited to Neville Staple AKA Judge Roughneck.

Neville then teamed up with former Specials Horace, Roddy and Lynval on the ill-received Desmond Dekker *King Of Kings* album. He had developed a taste for life in America through his time with Special Beat and got a big break when he went to America in the Nineties and became a citizen of Long Beach, California, where he got his own recording studio. He would remain in the States for ten years:

"I love it here in Long Beach," said Neville at the time, "and you can't beat the weather or the fans. I love it in America, it's beautiful, plus there really are so many more opportunities for me here. I'm able to perform all sorts of gigs and work on so many more projects than I ever could in Coventry. It's just that my passion is performing live and you know what it's like in the English music scene. It seems once you are no longer the 'flavour of the month' in England, they don't want anything to do with you. Don't get me wrong, I really love England. It's not the fans, it's that the promoters and buyers don't seem interested in much more than the bottom line. I certainly don't fit the boy-band thing that's happening these days!"

He began to carve a career for himself in the States, racking up plenty of shows and making headway on the recording front. He formed the production company 525 Music and developed a working relationship with producer Tom Lowry. He issued the preview album *Skanktastic* which featured the tracks 'Hypocrite', 'Simmer Down', 'Johnny Too Bad', 'Pressure Drop', 'Maga Dog' and 'Rude Boy Gone Jail', in the hope of being picked up by an independent label. He next appeared with his daughter, Sheena, on a 525 Music production for the hip-hop/trance outfit Bindu on the record 'We've Got Feelings Too'/'I Feel No Pain'. The writing credits show Neville, Sheena and Kendell Smith as contributors and both Sheena and Kendell went on to work with the Specials Mk2 on the *Today's Specials* album.

On his sporadic journeys back to England, collecting a good few air miles in the process, he joined his three colleagues Lynval, Roddy and Horace to reform the Specials. The story of the group's exploits is documented elsewhere in this book, but Neville enjoyed hogging the limelight as a charismatic frontman. He often played the Specials Mk2 shows bare-chested, looking ultra fit and belying his age, his displays putting his younger collaborators to shame.

In 1998 he hit a hiccup when, just before the secondary Specials ground to a halt, he became embroiled in an altercation that became well reported around the US. According to *Rolling Stone* magazine reporter Ari Bendersky:

"Neville Staple, lead singer of the influential English ska group the Specials, was arrested following a show Wednesday in Chicago at the Metro. Around 3:30 pm, the singer reportedly became irate and hostile toward Preston Graves, a production crew member, while Graves was telling the band members where to put their equipment. Staple reportedly began arguing with Graves, 29, and picked up a barstool and hit Graves in the back of the head and grabbed his throat. According to Chicago police spokeswoman, Arlene Mays, Graves went to Illinois Masonic Hospital where he was treated and released by doctors. Staple was charged with a simple battery misdemeanour. A court date is set for April 29th in Chicago, where the singer faces a possible fine and/or jail time."

Miles Woodroffe, who worked and travelled with the Specials Mk2 extensively as part of their production team (and who would later go on to create the website www.thespecials.com), recalled Neville's brush with the law:

"I remember the scuffle for sure. It was the Metro in Chicago and it happened early in the day as we arrived, not after the gig. I do remember he was arrested after the gig, but not what happened exactly after that. On that same tour, I was booked for mixing an outdoor show too loud on Long Island. I remember I was actually arraigned and had to divert from a tour stop in Philly to stand before the judge back there in Nassau County. He promptly dismissed it as ridiculous, so I raced back to mix the show and got a big shout out from Lynval, I recall. Good times! I'm just realizing that was ten years ago. Wow! Plus I never got my $100 bail money back now I think of it. Bastards!"

After the Specials Mk2 burnt itself out, the original rude boy's amazing work ethic saw him back recording with Sheena on a unique Jimi Hendrix tribute album that was being put together for Capitol. They appeared on both the album and the accompanying DVD with the track 'Up From The Skies' and Neville was extremely proud of being involved.

Not one to sit still long, he then supplied a couple of cuts for the soundtrack to the movie *Vampires Anonymous*, in which he even had a cameo role. During this same period, he teamed up with producer John Avila, better known as the bassist with US cult new-wave group Oingo Boingo. Nev relocated to Los Angeles for the project, as he and his backing band, known as the Hitmen, set about re-recording tracks from Staple's career with the original Specials and Fun Boy Three. The album, *Ghost Town – The Best Of The Specials And Fun Boy Three*, was put together at Avila's very own recording studio, Brando's Paradise. One track, a version of the Fun Boy Three hit 'Our Lips Are Sealed', even featured one of the song's co-writers, Jane Wiedlin from the Go-Gos on vocals. It was released on Anagram, a division of the Cherry Red empire, to mixed reviews but, fair play to Neville, the new versions were totally stripped and recorded in an original style.

After the record, he remained in LA a while:

"I'm based in Los Angeles. I live there, but I don't record there. All I do in LA is get the band together and rehearse. The only recording I do is for my daughter, Sheena. I do production and writing for her. So the only time I go in a studio is for her, not for myself. I like to record my stuff in Coventry at Planet Studios."

In 2000, Roger Lomas and Receiver released the album *Skinhead Girl*. The album consisted of 15 classic Trojan tracks, which had been recorded prior to the emergence of the Specials Mk2. The project, under the name the Specials, was a forerunner to the 1994 reunion and included Neville, Horace, Lynval and Roddy with a host of other backing musicians. Those musicians included ex-Selecter Neol Davies on guitar, former Paul Weller associate and Special Beat member Anthony Harty on drums and Leigh Malin on sax, (later a member of the Skabilly Rebels). It was generally considered by those involved to be a money-making exercise for Receiver. Lomas himself commented later:

"They were both good albums to work on, but a good idea in essence? In hindsight, possibly not."

The four Specials involved were offered in the region of £7,000 for the rights to the work, which they were persuaded to sell on. It was, Roddy Byers admitted later, "a silly move really."

A similar, but less effective, follow-up, *Conquering Ruler*, appeared a year later.

Neville's first major work on the solo front came via Cleopatra Records and the album *Special Skank Au Go-Go*, a 15-track collection which showed off his new rock/reggae approach to making music. The album showcased the unique style that Neville had refined, it really showed promise and sold modestly, bought mainly by fans, on both sides of the Atlantic. Ever busy, he appeared on the track 'Explosive' for Canadian ska band the Planet Smashers and then travelled to Miami to record the track 'Black Market Man' for Venezuelan Latin ska outfit Desorden Publico, which would appear on their album *Diablo*. The album went triple platinum and Neville's track was a big hit in the Venezuelan charts:

"Take the band from Venezuela," said Neville. "Anybody who asks me, who is in a band, who was brought up on the Specials music, and likes the feel of the music, real fans, they're inspired, and then I can do something on their record."

He also added his vocal talent to tracks on the album *Elva* for US grunge rockers Unwritten Law.

Neville then returned to Britain and put together a backing band for live performances in the UK. He also committed himself to writing new material for an album. Neville was also suffering from ill health, problems with his knees that required surgery, and was in a great deal of pain. The reason was simply years of wear and tear

Neville in Jerry's flat 1978. photo by R.Byers

Neville on train 1979. photo by R.Byers

from his high-tempo performances; jumping around, clambering onstage and plenty of dancing had all taken their toll. Undeterred, Neville continued to play his gigs through the pain and was often seen limping, but he was always committed and gave 100%.

He was asked to be the headline act for fashion house Ben Sherman's 40th Birthday celebrations scheduled to take place at the Canvas Club in Islington, London. The event was compèred by former Radio 1 DJ, Liz Kershaw. Neville, using a walking stick because of his knee problems, wowed the crowd with a set of Specials numbers and other covers. He was then joined by Madness' Chas Smash and the Beat's Ranking Roger onstage. Guest DJ that evening was none other than Jerry Dammers.

Neville's energy did not wane and, on his return to the UK, he created a new production company in conjunction with manager Jason Rothberg and in partnership with Alchemy Entertainment. This enabled him to create a new record label called Rude Boy Music; the intention was to release Neville's archive material, as well as new recordings, and to sign new bands. The spirit of Nev's earlier venture, Shack Records, was still alive and kicking.

There was no pause for breath, and he and other 2Tone stars then performed at the VIP party after the MTV European Music Awards at Leith Docks, Edinburgh in November 2003. The band consisted of himself, Lynval Golding, Roddy Radiation, Ranking Roger and Sixties music icon Donovan. Jerry Dammers was present as guest DJ, but didn't play as part of the group. Staple used the party as a platform to announce that he was going to launch his own line of clothing, Rude Wear, to tie in with the Rude Boy Music record label.

Work on the Rude Boy project began in earnest and he began to sign artists to the label such as Leicester punk trio Ictus, ex-Killing Joke members Jaz and Raven, US-based dance act Harry the Dog, Bermuda reggae star Mishka and reggae/dance act Saint and Campbell. He also organised promotional street teams to spread the word about Rude Boy Music and the Rude Wear clothing range.

Neville wanted Rude Wear fashions to celebrate the 25 years of 2Tone and to draw on the original 2Tone image, based around racial unity. The resurgence of ska had opened a market for fashionable clothes that echoed the original rude boy, mod and skinhead styles. He included suits, Harrington jackets, polo shirts, sweatshirts, T-shirts and hoodies:

"It's really great to know this type of clothing will soon be in shops again," Neville commented, "and maybe the kids will again walk down the street looking smart and trendy. No, seriously, the guys at Rude Wear have done a fantastic job and we have been working on this now for many months in order to bring together the music and the fashion once more."

Rude Wear was headed by entertainment and music executive Barry Sanders, along with fashion experts David Gold and Neil Wiseman. David Gold said:

"It's been an absolute pleasure working with Neville and his management team on the designs of the new range. We hope to have our first range in the shops by no later than the end of February 2004. We have had an absolutely amazing response from the European and American markets and we hope to have the product to present to our UK and Irish customers in the next few weeks. We started this really as fans of the music from our youth, but since the order books have filled up we are taking this very seriously and looking at a further range for late 2004 and 2005."

Neville's manic approach to live performance continued when he joined another couple of brief, hastily put together Special Beat tours of the US and Australia, with

Roddy Radiation joining up on one occasion. He also squeezed in a performance with Roddy and his Skabilly Rebels at BBC Radio Coventry's '25th Anniversary of 2Tone' bash: "To be honest, what can I do? I have to carry on," Neville explained. "When I first started on my own, eight years ago in America, I was panicking because people were used to seeing me in the Specials or they know of me in the Specials. So when I went to go and do it on my own, and I was used to the rest of the Specials around me, it was daunting. But as soon as you start playing two or three songs, you could tell that they [the crowd] didn't give a shit really. They just wanted to hear the music and they were glad that one of us was there. My set has Specials songs in it 'cos I've got to do those songs as well. So what I do is pick my favourite songs I like, the songs I like and enjoy doing in the Specials, and it's all favourites really. Mix it with some new stuff and most people agree, it goes down well. I love doing my new songs because then I get the reaction from the people to a new thing."

Neville's new touring band included Andy 'Angry' Perriss on guitar, Steve 'Sledge' Armstrong on bass, Joe Atkinson on keyboards, Warren Middleton on trombone and a succession of drummers, one being Winnie Marche (formerly of the Selecter and currently on sticks for Skaville UK). He played shows the length and breadth of Britain. His work on a new album eventually came to fruition in the October of 2004 with the release of his first true solo album, entitled *The Rude Boy Returns*. Old pals Rat Scabies of the Damned and Mick Jones of the Clash made guest appearances on a number of the tracks, and both played on a unique cover of the Specials' 'Do Nothing'. Other covers included Donovan's 'Yellow Star' and even the Specials Mk2's 'Place In Life'. The 15-track album received mixed reviews, but the general consensus was that it was a reasonable effort at creating something original. Dave Simpson of the *Guardian* wrote:

"All the trademarks are intact: the woozy saxophone, killer choruses and sense of boisterous bonhomie, despite lyrics which prick at the social conscience and send messages out to this generation's rude boys. Probably the most unexpected and rewarding comeback of the year."

The album flowed with all Neville's musical experiences and oozed with ska, reggae, Asian and even native US Indian influences, as in the track 'Nachna'. As part of the commercial package the album came with a free live DVD of the Ben Sherman 40th birthday bash and unseen footage of Neville around Coventry. There were also interviews with Neville, Roddy Radiation, Ranking Roger, Hazel O'Connor, the Libertines, TV and radio presenter Mark Lamarr, Don Letts, Pete Waterman and pioneering British DJ Norman Jay. In a benevolent gesture, Neville showed his support of the Mkombozi Centre for Street Children charity in Africa by donating ten percent of the proceeds from the album. With his knees repaired, a huge tour was undertaken to push the new release.

Neville's shows continue to receive rave reviews and the original rude boy never stops working. At the time of writing, Neville is still racing up and down the country playing to appreciative crowds. In 2009, along with Ranking Roger, he has organised a small Special Beat tour of Australia and Dubai, with Pauline Black appearing as a guest. Neville's energy never seems to wane, and as the man himself says:

"Fans are always asking my age and I say how old do you think I am? They usually come up with a nice figure, so I don't care. I'm not going to say I'm in my 30's, that just sounds stupid. I enjoy staying in touch with my fans; I do read all of my own emails personally. Without the fans, the Specials wouldn't have been so successful. As for me? I'll keep going till I drop!"

In Neville's case, it seems that rude boys don't get older, just more enthusiastic!

LYNVAL GOLDING

MOST OF Lynval's activities after the split of the Specials have been encapsulated within the previous descriptions of other band member's exploits. So, in an attempt to avoid repetition we will catch up with Lynval after his collaboration with Neville and their project Sunday Best that featured the backing band After Tonite. Lynval went on to manage the backing band for some time and they toured the clubs in London before Lynval shifted his attention to production work.

Being confined to the studio, however, didn't suit him and he was eventually rescued by the coming of the original Special Beat squad and their various global jaunts. In the middle of 1993 he left the group with keyboard player Sean Flowerdew:

"I got bored of reviving the Eighties," said Lynval, "especially the gimmicky songs like 'Monkey Man', although I think stuff like 'Ghost Town' still stands up today. I enjoyed it and it was an experience but all good things come to an end and I left to pursue other projects. I was replaced and the group continued to go on around the world. The fans were great."

After leaving Special Beat, Lynval stayed with Sean Flowerdew and they joined forces with Tony Finn in a new project called Arawak. Into the group came former Selecter drummer Charlie 'H' Bembridge and trumpeter Graeme Hamilton, who had played with the Fine Young Cannibals and the Special Beat and had recently performed on the massive worldwide hit 'Tired Of Being Pushed Around' by 2 Men, A Drum Machine And A Trumpet. 2Men, This consisted of a duo of Andy Cox and Dave Steele who had once played with the Beat and who had recently split from the Fine Young Cannibals, leaving that band defunct. Described as 'modern dance reggae' by Lynval, Arawak remained a studio project. After Lynval left, Arawak continued and developed over time and through various line-up changes into Skooby and then Skanga.

In 1993, Lynval's anti-racist masterpiece 'Why?' resurfaced on *The Shack – Volume One* compilation on Dojo in the form of a demo version credited to him and Neville Staple. It also featured a cover of John Holt's 'Wear You To The Ball', which was another late Specials demo that for legal reasons had Terry Hall's vocal removed. If you listen closely, Hall's voice can still be heard very faintly in the background as the track draws to a close.

As previously stated, Lynval was recruited on Trojan's Desmond Dekker project, and this led on to him become an integral member of the Specials Mk2 and their American and Japanese tours. When he returned to Coventry, he opened up the Glasshouse, a working studio in Earlsden. The studio was also opened as training centre where young people could come along and learn the basics of studio equipment, and it ran specialist music courses. The Coventry and 2Tone connection remained intact when Amos Anderson, a former member of reggae band Hard Top 22 (whose members provided most of the musicians in the first Selecter line-up), was made the studio's director.

Lynval remained close to Jerry Dammers and regularly appeared with him on the DJ circuit as well as on the Special AKA's 'Nelson Mandela' single and the SWAPO benefit single 'Wind Of Change'.

He was in constant demand as a special guest on other artists' work, often appearing live with the Pogues. He regrouped with Neville Staple to guest for the Scottish rock/dance crossover band the Soup Dragons, best known for their huge hit single 'I'm Free (To Do What I Want)', who were being guided on their album *Hydrophonic* by Rick Rogers. Neville's toasting skills and influences from the Asian music scene are prevalent, as is Lynval's characteristic rhythm guitar chop which all feature on the Soup Dragons track 'Rest in Peace'.

In 1996, during his time with the Specials Mk2 and their many journeys around the States, Lynval met a woman by the name of June Boland. As their relationship blossomed, Lynval became intent on settling in America. They eventually moved to the stunning location of Gig Harbor, a small town and former fishing village located near Seattle, and by 1999, they had married. Whilst enjoying a romantic time in America, it wasn't long before he was back into music in a big way. He set up Golding Productions with the intention of recording and releasing his own and other artists' material. His first was to be his wife's cousin, Christina Boland, whose stage name was Chela:

"I have done a lot of work with Lynval over the years," said Christina, "and he has been my mentor and producer in my musical ventures. We formed a band together called Chela and Georgetown, and did shows all over the Seattle area and other parts of Washington. I believe that Lynval and I have worked on 30 to 40 songs together, where he did mainly music production and I would come up with lyrics. I would spend the weekends over at their home and we would write and come up with new music the entire time."

Their working relationship thrived, developing Chela's ska/reggae/rock style with such outstanding tracks as 'Going Out Of My Head' and 'Take Me As I Am'. They even sampled the Specials' opening crowd murmurs from the beginning of 'Nite Klub' on their track 'Shine'. Their well-crafted live shows as Chela And Georgetown were performed regularly in and around the Washington state area. According to Lynval, Boland's first run on stage went a lot better than his own:

"I froze up on my first gig." he said, "She didn't."

Lynval was heavily into promoting and producing the Chela project and he remained sure that Boland would be the next big thing to come out of Washington (the last being Nirvana). As Chela and Georgetown maintained their run of well reviewed shows, Lynval donned his production hat again for US new wave band the Buttersprites for their debut album and, along with Chela, played at the album launch party. Shortly afterwards, he decided to flex his musical muscles still further with the formation of his own band, the Stiff Upper Lips. Their MySpace page describes them eloquently:

"Waft a bit of Jamaican breeze into the rainy, chilly clime of Seattle. Led by Lynval Golding, veteran of the UK's legendary Specials, impeccably dressed Stiff Upper Lips deliver a hefty helping of Saucy Brit beat. Seattle scenesters will recognize familiar fixtures on the stand, such as Saxophonist Andrew Sodt, currently of Lushy and formerly of Tiny Hat Orchestra and his counterpart on the sax, noted jazz musician and Wayward Shamans alum Craig Flory. No caravan of rockers would be full-length without a trombone and John Sampson fills the two-toned shoes of this role, while bassist Kirk Larsen and drummer Mike Daugherty (of Casey McGill's Blue 4 Trio and the Yes Yes Boys) complete this most rude of musical aggregations."

The band primarily played on a local level as an antidote to the grungy bluster of the Nirvana-type wannabes doing the rounds at the time. The band gigged and occasionally recorded for a couple of years before biting the dust in 2007, although sadly nothing was ever released,.

During their time with the Stiff Upper Lips, Lynval and Andy Stodt made guest appearances for another respected Seattle musician, Johnny Horn and his band Militant Rhythm Section on their album entitled *Mexican Weed Dub*, proving that Lynval was well in demand and possessed of as much energy as his former colleague Neville Staple. Lynval and Andy Sodt played on a few dates with Dave Wakeling's English Beat and Lyn

224

Original drummer Silverton & Lynval in Coventry pub 1979. Photo by R.Byers

was hailed by the ecstatic crowds as something of a hero. He was also now in constant demand as a father to his son, Dominic, and clearly very happy with life.

On his frequent trips to the UK, Lynval hooked up with Terry Hall on a number of occasions, the highlight of which was the Glastonbury festival where the duo appeared onstage in front of thousands, and on TV in front of millions, to spread the Specials' message in their collaboration with singer Lily Allen. Lynval repeated the experience with Lily when she played at Somerset House in London, and on her gig at the Showbox Theatre in Seattle during her US tour:

"I met Lily Allen through her MySpace." said Lynval, "I remember meeting her for the first time and doing 'Blank Expression' with her and she said 'Oh my God, I'm not worthy!' and I just said, 'Behave, you are embarrassing me!' She asked me to introduce 'Blank Expression' and I suddenly thought 'When I last did this song, she wasn't even born yet!' It was then I realised that, my God, we did have a big influence on people. Lily had said the Specials were one of her favourite bands. I turned up to her soundcheck with my guitar and started playing 'Blank Expression' and she was very excited about that. The audience weren't expecting to see me there, so it was great when she introduced me and the lights went on. We stayed friends and she wanted me to go out and do more shows with her, so I did another one in LA."

If having his own US outfit wasn't enough for the livewire Golding, he became a member of British dub reggae band Pama International, which reunited him with longstanding friends Tony Finn and Sean Flowerdew. Pama International included musicians who had previously worked with the likes of Galliano, Bentley Rhythm Ace, Steel Pulse, the Style Council and Pop Will Eat Itself, and had released a few albums prior to Golding's arrival. The band had also had one of their tracks 'Truly, Madly, Deeply' included in the soundtrack of the hit film *Lock, Stock And Two Smoking Barrels*, and the song was covered by UK traditional ska band the Dualers, who took it into the UK Top 25. Pama International then became the first band to be signed to the legendary Trojan record label in over 30 years when they released the critically acclaimed *Trojan Sessions* album, to which Lynval contributed, and which also featured the talents of many original ska stars such as Rico Rodriguez, Dennis Alcapone, Dawn Penn, Derrick Morgan and Dave and Ansell Collins:

"For the *Trojan Sessions*," said Lynval, "I never actually met any of the singers, I just did all my parts in Seattle and emailed them over to Sean!"

The Trojan link proved to be a help and a great promotional tool for Pama International, but as Sean Flowerdew recalled, it wasn't all wine and roses:

"Trojan approached us, I think they liked the fact we were taking the music to new generations and new crowds and the fact that we've built a huge grass roots following here. The old boss there, John Reed, had been aware of us from our first album and liked the way we worked. They were searching for new outlets for the music and in Pama International they saw a good vehicle. It was an honour to have something issued on Trojan, to be associated with that label and the music it's released over the years is amazing. The business side stinks. Unfortunately that seems a legacy that's been passed down through the years to whoever owns the label. Not towards us, but there was a massive lack of respect to the older artists. The way I see it, though, is the name and the logo is bigger than whoever owns it. Shame that doesn't relate to food on the table, but no-one remembers who's running it, they just remember the fantastic music. It happened to be Sanctuary running things when we were on the label, but Universal has now bought them out. No-one will look back and think 'Sanctuary were a great label, they ran Trojan brilliantly and put out some fantastic music.' No-one."

Their connection with Trojan lasted just the one album before they went back the DIY approach of recording and formed the record label Rockers Revolt. They released another album, *Love Filled Dub Band*, on which Lynval was included as a fully-fledged group member, and which featured his track 'Wonder Wonder':

"A few years ago, when a suicide bomber went into a wedding reception and blew himself up and killed people at the party, I was watching it on the news and the lyrics just came to me. Also, people talk about barbaric people in the Middle East, when we're blowing up innocent people, women and kids, with so called 'friendly fire'. Me and Sean talk about this stuff all the time and we decided we need to give this album a bit of oomph."

This recording featured a host of renowned guests including, from the Specials' camp, Horace Panter and Rico Rodriguez, and was co-produced by John Collins, the man responsible for the production of 'Ghost Town'. It also featured the talents of Paul Heskett, former Swinging Cats member and the flute player on 'Ghost Town'. Whenever Lynval found himself in England, he would team up with Pama International to perform live with them all over the country at many gigs and festivals. In 2008, with Lynval and Billy Bragg amongst others on board, the band embarked on a mission to spread the message of the rise of knife and gun crime in the UK with the new album *Highrise* accompanying the 'Highrise Campaign'. To help raise awareness, the band issued a statement to the press:

"It is very plain for everyone to see that knife and gun crime is out of control in the UK. Everyone involved with the making of *Highrise* is truly passionate about spreading a positive message, as well as providing funding, mentoring and opportunities to the younger generations. All the charities chosen by Pama International in this campaign do amazing work; Kids Company and London & Basement Studios actively give youths opportunities, support and guidance on a daily basis. In addition to the album's release, Pama International will be taking this vital message on the road. They will perform a series of club shows, as well as matinee performances and workshops for under-18s throughout 2009."

Lynval added: "If the Specials were around today, we'd be doing a song like 'Highrise'."

In an interview on Pama International's *Rockers Revolt* website, Lynval said of his time with the group:

"I've known Sean and Finny for about 15 years. After the Specials and Fun Boy Three broke up, I joined Special Beat and Sean was also a member. We both left that at the same time but stayed close. We've always been close. Good people bring out the best in you, you know? Although I now live in America, I record all my guitar parts and ideas and email them over. It's taken us three albums to get to where we want to be though. The set up is great. Good records take time to settle. We made a great record in *Love Filled Dub Band*, but not enough people heard it yet. The reviews and radio play speak for themselves. We do everything ourselves. Sean puts the music out and does all the press. We don't have big budgets to promote things or spend months in the studio. It's limited, but we're learning to work the limitations.

"We're not signed to a major, so we have no money for advertising, which isn't a bad thing. It means we work things from the grass roots. Now, we have very strong foundations and things will just build and build. We don't rely on anyone. No management, no label, no backing. All on our own terms. True DIY spirit. It's good. All the music industry don't know what to do, what the next format will be, all sales are down and they just sell off music cheaper and cheaper, devaluing everything. Through greed they'll lose everything, watch them get smaller and smaller. We'll outstay many because we're building something of quality. We have all the ingredients. Finny has one of the best soul voices. He gets better and better the more we do.

"Sean's writing gets better and better. He's got most of the next album written already! I'm looking forward to getting to the UK and hearing the ideas. I know it's going to be something incredible. The next level and playing with Pama International live is very enjoyable. First-class players. Fuzz Townshend and Ernie McKone our rhythm section are rock solid. Musically, how this band sets about things is for all the right reasons. We enjoy it. We enjoy playing live together. We enjoy recording together. We challenge each other, always try and make things better, always improving. We've put a tour package together with Rockers Revolt bands and we're calling it 'Reggae For The People', it's going to be a lot of fun."

Lynval is currently splitting his time between Seattle and the UK, with many trips across the Atlantic. He often spends time in his old stomping ground of Coventry and shows no signs of slowing down. His drive and enthusiasm cannot be matched and they're largely responsible for encouraging the Specials to communicate with each other:

"I love them guys, y'know? They are like my brothers. We don't always agree on things, but I love 'em all. They're wicked!"

EXTRA SPECIALS:

RICO RODRIGUEZ

NOBODY HAS worked harder at a music career than the talented man from Wareika Rico Rodriguez (Born Emmanuel Rodriguez in 1934 in Kingston, Jamaica). Before the Specials, he had a massive back catalogue of releases in his homeland and had appeared on many ska classics from the Sixties. After moving to the UK in the early Seventies, Rico had a quiet period. He subsequently signed to Island and released the seminal *Man from*

Wareika album, meeting his future partner in brass Dick Cuthell in the process. They both played on UK punk band the Members' reggae dub attempt 'Offshore Banking Business' in 1979. Also in 1979, they were approached to record with the Specials on their debut album, *Specials*. The duo continued to record and play live with the Specials until the band split in 1981.

Rico's long career gained him the accolade of playing on both the original and Specials cover of 'A Message To You Rudy'. He also guested for the Selecter on the *Too Much Pressure* album. He would go on to play with the Special AKA (although, surprisingly, was absent from the 'Nelson Mandela' single). He signed as a solo artist to the 2Tone label, for whom he released two singles and two albums, touring all over the world to promote his own music.

After the 2Tone involvement, he played on many artists' work, enjoying chart success again on Paul Young's cover of Nicky Thomas's 'Love Of The Common People' in 1983. He made guest appearances and did session work for artists including Cedric Myton and the Congos, Ian Dury, Kirsty MacColl, the Maytals, Chas Jankel, Joan Armatrading, Dennis Bovell and many more over the following years.

In the early Nineties he went on the road with a group of musicians under the name of Rico and his Band. In 1991, he then became a fundamental member of the jazz/ska band Jazz Jamaica, formed by Ernest Ranglin's nephew Gary Crosby. Rico played live and recorded with the group, before opting out to explore other avenues. He soon encountered another man to have a huge impact in his life, former Squeeze keyboard player and TV presenter Jools Holland. Rico said:

"I had my own band at the time, and the Police, they invited me to come an' do a gig with them, in other words I'm supporting the Police on these concerts. That's where I met Jools, at these concerts. He was supporting an artist with his piano playing, and that's where I met him at Sting's concert in the late Eighties. So when I came back from Jamaica an' played with a band name Jazz Jamaica, and Jazz Jamaica to me, everything wasn't so clear with we. I thought they want fe use my name, ya hear me good? I think they were tryin' fe use my name to big up themselves, and as the sufferer that I am, I don't want nobody to build up themselves off my name an' what I have done for music. Yeah?

"So, after I had been with them fe a lickle while I jus' leave them, and then I called Jools' office, an' I say 'You have any work fe me, sah?' And him sez 'Ohh, yes man!' So, from that I have been with Jools. Yeah. Oh God, man. The treatment, I have never been treated as good as any. I would say the best I have been treated in my musical career is by this man, Jools. He give you respec', y'know wha' I mean? I feel very good with Jools. And I say this, even though I'm with Jools' band so long, people still book me to play for them, individually. Ok? So I've always been respectful to him, say 'Jools, I have a gig on this an' that date, is it Ok, sah?' And he say 'Ok, its good man.'"

The Jools Holland Rhythm and Blues Orchestra regularly features on his BBC2 music show *Later...* and have recorded a few albums, including one called *Swinging The Blues, Dancing The Ska*, as well as releasing a big-band version of ska legend Lord Tanamo's 'I'm In The Mood For Love' (with vocals by Jay Kay from Jamiroquai). Jools' *Hootenanny* programme has been a mainstay of British New Year's Eve celebrations for some time, and on New Year's Eve 2008, Rico made a singing appearance. A sprightly 74 years old at the time, Rico enchanted the nation with his rendition of a ska-tempo version of the Nat King Cole track 'Love'. Rico has also appeared on the last two Pama International albums with Lynval Golding.

Legendary Rico Rodriguez on tour 1979. Photo by R.Byers

Talk of the Specials' reunion in 2009 has brought Rico's name back on to the lips of the 2Tone community. Messages of support from all over the world can be found on the internet, and there are many calls for him to reunite onstage with Coventry's finest. We can only keep our fingers crossed; at at the time of writing there has been no agreement between Rico and the Specials' management, but apparently, his name has been mentioned...

DICK CUTHELL

RICO'S CLOSE friend Dick Cuthell also played alongside the Specials. He is a master of all musical trades and as sound engineer, record producer and musician Cuthell's work can be found on hundreds of tracks by a host of artists. For a while, he was mainly involved in the reggae genre, especially whilst working at Island in the Seventies. He and Rico enjoyed huge success as part of the Specials and they would remain as part of the brass section with the Special AKA. Dick was very much in demand as a producer and engineer, his career having been given a lift through his involvement with the Specials. By the mid Eighties his list of clients read like a Who's Who of music, including Amazulu, Aswad, Blancmange, Elvis Costello, Frankie Goes To Hollywood, the Fun Boy Three, Julian Cope, Kirsty MacColl, Bryan Ferry, Chris Rea, Madness, Phil Collins, Ultravox and the Pogues. He worked extensively with Annie Lennox and Dave Stewart's futuristic group Eurythmics, and was at the desk for their groundbreaking *Sweet Dreams* album.

Dick would eventually, and somewhat bizarrely, simply fade away from the public eye and hardly any information remains on file about this mysterious genius. He was last heard of driving a taxi in London as well as being a chauffeur. He was rumoured to be suffering ill health but was recently rumoured to be producing again for new artists and working once more with Jerry Dammers. For many, if Rico and Dick rejoined the Specials on stage, even for one song, it would really be the icing on the cake. They added a big, beefy sound to the Specials that was second to none.

RICK ROGERS

AS MENTIONED elsewhere in the book, Rick Rogers had kick-started his career in the music industry with the establishment of his own PR company, Trigger, in the late Seventies. Trigger was responsible for guiding the early campaigns for both Stiff and Chiswick Records. He soon expanded into management, and through his management of the Damned became involved in the career of the Specials, where he assumed responsibility for taking care of the band and assisting with the running of the 2Tone record label. He was always regarded as the 'eighth Special', working away behind the scenes. He went on to manage and guide the careers of the Fun Boy Three, the Soup Dragons, Right Said Fred and High Fidelity (former Soupdragon Sean Dickson's band). He also spent time as marketing manager of Big Life Records and was the driving force behind the campaign for De La Soul's platinum-selling debut album *3 Feet High and Rising*.

Rick was also involved on the comedy circuit for several years, where he brought top American stand-ups such as Steven Wright, Emo Phillips, Sandra Berndhart, Dave Chappelle and the late, great Bill Hicks into the UK and thus to the attention of British audiences. Not content with that, he would also be responsible for launching the theatrical career of Paul O'Grady's alter ego, Lily Savage.

Rick is now the Business Fellow in Music at University College Falmouth, based at the Dartington Campus. As part of this role, he runs Dartington Recordings and South West Recordings, a stepping-stone label for South West based Musicians that releases one-off singles commercially. He also mentors young musicians and music businesses across the South West of the UK and presents seminars on the music business across the region. As well as his Business Fellow role, Rick is still active in the commercial music business and currently runs a specialist music management consultancy business, DLR Management, along with Dennis Smith (Sawmills Studio/Muse). Rick has often stated that he would like to see a reunited full Specials line-up, and he was involved with the early stages of the Specials reunion back in 2004. He is an integral part of the Specials' history.

DAVE JORDAN

ANOTHER VITAL ingredient to the Specials was engineer and producer Dave Jordan. In 1974, Dave worked with glam-rocker Barry Blue on the track 'Rosetta Stone', released by Bell Records (also home of the Bay City Rollers). He came to prominence in 1976 when he and Dick Cuthell were the assistant engineers for Aswad's self-titled debut album on Island. In 1977, he was engineer for ex-Fairport Convention singer Sandy Denny on her *Rendezvous* album. Later that year he remixed the Rolling Stones' double live album *Love You Live*, then worked with them the following year on the *Some Girls* LP. In 1979 he became involved with the Specials, and was a regular face on tour as well as working behind the scenes in the studio. He maintained his connection

230

Horn player and legendary producer Dick Cuthell on tour 1979. Photo by R.Byers

with the band after the split in 1981, taking on production duites for the Fun Boy Three. He became part of the 'Fun Four' production team with Terry, Neville and Lynval, but Jordan was the main man.

It was well known in the business that Dave was an habitual drug user and he developed a heroin addiction that made him unreliable at times. Despite his addiction he continued to work, and he produced and engineered for the Pogues, gaining success with tracks like 'The Irish Rover'. He went on to work further with Shane MacGowan in his post-Pogues set-up, the Popes. In 1995, after Jordan had been clean from drugs for some years, he went on tour with MacGowan and the Popes. MacGowan and his entourage reputedly dabbled in heavy drugs at the time, hardly the best atmosphere for Jordan. In 1995, the tour arrived in Paris, and Jordan's fate would be sealed. According to *The Independent* newspaper:

"In March, the Popes had played a gig in the Élysées Montmartre, Pairs. On the night of March 6th' the band and a number of the crew went back to the Regynes Hotel. In the early hours of the following morning, the band's promoter, Alan Lahana, received a call from the hotel informing him that one of the crew was dead in one of the hotel bedrooms. Lahana went straight to the hotel and called the police. When a member of the gendarmes examined the scene, it was clear to him that the body had been moved – perhaps in an effort to lift it on to the bed. The promoter identified the body as that

The SPECIALS – from conception to reunion

of Dave Jordan, a monitor engineer with the Popes, who had an association previously with the Pogues going back to the mid-Eighties. He was a gentle, quiet, shy man from the English Lake District who was married to a girl from Cork and had a previous marriage with two children.

"Jordan was a popular and well-liked man and his death would devastate a lot of people. While Lahana was dealing with the police, the other members of the band and crew got into the bus and drove back to London. Effectively, McGowan had abandoned one of his longest-serving crewmembers. He could have helped establish that Dave Jordan was a heroin addict, thus removing any doubt about the cause of death and hastening the return of his body to his native land. Only the intervention of friends of the dead man, and British Embassy negotiations, prevented the French authorities from keeping the body and recalling the Popes to France to complete their inquiries."

Four days later, Dave Jordan was buried in his native Kendal in the Lake District. In 1996, the re-formed Specials dedicated their 'comeback' album *Today's Specials* to Jordan's memory. Obviously a talented man, Dave's legacy will be measured by his work.

THE ROAD TO REUNION

"Time will heal, I hope that's true."
From 'Forgive 'n' Forget' – The Skabilly Rebels 2008

*M*ARCH 2008, and the music world was set alight by an interview on BBC radio with Terry Hall, who announced to the thousand of listeners that the Specials were on the verge of reunion:

"Well, we're still trying to put dates together, but hopefully September, October time. We need to spend the summer rehearsing. I think it's taken me 30 years to realise we could do it really well. It was seeing other artists on the reunion trail that has been an inspiration because I saw Patti Smith do *Horses*, and I saw the Pixies reforming."

The news spread like wildfire and the media swarmed on the story. Could it be that the most unexpected reunion of all time would actually happen? As in any relationship, things are not always plain sailing, and the Specials' archetypal rocky romance would never be resolved easily. But it seemed, tentatively, that the painful ghosts of the past could be exorcised by the powers of age and experience. The seven were talking, but this new-found accord had taken years, not months to achieve.

In 2004, Specials and 2Tone fans hoped in vain that the year of the 25th anniversary of the Specials and the 2Tone label would fulfil their dream of seeing their heroes on stage again. The 25th birthday of the first single 'Gangsters' would be in July and expectations for a commemoration of some form were high. Would there be new albums, new commemorative video releases, special one-off gigs? The year was, in the end, very disappointing and nothing of any real magnitude happened. Channel 4 aired the *TwoTone Britain* documentary, which had looked promising, but in the end just re-hashed old material and lacked any real depth. The highlight was probably a week-long run of programmes aired on BBC Radio Coventry and Warwickshire to celebrate the 25th Anniversary on home turf. The programmes featured interviews with 2Tone members, fan's stories and memories and an interview with this author (who incidentally was also the subject of a well-edited BBC Radio 4 programme called *Fashion Music* that covered the Specials and 2Tone and was aired around the same time).

The local celebrations were topped off by a night of live music by Neville Staple, Roddy's Skabilly Rebels and Norwich covers band the All-Skas. The following day the 2Tone Trail around Coventry, which takes in the sights of 2Tone history around the city, complete with guidebook, was officially opened by its creator, Coventry journalist and broadcaster Pete Chambers. Members of the 2Tone bands finished off the week with a quiz on the local BBC radio station. The two competing teams were the Judge Roughnecks, led by Horace Panter and the Three Minett Heroes led by Neville Staple and radio presenter Vic Minett. Simon Ward from 2Tone tribute band Special Brew and Specials' website forum co-administrator Mike Cornwell also took part. That was the sum total of the celebrations – or was it?

Unbeknown to the public, the Specials had come together, albeit tentatively, in March 2004. Slightly before this, Jerry Dammers had turned up at some of Neville's shows around London, as had Terry Hall and Lynval Golding. Speculation began that maybe something was happening.

"We had a meeting," said Neville, "just a chat in a pub. I hadn't seen Terry in 15 years. Afterwards he came to my show in London."

Terry added: "I saw Jerry DJ for the first time. I thought he was really good. I told him I was waiting for him to make another record. I know he loves DJ-ing but, whether it's with us or not, he should be really making records. It was seeing the Pixies in Brixton that made me think maybe we could do it one more time. I love the Pixies. When I was watching them, that was when I thought 'What would happen if the Specials did this?' With the Pixies there weren't any great laser shows, they just played the songs and they sounded brilliant. It made me very excited about doing something."

The first hurdle in the Specials reunion was to get all seven members of the band together in the same room for the first time in 24 years. Persistence by Lynval Golding to get the group to communicate was rewarded when a meeting was arranged and almost came about, but at the last minute Jerry Dammers pulled out, followed by Horace Panter. Everything seemed to be back at square one.

It was thought that the stumbling block was the involvement of Simon Jordan, the multi-millionaire owner of Crystal Palace Football Club and lifelong Specials fan, who was willing to fund a reunion if it could be achieved. A proposal had been put to the seven members that included a two night gig slot in June 2004 at Selhurst Park, home of Crystal Palace FC, a £60,000 pay packet for each band member and rights to a live CD and DVD to be discussed at a later stage. It seemed a mighty deal, but scepticism was rife in the camp. Old habits die hard, and, after all, the Specials weren't about the money. Of course, money would be a factor in any reunion, but it had always been a bone of contention with the band. However, the seven professional musicians, to be frank, deserved to earn whatever they could. Whatever the reasons for the wariness, it seemed that Jordan and his money were the root cause, especially for Jerry Dammers.

Jordan had befriended Terry Hall some time before and the pair had been together on Sky TV's football programme *Soccer AM*, which was presented by massive Specials fan Tim Lovejoy. Jordan had made it clear in many media interviews that he would love to see the Specials reform and he would help where he could. With the deal out in the open, time was taken to consider the matter, but as time passed Dammers seemed increasingly unhappy with Jordan's plan and also opposed involvement from various other management teams. He felt that there was not enough time to rehearse and get the Specials up to a high enough standard to play together as a cohesive unit before the proposed dates in June. He would also have preferred to find an alternative venue, and it was rumoured that he favoured Highfield Road, home of Coventry City FC, as a more suitable setting for their return.

To help soothe the situation, former Specials manager Rick Rogers was drafted in to deal with all the legalities of the proposed reunion. Dammers felt that he was being pushed aside and pulled out of the event before going on holiday to Europe. With the reunion hanging by the thinnest of fraying threads, Lynval Golding, the keenest advocate of a reformation, sent a heartfelt letter to all the remaining Specials asking them to forgive and forget and do it one more time:

"Without the fans we are nothing," he said. "We are not getting any younger and I think the time is right to go out there and do it for the fans. I want to celebrate what we achieved and share it with everyone. I think we owe it to the fans more than anything else."

While there were minor on-going hitches, Lynval remained a catalyst in keeping the fires burning in the reunion forge, dashing between the US and UK on regular goodwill missions and trying to ensure that the band members kept talking.

The original demise of the band in 1981, especially the defection of the Fun Boy Three, seemed to be the major reason for Jerry's initial reluctance to be involved. After all, it could be argued that Terry and Lynval were part of the team that had brought his dream crashing down, but there had been more to it than that. It wasn't just an argument over musical directions that split the band, the boys were exhausted and needed time away. Time away had become a permanent solution to their problems and we've already seen how, at that moment in time, Terry, Lynval and Neville were simply the closest to each other. Lynval told *Rockers Revolt* in 2008:

"How can I put this? How would you feel being in one of the biggest bands in England at the time and through bad vibes have to leave? It wasn't an easy decision. The Specials had become self-destructive. The nature of the band and the personalities in it were volatile at best. Anyone who watched a Specials show would know how volatile they could be, and that's what people loved, the energy, but the same energy burnt us out. We achieved a lot in a very short space of time. The more we achieved the more the seven of us had differing views on what to do and nobody communicated. At the time it was the only decision I could make, we could make, in order to keep moving forward. It was something we had to do. So, Fun Boy Three was a very good move and the right one at the time."

Lynval maintained his role as peacemaker, and although the project had been stopped in its tracks, there remained a general consensus that something could still be salvaged from the dying embers. The majority were still in agreement that 'something' needed to be done with the band.

With the planned reunion very much in the balance, back in Coventry producer Roger Lomas was asked by the City Council to organise a celebration for the 25th Anniversary, including a 2Tone Collective concert, made up of members of the Specials, the Selecter and the Beat. Jerry encouraged various 2Tone members to avoid the proposals that had been laid out, again on the grounds that it had been a long time since they had played together and they wouldn't perhaps be able to do justice to the 2Tone legacy. Dammers' PR, Jody Dunleavy, sent a statement to the Coventry Evening Telegraph:

"*A STATEMENT FROM THE SPECIALS: All the original band members of the Specials are very honoured and pleased that Coventry City Council have looked into the idea of 'A Concert in Coventry to Celebrate Twenty-Five Years of 2Tone.' It is not our intention to spoil anything, or interfere with anything anybody else may want to do, however, we are very sorry but we feel unable to take part. At this time we do not feel confident that we could deliver a performance worthy of the original band, or the reputation of the 2Tone label in the context of the proposed idea of a so called '2Tone Supergroup.' Most of the original members have never played with members of the other bands and we ourselves have not played together for 20 years. We think that our involvement with any 'super-group' would be unlikely to produce really good music without a great deal of commitment and rehearsal. This would not be possible due to lack of available time and other commitments.*

"*It's a shame that this rumour got out before we had agreed to anything. We think the idea could raise expectations unrealistically and would involve a high risk of leaving the public feeling slightly disappointed or let down, when they have shown so much goodwill and enthusiasm. We would again like to thank Coventry City Council and trust that they can understand why we feel unable to participate. We would also* like to make it clear that there are no plans for the original line-up of the Specials to perform anywhere in the foreseeable future."

Some at the Council felt a little rattled by the statement. Hilary Hopker, who was working on the team responsible for the planned event, said:

"Terry Hall, Neville Staple and Horace Panter had all expressed interest in playing an Anniversary show. They're saying they have not got time to rehearse but we haven't put a date on the gig. If they said they could not get their act together until January, we would say 'fine'. The Specials have got together to tell us they are not going to reform!"

Roger Lomas added to her comments by saying: "The only members not to have worked with other 2Tone bands were Jerry Dammers and Terry Hall. They have offered this statement as a band and it is a band that does not exist. Why offer it as a band when they were invited as individual musicians?"

It later became apparent that the statement, instigated by Jerry, was not a unanimous decision.

In early 2005, former Swinging Cat Paul Heskett raised the idea of the band playing as part of a charity event to bring in funds for those affected by the terrible Boxing Day Tsunami which had devastated parts of Thailand, but nothing more was heard of the proposal. Things remained quiet for a while, but Lynval worked to preserve interest amongst the band members through his many phone calls and trips back to the UK. Even so, it would be at least a year again before the rumour mill would churn out more gossip.

Renewed speculation was triggered by a trio of the group appearing together, very briefly, at the 100 Club in London in 2005. Roddy Byers was touring the country as part of the acoustic ska band Three Men And Black, where he was part of a line up that contained the Selecter's Pauline Black and Nick Welsh, along with the Beat's Dave Wakeling. Lynval and Terry turned up to catch the show and Lynval jumped onstage for a rendition of 'You're Wondering Now'. The fact that the trio were in the same room as each other reignited conjecture, and Suggs from Madness added fuel to the fire when he gave a full-page interview to *The Sun* newspaper dedicated to his thoughts on a possible Specials reformation:

"I've been encouraging them to do it, but it's not really my position to say. I know quite a few of them would like to get back together, but it's a bit like us in the eight years we had apart. Six say yes, then one says no, then the last one says yes and the first one says no. There's a lot of nervousness about spoiling your legacy, but I'm very grateful we did it. I've had a lot of joy from things like our Madstock gigs at Finsbury Park and the *Our House* musical and I'd love to come full circle by touring with the Specials again."

Around this period, Dammers was immortalised on vinyl by the band the Toy Guns. The Bethnal Green-based four piece issued a 7" single, 'Nice One Jerry', on Regal Records, described as 'an incendiary blast of ska-punk, delivering its anti-racist message with flair and intelligence.'

It would be another 18 months before life was breathed back into reunion plans. In early 2008, only one year away from the 30th anniversary, the band met as a seven-piece once more. An intensive rehearsal took place in London, and for those who attended, like Lynval's daughter and representative Michelle Golding, it was surreal:

"The sound was fantastic. It was like they had never been away," she said.

The Specials activity continued as EMI released *The Best Of The Specials*, a simple greatest hits package complimented by a DVD of the band's promo videos. The title and issue lacked thought and imagination, and EMI failed to search their Specials catalogue to check if there was anything new to entice fans and collectors. On the positive side, the release brought the band back into the public eye, and backed up by a limited TV advertising campaign, the album reached the Top 25 of the UK charts.

The group continued to meet, in one form or another, behind closed doors to keep the reunion moving forwards in what was hoped would be the right direction for all concerned. In Coventry, local journalist and 2Tone devotee Pete Chambers was the driving force behind a celebration of influential Coventry citizens throughout the ages that culminated in a Hollywood-style 'Walk Of Fame'. Each star bore the name of the recipient and the favourites were picked by readers of the *Coventry Evening Telegraph*. The Specials were one of the ten names to be honoured. The walkway was opened on 16th May 2008 at Priory Place in Coventry City Centre and Roddy Byers and Horace Panter represented the band. Horace took the personal 'star-in-a-box' memento home. Pete Chambers wrote of the event:

"Two of the biggest names in Coventry music are the Specials and Pete Waterman. Both were being honoured and the Specials' Horace Panter and Roddy Byers attended. Jerry Dammers phoned me on Thursday to tell me that sadly he couldn't make it. He did send me a message that read: 'I hope there might be an opportunity to read it out, or if not, maybe you could put it in the paper or something, thanks and thanks again for organising everything. I just want to say that I really appreciate the Specials being recognised in this way and want to thank all the people who voted for the band.' Back in 1979-80, the powers that be were less receptive to what I presume they considered to be just a pop band (not that the Specials would have ever called themselves that of course). Thirty years on and there are many 'movers and shakers' who actively think outside the proverbial box. This is probably a little off-centre to a world the Specials remember, but I think both Horace and Roddy were pleasantly surprised by the whole event."

Roddy, who had recently lost his father, said of the occasion:

"Yeah, I enjoyed the afternoon and it put me in a good mood for the gig we [Skabilly Rebels] played in Swindon that night. I wish my dad was still here as he would have been very proud of me."

Horace added: "I hadn't given the award thing too much thought really, but once it got going I must admit to feeling very proud and thankful to all the people who supported us. I wasn't born in Coventry and came here in 1972 as a student, so I never thought of myself as a 'Coventry Kid' like Terry, Roddy or Brad. I've lived here longer than I've lived anywhere else, so I suppose I'm an honorary Coventrian."

The occasion was promptly followed up with an award that would bring Coventry's finest in front of the paparazzi's flashing bulbs, and a stroll up the red carpet, for the prestigious 2008 *Mojo* Magazine Music Awards on 16th June. The band were to be inaugurated into the *Mojo* Hall Of Fame, an honour that had previously been bestowed on the likes of Arthur Lee, the Doors and Elton John. It must have been a tad galling, however, to be inducted after Madness, who were honoured in 2005 (Madness's pop longevity often overrides the Specials' short but explosive career). Looking proud but mildly uncomfortable in front of so many snapping photographers, six of the Specials historically appeared together in public for the first time in years. Neville had to miss the awards due to gig commitments in Ireland. The event was hosted by *Mojo* magazine's Editor-in-Chief Phil Alexander and, before introducing ska and reggae legend Dennis Alcapone to present the award to the group, he said:

"Everyone wishes that the Specials were still around now. Not only was their music

The Specials are inducted into Mojo Hall of Fame 2008. Photo by S Fernandez

terrific but they stood for something in terms of what they had to say. A British band whose tales of gangsters, ghost towns and teenage pregnancies are as relevant now as they were in the early Eighties. In four short years they united subcultures and made a lasting impact."

After tumultuous applause, Dennis Alcapone handed the award to Jerry Dammers, who on behalf of the band, said:

"I'd like to thank whoever it is who decides these things and it's a great honour. I'd like to thank all those people who backed and supported the Specials such as Rico Rodriguez and Dick Cuthell, Rick Rogers, Dave Jordan, Rex and Trevor and all the road crew and John Cooper Clarke, who we supported at Dingwalls the night Margaret Thatcher came into power. Thank you for giving us that support slot!"

Lynval Golding then stepped up to the microphone to address the audience:

"There are seven individuals that make up the Specials. With these guys, we brought culture together, this black and white multi-racial band, at a time when it wasn't the trendy thing to do. I also want to thank one man because without him we wouldn't have this here and that is Joe Strummer, who is no longer with us now, but he gave us a big break on the On Parole tour, a big respect to that man, y'know we love you. To the females in my family, my daughters and last but not least my little boy, Dominic, I hope this is going to be something for you to treasure for the rest of your life and follow. Thank you."

The final say came from Terry Hall, a lifelong Manchester United fan, who took the opportunity to air his sarcastic wit at the expense of Chelsea fans, who had just seen their side lose to United in the European Cup Final.

The band were well looked after, but Roddy for one found it an odd experience:

"It was a little bit strange but it was good to see some old faces. Although I saw Johnny Rotten being unkind to that young singer Duffy, which was a bit harsh!"

After the *Mojo* awards, (the actual award finding its way across the Atlantic to Lynval's home!) speculation about an upcoming reunion was rife. All that the band offered at the time was 'We are talking to each other' and 'No comment', but behind the scenes, the cogs in the workings of the Specials machine started to turn one more time. Terry Hall's manager Steve Blackwell, along with Michelle Golding, took on the unenviable task of pushing the reunion forward. There were hiccups along the way, but the internet bristled with fans eagerly waiting for something to happen. The good vibes from the first rehearsal brought about a second, attended by Roddy, Horace, Terry and Jerry, which took place in Kenilworth, just outside Coventry, but it was here that it became evident that there were problems musically.

Allegedly Jerry was unhappy with the speed and volume of the songs (too fast and too loud), and the situation wasn't helped by Jerry's chaotic drum machine which failed to keep time and skipped beats, reducing the rehearsal to a hit and miss affair. The vibes of the previous rehearsal didn't take long to turn into waves of negativity after a general meeting was called to discuss next steps. It was here that Jerry set out his ideas. He had wanted to try to aim for a proper reunion and 30th anniversary celebration, including the best part of both Specials albums, the 'Ghost Town' EP and a small amount of new material, in venues worthy of the band's status and legacy. Arenas such as the O2 in London were put forward, but the majority of the band favoured smaller, more intimate venues that harked back to the band's roots.

Jerry was convinced that a fair amount of rehearsal, for himself as much as everyone else, would be necessary, but others disagreed. A spokesperson for Dammers said that he had heard that former members were 'wanting to play mainly the first album'. Realistically, that seemed to make a lot of sense, a good block to build on. It also has to be said that, apart from Dammers, the majority of the group had maintained a steady playing career since the group split in 1981 and were still used to playing the chords and riffs of songs from the Specials catalogue.

Meanwhile, the band Hard-Fi was citing the Specials as an influence and their debut album *Stars Of CCTV* was laden with echoes of the Clash and the Specials. Lead singer Richard Archer met some of his heroes at a Love Music Hate Racism event in London 2008. Archer said:

"We worked with an organization in London called Love Music Hate Racism, which is a modern-day equivalent of the Rock Against Racism of the late Seventies and early Eighties. And the last show the Specials did was for Rock Against Racism, they played 'Ghost Town.' So we kind of sorted it out, that if we could get Jerry Dammers and Neville Staple onstage with us, we'd play 'Ghost Town' with them. Which was a huge moment for us. Actually, Terry Hall was there, and he and Jerry were talking about getting onstage with us for the first time in 21 years, and we're like, 'Come on, do it, do it, do it!' And they're like, 'Well, we haven't rehearsed' but we did a rehearsal with Jerry Dammers, and he's like, 'I don't remember the chords!' So we had to show him the chords to 'Ghost Town'."

So, it was understandable that Dammers felt time would be needed for everyone to get up to speed again on the Specials' tracks. After the meeting it was also alleged that Jerry wanted to re-record the classics of yesteryear in a slow jazz trance style not far removed from his current Spatial AKA Orchestra project, but this was denied in later comments by Jerry's spokesperson who countered with;

"It's not true that Jerry wanted to do 'slowed-down jazz versions of Specials songs.' This a complete lie. Jerry was expected to agree to other absurd proposals from Terry's manager including, for example, re-recording the entire first two Specials albums all over again."

Whether or not any of this was true, things were starting to look distinctly ominous. Neville Staple had been very keen to see Jerry on board and, as a mark of his respect for the commitment shown by Neville, Jerry began to appear as a 'special' guest whenever Neville was playing in London. Behind the scenes the story twisted and turned, and the notion that Jerry would never work with the present management was given substance when, at one of Neville's gigs, Jerry publicly lambasted Terry Hall's manager Steve Blackwell in a jaw-dropping tirade. The situation was deteriorating and the prospect of a reunion seemed to be fading away.

A decision was finally taken by six members of the group to take advantage of the initial ground covered by the Blackwell's team and proceed with reunion plans without Jerry Dammers, who could still not find an accommodation with regard to the band's current management position. More planned rehearsals came to fruition and the talk across the internet, media and gigs up and down the country crackled with reunion conversation. In the summer of 2008, those closest to the Specials camp learned, with great excitement, that a secret gig was planned for early autumn to test the band's mettle and the reception they would receive. So, 27 years on from the band's split, the reunion was definitely going ahead! Even though celebrations were slightly dampened by the fact that Jerry Dammers definitely wouldn't be involved, given the band's history, six out of seven wasn't bad going! As the legal eagles battled it out, the band continued with rehearsals, although a full line up was quite rare due to other commitments. Nikolaj Torp, a Danish keyboard player who had worked with successful UK chart act James Morrison, was recruited to play in Jerry's absence.

Whilst the band refined their songs, it became apparent that Jerry had trademarked the Specials band name along with that of the Special AKA, 2Tone Records, Tone Records and Tone Productions. The move made the situation uneasy and it was unclear whether the six remaining members would be able to appear under the Specials mantle. Nevertheless, things were still moving onwards and upwards. The 'secret' gig was to be held at Bestival, an annual three-day music festival on the Isle Of Wight on September 6th. With only a handful of people privy to the information, attempts were made to keep the lid on what was to be a monumental event. The band appeared on the Bestival bill as the festival's traditional 'secret act'. The previous year Madness had performed under the 'secret' banner, so it was a real coup for Bestival organiser Rob Da Bank to sign up the Specials and keep that 2Tone connection.

As the big day approached, one final rehearsal took place at the Assembly Rooms in Leamington Spa. The night before the gig, the Specials headed south. This author was honoured to be one of the few invited guests to attend the event and I was shocked to actually bump into Jerry Dammers at the festival entrance. He apparently came in as an ordinary punter to witness what must have been the surreal and painful sight of his old band perform. At 5.15pm the introduction began on the big screen, narrated by actor Nick Moran and accompanied by the dying fade of the song 'Jerusalem' and the familiar cry of 'Bernie Rhodes knows, don't h-argue!" rang out across the heads of 30,000 festival-goers. Despite the atrocious wet weather, those attending were in full festival spirit and had lived up to the festivals apt theme (given the weather) of '30,000 Freaks Under The Sea', with many dressed in nautical or sea-food-based fancy dress. As 'Gangsters' blared across the crowd, any doubt as to whether the band could still cut it was dispelled. They played a 47-minute set that consisted of tracks from the first album. The Coventry boys

240   YOU'RE WONDERING NOW had the audience bouncing and revelling with the pure 2Tone ska sounds. If you closed your eyes, you could have easily been transported back in time to their heyday. Terry Hall was on form with his one-liners and acknowledged the crowd with: "I've waited 27 years to play to a field full of prawns..."

After completing a fantastic version of 'Message To You Rudy', Terry referred to a recent TV commercial for crisps with 'Rudy' as a soundtrack (and a former professional footballer as the star): "I can't stop thinking of Gary Lineker now!"

The track saw the introduction of the three-strong brass section, which really added power to the show. Sadly, Rico Rodriguez and Dick Cuthell could not attend, but Warren Middleton (Neville's trombonist), Jon Read (former brass man for the Specials Mk2) and Tim Smart (trombone player who had played with Prince Buster) stepped in. As on the first album Roddy Byers took over lead vocals on 'Concrete Jungle' and the gig climaxed with 'You're Wondering Now'. They left the stage to rapturous applause and chants of 'Rude Boys!', which carried on for five minutes to an empty stage! The Rude Boys were back in town all guns blazing! The atmosphere backstage was triumphant and relieved, but no one was more ecstatic than Lynval Golding. His persistence, drive and enthusiasm over the last four years had paid off, and he told journalist Pete Chambers:

"It's amazing to be back! Its like its 1980-something again, it just feels so natural. It's all back, the sound, the vibe, the connection between each person and instrument. It feels like a little gang again and our unity is the glue that holds it all together."

"It was absolutely extraordinary," enthused Horace Panter. "The plan was always to concentrate on our first album but I was still uncontrollably nervous for a day and a half beforehand. Then the moment the roar went up and Neville launched into 'Bernie Rhodes knows, don't h-argue!' Wow!"

Backstage the party continued with Simon Jordan in attendance, along with TV and radio presenter and comedian Phill Jupitus, a big Specials fan who had been right at the front for the set:

"That was amazing. Absolutely fantastic!" said Phill. "You know, I was standing in the exact same place at a Specials gig in 1980 and when I closed my eyes out there it was like being in a time-warp. I opened me eyes and I still can't believe it. That was out of this world!"

No one can tell how it must have felt for Jerry Dammers to watch the group perform, but he told *Mojo* magazine after the gig:

"They did a fantastic job, but I think that one of the reasons I was excluded and didn't want to take part was because I had expressed the opinion that the real Specials would never do a gig where real Specials fans couldn't even get in. Bestival was already sold out. I went and it was very weird for me. Without my influence, it felt like they were playing themselves a bit. It was too much of a 'fun' thing, a bit of the stars of the Eighties nostalgia vibe, not what a real reunion would have been at all. There was something missing, but unfortunately, I'm the only one who knows what it is. The subtleties in the music were a bit lost on them. 'Doesn't Make It Alright' should have had the hairs on the back of your neck standing up, but compare it to the record and the heart and soul was a bit lacking. The best excuse for a reunion is if you can do some really good new music. The guy playing keyboard pulled his cap over his face so you couldn't see it wasn't me which says it all."

For one and all, however involved, it was a highly-charged emotional experience. The band did come in for some criticism for choosing Bestival as the platform for their comeback gig; however, it proved to be a great test. A trial gig in front of a thousand

YOU'RE WONDERING NOW

The Specials reunite for Bestival, September 2008. Photo by L. Heyman

The SPECIALS – from conception to reunion

YOU'RE WONDERING NOW

The SPECIALS – from conception to reunion

Specials fans would have be an easy option, and possibly given a false sense of achievement, but to win over the best part of 30,000 impartial music fans? Job done.

The news that the band had played their first show in 27 years raced around the world in seconds courtesy of the internet. During the Specials' set, people posted immediately to their blog sites via mobile phones:

"I can't believe this! As I type the Specials are playing!"

Thousands of text messages flashed on to phones up and down the country to announce that the band had played. The response to the gig was huge and must have been way above any expectations the group might have had.

After the euphoria of the gig had died down, reality struck home when an aggrieved Jerry Dammers responded with a legal embargo on the use of the name of the band. He wanted to ensure they could not play under the name of the Specials. The situation was further inflamed when Simon Jordan told Will Buckley of news and information website buzzle.com;

"I can't overcome the obstacle of Jerry Dammers, who has been away with the fairies in Middle Earth spending the last 15 years remixing 'Ghost Town'."

The war of words became intense but, while the legal teams crossed swords, within two and a half months the Specials were back, officially, and with the name intact.

On December 2nd 2008, a press statement was released to announce the Specials' 30th Anniversary Tour in April 2009. The statement was prepared by the group and issued by PR Company Hall Or Nothing, owned by Terri Hall, who had previously worked with Terry Hall and other artists on the *War Child* album. It read as follows:

"We are proud to announce that 2009 will see the live return of Coventry's finest, the Specials. One of the most important bands in the history of popular music and recognised as one of the greatest live bands the world has ever seen, the Specials have been the subject of continuous rumours and demands for their reformation since their split in 1981. It would be impossible to overstate the importance of the Specials to the UK music scene. Despite a brief career, the Coventry band lit up the late Seventies like a comet, their melding of punk and ska creating the 2Tone sound that is still today held up as an influence by bands across the world. Now, 30 years since the release of their debut single, 'Gangsters', the Specials will take to the road for a UK tour starting in April.

"Over two studio albums, the Specials scored eight Top 10 singles, including two Number 1s for the 'Too Much Too Young' live EP and the era-defining 'Ghost Town', two Top 5 albums and spawned a retrospective list of compilation and live albums from official releases, to much sought-after bootlegs. The band were rightly regarded as the starting point of the ska scene that swept the UK through 1978 and, in many ways, were emblematic of their times. Their songs dealt with the confusion of a country in industrial decline whilst struggling to come to terms with multi-culturalism and a new creed which became known as Thatcherism. Their re-emergence into a Britain teetering on the edge of recession, and still plagued by the same divisions and problems that they so memorably highlighted in 'Ghost Town', could not seem more apt, the songs from 'The Specials' and 'More Specials' seem as relevant today as they did 30 years ago."

Five dates were announced for the end of April to be held at the chain of Academy venues (now owned by O2, the mobile phone giant, and formerly better known as the Carling Academies) in the cities of Newcastle, Sheffield, a two-night stint at Birmingham, and then Glasgow. The start of May would see them at the Manchester Apollo and then two nights at the Brixton Academy in London. Tickets went on sale through various agencies from 9am on Thursday 12th December and no doubt there were a few sick days planned across the country, and even the world, as fans young and old, prepared to man the telephones and websites in order to get their hands on tickets for the comeback of the last ten years. In the media whirl around the comeback the Specials found themselves back in *New Musical Express* after a 27-year absence. In the interview, Terry Hall said:

"We did a secret slot at Bestival as a trial to see how we felt about it. We came away thinking we should celebrate our 30th Anniversary next year. It's the right time to do it, we talked about it at 25 years but we weren't together enough. Now we are all getting on and it feels comfortable again. When we did Bestival we didn't go near the second album, so I'm looking forward to playing 'Ghost Town', and 'Stereotype' will also be fun to play and I think we might be doing 'Maggie's Farm' too."

When pushed on the Jerry Dammers saga, Hall replied: "Jerry doesn't want to do the tour but the door remains open to him. I think he wants to do stuff with the Spatial AKA too, so the door is definitely not closed."

Terry's statement provoked a bitter response from Jerry:

"*A recent press release concerning a proposed tour by what has been described as 'The Specials', failed to clarify the actual line up of the band. Not surprisingly therefore, many people are under the impression it is the original Specials. As was common knowledge at the time of their success, Jerry Dammers was the founder, main songwriter and driving force of the Specials. He recruited every member individually, and the musical and style direction was guided by him. He designed the 2Tone logo and formed the 2Tone record label. Jerry has a duty to inform anybody who may be interested of the true situation, which is that he was not invited to take part in this proposed tour, or even told about it. He also has to say that claims that "the door is still open" to him fail to mention that Jerry has been driven out every time he has attempted to get involved over the last year. He also wonders why this appears in the newspaper when former band mates have his phone number. 'The prodigal sons came home, kicked me out, and have left the door open, great' says Jerry. These claims also contradict lawyers' letters stating that former members have resolved to go ahead without him, and that Jerry is not to speak to any of them.*

"*Attempts to imply that any proposed tour has Jerry's 'blessing', at this stage, are also highly misleading. These seem to be part of a wider attempt to rewrite the whole history of the band, in order to try to justify what is currently going on. Jerry does not wish to go into too much detail at this point, except to say that for over 25 years he had dreamed that his former band mates might come back one day, and was deeply shocked to find that when they did, for some of them, it was apparently to kick him out. Jerry had already started recording with a couple of them and the results were good. Jerry sees this whole thing as a takeover, rather than a proper reunion, representing primarily Terry Hall and his manager's (not to mention Simon Jordan's) ideas of what 'The Specials' should be and do. Press claims that this proposed band is now 'led by Terry Hall' seem to back this up.*

"*Jerry does not believe it represents what the real Specials stood for, politically, or in terms of creativity, imagination or forwardness of ideas, and he does not think the proposed venues would really be appropriate to a band of the status of the real Specials. He thinks the real test will come if or when another album is ever made. At the moment this is not the proud reunion and thirtieth anniversary celebration Jerry had hoped for. Although a lot of the responsibility lies with Terry's manager (who now apparently*

The Specials in Newcastle 2009. Photo by Pete Chambers

Roddy Byers, Birmingham 2009. Photo by Joe Kerrigan

YOU'RE WONDERING NOW

John Bradbury of the Specials, Newcastle 2009. Photo By Pete Chambers

The SPECIALS – from conception to reunion

manages the whole project), these are grown men too, and they are more than responsible for the actions of their manager. Neville Staple is the only former member who demonstrated real commitment to Jerry's involvement."

David Hepworth, former presenter of TV music programme *The Old Grey Whistle Test* and now of *The Word* magazine, who released the statement, said:

"The statement was very copious. I haven't seen anything like that before, but you know this is the Specials without Jerry Dammers, and to be honest, the fact that Jerry won't be there will only upset the anoraks. Thirty years have passed and unfortunately, it's sort of no longer his group. Its kind of whatever it is, you know, it's a case of you've released it into the world and it is what people think it is."

Hepworth's point is a valid one. Like a poet who writes a poem, whatever the writer intends it to mean, it is open to interpretation by the reader. Jerry found support for his position over the reunion from different areas, but not everyone was convinced; the music section of TV's Teletext announced him as their 'Chump Of The Week' stating:

"Fair enough, it's sad he isn't part of the Specials reunion, but his extraordinarily vitriolic statement against the other members was so downright bileful, it's little wonder they wanted nothing to do with him again. So sad it's come to this."

The reunited Specials remained tight-lipped and refused to be drawn into public verbal warfare, although the band's PR agency released a small statement in response:

"We don't agree with what Jerry has said, but we don't want to talk about it, not least because it is in the hands of our lawyers. We are all very excited about the overwhelming support shown to us, and the rush to buy tickets would appear to prove that the fans are looking forward to joining us in these dancehalls across the country next year as much as we are looking forward to playing them."

With limited tickets available, people sat nervously awaiting the very minute that they were due to go on sale. The Specials' website co-administrator, Mike Cornwell, contacted the management team with a proposal to ensure dedicated fans would be able to purchase tickets before the anticipated rush. The proposal led to a pre-sale of tickets aimed at members of the Specials' website forum and the band's Facebook page, run by Michelle Golding, giving anxious fans access to tickets 24 hours before the main sale. Just as well, because when the main sale of tickets opened at 9am the following day, the two nights at Birmingham sold out within four minutes, and the entire tour within two hours. To cope with the demand a further five dates were added, these being additional nights at Glasgow and Manchester and three more in Brixton. Demand was so high for the Specials' two shows in Birmingham that just minutes after they sold out, tickets went on sale on internet auction site eBay for more than twice their face value. Finally, after much speculation, a massive homecoming gig was announced at the Jaguar Hall at the Ricoh Arena in Coventry.

Coventry music historian and huge Specials fan, Pete Chambers said:

"I had an inkling the reunion tour would prove popular, but even I was surprised by the demand! If you turned the clock back to 1979 the tickets would definitely have sold out, but 30 years down the line, we couldn't be sure. This shows that the Specials' music, and what they represent, is as relevant as ever."

To further promote the tour, Terry and Lynval appeared on radio stations across the UK and Roddy and Horace took on the local media in the Midlands.

Shortly afterwards, on December 21st 2008, with one eye on the future, Horace left his teaching post at the Corley Centre in Coventry. He said reluctantly:

"I've absolutely loved being an art teacher, it's the second best job I've ever had. We're going to start rehearsing seriously again as a band in February, so I would have had to leave at half-term anyway. I thought it would be better to leave at the end of term like this."

He had worked at the special school for ten years, so his departure caused him some sorrow. He told the *Coventry Evening Telegraph*:

"The job has changed a lot over the years and some days it's absolute chaos, but I'm really going to miss it. A lot of the children can't really read and write but art is more of a level playing field, everyone can have a go."

With that, and with a heavy heart, Horace left to concentrate on work with the Specials. Lynval reflected on the tough five years that had passed since the reformation was initially conceived:

"It's been a journey into where we are right now. It's been five years in the making to get to this stage. I made a promise that I would never give in, y'know. I kept on and on and on and I know that people now have their tickets and its going to be great. It's been an amazing journey. It's now 30 years, we released our first our first single in 1979 and now its 2009! So obviously we are gonna have a hell of a party to celebrate that. When you think back to 1979, when Margaret Thatcher was in power, the Conservative Government, there was unemployment, there was racism, there was all sorts of things happening. The one thing I feel bad about is that 2009, nothing has changed but y'know we are not giving in.

"So for the next generation, listen, think, we are gonna make a change, make things better, we have to stand up for our rights, so remember, we are coming, we are gonna have a great time and I would like to thank everyone for the support out there. To the fans who bought our records, because if it wasn't for those guys we wouldn't be here today."

The band have influenced so many musicians, the list is almost endless. To prove their long-lasting legacy, one such artist, Ted Leo, of American punk rock band the Pharmacists, doffed his cap to the Specials on their 2003 track 'Where Have All The Rude Boys Gone?' in which he immortalised the Specials' band members with the lyrics:

"It's times like these when a neck looks for a knife,
A wrist for a razor, a heart is longing for bullets.
Tension is high under sea and over sky.
Pressure drop, people are acting foolish.
Ooh – but it's easy to see!
Ooh – we could dance and be free.
Ooh – to that 2Tone beat!
But it looks like it's gone…
Gangsters and clowns with a stereotyped sound,
It's coming like a ghost town – someone always knew it.
Hatred and shame, a racialist game,
Cycles of blame – someone sang me through it.
Who? well it's easy to see.
Ooh – we could dance to be free.
Ooh – to that 2Tone beat!
But it looks like it's gone…
I asked Jerry, he told Terry, Terry sang a song just for me,
Lynval gave a message to me,
Rhoda screamed and then she asked me,
Where have all the rude boys gone?"

The SPECIALS – from conception to reunion   *251*

At the time of writing, as one page in the Specials' history book ends, we can look forward to the next page and the band's upcoming tour with tingling anticipation. We have waited 30 years for this, and it seems ironic that, after such a long time, so many of the issues that the Specials highlighted are still dogging society today. The present financial climate harks back to the bad old days of the late Seventies, and the social problems of racial hate and un-protected casual sex have never truly been addressed. But let's not be downhearted; let's hope that the influence and legacy of the Specials can be as politically and personally motivating to a new generation. And for those of us whose lives were unutterably altered when we witnessed their fire and inspiration the first time around, let's relive our youth and revel in one of the finest live bands the world has ever seen. As the band once said, 'You can stand there like parked cars if you want to. It's up to you what you really wanna do.'

A TESTAMENT OF YOUTH
"It's good to be wise when you're young…"
The Specials, 1980

*t*HE INFLUENCE that the Specials had on the country's young minds at the time is often overlooked, but since the 2Tone explosion there has not been a youth cult like it on the shores of the UK. Ok, we have had other short bursts, like Madchester and Brit-pop but nothing on the scale, on the countrywide scale, of 2Tone.

The birth of 2Tone and the Specials came at a very important time, when the country was going to the dogs, as communities were torn apart by Margaret Thatcher and her cohorts in the Conservative Party. Add to the mix the right wing extremists, who fed off the simmering discontent and disillusionment, and the UK was teetering towards chaos. The music of the Specials became a positive beacon in a negative era. Not only did it carry a message that undermined the government, it carried a message of unity; let's stick together, black or white. If the powers that be were trying to destroy all that the people had, why should the people destroy themselves?

The effect of the times and the music can never fully be measured, but the recording stars of today, the ones that possess a spirit of anarchy, punch and lyrical bite (not the manufactured *X-Factor* sugar squad members), more often than not cite the Specials and their ilk as major influences on their musical careers. I could talk until the cows come home about the effect the Specials and 2Tone had on Joe Public, but the testimony of others will lend my convictions weight. Below are personal stories and quotes about why the Specials really were so special.

DAMON ALBARN – Musician (Blur, Gorillaz), London: "I discovered the Specials during my early youth as well as other bands like Madness, the Jam and the Kinks and I just thought they were great. Music was pretty much dull for me until I found the likes of the Specials. Their style was cool and their message made me sit up and take stock of the world around me. It helped propel me on a creative journey and the Specials philosophy? Well, I could take that in there with me, it has served me well. The band's importance as a contribution to the rich heritage of British music can never be overstated."

MIKE CORNWELL – Co-administrator, thespecials.com, Lincoln: "Thirty years ago, when I was nine years old, I saw the Specials on TV. They were smart and sounded great, I liked what I saw and decided to see what they were all about. Not only did I discover them, I discovered 2Tone and the other bands out there who dressed and sounded the same. I soon noticed that they must have been something big, as all the kids at school were wearing black Harrington jackets with sew-on patches and pin badges on, Sta-prest trousers, white socks and black loafers. Soon there was a gang of us, all into the same thing.

I wanted to go and see the Specials live but my parents said that I was too young and I had to make do with seeing them on TV and playing their vinyl. I played both of the Specials' albums over and over, I would listen to the lyrics so that I could sing along. At that age, I didn't really take any notice of any political statements in the songs, and you wouldn't believe what I thought some of the lyrics were! As time went on and I grew older, I began to work out what some of the songs were about, what the messages were. Although I never got to see the Specials live at the time, I can remember one bank holiday when the BBC broadcast *Rock Goes To College*, the Specials live at the Colchester Institute. I watched it on the edge of my seat. I remember watching Terry throwing his tambourine into the crowd, annoyed with the security, and there was a stage invasion by the fans. It was just one of those 'Wow!' moments. I followed the band and tried to collect as much as I could to do with them, whether it was a badge, poster, record or a magazine that featured them.

Then, shock and horror, after topping the charts with 'Ghost Town' I heard the sad news that the band were to split. I remember feeling gutted to say the least. I continued to follow the different spin-offs from the band and the ska scene in general. I tried listening to different styles of music, some of which I liked, but nothing topped the Specials and 2Tone. In the days before the internet, I kept in touch with what was going on by reading fanzines and in the late Nineties I found out that some of the band were to reform. To me this was fantastic news, it was not the same feeing for all, but I had the chance to go and see them, exciting times! Whilst the band were together I went to see them five or six times, all over the country. Although it wasn't the full, original line-up, the music was still there and the atmosphere at the gigs was electric.

I was going to more and more ska gigs and meeting some great people along the way, some of whom are close friends to this day. The new age of the internet came and one of my first experiences of surfing the web was to look up the Specials. I remember finding their website and various other fan sites, finding them made me realise just how great this band was and how many people loved them. I joined the website forum where fans came to chat and it became addictive and because of my passion for the band. I contacted the webmaster to see if I could get involved with the site in a bigger way and I was lucky enough to become one of the administrators who look after the forum. I got to meet various members of the band over the years, some of whom also make their contributions to the forum. It was unreal to meet some of your idols.

One thing that was always in my mind and has been a topic of conversation for many years was 'What would it be like if the Specials full line up re-formed?' I can remember one of my first posts on the forum asked the same question and I discovered that it wasn't just me that felt the same way. We endlessly discussed the possibilities and the reason why, or why not. I was always hopeful and my involvement with the website meant I sometimes got to hear an extra bit of news. Over the years rumours of a reformation would arise, especially on the 25th anniversary, alas it wasn't to be. Towards the 30th anniversary, the rumours began in full flow again, especially as various members had done guest appearances, sometimes together. When I was privileged to learn that something was definitely on the cards and the band were rehearsing the excitement for me was unreal, having followed the band for so long, wondering if the day would ever come.

Wow! It was happening, and more to the point, I was on my way to see them at their secret gig at Bestival. On September 6th 2008, after weeks of sleepless nights and a long nail-biting trip to the Isle of Wight, not only did it happen but I was on the sidelines of the stage! It was unreal, I still couldn't believe it, there I was in close proximity, it brought tears to my eyes! I was overjoyed to say the least and I got to meet the band members afterwards. Still to this day, it seems like it was part of a dream. As the 30th anniversary approaches and with the tour announced in 2009, let's hope it'll only get better!"

NICK WELSH – Musician (Bad Manners, the Selecter, Skaville UK), London: "The first time I saw the Specials (or the Coventry Automatics) was in the summer of 1978 in London. They looked and sounded like no other band around at that time. I filed them away in my head as 'must check them out again', which I did a few months later. They were now called the Specials, at a venue which escapes me now (I think it was the Nashville). I then heard the first single 'Gangsters', I was hooked, it was retro but new, I also liked the B-side 'The Selecter', a band I would later go on to play with. I have been lucky enough to play on stage with Brad, Roddy and Nev and I have to say it was a pleasure. If I had to name my favourite Specials track, it would have to be 'Friday Night, Saturday Morning' for the lyrics and Jerry's keyboards. The Specials are a big footnote in British musical history but their influence can be heard worldwide."

TRICKY – Musician, Bristol: "When I was a kid I always wanted to be in the Specials. I dreamed I was onstage with Terry Hall. There ain't been real music since the Specials. Everybody's living a lie now. Everybody's pretending. Everybody wants to be a lad. Everybody wants to be street. Writing lyrics about stuff they couldn't even know about. I can see right through it. Why are these people so ashamed of going to art school and music college? Terry Hall and the Specials wrote about things they knew. They came from those streets. They were boss."

STEWART RENNIE – Musician (Orange Street), Portsmouth: "I was ten when I first heard the Specials' 'A Message To You Rudy'. It was being sung at the front gates of my school by a new kid in my class who had only recently moved to Glasgow from Coventry, his name was Gavin Dow. I knew Coventry was in England, but couldn't tell you where. I went down my local Woolies the following Saturday and bought the single and played it to death on my hand-me-down mono record player. All the rest of the lads in my class had done the same. I remember watching *Top Of The Pops* on Thursday and seeing the Specials in the flesh, well through a colour TV, but it was good enough for me. The video was good, all these black and white kids mucking about on the streets of Coventry and the band playing in a studio with a white backdrop. It seemed really strange to see black kids; we never had any at my school, not to mention Glasgow!

I remember thinking how good the clothes looked, those hats, the long jacket the keyboard player with no teeth was wearing which my dad told me was called a 'Crumbie'! Most of the lads in my classroom had black Harringtons with patches of all the 2Tone bands on. That's how we used to separate the teams for football at break time, all the rude boys with the black Harringtons in one team against the rest, we were more than a football team, we were a movement! I got the Specials' LP and the Madness LP for Christmas that year and they went straight on to my mono record player. Even at that young age I could tell that the Specials had something to say politically and socially, whereas Madness were more of 'good time' band. It wasn't the political aspect that first attracted me to the Specials; it was the songs and the being in a gang thing. I knew that Thatcher and the Tories were in power, and that it was a bad thing, those days and those lyrics were to make my mind up on my political persuasion for the rest of my days, (that and the fact that my father was a Labour Party activist!)

I never saw the Specials play live, as my parents wouldn't let me go, but I knew a few of the older lads that did and I was always jealous of them. One of them had a drumstick belonging to Brad that he had thrown into the audience at the Glasgow Apollo. I remember the *More Specials* LP and thinking that they had changed the style of music on some of the tracks and that I wasn't so keen on 'Escalator Music' as Neville would call it. When you're young you always want things to sound the same, but things need to evolve, it's not until you're much older that you get it, truth be told some people would never get it. By 1981, the playground was less full of Harrington jackets and more full of leg warmers and Y cardigans, but 2Tone and the Specials were still out there. It all ended in the summer of '81, I first heard about the demise of the Specials on Radio 1 whilst on holiday in Dawlish. Gutted, Gutted, Gutted!

I would remain a fan throughout the Eighties and early Nineties, but we never had the internet in those days and I never really knew about fanzines. I did follow Glasgow-based band Capone and the Bullets about a bit and we'd hear the odd snippet of ska gossip every now and then. It was at one of those gigs that I learnt some of the Specials had re-formed; I bought the album *Today's Specials* and then learnt they were playing in Glasgow in December 1997. By this time, I was living in the south of England, but I wasn't going to miss it. I drove home, caught the gig, and drove back the next day. The gig was magic; I had actually managed to see some of the original Specials at last!

It hadn't been until I moved south in 1996 that I discovered that ska was still big in certain places and the south coast had a band called Loonie Toons who had a big following. I caught up with them in 1998, it was a great gig and the black Harringtons were out in force again. I caught several of their shows before they went their separate ways. Out of Loonie Toons came 2-Tonic and by this time I knew the lads in the band. By 2001, I was their manager and I made some great contacts and had a great time. However, I wanted to be on that stage playing those Specials songs, I wanted in! I was told to learn an instrument, so I bought a battered old trumpet from Cash Converters for £65, took lessons, and gradually made some progress. I would eventually join Orange Street in 2004 after playing at an audition where I only knew 'A Message To You Rudy' I was told 'you're in and your first gig is less than 2 weeks away!' Thanks lads.

There was me at 35 years of age, wearing my first ever tonic suit, playing some of those songs I had been listening to for 25 years, there was no excuse for not knowing the structure of the songs. The gig went well and I've been playing ever since. We change our set from time to time and have brought in more of our own songs, but those Specials songs remain in the set and always will do, they are just great to play and I never tire of them, nor does the audience. We played a gig In Coventry and Roddy Byers came along and played with us, we were made up. It was surreal playing with one of your heroes, but Rod was a top bloke and fitted in straight away, so we all felt at ease.

I was lucky enough to be 'in the know' and saw the Specials at Bestival in 2008, along with the author of this book and his right-hand man Mike Cornwell. I had trouble sleeping in the week running up to the gig; my missus thought I was mad! What a day we had. At different points through the set, we all had tears in our eyes, grown men all nearing middle age with tears in our eyes! God knows how the boys in the band felt! I wonder if that Coventry kid, Gavin Dow, was watching?"

GARY 'MANI' MOUNFIELD – Musician (the Stone Roses, Primal Scream), Manchester: "Take the Specials' first LP, I mean, it's special innit? That first album was brilliant. All us lads learned to dance 'cos of the Specials. A very influential band."

DEAN 'HAZZA' HARRISON – Musician (the Rough Kutz), Stoke-on-Trent: "I remember I was into punk, just me and my mate Rat really, from round our way. When I first heard 'Gangsters' I couldn't believe the sound was coming from the same radio that was

256

usually blaring out crap like Abba. It was a life-changing time, off came my hair, and on went the boots and I'm still the same to this day. Being massively into the Clash I really got into this new sound as it crossed reggae, ska and punk, something which I loved hearing the Clash do. I loved all the 2Tone and related bands but for me the Specials stood above all as their pure, raw energy and hard-hitting lyrical content, topped off with sheer danceability was unrivalled. I still went to gigs after 2Tone's demise, but the quality of what we now widely term ska was disappearing fast. It was the early Nineties when me, Rat and another mate Brigga decided to form a band, as we hated the poppy circus-sounding ska about at the time. Barring a few bands I couldn't make out where the others were getting their influences from, they certainly weren't taking any of the anger and energy from the Specials' sound. As the band progressed to be the Rough Kutz, we nailed our colours to the mast straight away, stating our influences as all things 2Tone, the Specials, the Clash, Stiff Little Fingers etc. We initially got slated by the other poppy ska bands, saying we were too fast and aggressive, something that we were more than proud of being labelled as. So to me, the Specials are the very reason I have spent hundreds of pounds buying records, having discovered all the Jamaican reggae artists through 2Tone: the one defining moment that changed my musical life and also why the Rough Kutz were born."

JAKE BURNS – Musician, (Stiff Little Fingers), Chicago: "I first became aware of the Specials (or the Special AKA as they were billed) when our manager, Gordon Ogilvie, handed me a copy of 'Gangsters' in the back room of the Rough Trade shop in 1979. 'Have you heard this?' he asked, 'This lot are the real deal.' And he was right. What neither of us could know at the time was that we would end up on (roughly) the same label and becoming pals with quite a few members of the band. By the time I saw my first Specials gig at Hammersmith Palais, I'd already become friends with Brad and was completely blown away by how infectious the band were live. In fact, at a later date a few of the more er… 'refreshed' members of their audience came back to the studio SLF were working in and added handclaps etc. to our cover version of the Heptones' 'Mr Fire Coal Man'. It was immediately after that first Hammersmith Palais show that I had the idea of SLF covering 'Doesn't Make It Alright.' Around this time, gig-going in the UK could be a hazardous experience. There was the whole battle line between right-wing skinheads and the (perceived) Rock Against Racism bands. Sham 69 suffered horribly from this and it looked for a while like we might be next in line. Then 2Tone and the Specials happened and they, sadly, got that unwanted attention. After all, it's one thing for me to talk about Rock Against Racism, but the Specials were the living embodiment of it. Luckily, they weathered that storm. As the years went on we both got on with our separate careers, although I would still see Brad from time to time for a beer or two. Roddy had also become a good mate by this stage and his subsequent band, the Tearjerkers, actually did a UK tour with SLF. More recently, he and I, along with Pauline Black and Nick Welsh have played together acoustically as Three Men and A Black. So, it was a personal pleasure to hear from Rod that the reunion was taking place. I really hope I get a chance to see them play once more. It's been too long!"

ERIN BARDWELL – Musician, (the Skanxters, More Specials, the Erin Bardwell Collective), Swindon: "Back in 1979 my Dad hired a black and white TV for the first time and we all got to see the Specials on programmes like *Top Of The Pops*. When the 2Tone tour came to Swindon, my Dad and his mate put up some posters round town for the promoter in exchange for a couple of free tickets for the gig. I was sure I was coming along to the show too, until my Mum introduced me to my baby sitter. I was so disappointed, but I was too young to go. Their debut LP quickly found its way into our record collection. I eventually managed to see the band live in 1980 when I was just seven years old. They changed my life forever. They encouraged my interest in West Indian music in general and sent me in a positive, decisive direction when it came to fashion and thinking. So I guess I have the Specials to thank for that.

By the late Nineties I wanted to see a Specials tribute band up on a stage. Nobody was doing one and the time felt right. I'd been running the Skanxters throughout the Nineties, but needed a break from doing original material. I needed to play somebody else's songs. The Specials' live repertoire was a good mix of their own self-penned tunes, and a healthy dose of original Sixties ska and reggae. Good ingredients, I thought, to take out and play some bigger gigs. I didn't want it to be just a band doing Specials covers; I wanted it to be the 1979-81 era, when the Specials were a proper live concern. A full seven piece plus two horns for the visual effect, nine guys with the right look. As well as the clothes it was important to get the instruments right. The Vox Continental organ, the light-coloured Telecaster, the Pearl drum kit, tribute bands who overlook the make of instruments can fall short of completion, as it all adds to the look and the sound. Being in the right stage positions was also important. We had fun with it too; I even blacked out my teeth to look more like Jerry Dammers!

We did our first gig in July 1999, a few months previous to that the band didn't really exist, we were just in time for the 20th Anniversary of the single 'Gangsters'. We used to go off in a van on weekend tours around the country. We had a really good time. One of the best bunches of guys I have ever played music with. The attention to detail was important, but too intense, and came with its limitations, so it was probably inevitable I left the group after three years. Some of them still do stuff with me now. I'm so glad I did More Specials. I wanted it to be a proper tribute, something that I would have paid to see if I had been in the audience."

JASON O'BRYAN – Musician (the Dub Pistols), London: "The Specials were a major influence on us. How chuffed were we to get to work with Terry Hall? He became a regular guest vocalist for us on tour, usually coming on for the last three songs to close the set. Before our headline show at our record label Sunday Best's Bestival 2007 show, Terry asked if Lynval Golding could come and play a few songs with us. It was a real honour to have the two of them together again onstage for the first time in years. As the finale to the show, we performed 'Problem Is', 'Gangsters' and 'Our Lips Are Sealed' and blew the roof off the place. I was lucky enough to be side of stage when six of the seven of the Specials re-formed at Bestival 2008, thanks to the kindness of Lynval's daughter Michelle Golding. Just before the guys went on, I asked Terry if I could join them onstage for a joke; 'Last three songs,' he replied."

PETE CHAMBERS – Journalist and Author, Coventry: "I'm sure most people reading this will have had an early music experience in their life. Mine begins predictably with the Beatles, and the wonder of a Dansette record player in the corner of our living room kicking out a sound that would stay with me forever. So with music well and truly bolted on to my life, I continued to soak up a plethora of musical influences along the way. Some I'm mighty proud to have enjoyed, others I can only put down to an age thing. Coventry through the Sixties and the early Seventies was not yet ready to take its place on the musical map. Come 1979 it all changed for me and my city. Ok I'm not about to tell you that, on seeing the Coventry Automatics for the first time I knew I had seen the future of Coventry music. Much as I would love to say I had, the fact is the whole thing remains a bit of a blur until a few months on, when it all fitted into place on hearing 'Gangsters' for the very first time.

The Eighties were an exciting time for the Coventry music fan; with the success of 2Tone, we at last had our own music scene. A scene that was brimming with talent and not just the black and white check variety either. Bands like Urge, Reluctant Stereotypes, Gods Toys, the Wild Boys and dozens of others all shared the dream of being the next big band to come out of Coventry. A huge bonus for Coventry was the publication of our own fanzine *Alternative Sounds*; at last, the scene had some cohesion to it. Band members became recognisable, and you never had to miss a gig again, because the *Alternative Sounds* always kept you up to date with all that was happening. On a personal note, it was the start of my journalistic career with a first review of Bad Manners. Half of Cov was watching the Clash at Tiffany's, I was down the Dog & Trumpet, watching Bad Manners and predicting big things for them.

By the early Eighties I was writing a music column for the *Coventry Weekly News*, keeping the free-sheet readers of Skaville up-to-date with what was occurring musically in the area. My column 'Surround Sounds' served me well for a number of years, until the paper did a front-page exposé of Horace Panter being involved in a mind-expanding cult (actually the self-improvement course Exegesis). My editor at the time got a whiff of my friendship with the Specials bassist, and suggested I did a little bit of insider digging and do a follow up on the story. I was of course appalled by his suggestion, and his subsequent advice that, to get on in the world of journalism, one had to be prepared to stab your best mate in the back! I left the paper, and concentrated on my newly acquired 'Coventry Gazebo' column in the Midlands music-paper *Brum Beat*.

It was a joy to be part of the scene in those heady days, when so much was happening. We were far from the 'Ghost Town' the media loved to portray us as, the city was buzzing. For about 12 glorious months, we became the epicentre of the UK music industry. Amazing as it sounds now, everyone wanted a piece of Cov in the Eighties, with Horizon studios being the place of choice for many artists to record and create the 'Coventry Sound'. All thanks to our 2Tone heroes, yet the city fathers at the time had a considerable problem getting their heads around the concept of the Specials and company putting the city they represent well and truly on the musical map. In their defence, the Specials never wanted to be civic property, and were content to be just a hit pop band.

Fast forward some 30 years, and hey presto 2Tone is part of our social history, and the current movers and shakers who had grown up with the Specials and the Selecter in their ears were ready to listen to what I had to say. That was a good thing, because I was more than a little aware that, if Coventry didn't celebrate 30 magnificent years of 2Tone, then who would? As Coventry's only music historian and a Coventry ambassador, I consider it my job to promote all Coventry and Warwickshire music in all its forms, but especially 2Tone of course. (Though I have to say, my knowledge of the genre is somewhat inadequate compared to that of the legendary Mr. 'Willo', the author of this book.) Apart from my *2-Tone-2* and my *2-Tone Trail* books, I'm also proud to have initiated Jerry Dammers' honorary degree, and for getting the Specials a star on the Coventry Walk of Fame, not to mention securing eight 2Tone plaques up around Coventry at pertinent and historic sites. It's an absolute joy to see so many people embrace something that was 'Made in Coventry', and it's an honour to have many of band members as friends, because they are the ones that have gone out and created history and put my beloved city on the map. The least we can do is try to spread the word a little. Here's to a Special 2009."

BOBBY HEATLIE – Producer and Musician (Ska Dance Craze Collective), Edinburgh:
"My first real memory of the Specials came when I first saw the black and white video of 'Gangsters' aged nine. As a budding youngster, I related instantly to what I was hearing. The sound was direct and fresh, the look was sharp and the band members played with an edge that got me brain and body moving. I couldn't sleep that night, as I wanted to hear it again and again. The following day I managed to get a copy from Trax Records in Gorgie Road, Edinburgh. Me and mate Stuart Auld from school went back to his house in Morrison Street and played the single and the B-side 'The Selecter' all night. The offbeat sound and the image of Walt Jabsco on the sleeve got us hooked with immediate effect.

Now a fully-fledged rude boy, I can't remember any happier times. With the 2Tone bands in full flow, every release seemed a major event in our lives. The school playground was awash with black and white and for once, the kids were united in a love for a musical identity. I was fortunate to have a musical family, my dad, Bob Heatlie senior and Grandad, Tommy Heatlie, were both musicians, playing keyboards and sax with various bands. I had to do that now, as I had found my place in music. I got my mates together and formed a band, the Semi-Tones. It wasn't the greatest band you'll hear, but for the school youth we had a purpose and it kept us out of trouble.

Looking back, the one major thing that 2Tone taught me was through the lyrical content. At the time, we didn't fully understand what was being said, but I personally learnt more from these songs than the education from Tynecastle High, where bigotry and racism were rife. One of our friends was half-caste, and he took hellish abuse and violence on a weekly basis, in which we always had to help him. Through songs like 'It Doesn't Make It Alright' and 'Why?' we managed to get through to some of the kids, because the Specials were cool and current. Some got it, some never did, but it definitely made his and others' lives easier. I don't believe 2Tone ever got the credit it deserved for the issues that politicians and the public avoided. Through music, they changed a high percentage of young attitudes, and whether it was then or even now, the message still gets through.

In the summer of 1981, and with unemployment, poverty and violence soaring through the working classes, 'Ghost Town' came along and provided the soundtrack to that period. A memory that still holds strong, was when visiting my Granny on a late Saturday afternoon, walking along the top road of Robb's Loan, Gorgie, I could see the blue flashing lights of the police and hear very loud angry voices, at the bottom of the street. It was a scene from the Wild West, people were fighting with anybody, cars and houses being destroyed, the area had lost control. It wasn't to do with race, but what was happening in their lives. Whilst the race riots were on the television, a copycat effect filtered through. People were leaving their houses and joining in the carnage, as they had enough. It lasted all night and the damage was scary. In that time, the area of Leith had kicked off too, in a similar fashion. It felt like revolution, but in the end, frustration and madness took over for the day, replacing containment and depression in those people's worlds. Later that year, the Specials split up, and whilst the Fun Boy Three's 'The Lunatics (Have Taken Over The Asylum)'

260

was a fitting song thereafter; something had gone and has never been replaced.

I've been involved in the professional music industry for 20 years and the influence of 2Tone in my life has always been there. In two very successful years their belief in themselves, to go forward and do what they wanted, on mostly their own terms, whilst tackling difficult issues, was a phenomenal and underrated achievement. I currently have a popular rehearsal and recording studio business in the centre of Edinburgh, an idea that stemmed from Jerry Dammers in the *2Tone Book For Rude Boys*. They wanted to build such a place in Coventry, but it didn't happen unfortunately. I also co-organise a music club, started in 2004, called Ska Dance Craze which features local original bands like Bombskare, Big Hand, the Amphetameanies and Big Fat Panda, to name a few, supported with the visuals from the era. Most nights merit a full house of 400, proving that ska still makes a vibrant and happy night for all."

SIMON WARD – Singer (Special Brew), Coventry: "I got my first Specials record at the age of 11 and never really looked at music in the same way again. The sound and the look just made perfect sense to me. I then spent the next few years collecting anything even remotely connected to 2Tone artists. After growing up listening to and loving the music of the Specials it was almost inevitable that Special Brew had to happen. We formed the band because the music of the 2Tone label wasn't being celebrated enough in the city where it was created. The response we have had at our gigs has been incredible. There have been so many great times, but I think what has to be the pinnacle of our five years together was standing on a stage in Coventry last year, skanking the soles off my loafers, with Roddy, Horace and Lynval playing together with us. A truly amazing moment and I look forward to many more in the years ahead. Stay Special."

MICHAEL 'MIGGY' SINCLAIR – Ska/Reggae DJ, Edinburgh: "The 2Tone movement basically shaped my life. From the age of seven, I was hooked, totally. I love my ska (my missus says I'm married to it) and I like the lifestyle of being a skinhead, going to the gigs, meeting new ska people, the clothes etc. I always stayed clued up by reading the ska and 2Tone fanzines, especially *Street Feeling* (a 'zine edited by the author of this book) and have spent so much money on my record collection, I daren't think about it! It was 2Tone that made this all possible, it also made me become a DJ and play at many well attended festivals all over the country. Now I also promote ska through my club night in Edinburgh called One Step Beyond. My life has been shaped by the Specials and Madness, and without a doubt they helped me become the man I am today."

GARRY BUSHELL – Journalist, TV presenter, Musician, London: "[The Specials] were the real thing, not just a working idea but a whole new music, a punky reggae party. Punk in feel and bite, ska in the beat. The punk made danceable, the ska intensified. The message? 2Tone. They were brilliant."

LINDA LEE – Executive Producer/Director, ska Documentary, New York: "As we listen to the lyrics from the 2Tone era, we are soberly reminded that, 30 years on, history can repeat itself: poor economics, recent gas shortages, rising unemployment, senseless acts of war (the Specials' 'Man At C&A'), teenage pregnancy (the Specials' 'Too Much Too Young'), racial intolerance and knife crime (the Specials' 'Why?'), and a growing sense of helplessness and apathy in youths (the Specials' 'Do Nothing'). Ska not only helped to unite the races and illuminated social conditions, but went on to span countries, cross cultures, and now helps bring the ages together. Today's youth can listen to Amy Winehouse singing the ska classic 'You're Wondering Now' and learn that it was also sung by the Specials in 1979, and then track that back to the original version sung by Andy & Joe recorded at Coxsone Dodd's famed Studio One in 1964. Ska is a musical and historical lesson in one song! And the Specials contributed to that fully."

JASON WEIR – 2-Tone.Info website, Northern Ireland: "Racism was never a big deal in Northern Ireland for the simple reason we didn't have many immigrants (let's face it, in the Seventies and Eighties who would have wanted to move to the place anyway?) but what the Specials and 2Tone did for my friends and me was help break down sectarian barriers. Having the same taste in music and clothes did more to reach across the religious divide than any crackpot politician could ever hope for. At the time the Specials were more than just a band, they (and 2Tone) became a way of life. Buying button badges at the weekly market, bleaching white socks, polishing Doctor Martens and loafers, and the look of utter disbelief on my Mother's face when I said I wanted a dogtooth suit for my birthday are my abiding memories of that time. But above all else the memories and excitement of buying such great records will stick with me for the rest of my life."

BIG MITCH – Singer (the Communicators), South West: "The Specials – what can I say that many more eloquent individuals haven't already said about this truly inspirational bunch of people? For me, within my lifetime, the most courageous, strong minded and individual band I have seen. I remember hearing 'Gangsters' for the first time and thinking 'something has changed'. At the time, I didn't know what that was but I knew I loved it. What I love about the Specials, apart from the unbelievable energy, amazing tunes and presence, is their knack of giving you a song that you could relate to as well as many songs with a message. For example, I remember hearing 'Friday Night, Saturday Morning' for the first time and when I heard Terry Hall sing that line 'I hope the chip shop isn't closed, 'coz their pies are really nice' I thought, 'that is how I feel walking back from the pub, he knows, he's done it, he's one of us, he's actually been out on the pull and only gone home with a slap in the gob too!' I also remember laughing outrageously to 'Pearls Café' when he talks of her being a 'wet dream come true' and knowing that woman he speaks of. And yet, from these lyrics so simple, yet so effective, the Specials would write a song like 'Why?' which would make you feel haunted and disturbed whilst making you question the very society that we lived in. The Specials inspired me by making me believe that I could achieve anything, and I could do it my way and that I did not have to follow (like sheep in a wolf's clothes!) in order to do it! I would like to personally thank Neville Staple. I had the pleasure of sharing a stage with Neville not so long ago, and I have to say the man was a gent. I also thank Jerry for the songs and the amazing 2Tone label. I thank Horace for some of the most underrated bass lines of our century. I thank Lynval for his enthusiasm, old-skool licks and gentlemanly manner. I thank John Bradbury for his crossover beats that were the backbone of every track. I thank Roddy Byers for adding that difference that every great band has! I finally I thank Terry, for being Terry Hall. The Specials are just that: SPECIAL! They should be held in the highest esteem throughout the world and used as an inspiration to anyone who feels that their circumstances hold them back. They were pioneers, influential – definitely, political – absolutely, but above all a great band. A *truly* great band."

TIM LOVEJOY – TV and radio presenter, London: "The Specials are one of my all time favourite bands. I love them. I can recall when Terry Hall came on the XFM show. I was excited! He walked into the studio, held his hand out and I went to shake it. Then he pulled it back, saying 'Schoolboy error'. I couldn't believe he was a *Soccer AM* fan and had picked up on the gag I did every week!"

PAUL FLANAGAN – A Specials fan, Ireland: "I can remember buying 'A Message To You Rudy' by the Specials when I was 11. Not as a rude boy or anything, just because I liked the song. I then started to notice the kids in my area were wearing Harringtons with sew-on patches and Specials badges and I found this very attractive so I started wearing it. I also bought 'Ghost Town' when it was at Number 1. But it was the album *Dance Craze* that changed my life forever back in 1981 and, from that day, I have never looked back. I never got to see the Specials at the time, but that didn't stop me from loving everything they did. By 1982 most of the kids on my street had left 2Tone behind and moved on, but not me, I stood my ground and I'm still here today 29 years later, waiting for my second chance to see the greatest band in the world live and direct at a venue soon. 2009, for me, is a dawning of a new era."

MATT BILTON – Musician, (Ska-Boom), Redcar: "What can I say? My first memory of ska and 2Tone music comes from looking through my Dad's record collection and catching a flash of black and white checks amongst a mass of mundane album covers. On closer inspection, it was an album called *Specials* by a band called the Specials. The year was 1980 and I had just returned home from another long day at school. After listening to the first track, 'A Message To You Rudy' and being intrigued by the strange 'offbeat' sound coming from the speakers, I had to listen to some more and found it hard to believe that the seven strange-looking lads on the cover were behind this new music I had found. Later that day that I went on to find such tracks as 'Concrete Jungle', 'Too Much Too Young' and 'Little Bitch'. I didn't understand the lyrics but the beat and overall sound that was infectious. Unknown to me, this was later to form the soundtrack to my life. Years passed, and my love of ska music was as strong as ever. Other kids at school could not associate with the shaved head, Crombie and oxblood Dr Martens I sported, but it didn't really matter. On leaving school and starting my first job, ska took second place for a while as I was attracted to big money working as a DJ in various clubs and bars across the North East of England (the house music generation had arrived but the oxblood DM's and shaved head stayed, old beliefs and habits die hard.) After many years away from home DJing, playing percussion and playing drums in various bands, things turned full circle. I put the feelers out to start a ska and 2Tone band, and not thinking there would be much interest, posted the adverts and forgot all about it. The response was unbelievable and eight other musicians were selected from many, along with myself, to form Ska-Boom! playing the ska and 2Tone music that meant so much to me. I have been truly blessed, and we are still able to go out and give our interpretation of such hits from the *Specials* album that I had found by a complete accident. Funny how things turn out, but those tracks from the late Seventies and early Eighties are still as relevant now as ever. My three young children are all familiar with what ska music is and who the Specials are, and so they should be. My band still goes out every week to play these tracks, amongst many others, with more enthusiasm than the previous week, but not as much as the next, which is a true testament to ska music. That resonant beat has been with me through good times and bad, and still remains."

CHALKIE DAVIES, Photographer, New York: "It's hard to believe that it's 30 years since our friend Elvis Costello told us about a great new band called the Specials and their label called 2Tone. We went straight out and bought the singles and were so impressed that we lobbied to do their album sleeve. When we were told that we could do it, we did our normal routine of checking out the band; we went to *Top Of The Pops* and observed them from afar. Immediately we realized that they were seven distinctively different people and so the following weekend we went to Coventry to shoot the pictures for the first sleeve. We found ourselves on top of the roof of the Odeon Cinema as well as in the derelict Canal Basin. The place was pretty run down, with an abandoned boat and prisoners from the local jail cleaning the place up. We positioned the band in front of one of the old buildings and while I shot a photo of them from an upstairs window and Carole Starr shot the same photo from the side; those two views of the same group shot became the first LP sleeve. Did we know then that the sleeve would last 30 years? We always felt that our work for the Specials was the best we had ever done, but let me also put it this way, I doubt if any of us expected to be alive in 30 years! Those were the days! We have lived in New York for the last 20 years, but allow us to salute, Terry, Jerry, Brad, Roddy, Lynval, Neville and of course, Sir Horace Gentleman."

THE COMPLETE DISCOGRAPHY

This discography provides a complete list of all Specials and Special AKA releases, and includes more recent additions and also the Specials Mk2.

7" SINGLES

GANGSTERS / THE SELECTER by The Selecter
(2Tone TT1 & TT2)
Released – July 1979
Chart placing – 6

A MESSAGE TO YOU RUDY / NITE KLUB
(2Tone CHS TT5)
Released – October 1979
Chart Placing – 10

THE SPECIAL AKA LIVE! EP
Features the tracks: Too Much Too Young / Guns Of Navarone / Long Shot Kick De Bucket / Skinhead Moonstomp
(2Tone CHS TT7)
Released – January 1980
Chart Placing – 1

RAT RACE / RUDE BUOYS OUTA JAIL
(2Tone CHS TT10)
Released – May 1980
Chart Placing – 5

STEREOTYPE / INTERNATIONAL JET SET
(2Tone CHS TT13)
Released – September 1980
Chart Placing – 6

DO NOTHING / MAGGIE'S FARM
(2Tone CHS TT16)
Released – December 1980
Chart Placing – 4

GHOST TOWN / WHY? / FRIDAY NIGHT SATURDAY MORNING
(2Tone CHS TT17)
Released – June 1981
Chart Placing – 1

THE BOILER / THEME FROM THE BOILER
(2Tone CHS TT18)
With Rhoda Dakar
Released – January 1982
Chart Placing – 35

JUNGLE MUSIC / RASTA CALL YOU
(2Tone CHS TT19)
With Rico Rodriguez
Released – March 1982
Chart Placing – Unplaced

WAR CRIMES (The Crime Remains The Same) / VERSION
(2Tone CHS TT23)
Released – November 1982
Chart Placing – 84

RACIST FRIEND / BRIGHT LIGHTS
(2Tone CHS TT25)
Released – August 1983
Chart Placing – 60

NELSON MANDELA / BREAK DOWN THE DOOR
(2Tone CHS TT26)
Released – March 1984
Chart Placing – 9

(What I Like Most About You Is Your) GIRLFRIEND / CAN'T GET A BREAK
(2Tone CHS TT27)
Released – September 1984
Chart Placing – 51

NELSON MANDELA (70th Birthday Remake) / NELSON MANDELA (Original)
(Tone Records FNMX1)
Released – 1988
Chart Placing- 93
The remake of the Special AKA classic saw African musicians Ndonda Khuze and
Jonas Gwangwa make the record their own with Jerry Dammers on keyboards and
production. The former Swinging Cats member Chris Long AKA Rhythm Doctor
added the DJ scratching.

GHOST TOWN REVISITED
(2Tone CHS TT30)
This was a tenth anniversary release credited to the Specials and Special Productions
that featured the original Ghost Town track on side one and the track Ghost Dub 91 as
side two, remixed by Andre Schmidt and Matt Clarke.
Released – June 1991
Chart Placing – Unplaced.

266

THE 2TONE EP
(2Tone CHS TT31)
This four-track EP was a commercial success and featured the four debut songs from the major 2Tone bands. Side A included Gangsters by the Special AKA
Released – October 1993
Chart Placing – 30

HYPOCRITE / HYPOCRITE REMIX (6 versions)
(Kuff Records KUFFD3)
The first single by the Nineties re-formed Specials – CD single format
Released – 1995
Chart Placing – Unplaced.

PRESSURE DROP / PRESSURE DROP (Handbaggers Remix) / DO NOTHING (Live) / HEY, LITTLE RICH GIRL (Live)
(Kuff Records KUFFD4)
Released – 1996
Chart Placing – Unplaced.
Again CD single format

Another three-track CD single was issued for A Little Bit Me, A Little Bit You from the *Today's Specials* album, but only in the US. The track listing was: A Little Bit Me, A Little Bit You (single edit) /AC HOT ASC Mix / Album version.

10" SINGLES

WAR CRIMES (The Crime Remains The Same) (Extended) / VERSION
(2Tone CHS TT 1023)
Released – November 1982

12" SINGLES

GHOST TOWN (Extended) / WHY? / FRIDAY NIGHT SATURDAY MORNING
(2Tone CHS TT 1217)
Released – June 1981

JUNGLE MUSIC / RASTA CALL YOU / EASTER ISLAND
(2Tone CHS TT 1219)
Released – March 1982

RACIST FRIEND / BRIGHT LIGHTS / RACIST FRIEND (Instrumental) / BRIGHT LIGHTS (Instrumental)
(2Tone CHS TT 1225)
Released – August 1983

NELSON MANDELA / BREAK DOWN THE DOOR
(2Tone CHS TT 1226)
Released – September 1983

THE PEEL SESSIONS:THE SPECIALS
(Strange Fruit Records SFPS 018)
Released – August 1987
This 12″ was issued by Strange Fruit as part of a long-running programme of releases
of material by artists who had appeared in session for the legendary John Peel. The
tracks were recorded on 23rd May 1979.
Side One : Gangsters / Too Much Too Young
Side Two : Concrete Jungle / Monkey Man

NELSON MANDELA (The Whole World Is Watching Dance Mix) / NELSON MANDELA (Original)
(Tone Records FNMX1)
Released – 1988

HYPOCRITE / HYPOCRITE REMIX (6 Versions)
(Kuff Records KUFF T3)
Released – 1995

PRESSURE DROP / PRESSURE DROP (Handbaggers Remix)
(Kuff Records KUFF T4)
Released – 1996

ALBUMS

SPECIALS
(2Tone CDL TT 5001)
Released – October 1979
Side One: A Message To You Rudy / Do The Dog / It's Up To You / Nite Klub / Doesn't
Make It Alright / Concrete Jungle / Too Hot
Side Two: Monkey Man / (Dawning Of A) New Era / Blank Expression / Stupid Marriage /
Too Much Too Young / Little Bitch / You're Wondering Now

MORE SPECIALS
(2Tone CHR TT 5003)
Released – September 1980
Side One: Enjoy Yourself / Man At C&A / Hey, Little Rich Girl / Do Nothing / Pearl's
Café/ Sock it To 'Em, J.B.
Side Two: Stereotypes (Parts 1 & 2) / Holiday Fortnight / I Can't Stand It / International
Jet Set / Enjoy Yourself (Reprise)

IN THE STUDIO
(2Tone CHR TT 5008)
Released – June 1984

Side One: Bright Lights / Lonely Crowd / Girlfriend / Housebound /Night On The Tiles
Side Two: Nelson Mandela / War Crimes / Racist Friend / Alcohol / Break Down The Door

THE SPECIALS SINGLES
(2Tone CHR TT 5010)
Released – August 1991
Side One: Gangsters / A Message To You Rudy / Nite Klub / Too Much Too Young /
Guns Of Navarone / Rat Race / Stereotype / International Jet Set / Do Nothing
Side Two: Ghost Town (12" version) / Why? / Friday Night Saturday Morning / War
Crimes / Racist Friend / Nelson Mandela / Girlfriend

LIVE AT THE MOONLIGHT CLUB
(2Tone CHR TT 5011)
Released – 1992
Side One: It's Up To You / Do The Dog / Monkey Man / Blank Expression / Nite Klub
Side Two: Concrete Jungle / Too Hot / Too Much Too Young / Little Bitch / Longshot
Kick De Bucket
This was the official release of the band's most famous bootleg LP

TOO MUCH TOO YOUNG
(Receiver RRLP 161)
Released – 1992
Side One: Gangsters / Do The Dog / It's Up To You / Monkey Man / Blank Expression /
Stupid Marriage / Doesn't Make It Alright
Side Two: Concrete Jungle / Too Hot / Nite Klub / Too Much Too Young / Little Bitch /
Skinhead Moon Stomp / Liquidator / Long Shot Kick De Bucket / You're Wondering Now
This album, issued by Receiver (a Trojan subsidiary), is a good example of the
band's early live set and was recorded at Aston University in 1979. The only
drawback to it is that the banter with the audience has been replaced by a loop of
cheering which was sampled from the Selecter's live comeback album, Out On The
Streets (also on Receiver).

DAWNING OF A NEW ERA – THE COVENTRY AUTOMATICS AKA THE SPECIALS
(Receiver Records RRLP 178)
Released – March 1993
Track Listing: Wake Up / Nite Klub – Raquel / Rock 'n' Roll Nightmare / Look But Don't
Touch Me / Concrete Jungle / It's Up To You / Stupid Marriage / Blank Expression /
Too Much Too Young
Receiver Records came up with the most classic of Specials releases in 1993. On this
album there are 12 early demos taken from a trip the group made to London when
they were still known as the Automatics in 1978. John Bradbury is missing from the
line-up and Silverton Hutchinson plays the drums on this collection. The novelty value
is held in the previously unheard tracks of Wake Up, Rock'n'Roll Nightmare and Look
But Don't Touch Me.

TODAY'S SPECIALS
(Kuff Records CD KUFF2)
Released – 1996

Track Listing: Take Five / Pressure Drop / Hypocrite / Goodbye Girl / A Little Bit Me, A Little Bit You / Time Has Come / Dirty Old Town / Somebody Got Murdered / 007 / Simmer Down / Maga Dog / Bad Boys
The much-maligned comeback album of covers by the Nineties version of the Specials.

GUILTY 'TIL PROVED INNOCENT
(Way Cool /MCA Records GRL 009)
Released – 1998
Side One: Tears In My Beer / Call Me Names / Fearful / It's You / Bonediggin' / All Gone Wrong / No Big Deal
Side Two: Leave It Out / Keep On Learning / Fantasize / Place In Life / Stand Up / Tears Come Falling Down Like Rain / Man With No Name / Running Away
The second, and far superior, Nineties Specials album. The American version featured three extra live tracks: Rat Race, Concrete Jungle and Gangsters.

THE BBC SESSIONS
(EMI Records EMI7423 497791 29)
Released – November 1998
The complete Peel Sessions, featuring a great version of Rico's Sea Cruise. A total of 16 tracks that also includes three Special AKA sessions.

STEREO-TYPICAL – A's, B's and Rarities
(EMI Records EMI7423 527154 28)
Released -August 2000
CD1: Gangsters / Message To You Rudy / Nite Klub / Too Much Too Young / Guns Of Navarone / Skinhead Symphony / Rat Race / Rude Boys Outa Jail / Stereotype / International Jet Set / Do Nothing / Maggies Farm / Braggin'And Tryin' Not To Lie / Rude Boys Outa Jail (Version) / Ghost Town / Why? / Friday Night Saturday Morning / Concrete Jungle (Live) / Raquel
CD2: The Boiler / Theme From The Boiler / Jungle Music / Rasta Call You / Easter Island / War Crimes / War Crimes (Version) / Racist Friend / Bright Lights / Nelson Mandela / Break Down The Door / Girlfriend / Can't Get A Break / Nelson Mandela '88 / Ghost Dub'91 / Let Us Unite
CD3: Ghost Town (Extended) / Why? / War Crimes / Racist Friend (Instrumental) / Bright Lights (Instrumental) / Nelson Mandela / Break Down The Door (Extended) / Girlfriend / Can't Get A Break / Nelson Mandela '88 (The Whole World Is Watching Dance Mix) / Ghost Dub '91 vs. Let Us Unite
A 46-track extravaganza of all Specials and Special AKA recordings on three compact discs. With sleeve notes by journalist Adrian Thrills, the compilation gives the collector / listener nothing new apart from the inclusion of the 1988 Mandela single and the Ghost Town Revisited tracks but, again, this was still old hat. EMI, who now owned the Specials and 2Tone back catalogue, fell very short with this release, which was simply another attempt to cash in on the Specials' legacy.

SKINHEAD GIRL
(Receiver Records RRCD 295)
Released – October 2000
Track Listing: I Can't Hide / Blam Blam Fever / Jezebel / El Pussycat / Soldering / You

Don't Know Like I Know / Memphis Underground / If I Didn't Love You / Them A Fe Get A Beatin' / Napoleon Solo / Skinhead Girl / Fire Corner / Bangerang Crash / I Want To Go Home / Old Man Say
Part one of the Sessions recorded with Roger Lomas featuring Roddy Byers, Horace Panter, Lynval Golding and Neville Staple.

CONQUERING RULER
(Receiver Records RRCD 292)
Released – February 2001
Track Listing: Jezebel / Tom Drunk / Take Me As I Am / Conquering Ruler / Decimal Currency / Promises / Double Barrel / Keep My Love From Fading / Rough & Tough / Foolish Plan / I Am A Mad Man / Salvation Train / Lorna Banana / Return Of Django / I Don't Need Your Love Anymore
Part two of the Lomas sessions.

THE BEST OF THE SPECIALS
(EMI Records 50999 520398 29)
Released – April 2008
With all the talk about the 2Tone 30th Anniversary in 2009, and the accompanying rumours of the Specials negotiating with each other, EMI cashed in yet again with a 20-track standard greatest hits package and a 16-track DVD to complete the marketing ploy. Reached the Top 30 in the UK.

OTHERS

There have been a vast amount of Specials-related albums released in the last ten years or so, but none that really contribute anything to the band's heritage. They tend to be re-packaged and re-badged CD albums that have been released previously, and some collections are somewhat farcical. Below are listed some of those which are more commonly-known:

THE SPECIALS – GANGSTERS LIVE (Hallmark) 1996 – Quite simply, a chopped-down version of the album *Too Much Too Young* that had appeared earlier on the Receiver label. The Hallmark album re-appeared with a new cover and the title *Too Much Too Young Live* (to confuse matters even more!) on Castle Music in 1999, but the music is exactly the same as the Hallmark CD issue.

TOO MUCH TOO YOUNG (EMI) 1996 – A mix of tracks from the two studio albums.

THE BEST OF THE SPECIALS (Disky) 1999 – 16 tracks containing a mix of singles, album tracks and one Special AKA track, War Crimes.

THE SPECIALS – A SPECIAL COLLECTION (EMI) 1999 – An out-and-out EMI cash, containing 16 album and single tracks. The words 'bog standard' spring to mind.

THE SPECIALS – ARCHIVE (Rialto) 2001 – A bizarre 23-track mix of original Specials and the covers from the *Skinhead Girl* and *Conquering Ruler* albums.

There are numerous albums around that include tracks from the Specials amongst music by other bands, particularly in last 20 years when the CD has become the most common format. It seems that every time a record company wants to release a ska compilation they opt for the same tracks that have appeared countless times before, and you can guarantee that the Specials are in there somewhere. They are of little real value to collectors, and so the compilations listed here are either on the hallowed 2Tone label or are of genuine interest to collectors:

DANCE CRAZE
(2Tone CHR TT 5004)
Released – February 1981
Everyone knows the story behind the release of the live *Dance Craze* album. It was the soundtrack to the movie of the same name. Not all the tracks in the film were issued on the album, which was released with a free poster of all the bands that appeared in the project. The poster was recently used in the 2007 hit UK film *This Is England* (the Specials also appeared on the soundtrack). For legal reasons, the subsequent US version of the album omitted Madness, but added Skinhead Symphony by the Specials and Carry Go Bring Come by the Selecter. The Specials' contribution to the UK version of the *Dance Craze* album was:
Side One: Concrete Jungle
Side Two: Man At C&A / Nite Klub

THIS ARE TWO TONE
(2Tone CHR TT 5007)
Released – November 1983
A 2Tone compilation released by Chrysalis to recoup some of the cash that had been pumped into the costly production of the Special AKA's *In The Studio* album. It was issued with a blue and pink cover and came complete with a poster of all the 2Tone acts. Listed below are the tracks credited to the Specials and Special AKA:
Side One: Gangsters/ A Message To You Rudy / Too Much Too Young
Side Two: Stereotype / Do Nothing / The Boiler / Ghost Town

THE 2TONE STORY
(2Tone CHR TT 5009)
Released – July 1989
This double vinyl album was released by Chrysalis to mark 2Tone's tenth anniversary. It mixed studio tracks with live cuts, all taken from *Dance Craze* except a previously-unissued superb live rendition of Stereotype, which for some inexplicable reason was omitted from the CD version. Note also there are no tracks from the Apollinaires or the Higsons. The Specials and Special AKA contributions are as follows:
Side One: Gangsters / A Message To You Rudy
Side Two: Blank Expression / Do Nothing / International Jet Set / Why? / Ghost Town
Side Three (Live): Stereotype / Too Much Too Young
Side Four: The Boiler / War Crimes / Nelson Mandela

THE BEST OF 2TONE

(2Tone CHR TT 5012)

Released – October 1993

Another Chrysalis re-hashed compilation. It did at least boast a very smart cover depicting a 2Tone record being played on an old Dansette record player. On the back of the cover were witty anecdotes courtesy of Specials manager Rick Rogers. This album followed hot on the heels of the successful *2Tone EP* which hit Number 30 in the charts. It does, however, contain nothing new apart from the rare 2Tone Elvis Costello single. This was the last vinyl album ever to be released on 2Tone.

Side One: Ghost Town / Too Much Too Young / Do Nothing/ Stereotype

Side Two: Rat Race / The Boiler / Gangsters / Nelson Mandela / A Message To You Rudy

THE COMPACT 2TONE STORY

(2Tone CHR TT 5013)

Released – November 1993

The daddy of all 2Tone compilations, this special four-CD set came complete with the book *The Two Tone Story* by George Marshall. The Specials' drummer, John Bradbury, was involved in getting this release out and, as he considered that the book was the best source of information with regard to 2Tone, he thought it would be ideal for inclusion. It contains every 2Tone single issue (not album), including B-sides and 12" versions and live tracks. A total of 68 numbers featuring the Specials, the Special AKA, the Selecter, the Beat, Elvis Costello, the Bodysnatchers, the Swinging Cats, Rico, Rhoda Dakar, the Apollinaires, the Higsons, JB's Allstars, the Friday Club and the two tracks from the freebie More Specials single by Neville and Roddy. The most outstanding features were the addition of two cuts never released in any format. The Bodysnatchers gave a live performance of Desmond Dekker's 007 (Shanty Town) in the film *Dance Craze* and it was finally released here, along with a rollicking version of Raquel credited to the original Specials, which had been released as the B-side to the Dutch Concrete Jungle live single.

AND SOME MORE

That concludes the 2Tone releases/compilations of note but below are a few albums that feature the Specials' recordings.The only ones of real value to the collector are:

CONCERTS FOR THE PEOPLE OF KAMPUCHEA

(Atlantic ATL 60153)

Released – March 1981

This double LP featured live recordings of groups like Queen, Wings, the Pretenders, the Clash and the Who, with all proceeds going to the famine relief fund for Cambodia (or Kampuchea as it was known then). A colour image taken from the 'Gangsters' promo video appeared on the inner sleeve. Only one track from a brilliant Specials set appeared on the LP:

Side Three: Monkey Man

LIFE IN THE EUROPEAN THEATRE

(WEA K58412)

Released – October 1981

The sleeve notes say it all about this politically-sharp compilation of British artists who all donated tracks to the record, the proceeds of which went to the Campaign For Nuclear Disarmament. The sleeve note reads:

"NUCLEAR POWER – No single civil industry threatens our lives and the lives of future generations with such brutal finality as Nuclear Power. It will have a deep and damaging effect on all of us. An enormous, appalling expensive risk. Despite the soothing words of the nuclear industry, accidents will happen. Everyday, the radioactive rubbish dump of lethal nuclear waste grows bigger, in spite of the fact that no one yet knows how to dispose of it with safety and certainty. It is a deadly inheritance to leave our children and their children. Of course, everyone needs energy, now and in the future. But heat from atom splitting will fail to provide the kind of secure source of energy we all need because it is complex, over-centralised, and unreliable, and also creates the materials for any country to assemble an atomic bomb. Meanwhile, it is diverting vast sums of money and scientific research resources away from the only true long term solutions to our needs: an energy conservation programme, coupled with the harnessing of the only abundant source of energy the world will always have: the sun. Half of the recording artists royalties from this album go into a fund for projects opposing nuclear arms and power."

The Specials appeared on the record with a track lifted from *Dance Craze*. The Police and the Jam were also amongst those who contributed.
Side One: Man At C&A (Live)

THE SPECIALS / THE SELECTER – LIVE IN CONCERT
(Windsong International WINCD 030)
Released – 1992
The Specials' contribution: (Dawning Of) A New Era / Do The Dog / Rat Race / Blank Expression / Rude Boys Outa Jail / Concrete Jungle / Too Much Too Young / Nite Klub / Gangsters / Long Shot Kick De Bucket
Windsong Records released this CD-only album that offers a joint package from the Specials and 2Tone colleagues the Selecter. Recorded at the Paris Theatre, London in December 1979, the concert was originally broadcast on BBC Radio 1 as part of the long-running *Live In Concert* series. that went on air at 6.30 every Saturday evening and featured a great variety of artists.

THE SHACK
(Dojo CD145)
Released – September 1993
This boasts a few little gems with Specials connections and items relevant to this book. Compiled by Sean Flowerdew of Pama International who also played keyboards for the Special Beat, this collection featured 'new' ska stars as well as the old guard. On the CD, there are two tracks credited to Neville Staple and Lynval Golding but both songs are actually Specials / early Fun Boy Three demos from 1981. The first is a cover of Wear You To The Ball which, as mentioned previously, is an intriguing number because neither Jerry Dammers or Horace Panter play on it and Terry Hall's voice was removed for legal reasons. The other track is a demo version of Why?. As an aside, in 2004, another Specials 1981 demo was uncovered, a cover of 96 Tears, originally recorded by Question Mark and the Mysterians, which was aired by Lynval Golding on his own website to commemorate the 25th anniversary of

2Tone. Neville also makes a solo appearance on this compilation as his alter-ego Judge Roughneck on the track 007 (Rude Boy Pon Probation). Also on the listings you will find Hypocrite by the Special Beat and Maroon Town's Nostalgia, produced by John Bradbury.

SPARE SHELLS – A TRIBUTE TO THE SPECIALS
(Pork Pie EFA 05643-2)
Released – April 2002
I have included this release for its novelty factor. German ska label Pork Pie released this CD album featuring 23 Specials tracks covered by ska, punk and psychobilly stars of the 21st century from all over the world. The cover was a great replica of the first Specials album.
Track listing is: Enjoy Yourself – The Busters / Nite Klub – Citizen Fish / Little Bitch – The Porkers / Hey, Little Rich Girl – Skavenjah / Gangsters – The Louisville Sluggers / Racist Friend – The Upbeat / A Message To You Rudy – The Allniters / Stereotype – The Skalatones / Do The Dog – The Amazing Crowns / Dawning Of A New Era – Area 7 / Ghost Town – Desorden Publico / Liquidator – The Bakesys / Friday Night Saturday Morning – The Allstonians / Doesn't Make It Alright – Dr Raju / Stupid Marriage – Skarface / Concrete Jungle – The Frits / Do Nothing – 78rpms / Man At C&A – Ballistic Allshorts / Blank Expression – Voodoo Glow Skulls / Too Much Too Young – Dave Smalley / Rat Race – Rude Bones / Sock it To 'Em, JB – The Butlers / You're Wondering Now – Skanic Ft Lynval Golding

RARITIES & BOOTLEGS

This section has been graciously compiled by Jason Weir from the superb 2Tone collectors website, 2Tone.info

RARE'N'TASTY

GANGSTERS

The band's debut has the honour of offering up some the most highly collectible and desirable Specials' items. First off the mark is the hand-stamped sleeve which accompanied the Rough Trade release of the single. Pressed on rather flimsy paper, not many of these have survived in any sort of presentable form, although Horace has stated that he and Brad stamped up the initial copies on much more robust card sleeves which ups the ante even more for the avid collector. 'Gangsters' also bucks the trend with regards the paper label version being much more desirable than its rather bland silver plastic counterpart. Paper label versions of 'Gangsters' are frankly as common as muck, but the silver label versions are a different story completely. There are also two UK label misprints out there. One has the Gangsters labels on both sides while the other has the Selecter labels on both sides. Of the non-UK releases, the Dutch mispress, which plays 'Banana Split' by teenage Belgian singer and actress Lio, should be of interest to most. As should the rather tasty Japanese 12" promo. The rather bland US 12" promo is hardly an essential item, but worth picking up nonetheless. Add to the list the numerous non-UK picture sleeves and it's easy to see why collecting versions of 'Gangsters' alone could become a lifetime's endeavour

A MESSAGE TO YOU RUDY

Apart from a UK label mispress, which features the 'Nite Klub' labels on both sides, and the Spanish version, which comes in three different formats (one 7" promo features the cover shot used on the band's debut album, while another 7" promo comes with a rather strange Technicolor label) the band's second single doesn't offer up a great number of collectibles. As always, the non-UK releases came with picture sleeves, which, although collectible, are reasonably easy to come by and are therefore not particularly rare.

TOO MUCH TOO YOUNG

The bands' first UK Number 1 was released as a two-track Promo/Jukebox single with the title track on the A-side and 'Skinhead Moonstomp' on the flip and offers an interesting variation to the commercially-available five-track EP. 2Tone's first picture cover features on most non-UK versions of the release, with the exception of the German version. For some reason this version uses a type of pencil sketch shot of the band on stage and will be of interest to the more discerning collector. Germany also saw a 12" version of the single, as did Japan. Same track listing as the 7" release in both cases.

RAT RACE

The Japanese release features a great picture, using artwork from the Specials' Seaside Tour poster of 1980. As always, most European releases of the single offer a picture sleeve, with the German release, or should that be one of the German releases (there are three versions available) taking the prize for perhaps the worst sleeve ever to grace a 2Tone release. It's difficult to imagine that cartoon rats on a zebra crossing are what Roddy envisaged when he wrote this track, but that is exactly what someone in Germany decided was a fitting sleeve for this release. For avid collectors only.

STEREOTYPE
Nothing much in terms of rarity, but the non-UK picture sleeves are a nice addition to any collection and are easy to come by.

DO NOTHING
As with 'Stereotype', not much offered in terms of rarities, although the Italian pressing has 'Man at C&A' as a B-side, while the French 7" pressing has 'Do Nothing' relegated to the B-side, with 'Sock It To Them' (sic) as the title track. Both discs would be a worthwhile addition to any collection.

GHOST TOWN
The band's final single offers up another curious blue plastic label, which had previously cropped up on the Selecter's 'On My Radio' and Madness' debut 'The Prince'. No one is quite sure what the story behind these labels is, although the various shades of blue do suggest something not going quite as planned at the pressing plant. 'Ghost Town' was the label's first 12" single and, as would be expected, offers up some interesting items for the collector. The standard UK 12" pressing is easy enough to come by but the die-cut 2Tone sleeve version, not to mention the white label promo, should be the preferred option for the more avid enthusiast. As would be the commercial 12" releases from the likes of America, Australia and Japan. In terms of European releases of 'Ghost Town', copies are easy enough to come by and can be picked up at a reasonable price. A real oddball release is the Japanese cassette single version.

THE BOILER
The subject matter of this release guaranteed that it wouldn't receive much airplay in the UK, and the rest of the world was no different. So far, the only non-UK copies to surface are from Ireland and Spain. The Spanish pressing comes with a unique picture sleeve, while the Irish pressing has the standard Walt Jabsco paper label. The mythical UK 12" pressing remains just that: a myth.

JUNGLE MUSIC
As this marks the last time Walt would appear on a UK 2Tone release, at least until his welcome return on the 2Tone Story LP, owning the paper-label version will no doubt keep the sentimentalists happy. As with 'Ghost Town', 'Jungle Music' was released in the UK on 12" format and both the commercial and white label promo versions are well worth getting hold of. 'Jungle Music' wasn't given as wide a release throughout the rest of the world as previous singles on 2Tone had, so editions from countries which did see its release, such as Germany, Ireland and Australia, are always sought-after.

WAR CRIMES
'War Crimes' was the first and only 10" single released on the label, which is an interesting, though hardly essential item. At the time of the singles Dammers had moved

2Tone away from its black and white roots and was working with an altogether less fetching brown and gold label design, which makes both the German and Irish pressings of this single all the more desirable as both of them were released with the much more appealing Walt Jabsco label.

RACIST FRIEND
By the time of this single's release, Chrysalis Records were doing as all other record companies were doing at the time and releasing singles in every conceivable format. 12" singles were now the norm on 2Tone and this release is no different. What should be of interest to collectors is the picture-disc version of this single, the first of its kind on 2Tone and worth picking up for that reason alone. Walt Jabsco proved that he was down but not out with a sneaky appearance on the German version.

NELSON MANDELA
Spain and Australia offer up Walt on their versions of this single, with the Aussie version offering the only post-'Jungle Music' 12" appearance of the man in question, which should keep the most meticulous of collectors on their toes. This Australian 12" pressing also features a 'Club Mix' of the title track, which, apart from the US 12" Promo pressing, is unavailable elsewhere.

(WHAT I LIKE MOST ABOUT YOU IS YOUR) GIRLFRIEND
The last single by the band offers up only the second picture disc to appear on the label along with a 'Free Single' version that for some reason included the 'War Crimes' single. And to round it all off yet another of those mysterious blue plastic label versions found their way on to the market.

THE SPECIALS ALBUM
As with most Specials vinyl output, non-UK editions of the band's debut album are easy to come by and, interestingly, feature 'Gangsters' at various different positions in the track listing. The US and Canadian pressings have what was the rear of the UK sleeve as the front cover and vice versa. The Japanese pressing comes complete with a fold out type booklet featuring the lyrics of all tracks and is well worth picking up. Pressings of the album from the likes of Israel and Argentina are of more interest, not to mention much rarer, than the standard European versions.

MORE SPECIALS
The must-have item for any collector is the initial UK pressing complete with free poster and free single. Easy enough to come by, but a poster that hasn't been Blu-Tacked to the owner's bedroom wall might be a different story. As with the band's debut, non-UK copies are easily picked up, although the Italian *Ancora Specials* and the Spanish *Mas Specials* (complete with free 'Rat Race' single) should top most collectors' wish list. Again, the Japanese version comes complete with a booklet and Obi if it has been well cared for. Meanwhile, both the cover and track listing of the US cassette version on the 747 label have to be seen to be believed.

IN THE STUDIO
The original 1984 Chrysalis CD pressing was released at a time when the format was very much in its infancy and as such makes it one of the very few sought-after variants

of this album. For those who hanker after the glory days of 2Tone, the Walt Jabsco labels were used on a few of the non-UK versions of the album and make pleasant additions to any collection.

LIVE AT THE LYCEUM
With superb sound quality and a great sleeve, this is perhaps one of the most sought-after Specials items. French in origin, this LP contains 16 tracks of the band on top form recorded live at the Lyceum on the 12th December 1979. The only drawback is that it will cost the average collector an arm and a leg.

CONCRETE JUNGLE
This Dutch-only single release comes with a great picture sleeve and offers up the first vinyl outing for the track 'Raquel', on the B-side. The title track is lifted directly from the *Dance Craze* soundtrack album, with the album itself plugged heavily on the rear of the sleeve.

HEY, LITTLE RICH GIRL
Housed in a unique sleeve and backed by 'International Jet Set' this single does everything to whet the appetite of any collector of the band's output. Why Japan was treated to this track from the band's second album remains a mystery, but that matters little when a gem like this is up for grabs.

BOOTLEG BOOTY

SKINHEAD SYMPHONY 7"
One of the more recent bootlegs to appear on the market, this 7" is something of a disappointment. Bootlegging tracks which are commercially available elsewhere is never going to be a great selling point, although the packaging will no doubt ensure that it remains a highly sought-after item. Housed in an alternative shot from the photo session which provided 'Do Nothing' with its picture sleeve, the vinyl bears a faithful reproduction of a Walt Jabsco paper label, although the more discerning collector will notice that the font used for the '2' is not identical to the one used on the official releases. The tracks themselves are without fault, although better quality live versions of 'Madness' are available elsewhere. The version of 'Skinhead Symphony' is lifted directly from a John Peel session and proves that it certainly lost none of its punch when confined to the studio.

NITEKLUBBING MONKEY MAN
Of German origin, this is a pretty nondescript release of what sounds like a decent audience recording of the band at the Markthalle, Hamburg. With 18 tracks of the standard set list of the time, it does offer another vinyl outing for the 2Tone standard 'Madness'. The recording is of such quality that the brass section is just about inaudible during the likes of 'Guns Of Navarone', although for some reason Rico's solo sounds loud and clear. The sense of disappointment is only compounded by the shoddy artwork. Far from essential.

LIVE IN MANCHESTER
It's a measure of the stir the Specials were causing at the time that a bootleg album should surface so early in their career. In fact, by the time this LP appeared the band had

made only one recording, 'Gangsters', which Neville proudly introduces on this recording as 'our new single'. It therefore preceded the band's official debut album and was even given favourable reviews by some music journalists. The fact that the band's official debut album was yet to appear may go some way towards explaining the rather bizarre song titles listed on the rear of the sleeve. The recording itself is of a pre-Rico and Dick Cuthell version of the Specials and only serves to highlight what essential components they both were to the overall sound of the band.

GANGSTERS

Another bootleg from recent years, this album is a definite case of presentation over substance. The high-quality glossy sleeve and super thick vinyl will no doubt have collectors of the format swooning with delight, but the track listing is a major disappointment and is only salvaged by the inclusion of the five live tracks recorded for US college radio show, *The King Biscuit Flower Hour*. All other tracks have been commercially available for many years and it even includes a UK Number 1 single, which only serves as a reminder of just how pointless this release is. The bootleggers seem only too keen to reiterate this with the inclusion of the official 2Tone catalogue numbers of the tracks included on the album, although someone should have pointed out to them that 'Too Much Too Young' was never a UK 12" release. Not that it matters, as the tracks listed as such are from the Aston University recording and not from the flip side of the 'Too Much Too Young' EP.

GANGSTERS DOUBLE LIVE

Yet another bootleg with the 'Gangsters' moniker. This time it's a double vinyl effort, a recording of a gig at the Boston Paradise during the band's first visit to the US. While the band were playing this gig on January 30th 1980, 'Too Much Too Young' had just been released and was beginning its upward trajectory through the UK singles chart. The track is introduced here by the now customary advice on the use of contraception from Terry Hall and is followed by Neville experiencing some problems with his microphone. Not exactly a perfect quality recording, as it suffers from some distortion now and again, but it's still worth tracking down for Terry Hall's bizarre Jimmy Cagney-based intro to 'Rat Race', if for nothing else.

Note: in a move that bootlegs the bootleggers, a single-disc version of this album has recently surfaced. The track listing is simply the first disk of the album with the track listing altered accordingly and appearing on the front instead of the rear of the sleeve.

RUDE BOYS OUT OF JAIL

Another outing for the Boston Paradise recording. As before, it's a double LP, this time released on Centrifugal Records, who also released the Madness bootleg 'Mistakes', which was recorded at the same venue some five weeks after the Specials gig. Unfortunately it has been mastered at the wrong speed and as a result the tracks are slowed down, causing Terry to sing in baritone. The rear of the sleeve features a group photo from what must have been a very strange photo shoot indeed.

UNRELEASED '2TONE TOUR' BBC BROADCAST 1981

Another recent bootleg to appear on the market, this is a recording of the *Rock Goes To College* broadcast of the Colchester Institute gig in December 1979, which was transmitted in early 1980 and not 1981 as listed on the label, a label which also lists a track titled 'Talk Each Other'. Considering that bootleg videos of this gig have being doing the rounds for years it's perhaps surprising that this is the first audio version to appear on vinyl. As you would expect with recent digital TV broadcasts of the gig, the bootleggers couldn't really go wrong with sound quality.

LIVE AT THE MOOLIGHT CLUB

Horace Panter shed light on the origins of this recording in his excellent account of his time as a Special, and quite rightly questioned how a bootleg recording ended up in the hands of Chrysalis Records, who officially released it on 2Tone in 1992. The intention was to include the track 'Long Shot Kick De Bucket' on a live compilation album of various bands recorded at the Moonlight. The project itself never got off the ground, although the famous soundbite intro 'this one is for all the bouncers' was used for the band's studio recording of 'Monkey Man'. The bootleg has an identical track listing to the official release, but for reasons best known to themselves, Chrysalis have removed most of the inter-song banter. This bootleg is also available as a clone of the official release complete with high quality sleeve and label design, the title of which has been expanded slightly to 'Live At The Moonlight Club 1979'.

GANGSTERS CARNIVAL CD

This Japanese CD bootleg is said to be 'limited to 250 copies' which should be viewed with some scepticism as copies appear on the market on a regular basis. It is, however, an excellent quality recording of the band in action, and what's more, offers tracks from the *More Specials* set, which for some reason was never bootlegged to the same extent as live recordings from the bands debut album. Curiously, the extended intro to 'Nite Klub' is listed as 'Ska-Blues-Jam', but in reality this is the same arrangementof the number as the one on the *Dance Craze* album.

LIVE AT THE LYCEUM CD

Although the sound isn't as crisp as the vinyl promo recording of this gig, this is still one of the best examples of the Specials doing what they did like no one else; playing live. From the opening track, 'Dawning Of A New Era' to the closing bars of 'Madness', this is the sound of a band that, in its day, was peerless. The pace is relentless and Terry Hall seems to spit out the lyrics of songs like 'Concrete Jungle' and 'Too Much Too Young' with real venom. As an added bonus, the album includes some live tracks recorded in the US, and a demo version of 'Stupid Marriage'. Duff artwork aside, this CD bootleg is an essential addition to any Specials collection.

ALL THE REST

The other collectables or items worth considering include the 'Too Much Too Young' 12" formats from Germany and Japan. The German record was simply the five-track UK EP version in 12" format, but the Japanese vinyl looks very smart, and comes complete with the quintessential Japanese Obi strip, a strip of paper looped around the left side or folded over the top of Japanese LP albums. Obi strips are also found folded over the left side of music CDs, video games, DVDs and even on the covers of books when they are sold new. The Japanese word Obi refers to the traditional sash or belt worn with a kimono. Obi strips normally carry the title of the product (usually in phonetic Japanese), the track listings, other information such as price and catalogue number, and information on related releases or artists from the same record company. The 'Too Much Too Young' 12" features a paper label centre and a delightful lyric sheet on which the lyrics are obviously quite wrong! Any Japanese release, whether it be 7", 12" or album format (as mentioned in the rarities section) is a valuable commodity.

There are also some little 'cash-in' 2Tone-related items that are worth noting. In 1981, the Rush Release label put out the nicely-titled 'The Clash And The Specials Go To Jail' (NIBZ 001). Credited to Don Drummond Junior and The Ska Stars, it is a traditional ska instrumental with a hand-drawn cover complete with the compulsory 2Tone black and white check, the familiar features of Walt Jabsco down the left side and the Clash rude boy looking across from the right.

As for live recordings, the most famed or rarest have been documented above, but many gigs were captured on cassette by audience members and over the years many of these recordings have come to light. Also, some gigs which were recorded direct from the sound desk have only recently surfaced, much to the collectors' delight. Some of the bootleg shows are of poor sound quality – *Live At The Pavilion Boultard, Paris* is an example – but there are recordings of gig in the US, France and Netherlands, as well as the UK. For a comprehensive list, visit www.skascene.co.uk

The Specials Mk2 were also often captured on live recordings, the most well-known being the *Princes at The Palace*, a gig at The Palace in Hollywood, US. The sleeve is full of song title mistakes, the most amusing being 'Man At C&A' labelled as 'Shark Attack'.

The Special AKA are worth collecting on imports only as the odd Walt Jabsco paper label tends to crop up (these were never used on the UK releases after 'Jungle Music'). The big debate over whether there is actually a 12" version of 'The Boiler' seems to rumble on, but the likelihood is that no 12" copies were ever pressed.

The video age gave us the chance to see the Specials play from the comfort of our own homes. Specials videos took a long time to be released, especially considering that the Beat, Madness and Bad Manners had all had video cassettes issued a few years earlier. *On Film*, featuring videos by the Special AKA, was made available in 1984. It wasn't until the late Eighties/early Nineties that the original Specials made it into the video arena. First came the long-overdue release of *Dance Craze* by Chrysalis (Chrysalis CVHS 5022) in 1988, which was soon followed by a compilation called *Specials* (Chrysalis CVHS 5034), which included the group's promo videos as well as the Special AKA videos from the *On Film* release. After the release of *The Specials' Singles* album in the early Nineties, Chrysalis revamped the cover to the video and re-issued it under the title of *The Specials* with the same catalogue number (Chrysalis CVHS 5034).

Before the arrival of DVD, a popular haunt for collectors were the many record fairs held all over the country, where you could find many Specials videos containing footage transferred from TV and, more often than not, featuring post-Specials bands like Fun Boy Three and the Colour Field. These, at the time, were little gems of long-forgotten shows and appearances that have since been etched on to DVD. Three concerts that have benefited from the DVD treatment are the *Rock Goes To College*, *Live At The Montreux Festival 1980* and *Live In Tokyo 1980* shows, which, using home movie editing suites on computers, have been cleaned up and made available to the public. There is a great deal of pressure on EMI to release *Dance Craze* on DVD, but at the time of writing there seems to be no willingness on their part to comply, even in light of the activity surrounding the band's 30th Anniversary.

For those with literary interests, there are a few books detailing 2Tone and the Specials. With most of the books now only being available through the modern collector's tool, the internet, and hours of surfing eBay in particular, I would recommend the readily-available Ska'd For Life, Horace Panter's own account of life in the Specials. Published by Pan Macmillan in 2007, it gives a rare and fascinating insight into life in the Specials and the band's early days, told in Horace's uptempo style. Next has to be The Specials Illustrated Songbook by Nick Davies and Ian Haywood, published by the Specials' music publishers Plangent Visions Ltd in 1981. It contains hilarious and superbly sketched caricatures of the band and of Coventry and also depicts the stories told in the songs. It covers tracks from both albums and comes with essential guitar chords (for the budding musical rude boy) and some fantastic full-page photos from Allan Ballard. Trevor Teasdel, who manages The Hobo, Coventry's music and arts magazine recalled:

"One night while working on some songs with Coventry jazz guitarist Andy Cairns, artist Nick Davies came round (he was a friend of Andy's) with the drafts of the Specials Illustrated Songbook asking what we thought of them. They were incredible illustrations, cartoon-style with the Specials typified as Boris, Tommy, Winston, Slug, Noddy, Leroy and Corky! And the band were called the Spare Shells on the Syphilis label! Nick had been working day and night on the book and it was very creative, better than the average songbook. Nick gave us the option of being immortalised in the book by scrawling our names on the cartoon wall of a urinal. As it was a urinal, our mention wouldn't be too flattering: Andy's name is on it [Look for 'Andy is a baldy wimp' on the urinal wall on the 'Nite Klub' page] I declined, not knowing what he might write! It was a fantastic work and Nick was making last-minute adjustments as we talked."

Davies went on to design the front cover for the '(What I Like Most About You Is Your) Girlfirend' single for the Special AKA. Both Davies and Haywood had attended Lanchester Polytechnic Arts College in Coventry, some four years after Dammers and Panter. To this day, Davies continues his brilliant cartoon work, and lives in Burry Port, South Wales. Haywood is now a graphic designer and Brand Communication Consultant in Coventry. The Specials Illustrated Songbook always sells for high prices on eBay, commanding anything from £25 upwards.

Next on the list comes the somewhat bemusing Two Tone Book For Rude Boys by Perry Neville and Jimmy Egerton (with words by Miles) published in 1981 by Ominbus Press. It tried to cash-in on the 2Tone boom, but by the time it was issued, 2Tone was beginning to fade. Again, this book commands big money when copies appear on eBay. The Two Tone Story by George Marshall, published by ST Publishing in 1990, gives great coverage to the 2Tone label and the Specials, and was re-issued in style when it was included in the four-CD package The Compact 2Tone Story in 1993.

The first edition of this book You're Wondering Now – A History of The Specials was issued in 1995, again by ST Publishing. With its story of the Specials and what happened to the band members after the split in 1981, it became the first biographical account of the band.

In 2004 two books crept on to the market, more directly aimed at 2Tone as a whole than the Specials specifically. First came Richard Eddington's Sent From Coventry – The Chequered Past of TwoTone. A somewhat padded out version of The Two Tone Story, its

284

only really exclusive point comes from the Coventry-born author's contemporary descriptions of the atmosphere around Coventry at the time. The second was Dave Thompson's *Wheels Out Of Gear – 2Tone, The Specials And A World In Flame* published by Helter Skelter. This was the story of many other musicians as well as the 2Tone story, but included no new revelations.

There were two magazines printed in conjunction with the *Dance Craze* movie back in 1981. The first was an official publication with a foreword by Garry Bushell, the man who made Oi! music a big success in the Eighties and would go on to work at *The Sun* newspaper and on TV. The mag included interviews and features on the 2Tone bands and a significant piece on skinheads. The second was published by *Movie Realm*, a specialist film magazine that did 'special' souvenir publications of movies in general. The 2Tone special was designed like a programme and had some great photographs of the 2Tone bands and the fans at venues around the country. Another magazine worthy of mention was *Ska 80* which was intended to be a long-running concern, but in fact lasted only one edition. Its pages featured band info, song lyrics and photos. As well as focussing on the 2Tone brigade, it also covered UB40 and Dexys Midnight Runners. The mag developed into *Flexipop!*, a music publication that gave away rare and tasty treats on a flexi disc every month. It was founded in 1980 by ex-*Record Mirror* writers Barry Cain and Tim Lott, who employed reporter Huw Collingbourne as a contributor:

"I started writing for *Flexipop!* magazine in early 1981," said Collingbourne. "This was at the time when the New Romantic bands such as Duran Duran and Spandau Ballet were just emerging out of the clubs and into the charts. At the other extreme of the music scene, there were the New Wave and Old Wave punks, ska bands, goths and bands with no category: The Stranglers, The Specials, The Exploited, The Banshees, Bauhaus, The Cure, The Clash and others. *Flexipop!*'s great idea was to get exclusive recordings from the top stars of the day and put them on to a free cover disc. These days those flimsy plastic discs and the magazines on to which they were stuck are collector's items. Back in the '80s they were considered to be here-today-gone-tomorrow trash. Disposable pop for the throw-away generation."

The flexi disc was a record made of a thin vinyl sheet with a moulded spiral groove, and was designed to be playable on a normal record-player turntable. Because of their minimal cost they were often included free with magazines as a promotional or educational tool. The Selecter's rare clear vinyl 'Ready Mix Radio' was a *Flexipop!* freebie, as was Bad Manners' blue vinyl 'No Respect'/'Only Pretendin'' and Madness' green vinyl offering of 'My Girl (Ballad)'. Despite early success, *Flexipop!* ceased publication in 1982.

We still await any official Specials releases on DVD, but 2007 saw the unofficial release of the American import DVD *The Specials – Too Much Too Young* by SMore Entertainment. This item was hastily pre-ordered by many Specials and 2Tone fans alike, but the final product was very badly put together, relying on stills taken from the internet, coupled with monotone narration that included many off-kilter facts, and interspersed with the Specials and Special AKA promo videos. It was a terrible production, its only saving grace being the inclusion of some previously unseen Super8 film footage of the band in concert at Hurrah's in New York and the Speaks Club, Long Island, NY in 1980, shot by Brian Zabawski. The DVD was to be released in the UK with television and radio presenter Tim Lovejoy as the narrator. Lovejoy found it a bit peculiar:

"All I remember was, I just got asked to do it. The script was poor and I was ill. I think it sounded a bit wordy and weird."

That aside, Jerry Dammers caught wind of the US and UK versions and had an injunction put on it preventing its release, and the item was withdrawn from sale. Despite the move, many of the US copies made their way to the UK mainland before the ban was in place.

Whether or not 2009 will see any new 30th Anniversary commemorative releases remains to be seen, but with the tour imminent, a live DVD has to be on the cards—and not before time!

COMPREHENSIVE GIG GUIDE

"I won't dance in a place like this..."
'Nite Klub' – The Specials 1979

This fantastic guide has been kindly compiled by Specials' fan Michael Sanderson. It documents virtually all the shows played by the Specials, including their very early years as the Hybrids and the Automatics. Although there are some gaps in the information, this is the most comprehensive list ever compiled.

The Hybrids – 1977

Oct	Coventry – Heath Hotel (supporting the Shapes – first-ever gig)
Oct/Nov	Coventry – Heath Hotel (supporting Urban Blight)

The Hybrids then played a fortnight residency

The Automatics – 1978

Jan 31	Coventry – Locarno (supporting Ultravox – Terry Hall's first gig)
Feb 23	Coventry – Hand and Heart Inn
Mar 7	Coventry – Locarno (supporting Sham 69 and Menace)
Mar 17	Derby – Kings Hall (supporting Generation X)
Mar 18	Huddersfield Poly (supporting Generation X)
Mar 20	Coventry – Mr Georges (Monday night residency)
Mar 26	London – Marquee (supporting the Saints)
–	Birmingham – Golden Eagle (a residency, possibly on a Friday)
–	Coventry – Tiffanys Ballroom
May 1	Birmingham – Barbarella's (with the Clash)
May 11	Birmingham – Mayfair Ballroom (with Sham 69)
–	Birmingham – Barbarella's (the Clash failed to turn up, so the band headlined)
–	Birmingham – Golden Eagle (still playing residency)
–	Newcastle (on a Monday)

The Special AKA / The Specials 1978

Jun 28	Aylesbury – Friars (supporting the Clash)
Jun 29	Leeds – Queens Hall (supporting the Clash)
Jun 30	Sheffield – Top Rank (supporting the Clash)
Jul 1	Leicester – Granby Halls (supporting the Clash)
Jul 2	Manchester – Apollo (supporting the Clash)
Jul 3	Manchester – Factory (supporting the Clash)
Jul 4	Glasgow – Apollo (supporting the Clash)
Jul 5	Aberdeen – Music Hall (supporting the Clash)
Jul 6	Dunfermline – Kinema (supporting the Clash)
Jul 7	Chester – Deeside Leisure Centre (supporting the Clash)
Jul 8	Crawley – Sports Centre (supporting the Clash)

Jul 9	Bristol – Locarno (supporting the Clash)
Jul 10	Torquay – Town Hall (supporting the Clash)
Jul 11	Cardiff – Top Rank (supporting the Clash)
Jul 12	Birmingham – Top Rank (supporting the Clash)
Jul 13	Liverpool – Empire (cancelled)
Jul 13	Blackburn – King Georges Hall (supporting the Clash)
Jul 14	Bury St Edmonds – Corn Exchange (supporting the Clash)
Jul 15	Edmonton – Pickett's Lock Sports Centre (cancelled)
Jul 22	Liverpool – Eric's (matinee & evening – supporting the Clash)
Jul 24	London – Music Machine, Camden (supporting the Clash)
Jul 25	London – Music Machine, Camden (supporting the Clash)
Jul 26	London – Music Machine, Camden (supporting the Clash)
Jul 27	London – Music Machine, Camden (supporting the Clash)
Aug 28	Birmingham – Cannon Hill Park (with Steel Pulse)
Nov 14	Paris – Club Gibis (cancelled)
Nov 15	Paris – Club Gibis (cancelled)
Nov 16	Paris – Club Gibis
Nov 17	Paris – Club Gibis
Nov 18	Paris – Club Gibis
Nov 19	Paris (supporting Devo – but Specials did not play)

The Special AKA / The Specials 1979

–	Birmingham – University (supporting the Au Pairs. Brad's first gig)
–	Warwick – University
–	Worcester
–	Sheffield – Limit Club
Mar 14	London – Moonlight Club (reviewed in *Sounds* music paper)
Mar 16	London – University College Student Union (Rock Against Racism)
Mar 16	London – North East Polytechnic (Rock Against Racism)
Mar 18	London – Hope & Anchor, Islington (Rock Against Racism)
Mar 21	Coventry – Lanchester Polytechnic
-	London – Nashville Rooms, Kensington
Apr 7	Halifax – Good Mood Club
Apr 8	London – Lyceum Theatre (with the Damned and UK Subs)
Apr	London – Nashville Rooms, Kensington
Apr 24	London – Music Machine, Camden (reviewed in *NME* music paper)
Apr 27	Birmingham – Aston University
Apr 28	Liverpool – Eric's
Apr 30	Milton Keyes – Crawford Arms
May 2	London – Moonlight Club
May 3	London – Dingwall's, Camden
May 5	London – Hope & Anchor, Islington
May 7	Kingston-upon-Thames – Noise Factory
May 8	Fulham – Greyhound
May 17	Telford – Town House
May 21	Birmingham – Barbarella's
May 26	Norwich – Boogie House

May 27	London – Lyceum Theatre (with the Gang of Four)
Jun 2	Cross Hands, Wales – Martletwy Working Men's Club
Jun 3	Newbridge, Wales – Memorial Hall
Jun	Swansea, Wales – Working Men's Club
Jun 7	Canterbury – College of Art
Jun 8	London – Nashville Rooms, Kensington
Jun 9	Wolverhampton – Polytechnic
Jun 15	Manchester – Russell Club (possible Manchester bootleg LP gig)
Jun 16	Huddersfield – Polytechnic
Jun 18	Worcester – Hideaways
Jun 22	Lincoln – AJ's
Jun 23	Jacksdale, Nottingham – Grey Topper
Jun 26	London – Hammersmith Palais
Jun 27	Bournemouth – Town Hall
Jun 28	London – Nashville Rooms, Kensington
Jun 29	Shropshire – Newport Village
Jun 30	Cheltenham – Whitcombe Lodge
Jul 2	Edinburgh – Tiffany's
Jul 3	Aberdeen – Russell's
Jul 6	Bournemouth – Capone's
Jul 7	Cheltenham – College of Art
Jul 10	Leeds – Fan Club
Jul 11	Shrewsbury – Cascade Club (cancelled)
Jul 13	Wolverhampton – Lafayette
Jul 14	Liverpool – Erics (matinee and evening shows)
Jul 16	Chester – Smartyz
Jul 21	London – Electric Ballroom, Camden (with Madness and the Selecter)
Jul 21	Nottingham – Sandpiper (cancelled)
Jul 24	Norwich – Boogie House
Jul 25	York – Pop Club
Jul 26	Bishops Castle – 3 Tons
Jul 27	Birmingham – Barbarella's
Jul 28	Dudley – JB's
Jul 31	Coventry, The City Centre Club
Aug 1	Newport – Stowaway's
Aug 3	Sheffield – Limit Club
Aug 4	Blackpool – Norbreck Castle
–	Retford – Porterhouse
–	Chesterfield
–	Barnsley – Town Hall
–	Ross on Wye
–	London – Hammersmith Palais
Aug 17	Belgium – Bilzen Jazz and Rock Festival
Aug 21	London – Hammersmith Palais
Oct 19	Brighton – Top Rank
Oct 20	Swindon – Oasis
Oct 21	Bournemouth – Stateside

The SPECIALS – from conception to reunion

Oct 22	Exeter – University
Oct 23	Plymouth – Fiesta
Oct 24	Cardiff – Top Rank
Oct 25	Nottingham – Kimberley Recreation Hall
Oct 26	Norwich – University of East Anglia
Oct 27	Hatfield – Polytechnic
Oct 28	Wolverhampton – Civic Hall
Oct 29	Birmingham – Top Rank
Oct 30	Blackburn – Golden Palms
Oct 31	Hanley – Victoria Hall
Nov 1	Manchester – Apollo
Nov 2	Lancaster – University
Nov 2	Manchester – The Factory
Nov 3	Manchester – The Factory
Nov 4	Sheffield – Top Rank
Nov 5	Leicester – De Montford Hall
Nov 6	Plymouth – Guildhall
Nov 8	Derby – Kings Hall
Nov 9	Newcastle – Mayfair Suite
Nov 10	Stirling – University
Nov 11	Glasgow – Tiffany's
Nov 12	Edinburgh – Tiffany's
Nov 13	Aberdeen – Ruffles
Nov 14	Ayr – Pavilion
Nov 15	Carlisle – Market Hall
Nov 16	Wakefield – Unity Hall
Nov 17	Loughborough – University
Nov 18	Bristol – Locarno
Nov 19	Shrewsbury – Music Hall
Nov 21	Liverpool – Mountford Hall
Nov 22	Dublin, Eire – Olympic Ballroom (with Dr Feelgood)
Nov 23	Belfast, N. Ireland – Queens University (with Dr Feelgood)
Nov 25	London – Lyceum Theatre
Nov 26	Hemel Hempstead – Pavilion
Nov 27	Great Yarmouth – Tiffany's
Nov 28	Cleethorpes – Winter Gardens
Nov 29	Coventry – Tiffany's
Nov 30	Malvern – Winter Gardens
Dec 1	London – Lewisham Odeon
Dec 2	London – Lyceum Theatre (recorded and made into bootleg LP)
Dec 3	Guildford – Civic Hall
Dec	Blackburn
Dec	Stoke-on-Trent
Dec	Colchester – Institute (Rock Goes to College)
Dec 20	Coventry – Tiffany's (2 shows)
Dec 21	Edinburgh – Odeon
Dec 23	Glasgow – Apollo
Dec 28	London Hammersmith Odeon (supporting the Who)

290

The Specials 1980

European Tour

Jan	Paris
Jan 12	Brussels – Ancienne Belgique
Jan	Berlin – Metropole
Jan	Hanover
Jan 16	Hamburg – Markthalle
Jan 21	Amsterdam – Paradiso
Jan	Rotterdam
Jan	Cologne

American Tour

Jan 25	New York, NY – Hurrah's
Jan 26	New Orleans, LA – Warehouse (supporting the Police)
Jan 28	Norman, OK – Boomer Theatre
Jan 30	Denver, CO – Rainbow Theatre (supporting the Police)
Jan 31	Salt Lake City, UT – Terrace Ballroom (supporting the Police)
Feb 1	Seattle, WA – The Showbox (supporting the Police)
Feb 3	Vancouver, BC – (supporting the Police)
Feb 4	Vancouver, BC – Commodore Ballroom
Feb 6	Portland, OR – Paramount Theatre (cancelled)
Feb 8	Los Angeles, CA – Whiskey a Go-Go (2 shows)
Feb 9	Los Angeles, CA – Whiskey a Go-Go (2 shows)
Feb 10	Los Angeles, CA – Whiskey a Go-Go (2 shows)
Feb 11	Los Angeles, CA – Whiskey a Go-Go (2 shows)
Feb 13	San Francisco, CA – I-Beam (cancelled)
Feb 14	Davis, CA – University (2 shows)
Feb 15	Palo Alto, CA – University (2 shows)
Feb 16	Santa Cruz, CA – Catalyst
Feb 17	San Francisco, CA – Warfield Theatre
Feb 18	Minneapolis, MN – Duffy's
Feb 19	Madison, WI – Merlyn's
Feb 21	Shaumberg, IL – B.Ginnings
Feb 22	Chicago, IL – Park West (2 shows)
Feb 23	Detroit, MI – Centre Stage
Feb 24	Toronto, ON – Maple Leaf Ballroom
Feb 26	Albany, NY
Feb 27	Lynway, MA – The Main Act
Feb 28	New Haven, CT – Great American Music Hall
Feb 29	Cherry Hill, NJ (cancelled)
Mar 1	New York, NY – Diplomat Hotel
Mar 2	Long Island, NY – Speaks

Europe

Mar 14	Paris – Pavilion Boultard
May 26	Holland – Pink Pop Festival

Seaside Tour UK

Jun 4	Great Yarmouth – Tiffany's
Jun 5	Skegness – Sands Showbar
Jun 6	Bridlington – Royal Spa Pavilion

Jun 8	Redcar – Coatham Bowl (cancelled)
Jun 8	Leeds – University
Jun 9	Barrow in Furness – Civic Hall
Jun 10	Blackpool – Tiffany's
Jun 11	Colwyn Bay – Pier Pavilion
Jun 12	Aylesbury – Friar's (2Tone birthday party)
Jun 13	Worthing – Assembly Rooms
Jun 15	Bournemouth – Stateside
Jun 16	Hastings – Pier Pavilion
Jun 17	Margate – Winter Gardens
Jun 18	Southend – Cliffs Pavilion
Jun 19	Portsmouth – Guildhall

Japanese Tour

Jun 25	Tokyo – Konen Hall
Jun 26	Kyoto – (outdoor arena)
Jun 27	Osaka – Expo Hall
Jun 28	Osaka – Expo Hall
Jun 30	Tokyo – Shibuya Hall
Jul 1	Tokyo – Shibuya Hall
Jul 2	Tokyo Carnival (2 shows, rearranged Sun Plaza Hall & Tsubaki House)

Europe

Jul 5	Belgium – Torhout (Woodland Festival)
Jul 6	Belgium – Werchter (Woodland Festival)
Jul 11	Montreux, Switzerland – Montreux Jazz Festival

UK

Sep 13	St Austell – Riviera
Sep 14	Bristol – Locarno
Sep 15	Cardiff – Sophia Gardens
Sep 16	Stoke – Trentham Gardens
Sep 17	Sunderland – Mayfair
Sep 18	Newcastle – Mayfair
Sep 20	Edinburgh – Playhouse
Sep 21	Glasgow – Apollo
Sep 23	Leicester – De Montfort Hall
Sep 24	Sheffield – Top Rank
Sep 25	Coventry – Lanchester Polytechnic
Sep 26	Coventry – Lanchester Polytechnic
Sep 30	Derby – Assembly Rooms
Oct 1	Manchester – Apollo
Oct 2	Bradford – St George's Hall
Oct 3	Blackburn – King George's Hall
Oct 5	Poole – Arts Centre
Oct 6	London – Hammersmith Palais
Oct 7	London – Hammersmith Palais
Oct 8	Uxbridge, Brunel University
Oct 9	Cambridge – Midsummer Meadow Supertent
Oct 10	Brighton – Top Rank
Oct 11	Swindon – Oasis

Oct 13	Doncaster – Rotters
Oct 14	Liverpool – Rotters
Oct 15	Liverpool – Rotters
–	Bracknell
–	London – Brunel University
–	Nottingham – Kimberley Leisure Centre
Oct 16	Birmingham – Odeon

Europe

Oct 18	Amsterdam – Jaap Endenhal
Oct	Rotterdam
Oct	Barcelona (in a bull ring on a Saturday)

UK

Oct 26	London – Trafalgar Square (CND)
Oct 30	London – Hope & Anchor, Islington
Oct 31	London – Hope & Anchor, Islington

The Specials 1981

Jan 14	Belfast – Ulster Hall
Jan 15	Dublin – Stardust Ballroom
Jan 16	Galway – Leisureland
Jan 17	Cork

Europe

–	Amsterdam (an ice rink with Madness)
Apr	Zwolle, The Netherlands
Apr	Berlin – Metropol

UK

May 1	London – Rainbow Theatre
Jun 20	Coventry – Butts Athletic Stadium

Europe

Jun 26	Horten, Norway – Horten Festival (with Ian Dury)

UK

Jun 27	Rotherham – Herring Thorpe Playing Fields
Jul 4	Leeds – Potter Newton Park (carnival against racism)
Jul 24	Liverpool – Royal Court (last ever UK gig)
Jul 26	Dublin – Dalymount Park (cancelled)

America

Aug	New York, NY – Pier 51
Aug	Pasadena, CA – Perkins Palace
Aug 21	Staten Island, NY – Paramount Theatre
Aug 22	Philadelphia, PA – The Liberty Bell Racetrack
Aug 23	Oakville, ON, Canada – The Grove
Aug 25	Long Island, NY – The Ritz
Aug	Boston, MA – Bradford Hotel Ballroom (last ever gig)

USEFUL LINKS

The Specials website	www.thespecials.com
The Specials Fans Forum website	www.thespecials2.com
2Tone Collectors site	www.2-tone.info
The Specials' Fans MySpace	www.myspace.com/thespecialsfans
Terry Hall website	www.terry-hall.com
Roddy Radiation website	www.roddyradiation.com
Neville Staple site	www.nevillestaple.co.uk
Lynval Golding site	www.lynvalgolding.com
Terry Hall MySpace site	www.myspace.com/baglady1959
The Skabilly Rebels MySpace	www.myspace.com/skabillyrebels1
The Neville Staple Band MySpace	www.myspace.com/nevillestaplefromthespecials
Lynval Golding MySpace	www.myspace.com/stiffupperlipsss
Madness website	www.madness.co.uk
The Selecter website	www.theselecter.net
The Beat MySpace site	www.myspace.com/officialbeatspace
Dave Wakeling website	www.davewakeling.com
Nick Welsh MySpace site	www.myspace.com/nickwelshmusic
Rhoda Dakar MySpace site	www.myspace.com/rhodadakar
Skaville UK MySpace site	www.myspace.com/skavilleuk
Bad Manners website	www.badmanners.net
Pete Chambers MySpace	www.myspace.com/2tonetwo
Paul Williams' MySpace	www.myspace.com/paulwillo
Mike Cornwell's ska site	www.skascene.co.uk
Special Brew Coventry	www.specialbrew.info

BIBLIOGRAPHY

Ska'd For Life – Horace Panter.
Pan Macmillan, London, 2007.

2-Tone 2-Despatches from the 2Tone City – Pete Chambers.
Tencton Planet Publications, 2008.

The Two Tone Story – George Marshall.
S.T. Publishing, Dunoon. 1990.

Passion Is A Fashion – The Real Story of The Clash – Pat Gilbert.
Aurum Press Ltd, London. 2005.

Mojo Magazine
'Q' magazine – 25 Years of 2Tone, Collectors Edition, 2004.
Record Collector magazine – Issue 300, August 2004.
2-Tone.info (website)
ReggaeVibes.com (website)
The Specials.com (website)
UKPressonline (website)
RoddyRadiation.com (website)

ALL THE YOUNG DUDES

Mott The Hoople & Ian Hunter

Campbell Devine

This, the official biography of Mott The Hoople, traces their formation and their inevitable rise to international stardom. Author Campbell Devine has successfully collaborated with Ian Hunter and members of 'Mott' to create a biography devoid of borrowed information and recycled press clippings but instead new, sensational and humorous inside stories, controversial quotes and an array of previously unpublished views from the band. With first hand input from members Hunter, Griffin, Watts, Allen and Ralphs, this book gives the complete insight into the legend of Mott The Hoople. Queen, The Clash, Kiss, Def Leppard, Primal Scream and Oasis have all cited Mott The Hoople as a major influence.

Queen's Brian May and Def Leppard's Joe Elliott have provided their own foreword to pay a long overdue tribute to a band who were simply one of rock's most treasured.

Already described as the 'definitive tome' on their careers, this unique and fascinating biography is by far the most scrupulously researched written work ever produced on Mott The Hoople. This book is welcomed by both the committed and casual rock reader as well as the ageing rocker and of course all the young dudes.

Relaunched in 2009 to coincide with the band's re-formation tour after more than 30 years.

 *Other must-read titles availab...*

All The Young Dudes: Mott The Hoople & Ian Hunter
Campbell Devine

Bittersweet: The Clifford T Ward Story
David Cartwright

Burning Britain – A History Of Uk Punk 1980 To 1984
Ian Glasper

Cor Baby, That's Really Me !
John Otway

Deathrow: The Chronicles Of Psychobilly
Alan Wilson

Death To Trad Rock – The Post-Punk fanzine scene 1982-87
John Robb

Embryo – A Pink Floyd Chronology 1966-1971
Nick Hodges and Ian Priston

Goodnight Jim Bob – On The Road With Carter USM
Jim Bob

Good Times Bad Times – The Rolling Stones 1960-69
Terry Rawlings and Keith Badman

Hells Bent On Rockin: A History Of Psychobilly
Craig Brackenbridge

Independence Days – The Story Of UK Independent Record Labels
Alex Ogg

Indie Hits 1980 – 1989
Barry Lazell

Irish Folk, Trad And Blues: A Secret History
Colin Harper and Trevor Hodgett

Johnny Thunders – In Cold Blood
Nina Antonia

Music To Die For – The International Guide To Goth, Goth Metal, Horror Punk, Psychobilly Etc
Mick Mercer

No More Heroes: A Complete History Of UK Punk From 1976 To 1980
Alex Ogg

Number One Songs In Heaven – The Sparks Story
Dave Thompson

Our Music Is Red – With Purple Flashes: The Story Of The Creation
Sean Egan

Quite Naturally – The Small Faces
Keith Badman and Terry Rawlings

Random Precision – Recording The Music Of Syd Barrett 1965-1974
David Parker

Rockdetector: A To Z Of '80s Rock
Garry Sharpe-Young

Rockdetector: A To Z Of Black Metal
Garry Sharpe-Young

rom Cherry Red Books:

Rockdetector: A To Z Of Death
Metal
Garry Sharpe-Young

Rockdetector: A To Z Of Doom,
Gothic & Stoner Metal
Garry Sharpe-Young

Rockdetector: A To Z Of Power
Metal
Garry Sharpe-Young

Rockdetector: A To Z Of Thrash
Metal
Garry Sharpe-Young

Rockdetector: Black Sabbath –
Never Say Die
Garry Sharpe-Young

Rockdetector: Ozzy Osbourne
Garry Sharpe-Young

Songs In The Key Of Z – the
Curious Universe of Outsider
Music
Irwin Chusid

Tamla Motown – The Stories
Behind The Singles
Terry Wilson

The 101 Greatest Progressive Rock
Albums
Mark Powell

The Day The Country Died: A
History Of Anarcho Punk 1980 To
1984
Ian Glasper

The Legendary Joe Meek – The
Telstar Man
John Repsch

The Rolling Stones: Complete
Recording Sessions 1962-2002
Martin Elliott

The Secret Life Of A Teenage
Punk Rocker: The Andy Blade
Chronicles
Andy Blade

Those Were The Days – The
Beatles' Apple Organization
Stefan Grenados

Trapped In A Scene – UK
Hardcore 1985-89
Ian Glasper

Truth... Rod Stewart, Ron Wood
And The Jeff Beck Group
Dave Thompson

You're Wondering Now – The
Specials from Conception to
Reunion
Paul Williams

*Please visit
www.cherryredbooks.co.uk
for further information and
mail order.*

CHERRY RED BOOKS

Here at Cherry Red Books we're always interested to hear of
interesting titles looking for a publisher. Whether it's a new
manuscript or an out of print/deleted title, please feel free to
get in touch if you've written, or are aware of, a book you feel
might be suitable.

richard@cherryred.co.uk
iain@cherryred.co.uk

www.cherryredbooks.co.uk
www.cherryred.co.uk

CHERRY RED BOOKS
A division of Cherry Red Records Ltd.
3a, Long Island House,
Warple Way,
London W3 0RG.